Design Paradigms

A Sourcebook for Creative Visualization

■

Warren K. Wake, D. Des.

John Wiley & Sons, Inc.

New York • Chichester • Weinheim • Brisbane • Singapore • Toronto

This book is printed on acid-free paper.

Published simultaneously in Canada.

Library of Congress Cataloging-in-Publication Data:

Wake, Warren K.
Design paradigms : a sourcebook for creative visualization / Warren K. Wake.
p. cm.
Includes bibliographical references and index.
ISBN 0-471-29976-6 (pbk. : alk. paper)
1. Design, Industrial. 2. Visualization. 3. Computer graphics. I. Title.

TS171 .W35 2000
745.2--dc21
99-048039

Printed in the United States of America.

10 9 8 7 6 5 4 3 2 1

Cover design: Paul DiNovo.
Cover photography: Warren K. Wake.
Editor: Margaret Cummins.
Assistant Managing Editor: Maury Botton.
Book design and layout: Warren K. Wake.
Set in ITC Stone® using QuarkXPress™.

To my children, Richard and Paulina

Contents

Preface

"Design paradigms" is a term that we use to talk about a thousand different great little ideas that are at the heart of natural and manufactured devices. This book is a "field guide" to the paradigms, introducing this powerful tool for design and creative visualization. It is intended for professionals, students, and instructors alike in design professions, including industrial and graphic design, architecture, and engineering. It will also be of use to persons interested in creativity, biology, and invention.

This is intended as a book that can be immediately put to work; it is filled with ideas you can apply to all types of design problems. For instance, the next time you face a question such as "How can I connect these two things?" turn to the design paradigms, in Chapters 7 and 8, and explore a host of different methods for attaching and joining that you can apply. The book is also suited to casual reading, providing insights into the structure of, and similarities between, the mechanisms of design, invention, and organisms.

The book is organized as follows: The first chapter is an introduction to design paradigm concepts, followed by twelve chapters of paradigms broken down into categories of more or less increasing complexity. The paradigm chapters begin with simple shapes, followed by the ways more complex forms can accommodate functions like enclosure, bending, and getting bigger and smaller. We then look at how multiple objects relate to each other, and how they can be joined, attached, or have passages between them. We also consider how multiple objects can relate to each other or how an object can have multiple functions. We also look at paradigms that operate in areas that are not readily apparent to the naked eye. In the final chapter we look at how to apply the paradigms in creative processes and endeavors. Design professionals might wish to skip around in the book, visiting paradigm categories as need or fancy strikes. Those new to design might wish to read the final chapter earlier.

This book focuses on the basic 3-D paradigms. It is neither a full treatment of design, nor a full treatment of design paradigms. Perhaps later volumes will explore design paradigms in areas including structure, 2-D composition, and color. A book of this type can never be complete, even within the selected categories I've covered here, for new paradigms will continue to be invented and discovered as time goes by. Rather, let this be a starting point. Each designer must ultimately develop his or her own collection of paradigms, thereby creating the mental toolbox you draw upon when designing. To those early in the stage of building this toolbox, this book aims to give you a head start, with the many wonderful paradigms collected here and organized into useful categories. Learning these will serve to help build your visual and conceptual vocabulary. To the seasoned professional, this book aims to close the gap on years of experience and time spent trying to figure things out. *Design Paradigms* offers you ways to connect many of the important things you've learned over the years, and a method to structure and utilize the knowledge you already possess.

You are invited to participate in this ongoing process of design exploration. As you explore each category of paradigms, look around you. Study your possessions, your tools, your pets, your body, and think. How do things bend? How are things joined? How do things get larger or smaller? As you pay attention to these questions, you'll find the examples discussed here are hard at work in things all around you. You might also discover other paradigms, other methods of accomplishing the goals defined in each chapter. You are encouraged to keep a sketchbook of these or at least draw in the margins of this book, for through drawing comes understanding and ownership. As we travel through the different domains of the design paradigms, you the reader will join in a design adventure and conversation that has been going on for centuries. Discover the paradigms, and make them your own!

Warren K. Wake, D. Des.
Belmont, Massachusetts
January, 2000

"And I hope that my nephews will be grateful not only for the things I have explained here, but also for those which I have purposely omitted, so that they find pleasure themselves in inventing them. . . . "[1]

–Rene Descartes

Fig. 0.1 Rene Descartes (1596–1650), mathematician, philosopher, and scientist. Descartes's appreciation for mechanisms led to his development of *cartesian mechanism* philosophy that attemped to explain virtually everything except god and human spirit through mechanical metaphor.

Acknowledgments

The author gratefully acknowledges the contributions of the many friends, associates, and family who helped bring this project to fruition. Thanks to my son, Rick, for his help, his comments, and his photography. Thanks to Susan Englert and Sally Levine, for their editing and suggestions on the manuscript, and for introducing me to QuarkXPress™. Thanks also to Rosanne Russell, for her suggestions on the design of the book, and her instruction in Quark. Thanks to Matthew Linton and Marc Lisle for their comments on the early manuscript. I am deeply indebted to Diego Matho, who helped immensely throughout the project, reviewing the manuscript, developing illustrations, and assisting with the photography.

Special thanks to Peter Cheimets, for his photographs of the Amundsen-Scott Station at the South Pole, to Dean Powell for his photograph of the Northwest Coast Nesting Tables, and to Kenneth W. Gardiner for his photograph of the spittle bug.

Thanks are also due to those who got me started on asking many of the questions I address here: my mother, Doris, who didn't fuss too much as I took apart my toys and our household telephones; my high school art teacher, Dr. Robert Burkey and my instructors in the Syracuse University Design program, Rolf Faste (now with Stanford University) and James Pirkl. Thanks also to Bill Mitchell, for his encouragement and advice at the start of this project; to Don Brown, who reminded me to tell the story with pictures, as well as with words; and to my editor, Margaret Cummins, for her support throughout the project.

Trademarks

It is the author's intention to acquaint the reader with the design paradigms in the many settings in which they occur. Many of these are employed in commercial products. Where possible, the familiar product names are used in the text, in order to properly acknowledge the commercial forms of these products. This is not an endorsement of these products, and none of these companies have underwritten this project.

AutoCAD® is a registered trademark of Autodesk Inc. Band-Aid® is a registered trademark of Johnson & Johnson. Barricade® is a registered trademark of Fire Protection, Inc. Bondo® is a registered trademark of Dynatron/Bondo Corp. Bubble Wrap® is a registered trademark of Sealed Air Corporation. Calphalon® is a registered trademark of Calphalon Corporation. Cheerios® is a registered trademark of General Mills. Coke® is a registered trademark of The Coca-Cola Co. DERMABOND® is a registered trademark of Johnson & Johnson. EMS® is a registered trademark of Eastern Mountain Sports, Inc. Fiberglas® is a registered trademark of Owens Corning Fiberglas Corporation. Frisbee® is a registered trademark of Wham-O Mfg. Co. GelRelease™ is a trademark of Cetacean Research Technology. Goodyear® is a registered trademark of the Goodyear Tire & Rubber Company. Gore-tex® is a registered trademark of W. L. Gore & Associates. Great Stuff® is a registered trademark of Insta-Foam Products, Inc. Greenlee® is a registered trademark of Greenlee Textron Inc. Gumby® is a registered trademark of Prema Toy Co. Inc. Hula Hoop® is a registered trademark of Wham-O Mfg. Co. L'eggs® is a registered trademark of Sara Lee Corp. LEGO® is a registered trademark of Interlego A.G. Levi's® is a registered trademark of Levi Strauss & Co. Liquid Nails® is a registered trademark of The Glidden Company. Lycra® is a registered trademark of E. I. Du Pont de Nemours

1

Introduction

This is a book about design, in the broadest and most basic sense of the word. *Design Paradigms* presents a new approach to solving design problems and thinking about the ways things work. We will explore the foundations of 3-D design to identify the forms and techniques that enable designs, inventions, and organisms to function. We will be particularly concerned with the reasons these solutions take particular forms, what their form tells us about their function, and what their function tells us about their form. We will explore how these basic mechanisms work, and we will look at how forms relate to each other, and to us.

In the earliest stages of design, a designer must ask some fundamental questions. These questions arise whether the design is for buildings, machine parts, clothing, toys, appliances, furniture, or bridges. What is the essence of the problem? What is the essence of the prior solution (if any)? Where did the prior solution fail? If it didn't fail, how can the prior solution be improved upon? What other ways might there be to do this? Are there other problems similar to this one? What form does this solution imply? What other forms or basic approaches might work as well?

In addressing questions like these, a designer draws upon a bag of tricks—knowledge gained over a lifetime of observing, drawing, and designing. We might divide these tricks, techniques, and knowledge bits into several categories, such as basic forms, functional relationships (such as the way two parts relate to each

par·a·digm
from Greek *paradeigma*, from *paradeiknynai* to show side by side. EXAMPLE, PATTERN; *especially:* an outstandingly clear or typical example or archetype.[2]

other), and behaviors (such as the ways in which an object can get bigger or smaller). Within each of these categories is a collection of distinct useful forms, mechanisms, techniques and relationships. Each of these embodies a fundamental design strategy. We will call these things *design paradigms.*

In both the natural and manmade worlds, we occasionally encounter these wonderful forms, mechanisms, and assembly techniques that we quickly recognize as essential or *quintessential* solutions. We realize they are essential both because the same solution appears in many contexts, natural and manmade, and because we can't remove anything from the device and still have something meaningful. Since we might find these paradigms combined in various ways to form more complex designs, we might think of these as *atoms* of design. These concepts are intrinsic to the idea of design paradigms. As quintessential solutions, they are found at the heart of design solutions. As atoms, they constitute the basic building blocks of design.

Each design paradigm exemplifies a distinct method of solving a problem. Design paradigms are characteristically quickly understood and embraced, and take on special significance in helping us to understand our world. Design paradigms become a framework for explaining the workings of natural and designed objects. When we first see a set of Russian nesting dolls, for instance, we quickly grasp the concept of *object-within-similar-object.* After seeing the second doll within the first, and the third within the second, we eagerly look for a fourth and fifth. Further, as we discover a set of nesting screwdrivers or slice open an onion to find effectively another onion inside another, we find that there are many things we might classify as *nesting like a set of Russian dolls.*

In addition to their role in helping us to understand designs, paradigms are also powerful tools for creating new designs. Each paradigm learned becomes a part of the designer's mental toolbox, a set of fundamental approaches to solving problems. Once a paradigm is discovered, it becomes ready at hand when faced with a design problem. For example, consider the task of designing a set of snack tables. Faced with the challenge of storing the tables compactly when they're not in use, you might call to mind the *Nested Spoons paradigm* (see Chapter 10) and create a set of tables that neatly stack one on top of each other. You might alternately turn to the *Russian Dolls paradigm* (see Chapter 11) and realize that the tables might also be stored compactly by nesting them each inside a slightly larger one (see Fig. 11.5c).

The full power of the *Design Paradigms* approach is realized by exploring and applying alternatives within and across paradigm categories as part of the creative-visualization phase of the design process. Consider the problem of designing a camera tripod that must be large when supporting a camera to take pictures, and small when not in use. How many ways can you think of to make something larger and smaller? Chapter 5 presents a host of methods of making things bigger and smaller, collected and grouped so that each can be applied in sequence onto a

Fig.1.1 a-e Icons representing the *Nested Spoons, Russian Dolls, Telescope, Scissors,* and *Boiling* paradigms. Each represents a fundamental design concept.

problem such as this. Some of these paradigms will suggest obvious solutions to a particular problem, such as the *Telescope paradigm* applied to the tripod. Another paradigm, such as the *Scissors paradigm* might suggest a design featuring legs that expand by a scissoring mechanism and fold compactly when not in use. This might not be an obvious or frequently seen structure for a tripod, but it doesn't seem like an outrageous solution either. The application of other paradigms in the same category, however, might be more surprising. While a paradigm such as *expansion due to boiling* might at first seem inapplicable in the design of a tripod, it deserves a moment's consideration. This paradigm might potentially be employed in a remotely operated tripod, say on an unmanned Martian landing craft.

Shifting paradigm categories can produce more radical design results. By shifting the category from *Bigger and Smaller* to *Attaching* (see Chapter 8), we are recasting the question rather than finding solutions to the problem as originally presented. Indeed, instead of designing a tripod that gets bigger and smaller, we can obviate the need for the tripod, by exploring ways to attach the camera to fixed objects like telephone poles and trees. We will return to the issues of applying design paradigms in Chapter 14, *Putting Design Paradigms to Work.*

Design paradigms are the truly fundamental ways of forming and doing things. Human designers invented some of these great little ideas, but most have evolved through natural processes, particularly biology. Some, such as the *basic geometrics*, are built into the fabric of matter. Akin to the laws of physics, there are inescapable meanings to form. A ball shape, for instance, will tend to roll. It is up to evolutionary or human design processes to discover these properties, however. Many paradigms have been discovered through both types of processes, and are consequently found both in the natural and in the constructed, or manmade, worlds.

> We will discover that the laws that rule design of any kind are the laws of nature. They all boil down to the fundamental principle of unity that pervades all creation.[4]

> *"We cannot expect to be a master designer before first learning all we can from these elemental conceptions, just as a navy captain must first learn the elementary rules of sailing before commanding a destroyer."*[3]
>
> *-Paul Jacques Grillo*
> Form, Function & Design

Because the paradigms are essential, we repeatedly encounter them at the heart of biological systems and as the basis for a myriad of designed objects. Both nature and human designers tend to return to solutions that work. As we explore the paradigms, we will intentionally weave back and forth between examples in the natural and manmade worlds, between art and nature, to start to appreciate the breadth of applicability of the paradigms.

Fig. 1.2 Mihaly Csikszentmihalyi. University of Chicago photo.

Although most of the paradigms should at first glance be familiar to the typical reader, a hallmark of creativity is to be able to take a fresh look at the familiar, as described by psychologist Mihaly Csikszentmihalyi:

> Creative people are constantly surprised. They don't assume that they understand what is happening around them, and they don't assume that anybody else does either. They question the obvious—not out of contrariness but because they see the shortcomings of accepted explanations before the rest of us do.[5]

It is important to try to try to keep an open mind as you explore the paradigms, to enjoy the spirit of discovery and allow for the many possibilities to be surprised by the familiar.

As you learn the paradigms, you will find it useful to explore the ideas through drawing. Drawing is an important tool for understanding the fundamental structures of the natural and built environments. Designers have long noted the relationships between art and nature, and have used drawing to capture and explain these ideas, often keeping sketchbooks of the clever natural and manmade devices they encounter. The best known of these are the wonderful sketchbooks of Leonardo da Vinci. Leonardo explored extensively basic geometry and natural form in plants, animals, and the human body.[6]

That artists and designers have much to learn from nature is unquestionable. Basic biology and life drawing are usually recommended, if not required, as part of many design degree programs. Learning from nature is only half of the message, however. There is much to learn from the built environment as well, particularly in comparing and contrasting natural and artificial solutions to similar problems. Leonardo saw this, too, and his sketches and notes frequently explored the manmade world as well, including the basic mechanisms of architecture, transportation, munitions, and other designed artifacts of his day.

Recognizing Design Paradigms

Design paradigms, you will find, are all around us, many yet waiting to be discovered. How do you recognize an encounter with a design paradigm? Think back to the first time that you saw a Swiss Army knife. Did you marvel as each blade was taken out and the entire knife became a different tool? Did you experience delight in the realization that this was the single best expression of this idea? If you look at a

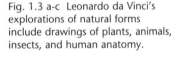

Fig. 1.3 a-c Leonardo da Vinci's explorations of natural forms include drawings of plants, animals, insects, and human anatomy.

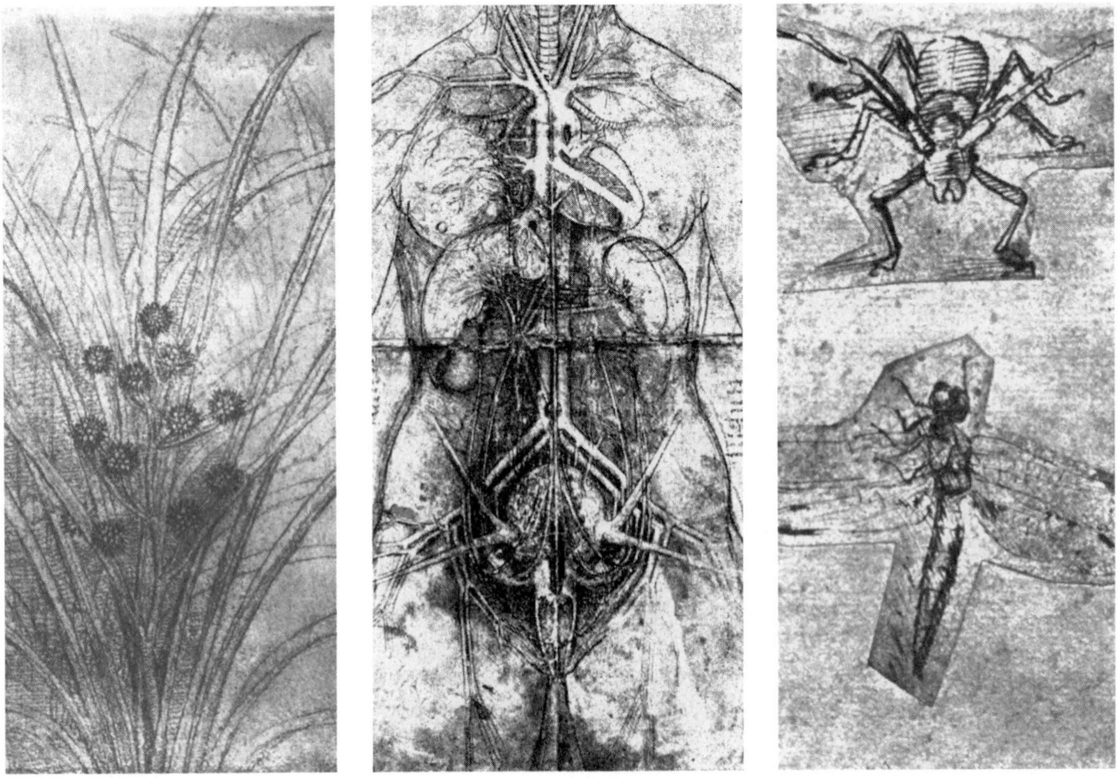

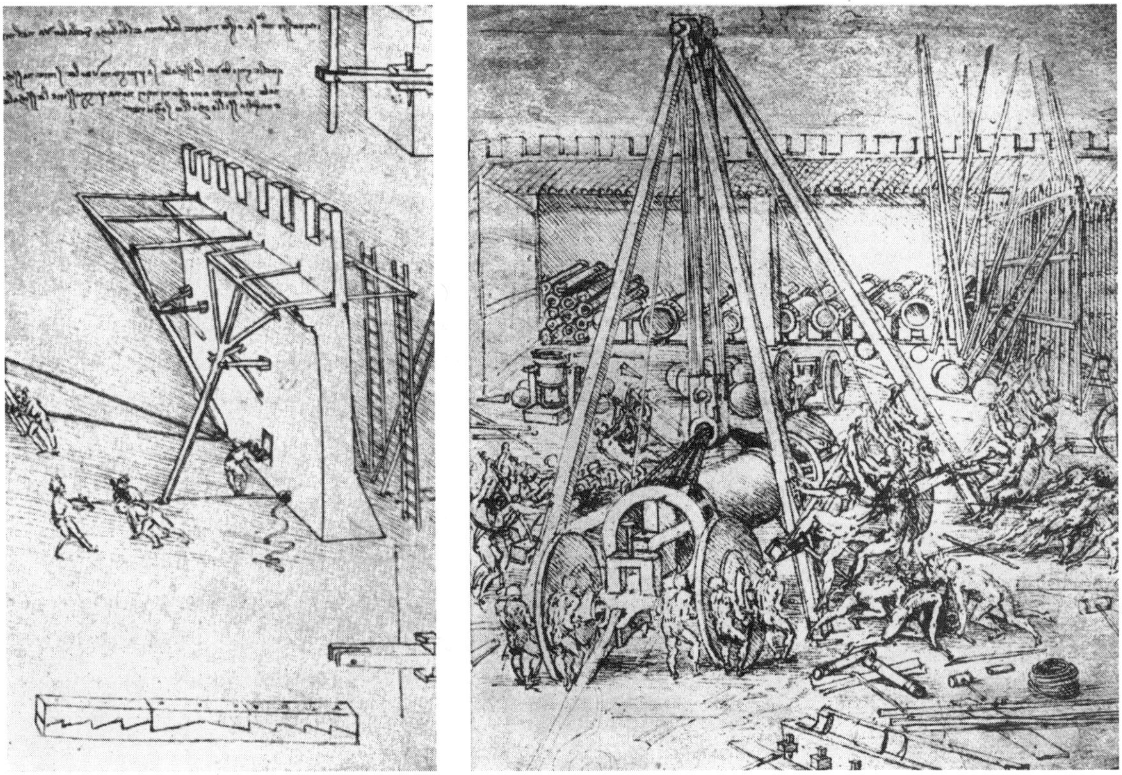

Fig. 1.4 a, b Leonardo's explorations also included studies of basic mechanisms, military devices (as in the mechanisms for scaling walls, left), and manufacturing systems (as in the foundry, right).

kitchen tool where a can opener has five or six gadgets that fold out of it, do you think to yourself, "This works like a Swiss Army knife?" Now try to remember the first time you discovered a piece of mica. Did you marvel at how you could separate nearly identical slices of the transparent mineral with your fingernail? Did you fantasize about what other things could be made in lightly adhered pads?

Experiences like these exemplify the feelings you get when discovering a design paradigm. These feelings, perhaps, come about at the discovery of a fundamental truth about the way things work. There is joy in the realization that a broad new group of existing and possible devices can be understood or invented now that this paradigm is known and understood. We may feel charged or empowered as we realize our thinking has been changing as a result of this understanding. The paradigm has given us a new way to categorize things we encounter and a new approach to formulating new ideas.

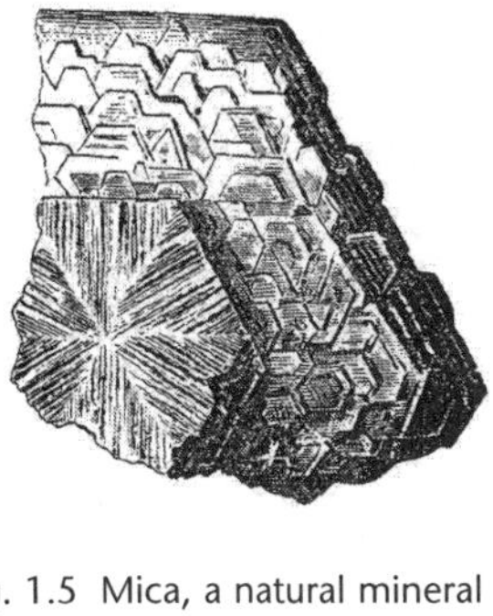

Fig. 1.5 Mica, a natural mineral composed of easily separable sheets, much like Post-it® notes.

Paradigms as Metaphor

> *"All thinking is metaphorical."*[7]
> *–Robert Frost*

Fig. 1.6 Robert Frost (1874–1963), American poet.

The role of the paradigms in thinking, at least for the tasks of designing and thinking about visual and functional relationships, is akin to the role of metaphor in language. Paradigms and metaphors enable us to introduce new ideas by explaining them in terms of more familiar concepts. While there is some overlap between paradigms and metaphor, the primary distinction is that metaphors operate primarily with verbal analogies, while paradigms act primarily nonverbally. Design paradigms function as physical metaphors, used as a basis for visual and functional analogies. They give us a handle on how to think of and talk about the ways that things operate, how they change, and how objects relate to other objects, when we might otherwise find such explanations impossible. They provide a foundation upon which to base our understanding of new and unfamiliar elements, just as metaphor does in language. Because of these similarities, it will be useful to review some of the ways in which metaphors work for us.

As a figure of speech, a metaphor embodies an implied comparison, in which a word or phrase ordinarily and primarily used for one thing is applied to another.[8] This simple definition, however, does not convey the significance of metaphor in human cognition. Metaphor is the bridge between what we know and what we wish to know. It has been suggested that metaphor and analogy might be the basis for *all* learning.[9] It is not merely used in language and the expression of ideas; it is at the root of how we understand, explain, and generate physical objects, devices, mechanisms, and art.

Metaphor has several important roles in thinking and speaking that are parallel to how we use paradigms in design processes. First, metaphor is used in explaining something you understand to someone else. Metaphor is a tool that enables you to recast these things in terms more familiar to your audience. Second, metaphor is a tool you use to try to understand things that are not yet familiar to you. You might form a hypothesis about the unfamiliar, liken it to something familiar, and then proceed to test that hypothesis. Third, metaphor is a bridge spanning gaps in our abilities, collapsing time, distance, and other barriers. By likening a seemingly impossible problem to a more familiar and solvable problem, we can superimpose a wide range of known solutions onto the solvable problem, and then try to expand them to apply to the new problem.

> *"The greatest thing by far is to be a master of metaphor. It is the one thing that cannot be learned from others. It is the mark of genius."*[10]
> *-Aristotle*

Fig 1.7 Aristotle (384BC–322BC). Greek philosopher, depicted in a fresco by Raphael.

Introducing new ideas to others frequently requires the use of metaphor. Metaphor can be applied in introducing new design concepts, new products, and new technologies. The clever use of metaphor, for instance, is credited with the widespread adoption of office computing. Explaining word processing as *a smart typewriter that automatically corrects your errors and lets you move words, sentences, and paragraphs around on a page* sold countless systems beginning in the 1960s, a time when most potential consumers felt that computers were useful only to scientists and engineers.

The second important function of metaphor is as a personal tool in developing an understanding of the unfamiliar. This is a problem frequently faced in design. Many design tasks attack problems that are at least initially unfamiliar. This is often the case in science as well: much of the objective in science is the exploration of the unknown. A most potent tool for exploring the unknown is casting the unfamiliar in terms we can understand, as pointed out by David Edge:

> In recent years, there has been a notable increase in interest, among philosophers of science, in the cognitive functions of metaphor. The process whereby we construe an uncertain, obscure, or puzzling area of experience in terms of one both familiar and apparently (in at least some respects) similar, the displaced patter acting as a metaphorical redescription of the unfamiliar, has been shown to be central to many key scientific innovations.[11]

Fig. 1.8 (right) Horseless carriage. The design of this early automobile was derived from the carriages it replaced.

Fig. 1.9 Horse-drawn carriage.

Fig. 1.10 Car designs soon diverged from the carriages of the past.

The third function, the bridge, is itself intentionally a metaphor. Just as bridges permit us to drive in a continuous path across previously uncrossable barriers like rivers, lakes, and gorges, metaphor can be used to span between the islands of understanding we have in the unknown, to form a coherent idea, path, or design.

Technology is the basis of many of our metaphors and is important in terms of how we think and how our ideas progress. The use of metaphor and the process of design and the evolution of science and technology are cyclic in the sense that metaphors help to shape technology, and new technology leads to new metaphors. Major changes arise periodically, such as moving from horse-drawn carriages to motor-driven vehicles. The initial description of the latter is naturally metaphorical, as in the term "horseless carriage." The association with the previous technology is both verbal and visual. The early designs of such vehicles show visual evidence of the metaphor, as they retained much of the appearance of horse-drawn carriages. The horse-drawn carriage was itself a technological innovation, as were the horseless carriage and later automobiles. We tend to not only base new inventions on old, but also explain and try to understand new inventions in terms of what we already know.

> Technological devices are significant components of our familiar everyday world: they therefore share in this process, forming the literal basis of metaphors which give implicit, tacit structures to our thought and feeling and that "fill our consciousness." Indeed, many of the most influential of the theories of modern science have an explicit origin in such "technological metaphor."[12]

Fig. 1.11 The *mind as a machine* metaphor is expressed both through words and through visual illustrations such as these.

As our technology progresses, so do our metaphors, and these in turn help us to gain an increasingly better understanding of complex concepts. This has been particularly evident in psychology, as we have seen explanations of the mind progress. *The mind is a machine* came into use after the Industrial Revolution, and was replaced by a series of metaphors reflecting both the progress of technology and the increased level of understanding of mental processes. Thus in later years the mind was compared to a telephone switchboard, television, computers, and most recently, the Internet. The importance of the appropriateness of metaphor choices is huge. The use of metaphors has actively shaped theories about behavior, in turn influencing courses of therapy and education. Comparing the mind to a machine, for instance, indicates that a pattern of training, such as the stimulus-response therapies of behaviorism, would be a more successful treatment than those depending on internal states, introspection, or chemical adjustment.

Often a simple metaphor isn't adequate to explain a complex idea. Frequently *composite metaphors* are used, or a *modified metaphor* is applied. In a composite metaphor, multiple metaphoric comparisons are made. The metaphors are often, but need not be, related to each other. In a modified metaphor, a comparison is made, with qualifications; it is the same, *but different.* Artificial intelligence pioneer Marvin Minsky gives an example of the modified metaphor:

> For example, suppose you need a hammer but can only find a stone. One way to turn that stone to your purposes would be to make it fit your memory of a

> hammer's appearance—for example, by making your description of the stone include an imaginary boundary that divides it into two parts, to serve as a handle and as head. Another way would be to make your hammer frame accept the entire stone as a hammer without a handle.[13]

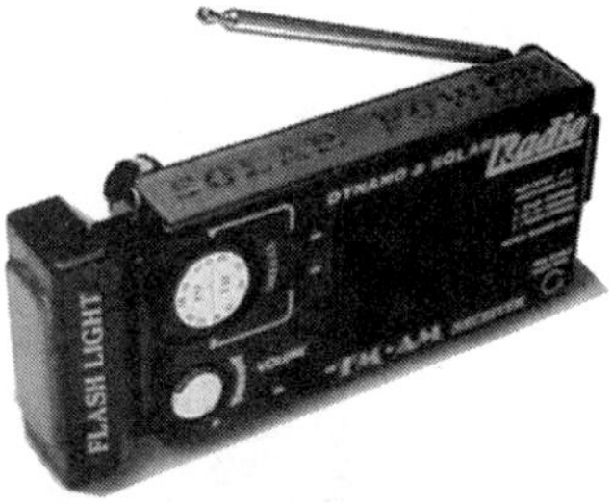

Fig. 1.12 What might be called the "Swiss Army knife" of portable radios, this device includes an AM-FM radio, a flashlight, a solar panel and alternative hand-cranked power.

The primary difference between paradigms and metaphors is that with paradigms, the association between domains is visual and functional rather than verbal. The two overlap, however, when we *talk* about a paradigm (making it verbal), for instance, or use *objects* in explaining metaphoric relationships (making it physical). Consider the situation of applying the *Swiss Army Knife paradigm* (see Chapter 12) to a design for a radio, by incorporating several other tools, such as a flashlight and a beacon. Understanding the association between the knife and the radio can be accomplished entirely without words, by looking at or using the two, and realizing that they share the same underlying structure, providing several functions within a single body. You can also explain the relationship with metaphor, suggesting that the invention is "the Swiss Army knife" of portable radios.

Application of both metaphor and paradigms requires that two domains be linked, usually the familiar and the unfamiliar, and that these two domains be different. Thus it is natural that metaphorical explanations of designed, technological, or manufactured things are often cast in terms of the biological, and that explanations of the biological world can be in terms of the technological.

Design and Nature

Nature, particularly biology, provides us with a wealth of design solutions. Many of these are paradigmatic, such as the layers of an onion or the way a kangaroo carries its young in a pouch. When we look at the way that the planets orbit around the sun, we see fundamental forces, such as gravity and inertia, at work, and certainly, orbiting may be considered a paradigm of how bodies might relate to each other. But in the case of biology, there is the sense that over millions of years of evolution, different approaches to problems arose and either succeeded or did not. The implication then is that the solutions found and employed in the structure of plants and animals are still in use because they have worked better than alternatives, giving these creatures evolutionary advantages.

> These relationships usually have an appropriateness about them which we attribute to evolution, but which resembles the appropriateness of structure to function characteristic of well-designed implements.[15]

> *"Though human ingenuity may make various inventions which, by the help of various machines answering the same end, it will never devise any inventions more beautiful, nor more simple, nor more to the purpose than nature does; because in her inventions nothing is wanting, and nothing is superfluous, and she needs no counterpoise when she makes limbs proper for motion in the bodies of animals."*[14]
>
> –Leonardo Da Vinci

Fig. 1.13 Leonardo da Vinci (1452–1519), self portrait.

There are limitations to evolution as a design process, however. One important limitation is that nature can't easily "back up." In human design processes we frequently arrive at a point where we realize that small "tweaks" won't achieve our objective, so we return to an earlier point in the design process to try something radically different. If we look at our own human evolution as bipeds, we might point out that the lower back is a weak point in human design, subject to frequent problems and occasional failure. This is the type of problem, however, that normal evolutionary processes cannot correct; it might imply backtracking to our prevertebrate ancestors and re-evolving a species parallel to our own.

Another important limitation to evolution as a design process is that nature must base evolutionary changes on available materials and structures, and can't look ahead in the design process. Harvard's Stephen Jay Gould discusses the ways in which evolution depends upon fortuitous circumstances. How could birds have evolved wings to fly, for instance? Since it is unlikely that an entirely wingless species gave birth one day to offspring with wings and the ability to fly, you might presume that some early ancestors of birds had half wings. These half wings could not have

Fig. 1.14 Rearing horse. Study by Leonardo da Vinci for *Battle of Anghiari.*

"The truly great designers arrived at their conclusions through the observation of nature: their masterpieces show close kinship of form and design with plants or animals which have a similar problem to overcome."[17]

-Paul Jacques Grillo
Form, Function & Design

"The deeper insight any Man hath into the Affairs of NATURE, the more he discovers of the Accurateness, and Art, that is in the Contexture of Things."[18]

-Sir Thomas Pope Blount, Baronet, 1693

enabled the creatures to fly, so what adaptive purpose might they have served? Since nature can't see ahead a thousand generations to plan creatures with steadily larger wings until they are able to fly, Gould speculates that the half wings must have served another purpose, perhaps as cooling structures for the ancestral birds.[16] You might also speculate that ancient birds with large cooling wings might also have started to realize advantages in air-propelling themselves along the ground or reducing incidence of injury in falls by using the half wings to slow their descent. This points out the advantage human designers have, being able to work directly on a design problem like flight, while nature might be described as stumbling upon good ideas that occasionally arise through fortuitous circumstance.

Some designers bristle at the suggestion that design exists in nature, claiming that design is a uniquely human activity. Others take a more abstract view of design, claiming that design is manifest in objects that are clever in their construction, regardless of the origin of the objects. This distinction will not be important here since the design paradigms are not design *per se*. Instead they are the basic forms, techniques and devices upon which design depends. Further, the distinction of human-made design is becoming increasingly less meaningful because machines are now regularly solving problems and designing useful devices. Advanced automatic design programs are used for tasks ranging from laying out circuitry to designing airfoil shapes. These programs have the advantage of being able to simulate forces such as wind and electricity, as well as to manipulate form endlessly based on a set of criteria, such as maximizing aerodynamic lift. The resultant solutions did not exist previously in nature and came about through no natural processes. Although they are not the direct result of human creativity, it is hard not to call the products of the program's efforts design. For our purposes, it will be useful to include in our consideration of design paradigms solutions arising from human, evolutionary, and automated processes.

The Human Body

Our first resource for finding and studying paradigms found in nature is the human body, first because it is most readily available for consideration and most familiar to us. It is also an incredibly rich source of paradigms. For example, think of a structure in your body that has a hard shell around a soft inside—exoskeletal, like a lobster—instead of the more usual arrangement of soft flesh around hard bone. When asked this question, surprisingly many people answer "*There is none!*" But, of course, this is the form of the skull, with its hard shell wrapped around the brain.

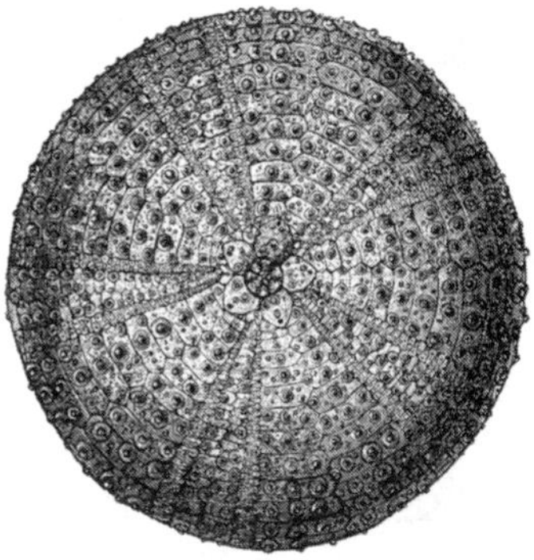

Fig. 1.15 Sea urchin. Exoskeletal creatures such as this protect their soft tissue with a rigid external structure.

Many paradigms are evident and don't require us to look inside our bodies. Some of these arise through the many ways we *use* our bodies. As children we learn to solve problems with our bodies. If we can't see something because we're too short, we learn to make ourselves taller by standing on our toes (see Fig. 5.23). If we also want to be seen by someone else, we make ourselves even larger by waving our arms. If we see a loose screw, we might try to tighten it with a fingernail. As we run into problems and situations throughout our lives, our bodies are always readily available and we're first inclined to consider applying our bodies to problems.

Fig. 1.16 Human skull. A bony structure envelopes the soft tissue within, as does the sea urchin's shell.

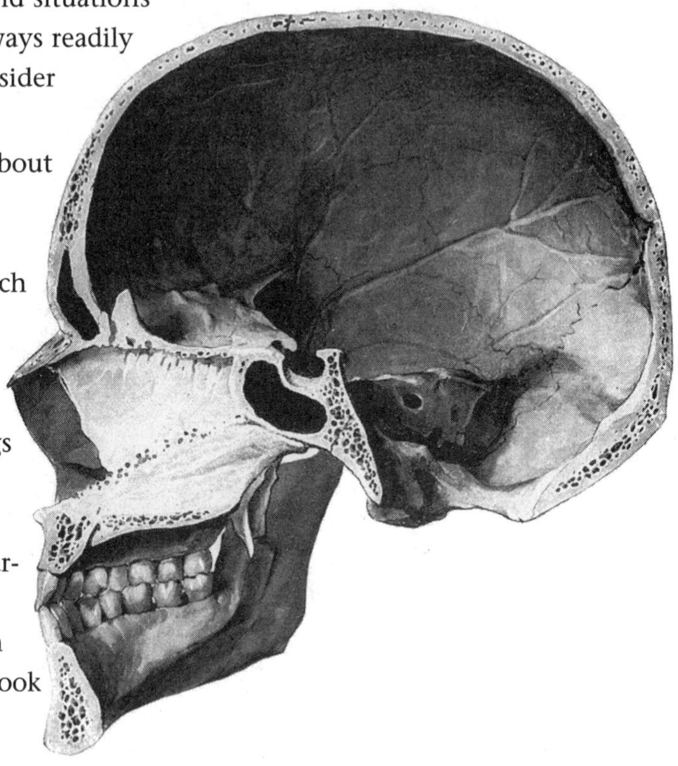

But many of the interesting things about the human body happen within. The many different structures, systems, and subsystems of the body can teach us much about design. An astounding variety of solutions to any given problem is at work within the body; for instance, consider how many different ways things are connected within our bodies. These include skin, bone, tendons, ligaments, and nerves, blood vessels, muscle and cartilage, to name just a few. Most of these mechanisms are hidden within. To learn more, you should refer to an anatomy book

"O speculator on this machine of ours, let it not distress you that you gain knowledge of it through another's death, but rejoice that our creator has placed the intellect in such a superb instrument."[19]

–Leonardo da Vinci

or software, or better yet, take a course on gross anatomy. For a designer, no verbal explanation can replace the learning that takes place seeing first-hand the internal form and function of the body's mechanisms.

Because of the importance of the body in how we think of design problems and solutions, we will return to the body many times throughout this book. Whenever possible, examples of paradigms will include a body-based example, in part to reinforce their personal relevance.

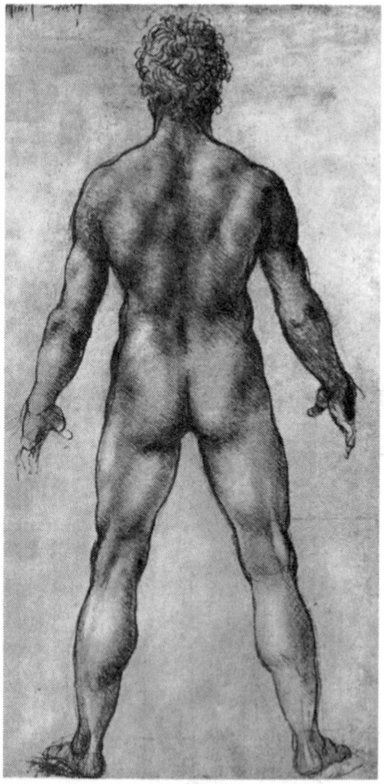

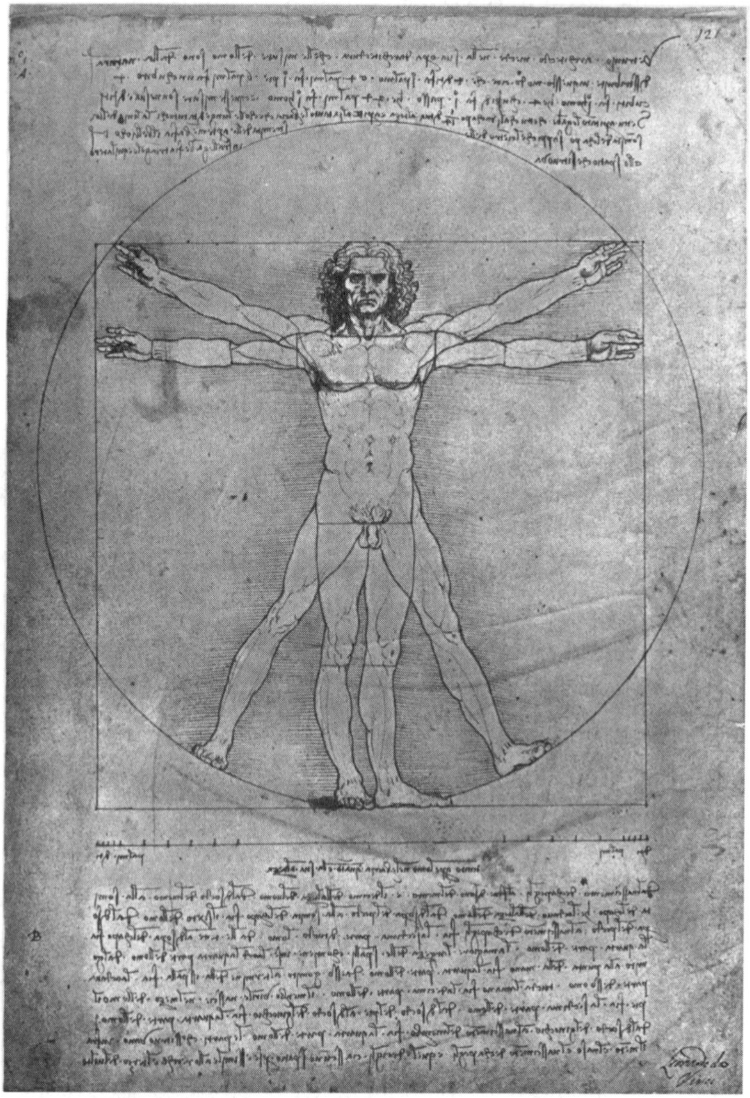

Fig. 1.17 a, b Leonardo da Vinci, drawings. a) (above) Sketch of a male figure. b) (right) *The Vitruvian Man.* In the quote above, Leonardo reflects on his knowledge of anatomy, gained through dissecting cadavers. Leonardo clearly also learned a great deal from drawing from life.

Where Does Form Come From?

Look around yourself, and look at the form of the things you see. Form is about shape, function, and material. In design, as in nature, most form is not arbitrary. But where does form come from? A wide range of opinions exists as to where forms *should* come from. A phrase popularized by nineteenth-century architect Louis Sullivan, *"form follows function,"* led to an architecture that eschewed eclecticism in favor of architectural form that expressed its environment, its structural system, and its purposes. Times and tastes change, however, and often architects have worked the other way, having function follow form, creating a sculptural form for a building, then fitting the functions and structural system into the form.

Fig. 1.18 Architect Louis Sullivan (1856–1924), famous for the dictum "form follows function."

In addition to these two options, a third possibility is that form might be independent from function, at least in the conventional sense of the word "function" (Or at least we might need to broaden our definition of "function.") Since designers first turned their attention to household products decades ago, many products have emerged with formal characteristics largely unrelated to their primary purposes. Beverage bottles started appearing in more or less woman-shaped bottles, and refrigerators came on the market sporting aerodynamic streamlining. While the shape of the bottle has little to do with its ability to function as a container for liquid, and the refrigerator doesn't refrigerate better with streamlining, it's important to recognize that part of the function of these objects is to appeal to the buyer. For retail products this is arguably of greater importance than the functionality of the product relative to its competition. Rather than drawing their formal cues from functional requirements, these things use form to elicit an emotional response. Using form merely to attract, though, is not purposeless, nor was it invented by Madison Avenue, nor even by humans. Charles Darwin's theory of evolution does not imply that only the strongest or the most functionally sensible will survive; rather, those individuals that attract mates and produce offspring have the advantage. So, too, products that

Fig. 1.19 Beer bottle with a "feminine curve."

"Form . . . and the changes of form which are apparent in its movements and in its growth, may . . . be described as due to the action of force. In short, the form of an object is a "diagram of forces," . . . from it we can judge of or deduce the forces that are acting or have acted upon it."[20]

-D'Arcy Wentworth Thompson
On Growth and Form

"What does make design a problem in real world cases is that we are trying to make a diagram for forces whose field we do not understand."[21]

-Christopher Alexander
Notes on the Synthesis of Form

through their form are able to attract buyers will survive in what we might call "retail Darwinism."

But getting back to the primary question here, "Where does form come from?", I will argue that most designed forms begin with a paradigm. This might be an object paradigm, such as a ball, or a concept paradigm, such as a type of connection. Designers will usually reshape the form after this point in response to many factors, including the physical interface points with the user and/or other parts, enhancing safety and comfort. Designs are also refined to meet a host of functional and aesthetic criteria. Functionally, a design can be refined to work with other parts—or may be modified to optimize its performance relative to various criteria.

Optimization usually involves altering a number of different parameters, such as size, material composition, and form, and studying the resultant effects on costs and benefits. If, for instance, we wish to improve the gas mileage of a car, we might alter the design to improve the aerodynamics. We might also alter the form by pushing and pulling the roof line, lowering a skirt close to the ground, and extending the line of the rear window to reduce turbulence. But these changes incur costs of various types; for instance, lowering the roof line reduces passenger space. As we move to lighter materials to

Fig 1.20 Pennsylvania Railroad's Engine 3768. Raymond Loewy's wind tunnel tests helped produce this streamlined design that lowered the wind resistance by one-third.[22]

reduce the weight of the car, we improve gas mileage—but might reduce crash safety. When refining a form to improve its performance relative to several criteria, the designer realizes that improvements to one aspect of the design might be at the expense of another. Optimization is, consequently, striking the right balance between them. Changing several variables at once can make it difficult to perceive the effect of a single variable. An important concept to simplify this analysis is called *ceteris paribus*, which is a Latin phrase indicating the assumption that all other things remain equal. In analyzing the effect of weight on gas mileage, for example, we plot its effect independently from other related criteria, such as costs and safety.

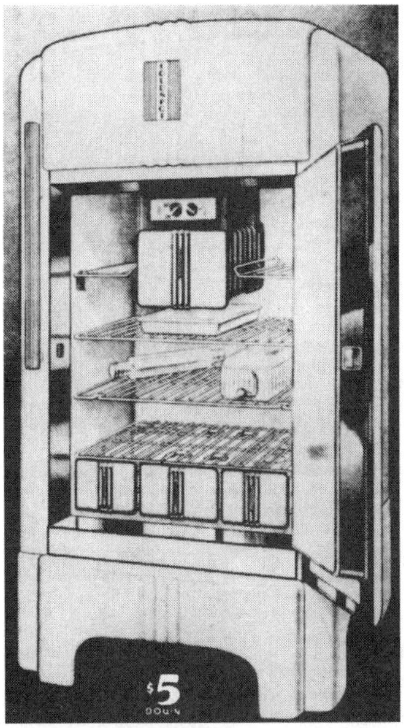

Fig. 1.21 Coldspot refrigerator. While the streamlining on Raymond Loewy's 1934 design doesn't help it fight wind resistance, its responsiveness to customer needs helped raise Sears Roebuck from tenth place to one of the top three companies in the industry.[23]

Meeting aesthetic criteria is the primary goal in styling a product. The semiotics of product form has an unquestionably powerful influence on purchase decisions and consumer satisfaction with products. Styling usually profoundly changes the perceived form of the product. Products might be styled to give them identity within a product line. For instance all BMW models are expected to have a BMW face, with distinctive grill elements and other cues. Design cues might alternately be "lifted" from other designs to attempt to ride the success of those other products. Visual sexual allusion might alternately be applied, as in the bottle example, to give the product a perceived gender bias to enhance its appeal to the consumer. Mechanical allusion might be applied as well, for instance, employing chromed engine parts, hood scoops, and bulges to convey an image of a high-performance automobile.

Fig. 1.22 Automobile grille. The design features quickly identify this as a classic MG. Like human facial features, these elements identify not only a particular model, but also its "family relationship," as similar features are maintained over generations of automobiles.

Products might also be designed to include visual metaphor, for instance, using a bridgelike aesthetic on a building intended to metaphorically function as a bridge between two departments at a university. While these styling processes are interesting—and constitute much of the work of designers, we will focus here on the phase that usually comes before styling: exploring the paradigms at the heart of design solutions. We begin with the simplest paradigms, the fundamentals of form, in the next chapter, "Simple Shapes."

2

Simple Shapes

Simple-shape paradigms are objects that achieve clever functional properties through their form. "Simple" shapes in this chapter refers to the way these paradigms are composed of a single form. The geometry of the forms themselves, such as the *platonic solid* dodecahedron or the Möbius strip described below, might actually be rather complex. But whereas other groups of paradigms involve interlocking, moving, or changing parts, or the relationships between many parts, the simple-shape paradigms accomplish interesting results *simply through shape.*

The simple-shape paradigms are forms we can easily recognize, grasp, describe, and appreciate for their simplicity and elegance. They are often, but not necessarily, made of a single material. And while their outward form might fit a simple-shape paradigm, it might also belie complexity hidden within. We might even encounter things that are complex both in form and in composition, such as the armadillo, which enters the simple-shape paradigms when it rolls into a simple ball to protect itself. We might also see a simple and elegant form, which is literally only a shell hiding a complex interior. This is the case with the chicken's egg, a pure and basic form that is often held up as an example of elegant simplicity. Yet the egg, as we will see in later chapters, also embodies higher-order paradigms, such as enclosure, encapsulation, and growth.

The simple-shape paradigms are important both as individual forms and as building blocks for more complex designs. Many things we'll explore in the higher-order paradigms, we will see, can be broken down and considered at some level under the simple-shape paradigms.

Basic Geometrics

The cone, the sphere, the cube, the torus and the cylinder—these basic shapes constitute a palette of the most familiar solid forms. The basic geometrics paradigm is characterized by irreducible simple forms. These forms are the building blocks of more complex form.

Many forms arise by modifying the basic geometrics in various ways: stretching them, pulling them, tilting them, twisting them, and slicing off segments. In high-school geometry, for example, you learn of the family of curves, circles, and ellipses that one finds by slicing a cone; we call these the *conic sections*. We can cut the corners off a cube or the point off a cone, but we end up with a more complex shape.

These basic forms can also be combined in various ways; for instance, the shape of a rocket might be

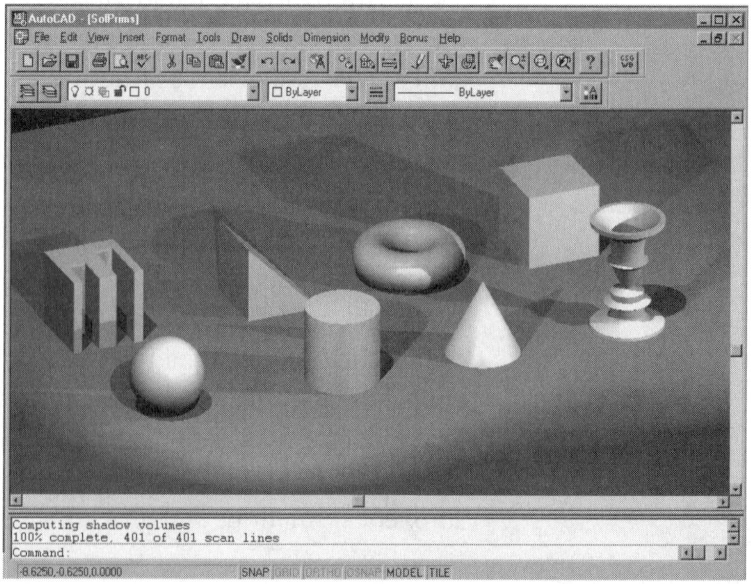

Fig. 2.1 Basic geometric forms are the building blocks of more complex forms in computer-aided design programs such as AutoCAD®.

described as a cone placed on top of a cylinder. Similarly a medicine capsule might be described as a cylinder with a half sphere attached on each end. A flat washer might be described as a short cylinder with a smaller-diameter cylinder subtracted from the center.

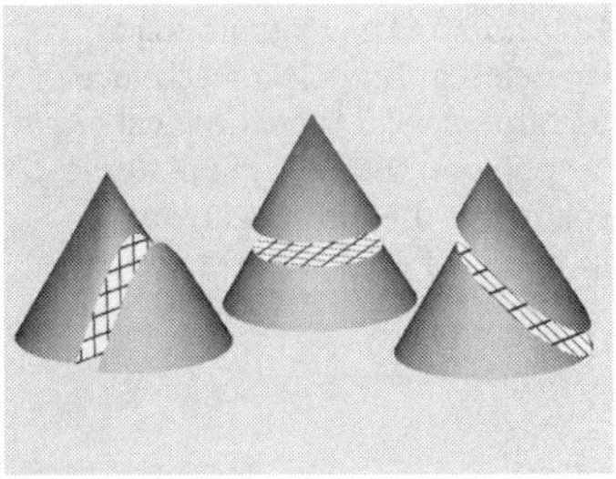

Fig 2.2 Conic sections. Slicing a cone reveals, from left, a parabola, a circle, and an ellipse.

The techniques of combining forms are essential to creating compound shapes. These methods are widely used in architectural design, for instance, in the process called *massing studies*, wherein rough geometric shapes representing the various spaces in a building are laid out spatially and start to give form to the building. These techniques are also at the heart of the modeling operations of computer-aided design (CAD) programs. In addition to a set of basic shapes, most CAD systems provide various manipulation commands, and often a set of Boolean operations—union, intersection, and difference—that enable new shapes to be created by repeatedly modifying shapes, joining one to another, subtracting out a third, and so on.

Fig. 2.3 The space shuttle. As with many manufactured devices, analysis of the form reveals a composition consisting primarily of cylinders, cones, and other simple shapes.

We'll revisit some of the basic geometrics in later sections of this chapter. For instance, the cube is also a platonic solid, and the sphere is also the general form of a ball.

The Platonic Solids

The platonic solids are the set of five solid forms described by the Greek philosopher Plato, having the properties that each is convex (ball-like) and composed of identical regular polygons, with each vertex alike. Each of the platonic solids fits neatly within a sphere, with all vertices touching the sphere. Similarly a sphere can be fit within each solid in such a way that the sphere would touch each face of the platonic solid. The simplest of these shapes is the tetrahedron, a four-sided solid bounded by equilateral triangles on all sides. The familiar cube is next, with six identical square faces. The octahedron, with eight equilateral triangles on all sides, is easily

Fig. 2.4 Tetrahedron "drink box." This platonic solid finds use in packaging, formed by crimping a tube at either end, rotated 90 degrees relative to the axis of the tube.

Fig. 2.5 a-f The Platonic solids, modeled in AutoCAD. Each face of a platonic solid is an identical regular polygon. Each of the platonic solids may be inscribed neatly inside a sphere, as shown below.

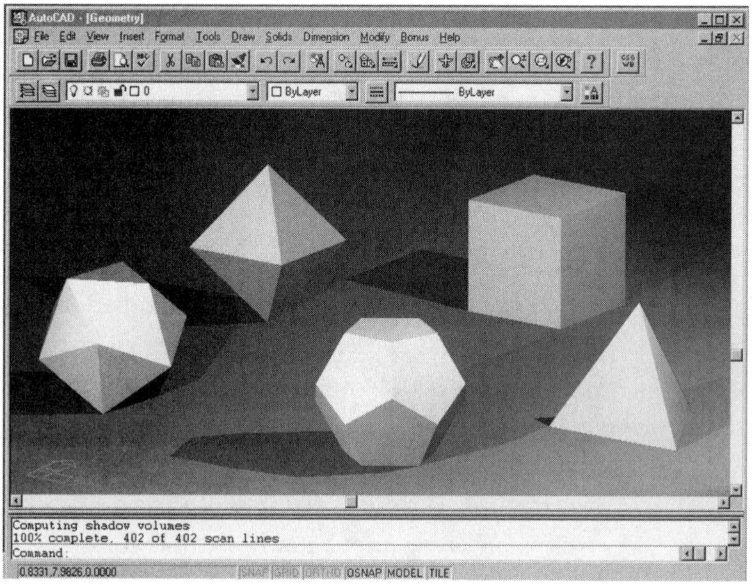

visualized as two square-based pyramids fused at their bases. As we move to the dodecahedron, with 12 pentagonal faces, and the icosahedron, with 20 triangular faces, we see the forms becoming increasingly spherical.

Another characteristic of the platonic solids and other polyhedra is that they can be "unfolded," or drawn on a flat plane, cut out, and refolded. This property was recognized by the artist Albrecht Dürer (1471–1528), who drew not only magnificent perspectives of the polyhedra, but also diagrams of their unfolded forms. You can exploit this property when constructing these forms out of paper: they may be die cut and scored as a single piece, rather than many small faces being cut, fitted and connected together.

Some of the platonic solids have found use in packaging and other applications. The tetrahedron, for example, is occasionally used for packing such items as macadamia nuts; it can easily be formed by crimping a tube top and bottom at 90 degrees relative to each other (see Fig. 2.4). The cube, and variations on it, of course, forms the basis for most boxes.

Polyhedra and Geodesics

The platonic solids are just the beginning of a vast array of convex and compound polyhedra. Polyhedra are captivating for a variety of reasons. Their geometries are interesting and thought-provoking. This has led to their study and their incorporation in artwork, particularly in perspective drawings, but also in models and even buildings, from Neolithic times to the present. Leonardo da Vinci, Albrecht Dürer, M. C. Escher, and Buckminster Fuller are among the many artists and architects captivated by polyhedral forms and their possible uses.

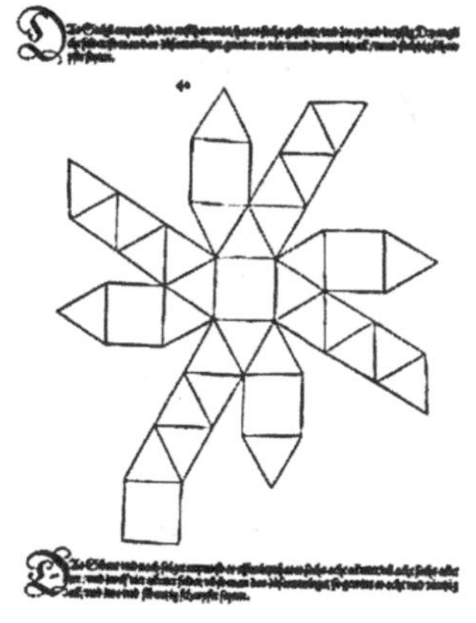

Fig. 2.6 Drawing by Albrecht Dürer (1471–1528) of an unfolded snub cube.

The higher platonic solids and other polyhedra approximate spheres, yet might be constructed of simple identical planar parts. This makes the components easily mass-producible. This was one of the arguments Buckminster Fuller made while promoting his geodesic dome structures and buildings. It has also proven valuable in making sphere-approximating objects, such as soccer balls, out of materials like leather that otherwise could not easily be made into a sphere.

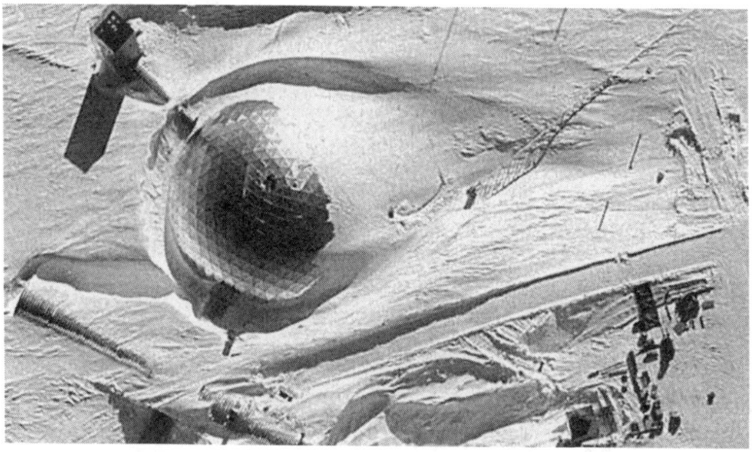

Fig. 2.7 a, b The geodesic dome, designed by Buckminster Fuller (1895–1983). This 150-ft. diameter dome, seen at left from the air, covers the Amundsen-Scott South Pole scientific research station. P. Cheimets photos.

One of the most exciting recent discoveries in chemistry and materials science was of a form of carbon quite different from the familiar graphite and diamond. Carbon molecules were discovered bonded as lattices reminiscent of Fuller's

Fig. 2.8 Polyhedron study by Leonardo da Vinci.

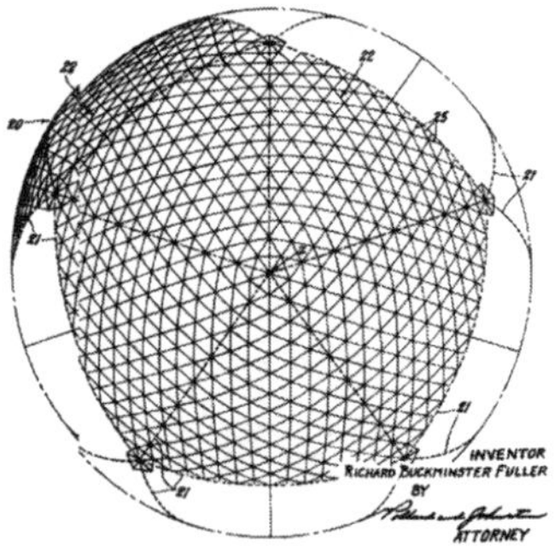

Fig. 2.9 Patent drawing, Geodesic dome. R. Buckminster Fuller, Inventor.

domes. These structures were consequently named Fullerenes, and their discovery led to the 1996 Nobel Prize for chemistry. One such form is the C_{60} molecule, playfully named Buckyballs. This molecule, made of 60 carbon atoms arranged as a *truncated icosahedron*, is bound by 20 hexagonal and 12 pentagonal faces, and coincidentally is also shaped like a soccer ball.

Ball

In a geometry textbook, a discussion of the sphere might follow the platonic solids, but a sphere, we will see, might actually have less to do with design than a ball. Most balls are more or less spherical in form, although, of course, there are exceptions, such as footballs. In the ball paradigm, we'll be concerned with roughly spherical forms, as well as other forms that may be rolled or curled into a ball. "Ball," both as a word and form, implies a number of things beyond what "sphere" implies. A ball suggests throwing and catching, bouncing and rolling. The ball form of our eyes enables them to

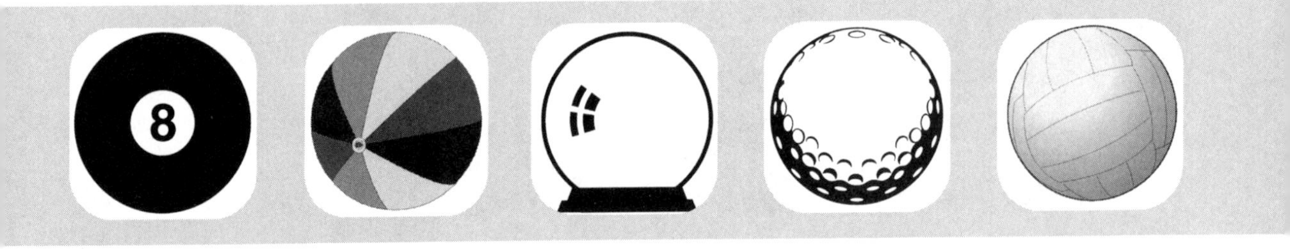

Fig. 2.10 a-e Icons representing several types of balls. Each communicates a different sport or activity.

move freely and smoothly in our eye sockets. Because they easily roll in any direction, balls placed under things, which we call ball bearings, make them easy to move. The balls' movement is often constricted by placing them in a channel, so we can construct such things as an easily moving file-cabinet drawer (linear), a Lazy Susan (circular), or a bicycle-wheel hub (cylindrical).

Beyond the uses for a ball as is, the paradigm is interesting in part for the ways we can form a ball out of

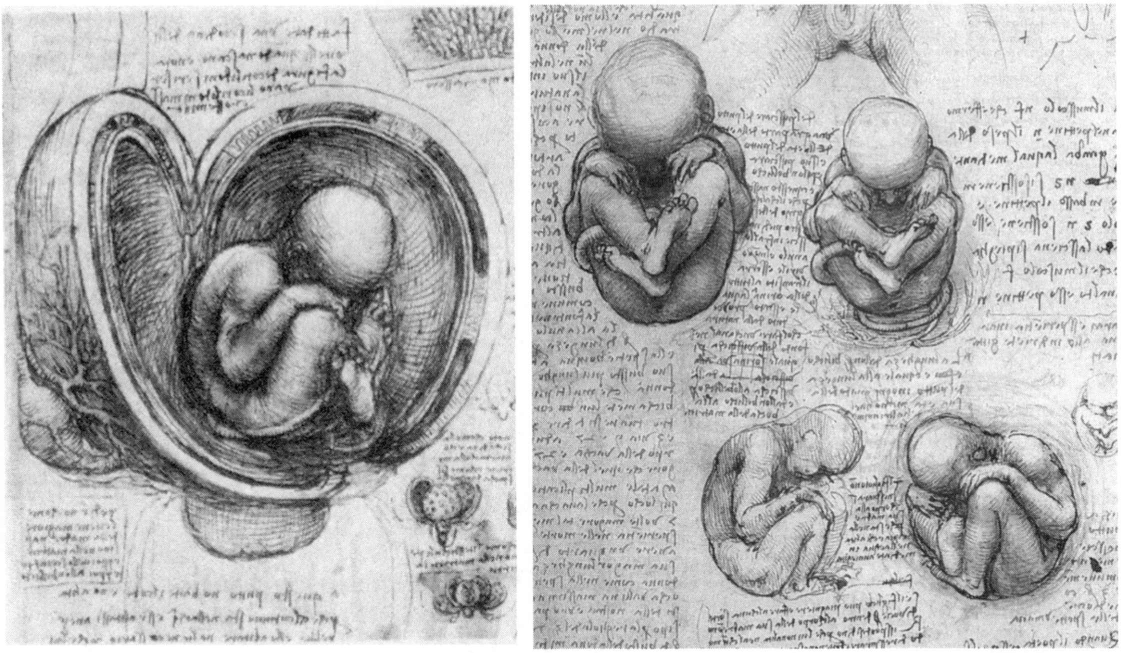

Fig. 2.11 a, b Studies by Leonardo da Vinci of how a fetus is curled into a ball shape within the womb.

things that are not ball-shaped to begin with. We start with what is most familiar to us, our bodies.

A ball will roll because its form has no elements protruding outwards to catch or prop the ball, thereby keeping it from doing so. Consequently if we have such protrusions, like arms or legs, we can protect them from such perils as injury or cold by drawing them close to our body and tucking our head in, forming a ball. We begin life curled into a ball, because we most easily fit in the womb that way. Divers form a ball while flipping—in order to spin faster by minimizing their rotational inertia. You also might assume a ball shape when preparing for a plane crash.

Ball-like products include not only balls for sports and ball bearings, but also a wide variety of products using balls in a socket of some sort. Ball joints are used to connect parts where a wide degree of directional freedom is desired, such as in desk penholders. Some of these applications are discussed in greater detail in the *Ball and Socket* paradigm sections of Chapters 4 and 7. Balls rotating in sockets are also used to dispense liquids, including roll-on deodorants, and

Fig. 2.12 Soccer balls. The truncated icosahedron form approximates a sphere, and enables construction using small patches of leather sewn together.

in the tips of ballpoint pens. Furniture casters are also sometimes made with a freely rotating ball in a socket, which allows the furniture to be easily moved.

Fig. 2.13 The armadillo protects itself by curling into a ball shape, exposing only its tough armor.

A creature particularly well adapted to take advantage of changing to a ball shape is the pill bug *Armadillidium vulgare*. This tiny animal, its name notwithstanding, is not a bug at all, but rather an *isopod*. Distantly related to shrimp, it is technically a crustacean that has adapted to life out of water. The pill bug, when bothered, rolls up into a near-perfect ball, with its tough shell outward, thereby serving multiple purposes. As a ball, it protects its soft belly and its legs. It also tends to roll, thereby possibly escaping predators. Similarly, an armadillo can also roll its body into a ball, leaving little but its tough armor exposed. Hedgehogs can also roll into balls when frightened, protecting themselves with sharp spines rather than armor.

Disc

A disc is something flat and circular. Geometrically many discs are cylinders with a small height relative to diameter, while other discs, such as Frisbees®, have rounded edges. A rounded disc can function similar to a ball joint, providing a flexible bearing between two moving parts. Discs in between

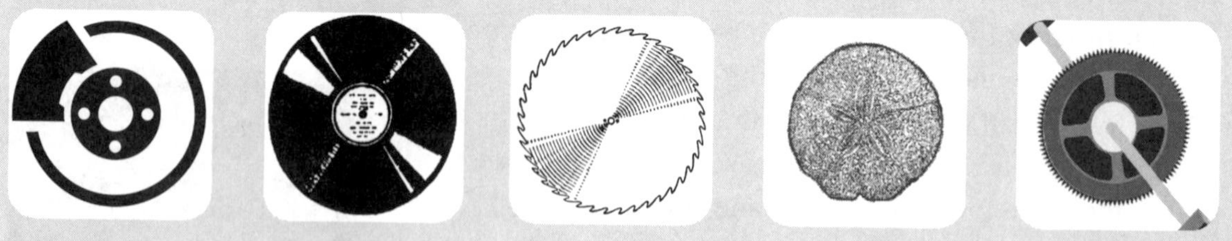

Fig. 2.14 a-e Discs as icons. As with balls, even simple graphics of familiar disc forms are instantly recognizable and evoke complex activities.

the vertebrae of the human spine provide both cushioning and a lubricated surface that permits flexible movement of the vertebrae relative to each other. We are usually unaware of these discs unless they become damaged (a "slipped" or herniated disc), causing pain or even paralysis as they press against the spinal column.

A disc might start with a ball that is then flattened. A ball of puttylike material will form a disc if it is dropped from a high place or pressed against a hard surface. This relationship is exploited in making tortillas, piecrusts, and a variety of other baked goods. When tortillas are made, a measure of dough is rolled in the hands and then rolled out flat or pressed in an iron. Discs can also be formed when a batter is poured and spreads out to a disc under its own weight. This is the process used in making pancakes.

Discs are widely used in recording, from the old analog records to magneto-optical computer discs. In all of these forms, the disc serves as a surface on which to place a linear track of information. The track itself is a spiral, whether of pits that deflect laser light—or of bumps which cause a needle to vibrate on an old-fashioned phonograph.

Sheet

The word "sheet" might first conjure images of bedsheets, but upon reflection, we find sheets all around us. We find sheets of paper, sheet metal, Sheetrock®, and sheet cakes. A sheet is a flat object that is separate or separable from its surroundings. It usually has clear boundaries, for instance, the 8½ by 11 inch boundary of a sheet of office paper.

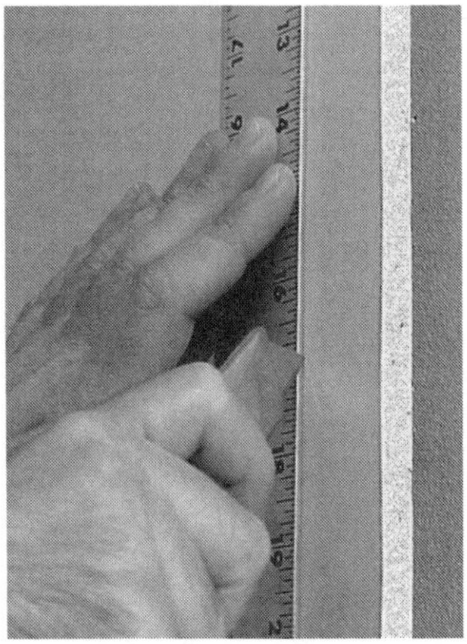

Fig 2.15 Sheetrock®, a popular building material, is composed of sheets of gypsum laminated between sheets of paper. It has largely replaced plaster and lath as a wall surface material.

There are several related terms for things that come in sheets, which vary by thickness. A *film* is a thin sheet or coating. The term is applied to plastic food wrap or a thin layer of oil over water. A *blanket* is a thicker sheet. A film will usually adhere to the surfaces underneath, taking on those exact contours. A sheet will follow contours, but not as well; its own tensile strength will maintain some form of its own, as when a sheet is draped over a chair. A blanket has thickness, or loft, of its own and, therefore, hides contours. We see this when a field—blanketed by snow—becomes a softly undulating surface.

Fig. 2.16 Drawing by Leonardo da Vinci. A sheet covers a human form, and conveys much to us through its wrinkles and the way it interacts with light.

Sheets are formed by a variety of processes. We can form a sheet by rolling a material out flat, as is done with dough or metal. Some materials, such as metal, can be pounded into sheets. Paper pulp in a water suspension forms a sheet when separated from the water by a screen.

Many sheets attached at one end become a pad or a book. Post-It® note pads are held together by light adhesive on the back of each sheet (see Chapter 8). Similarly, and much to the delight of children, mica is a mineral that naturally forms in sheets that are lightly adhered to each other and which may be separated with the fingernails.

Tube

A tube is a hollow, cylindrical form. It can function as a pipe or as a structural form. Tubes are quite common in nature. Pluck the flower off a dandelion, and you'll see that its stem is a tube. Our bodies have miles of tubes, to carry blood, bile, urine, and the like. Throughout the body, tubes—the esophagus, the windpipe and the intestines—serve as the passageways for the solids, liquids, and gasses that pass through and within our bodies. With veins, hoses, and the like, tubes are important for the spaces they enclose. We will discuss tubes as passageways again later in Chapter 9.

Tubes can have many other meanings and purposes, however. With flower stems, the substance of the tube is of interest rather than the space within it. The flower stem is a structural shape. The tube provides resistance to bending evenly in all directions, and resists torsion as well. It is also the tube itself rather than the space within that provides the passageways for liquids moving through the plant.

Just as dandelion stems are structural, cylindrical metal sections are frequently used as structural elements rather than as pipes. Pipe sections are commonly used for signposts and parking meters, and as the upright supports for chain link fencing, to name but a few applications. We have structural tube-like structures within our bodies, such as our arm and leg bones.

Short tubes offer a number of features that are advantageous as pasta shapes. The shape of elbow macaroni, for example, provides an interior surface through which water can pass. This encourages faster and more even cooking than an equal mass of a more solid shape.

Closely related to the Buckyballs mentioned earlier (see the *Platonic Solids paradigm*), Fullerenes have recently been discovered in tube form as well. Perhaps the smallest of tubes, these lattices of carbon atoms form tubes only a few atoms wide, but many thousands of times longer. The tubes

Fig. 2.17 a, b Plant stems. Many plant stems, from dandelions to bamboo, are structural tubes. Similarly tubing and pipe sections are used for structural purposes in goalposts, signposts, bicycle racks and many other objects.

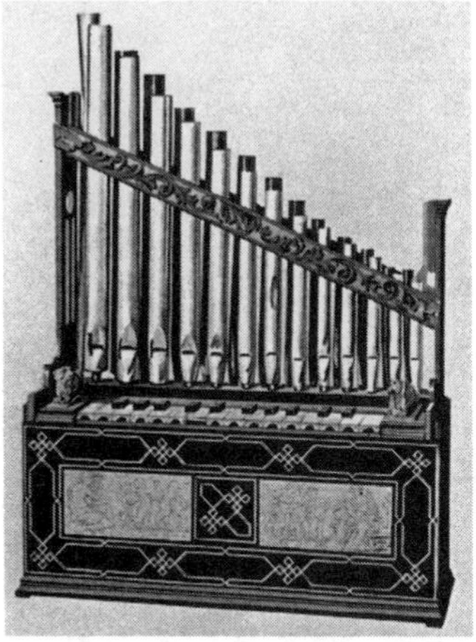

Fig. 2.18 Tubes or pipes are integral to the design of many musical instruments. Pan pipes and pipe organs employ tubes and pipes of various sizes to produce resonance at a progression of frequencies, producing a desired set of notes.

Fig. 2.19 A carbon nanotube, the smallest known tube structure. Like "Buckyballs," the tube is a lattice of carbon atoms.

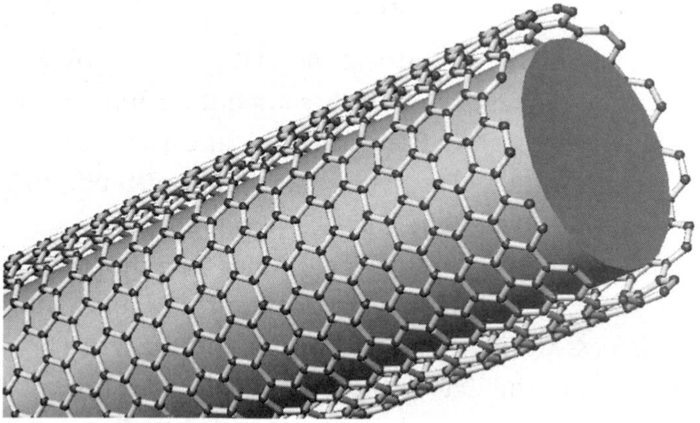

sometimes are formed concentrically, with tubes within tubes. This is a new discovery, and the properties and possible uses are not well understood yet, but researchers are speculating about superconductors and high-strength materials that might some day be made from them.

Torus

A torus is the shape most Americans would call "doughnut-like." Among the more familiar torus-shaped objects are bagels, doughnuts, and Cheerios®. O-rings are toroid gaskets that may be used to seal spaces between tubes. Inner tubes are torus-shaped, and even modern car tires, which are tubeless, enclose a toroid space.

Besides the inside of the torus (the doughnut, if you will), there is also the space within (the doughnut hole) that might be functionally important as well. This is the case when the torus shape is used in conjunction with tubes or rods. The space is important to the functioning of toroid curtain rings, for instance, which suspend a curtain from a rod. This is also the space where your finger goes when you wear a more or less torus-shaped ring.

Fig. 2.20 A breakfast cereal employing the torus shape.

A circle or a sphere moving radially around an axis will describe a torus. If, for example, we think of the torus-shaped toy—the hula hoop®, and the marble inside the hoop (as was done to make a "shooping" sound), in the course of a revolution around the hoop, the marble has traveled the full interior space of the hoop. This principle is employed in computer graphics, where a torus is frequently constructed by rotating a circle incrementally around an axis and connecting it to its previous position with polygons.

A related principle is employed in the human body to provide a sense of balance. If you place sensors around the perimeter of the hula hoop that are triggered when touched by the marble, you will have a device that can sense the orientation of the hula hoop, since gravity will draw the marble to the lowest point in the hoop. If you place three such hoops at right angles to each other along imaginary "xy," "xz," and "yz" planes, and you have a system that can detect almost any orientation. This is nearly identical to structures that evolved as our sensory organs for position, the semicircular canals located in the inner ear; the only significant differences are that the semicircular canals are not quite perfectly torus-shaped, and liquid, rather than marbles, triggers the sensors.

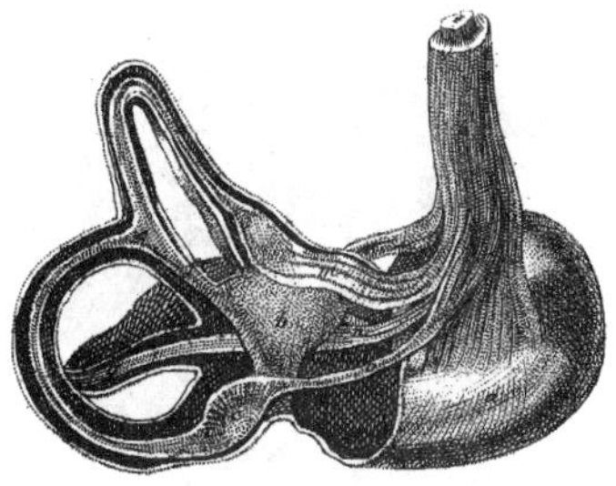

Fig. 2.21 The semi-circular canals of the inner ear. Three torus-shaped structures at right angles to each other provide information as the head tilts relative to the X, Y, and Z axes. This provides your sense of balance.

Fig. 2.22 a-e Icons representing several familiar torus forms.

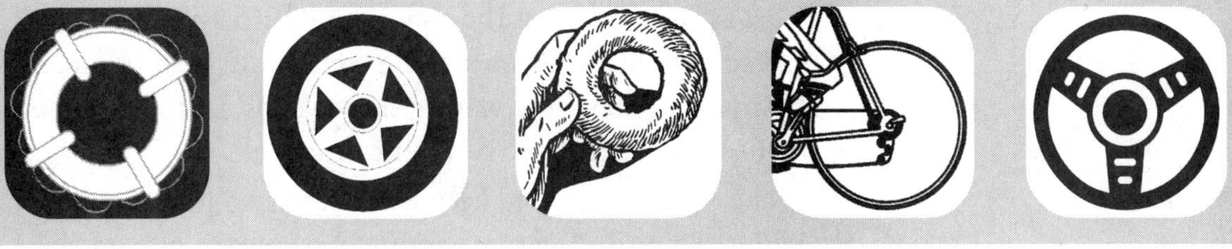

Coil

Coils and spirals are two closely related terms and ideas. In modern English the terms are used almost interchangeably. For our purposes, though, we'll define a coil as a series of loops of a material that is of more or less constant radius, as when wrapped around a cylindrical core, whereas a spiral is made of loops that steadily increase in diameter as they move outward from the center (see *Spiral paradigm*). A coil is

Fig. 2.23 A coiled rope. Ropes, hoses, and wires are among the things we keep compact and organized by coiling.

more or less synonymous with a helix. If the loops touch each other, as they do in an unstretched "Slinky" toy, we will more likely use the term "coil," while if they are stretched apart, either term might apply. If a coil is attached to a core, as are the threads on a bolt, the term "helix" is frequently used.

Coils occur commonly in nature. On the micro scale, we find coil forms at the very heart of life in DNA, the connected double helix that contains the blueprint for life. We begin life in utero fed through an umbilical cord, through which blood vessels are coiled. Vine plants, such as grape plants, ivy, cucumbers and peas, have coiled tendrils that tend to catch onto things to support the climbing plants.

Coiling is of interest as a design paradigm because it has a number of useful properties. Coils are a compact form for long things: we can compactly store ropes, wires, hoses, and the like by coiling them. Given this, it is not terribly surprising that the word comes from the French *cuillir*, to gather. Coils behave differently when turned than they do when pulled; for instance, a corkscrew when turned will enter the cork, and when pulled it pulls out the cork. Coils also tend to act as springs, when they are both pulled apart and pushed together. Coil springs are commonly found in many applications, including vehicle suspensions, pogo sticks, and the inside of retractable ballpoint pens.

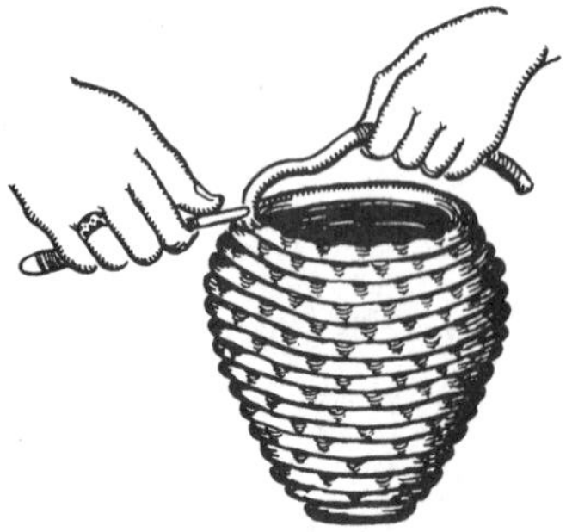

Fig. 2.24 Coiling is an important technique in many crafts, including pottery and basket weaving.

The desire or need to keep cords retracted in a compact form while providing some springiness makes coiling ideal for power cords for various appliances, such as hairdryers, shavers, and telephones. Careful specification of the properties of the plastic insulation used ensures that the cord can be stretched out with little effort, but still provides enough spring to retract the cord into a tight coil when not in use. Coiling the cord keeps a long cord from presenting a tripping hazard and tends to be tidier in appearance.

The *Coil paradigm* has also been applied to shoelaces (Fig. 2.27). Shoelaces have long presented a number of problems.

Fig. 2.25 Coil springs provide cushioning in a train suspension.

Learning to tie them has been a milestone in child development because of the difficulty of the task for young hands. Poorly tied knots easily come apart, leaving the laces dangling. Long dangling laces tend to get worn, wet, and dirty, and might even pose a hazard: they can cause you to trip and they can get caught in escalators. Coiling shoelaces for children's shoes is one approach to solving these problems. Pulling the coiled lace through the holes, the shoelace is easily tightened. The child then simply releases the lace and the lace snaps to its coiled shape and thus shortens to a length too short to trip over. Further, the spring nature of the coil keeps the lace from being drawn through the eyelet, so no knot need be tied.

Fig. 2.26 Coiled shoelaces. Coiling obviates the need to tie the shoelaces; just a tug on them tightens them, and coiled, they are not tripped over.

The coil form has some properties that makes it well suited to springs. Imagine a 2-foot-tall steel spring being compressed down to 1 foot. The coil, if it were unwound, might be a 10-foot steel rod. The deformation of the steel, therefore, as a coil form is 1 foot per 10 feet of length. Compare this to a 2-foot straight vertical length of the same steel rod being compressed to 1 foot. The rod will clearly be crushed and deformed while the coil spring will return to its original form as it is released. The purpose of coiling in a spring is to spread out the deformation along a greater length of material to keep deformations within what is known as the elastic

Fig. 2.27 The *Boa constrictor* coils its body to hold and kill prey.

range of the material. This is the range within which the material is able to snap back to its original form.

The coil has a number of other properties that a corkscrew exploits. A rigid coil, especially when sharpened at the end, will, when turned, enter a resistant substance about as easily as a straight implement will. The situation is quite different, however, when a corkscrew is pulled instead of turned. Here the resistance is akin to pushing a spike *lying on its side* through the cork. This is essentially the same idea as with screws and bolts: the threaded hardware enters easily when twisted but resists being pulled straight out.

Some coils turn in a left-handed manner, while others are right-handed. This is significant in a couple of circumstances. For instance, the pedals of a bicycle continually turn in opposite directions as you ride the bicycle. The pedal you push with your left foot continually turns in a clockwise direction, while the right continually turns counterclockwise. This action tends to tighten the right pedal over time and would tend to loosen the right pedal, if the same type of threads were used. Reverse threads are consequently used on the right side to prevent this problem.

Handedness also is significant in terms of how coils interact with each other. While coils of the same handedness are usually fairly easy to separate from one another, intermixing clockwise and counterclockwise coils tends to result in knots. For this reason, gardeners avoid planting honeysuckle (genus *Lonicera*), which employs left-handed coils, next to Tecoma, which forms right-handed coils. When next to each other, the two plants form a hopeless tangle of knots.

Helicoid

The helicoid is familiar as the shape of an auger drill. The helicoid is an extension of the *Coil paradigm*. A helicoid may be visualized as a helix, oriented vertically and centered around the z-axis, with each point on the helix connected to the axis by a line parallel to the x-y plane.

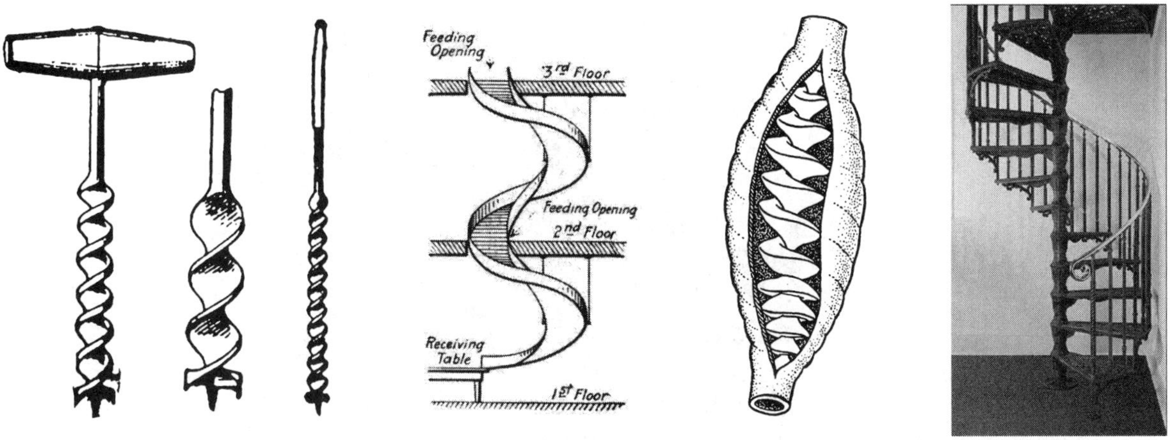

Fig. 2.28 a-d Natural and manufactured helicoid forms. a) Auger drills. b) Materials-handling ramp. c) The spiral valve found in the intestine of the spiny dogfish *Squalus suckleyi*. d) Spiral staircase.

Another method of visualizing the form, frequently used in computer graphics, is to place a line on the x-y plane passing through the z-axis. As the line moves outward on the z-axis, it rotates about the z-axis at a constant rate. The helicoid is a minimal surface. A wire loop formed in the shape of a helix and dipped in a soap solution will form a helicoid. Because the helicoid may be constructed of straight lines, it is, along with the hyperbolic paraboloid and the Möbius band, defined as a ruled surface. This has a special meaning mathematically; it also implies that manufacturing is facilitated as formwork or construction elements may consist largely of straight flat elements.

A spiral stair is a helicoid shape, as well as variations on the screw auger. The Greek mathematician and astronomer Archimedes (c. 285–212 BC) is generally credited with developing the Archimedes screw, a device that is used to raise water. The Archimedes screw is a helicoid within a cylinder tilted at about a 45-degree tilt. As the screw is turned, pockets in the form move steadily upward. The device is still widely used in such applications as pumping sewage, because its design is resistant to clogging. Variations on the Archimedes screw are widely used in agriculture and manufacture in applications such as moving grain and controlling the flow of materials from hoppers.

Fig. 2.29 Seven large Archimedes screws pump sewage at a Memphis treatment plant. Lakeside Equipment Corporation photo.

Among the helicoids found in nature is the so-called spiral valve, found in the intestines of certain animals, including sharks, rays and rabbits. These valves apparently serve to increase the surface area of the intestine within a region, thus facilitating digestion and absorption of nutrients without impeding flow.

Spiral

Spirals are closely related to coils, but a spiral usually starts at a center point and winds outward, gradually increasing in radius. The term is related to "spire," as in a church steeple, a form that comes to a point. Since "spiral" and "coil" are often used interchangeably, you'll unfortunately find terms like "spiral notebook," that don't fit our usage, though we probably would not succeed in a campaign to get people to call them helically or coil-bound notebooks.

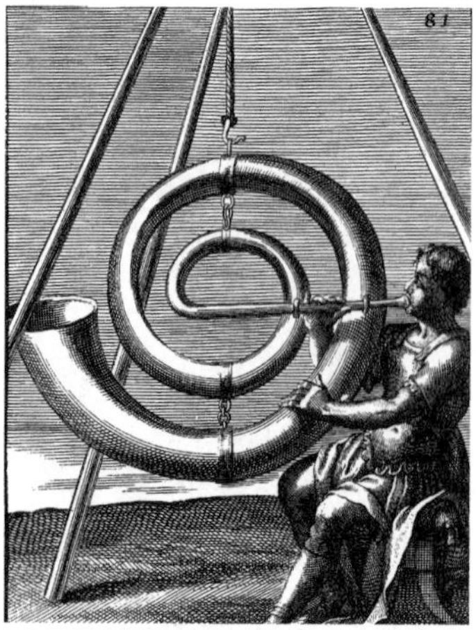

Fig. 2.30 This early tuba employed a spiral form.

A spiral continually changes in radius. The change might be linear, increasing at a constant rate, or the rate of change itself might increase at a steady rate, in which case we call it a *logarithmic spiral.* A linearly increasing radius can be demonstrated by winding a rope into a spiral. A logarithmic spiral can be seen on the underside of most snail shells.

Fig. 2.31 a, b Many shells grow in spiral forms, such as the chambered nautilus, left, and numerous species of snail.

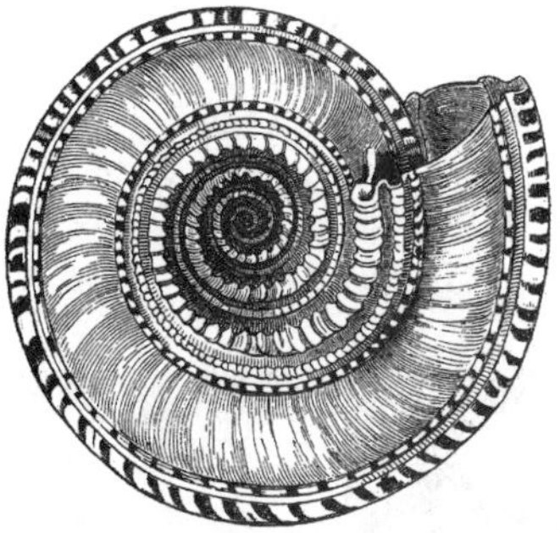

A spiral is a good way to compact something that would otherwise be long. Thus, as mentioned in the *Disc paradigm*, something like a music CD contains a linear track of information, nearly five miles in length. It is clearly made more manageable by winding it into a tight spiral, and imprinting the information on a 12 centimeter-diameter disc.

Fig 2.32 Spiral galaxy. Spirals arise naturally not only through growth, but also through the interaction of mass, gravity, and inertia. They are found in naturally occurring examples ranging from the microscopic to entire galaxies.

Fanfold

The model for the *Fanfold paradigm* is the classic paper folding fan. The folded paper fan accomplishes two primary functional requirements. First, folding and unfolding the fan takes it between a maximal and minimal size and exposed surface area. For the paper fan, the fanfold helps the fan fold to a minimal size, making it pocketable. In the fan's expanded state, the fanfold ribs increase its strength while the expanded size catches a great deal of air for cooling yourself.

As a means of packing a great deal of surface area into a compact space, the paradigm finds use in such packaging materials as paper towels and facial tissues. Paper

Fig. 2.33 A folding paper fan.

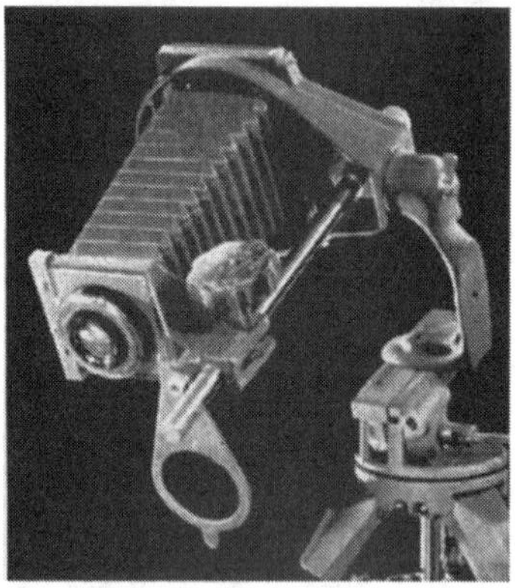

Fig. 2.34 Fanfold construction extended to a tube or prismoid shape creates a bellows. A camera bellows enables a change in size of the enclosed dark space separating the lens from the film plane.

towels, for instance, are usually sold as either rolls or "fanfold." Fanfolds enable accordion doors and Japanese screens to fold compactly. Cloth folded in this manner is called *pleats*, which are used to provide an expandable section of cloth, or to accomplish a distinctive or decorative visual appearance.

The strength of the fanfold configuration makes it useful for architectural roof forms, too. The *Fanfold paradigm* can be applied in several design variants. Beyond the flat fanfold, you might have intersecting fanfolds. This is useful where the objective is to enclose a space using a fanfold. One example of this is the roof of the Air Force Academy Chapel, shown below in Figure 2.35.

Intersecting fanfold surfaces connected together can form an expandable tube. This is usually called a *bellows*, as found on a camera or an accordion (see the *Bellows* section in Chapter 5). A fanfold variant can also be created in a cylindrical form, which is useful for variable-length, flexible-hose connections; these are sometimes used for enclosing wiring and for clothes-dryer exhaust hoses.

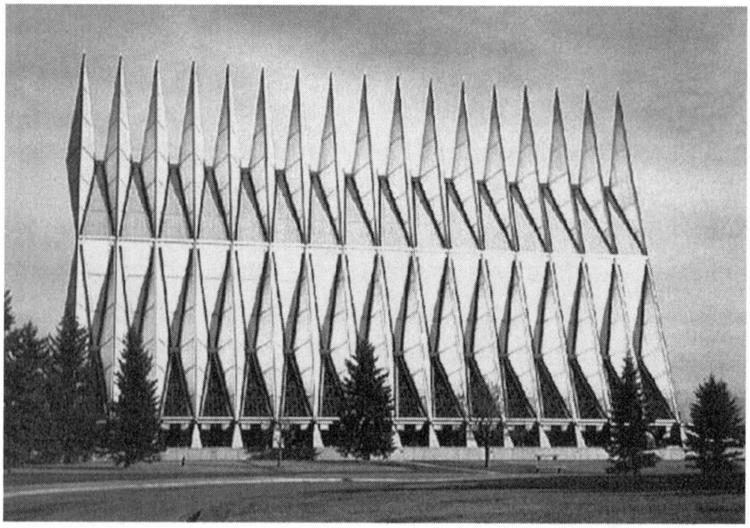

Fig. 2.35 The United States Air Force Academy chapel, designed by Skidmore, Owings and Merrill, employs a form composed of intersecting fanfold forms. USAF photo.

Corrugation

Corrugation involves undulating a surface in a wavelike manner. Corrugated cardboard is familiar as the material many boxes are made of. Although it is formed of a relatively small amount of craft paper, corrugated cardboard is quite strong with respect to compression, bending, and tension. Corrugating a surface applies alternate ridges and valleys to the surface in the manner of a sine wave. Corrugating changes a surface from 2-D to 3-D, and increases the surface area of the corrugated material covering a given area.

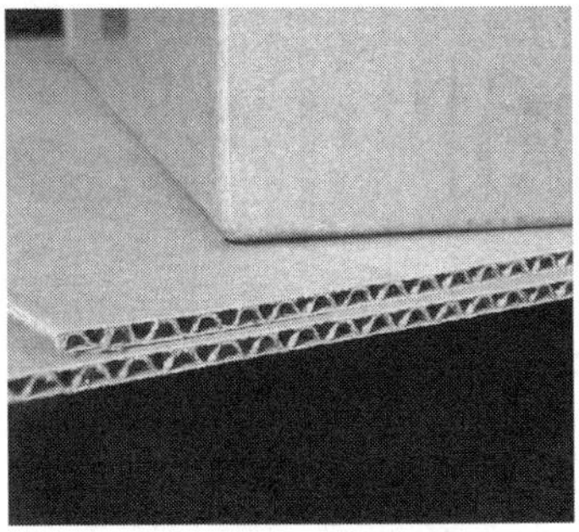

Fig. 2.36 Corrugated cardboard. Just as important as the corrugations is the lamination of the top and bottom paper sheets, which maintain the corrugations of the middle layer and provide substantial tensile strength.

Although cardboard is probably the most familiar corrugated product, corrugated plastic is also sometimes used in packaging as a stronger alternative to cardboard. An example can be found in the crates used in post offices for handling mail. A number of building materials are also corrugated to give them strength, including Fiberglas® and steel. Corrugated Fiberglas is sometimes used for skylights and lightweight garage, shed, or greenhouse enclosures. Corrugated steel and other metals are primarily used in industrial applications, such as for a roofing or wall-surface material. The corrugations on these materials, however, are usually more rectangular than sine wave in shape.

Fig. 2.37 Corrugated metal building. Corrugation gives thin sheet metal substantially greater strength, making it suitable for use as a building material.

Fig. 2.38 Corrugated surfaces can occur naturally in dirt, beach sand, and snow. They may also be produced intentionally in agriculture.

Although washboards are now rarely used in the United States, the term "washboard" is still synonymous with corrugation. A washboard, a frame holding a corrugated piece of glass or metal, was the once-common implement used for washing clothes. With the washboard resting in a pail of soapy water, clothes were alternately rubbed against the corrugations and rinsed in the pail to loosen dirt. The term is now more frequently used to describe the undulating appearance of idealized abdominal muscles.

Corrugations appear in many places in nature. A lake might appear corrugated with patterns of waves across its surface. When we're swimming, our fingertips become corrugated (wrinkled) as our skin absorbs water and expands. The corrugation accommodates the additional surface area of the expanded fingertip skin. Wrinkled skin might provide special benefits for elephants. Scientists have wondered how an elephant could have an adequate surface area to cool their substantial mass. Current theories suggest that their highly corrugated skin provides the additional surface area required for this task.

Oar

Oars and paddles imply motion in water. While you might quickly think of rowboats and assume that oars are strictly a human invention, they are in fact a long-standing natural means of achieving propulsion in water. Several species of water beetles made this discovery long ago. Perhaps the most striking of these is the Backswimmer, aquatic insects of the family *Nonectidae*, order *hempitera*. These insects are shaped like tiny rowboats, complete with oars. As they float on their backs, they paddle with their oarlike rear legs.

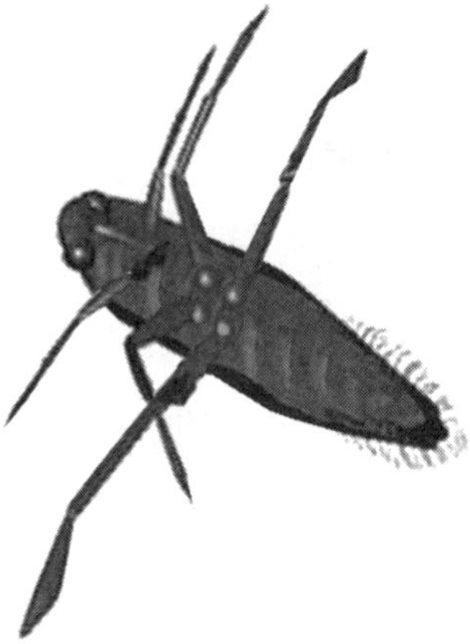

Fig. 2.39 The oar-equipped Backswimmer.

Whether you intend to move liquid or to move through liquid, the task remains the same, often best done by a paddle or oar. The greater the length of the oar, the farther you can move water and, thus, the greater the motion you can achieve. Consequently, oars tend to have a long arm attached to a paddle end. We use our arms as paddles when we swim: the width of the hand serves as a paddle and the length of the arm acts like an oar. In the kitchen, a spoon becomes a paddle when we stir a pot of soup, and in industrial kitchens, large vats are stirred by motorized paddles.

Fig. 2.40 a, b Scull rowing. With this equipment, the rower takes on a configuration remarkably similar to that of the Backswimmer.

Spoon

A spoon is an implement usually made of metal or plastic, with a bowl-shaped receptacle and a handle. A spoon usually acts upon a liquid. You can use a spoon to stir a liquid, in which case it functions like the paddle in the *Oar paradigm*. But the spoon adds a capability beyond the paddle: you can lift and drink liquids with it, such as soup. Spoons are used for solids as well, particularly with small particles like those found in granulated with sugar. Grains of sugar, however, behave like a liquid: they flow and can be poured. Most spoons nest; they fit neatly on top of each other, a property that we will explore later in the *Nested Spoons paradigm* in

Fig. 2.41 A cooking spoon.

Fig. 2.42 The Roseate spoonbill. The bird's bill not only resembles a spoon, it functions similarly as well.

Chapter 10.

Spoons, and silverware in general, carry with them cultural baggage and implied meanings. The way a table is set and your knowledge of how and when to use each implement are considered by some to be a mark of culture. In Western culture spoons represent a separation of the diner from the food; the food is lifted by the spoon, the spoon is raised to the mouth, and the head is never lowered to the food. Because a spoon implies a small quantity, a friend might make a joke about your appetite by asking whether you would prefer a spoon or a shovel. A larger spoon is called a ladle. Spoons are very much a part of the imagery of Western civilization. Their presence can represent nurturing and caring, as an image of a mother giving a spoon of medicine to a child might imply. We even see spoons in the stars, namely the Big Dipper (*Ursa Major*) and the Little Dipper (*Ursa Minor*).

Using implements and tools is primarily a human domain, so we don't find true spoons being used in nature; however a number of creatures use body parts in spoon-like ways. When a dog or cat drinks from a bowl, for instance, its tongue reaches down into the water and curves up at the tip, forming a spoon-like depression to hold the water. This is quickly lifted into the mouth, and the process is repeated.

Many birds use their beaks and bills as spoons as well. The birds drink by dipping the beak into water and lifting, then tilting the head back. The water then drains to the back of the mouth so they can swallow it. The most spoon-like of these is not surprisingly called the spoonbill, which comprise six species (subfamily *Plataleinae* of the family *Threskiornithidae)* of long-legged wading birds with spoon-shaped bills. Just as you might eat soup, dipping a spoon in to raise both solids from the bottom and broth, the spoonbill waves its bill across the bottom to catch, lift, and eat small fish and crustaceans.

Airfoil

If we look at a cross section of a typical airplane wing, we find that the top of the wing is curved, while the underside is relatively flat. The air that the wing passes through will be divided: some will pass over the wing; some, under. The air that passes over the curved upper section has a longer path to reach the rear of the wing. This means that the air above the wing is spread out over a greater area and is consequently at a lower pressure than the air below the wing. The formation of higher pressure below the wing and lower pressure above is one of several factors providing lift for the airplane. This is known as *Bernoulli's Principle*, named for its discoverer, Daniel Bernoulli (1700–1782). Another important contributor to lift, that is also a function of the shape and orientation of the wing, is the tendency of air to follow the surface of the tilted wing (called the Coanda effect), thereby forcing large volumes of air downward.[24]

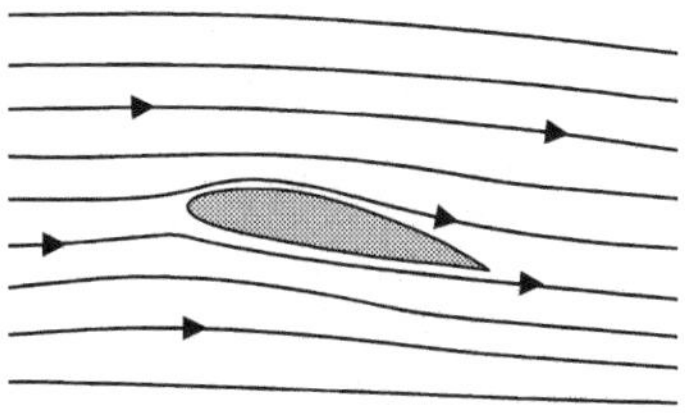

Fig. 2.43 A cross-section of a wing as an airfoil. Lines show air motion past the wing under lift condition.

The airfoil form is extremely important to making flight practical. The airfoil is also significant, in a symbolic way, as a design paradigm. The airfoil is a potent reminder that shape is not just a visual phenomenon. Different forms interact with forces in different ways, and the effective interaction with these forces will often determine the success of a design. In designing things that must interact with forces, the forces themselves can be used to help shape the design. Wind tunnels and supercomputer simulations are common in the design of airfoils because they enable us to study the interaction between form and force to optimize designs.

Controlling the interaction of a designed artifact with forces caused by moving through a medium is an important concern in the design of most moving vehicles, including not only airplanes, but also sail- and powerboats, propellers, automobiles, and even bicycles and golf balls. This is a particular concern where such factors as speed or fuel economy are to be optimized. Consequently some of the best aerodynamic and hydrodynamic design and engineering is applied to America's Cup yachts, Olympic bicycling equipment, and Formula 1 racing cars.

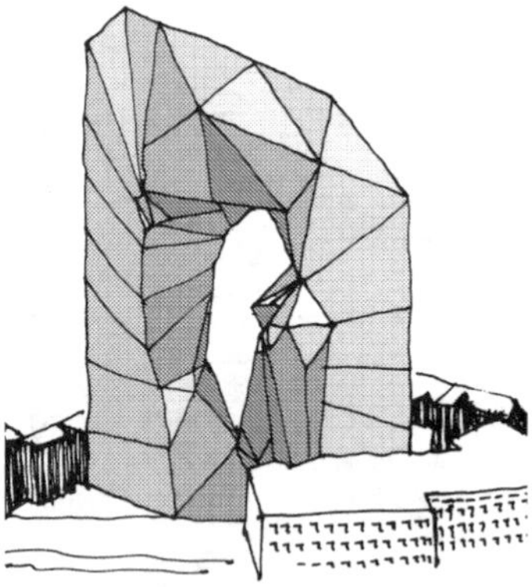

Fig. 2.44 Building design by architect Peter Eisenman based on the *Möbius Strip paradigm.*

Möbius Strip

A Möbius strip is a one-sided 3-D object, discovered by and named for German mathematician August Ferdinand Möbius (1790–1868). You can make a Möbius strip by taping together two ends of a paper strip after giving a half twist to one of them. If you attempt to draw a line down one side of a Möbius strip, a magical transformation happens. Half way through drawing the line you discover the line is now being drawn on the other side of the paper, and shortly thereafter the line continues back to the original starting point.

Fig. 2.45 The international recycling symbol, designed by Gary Anderson, is based on a Möbius Strip.

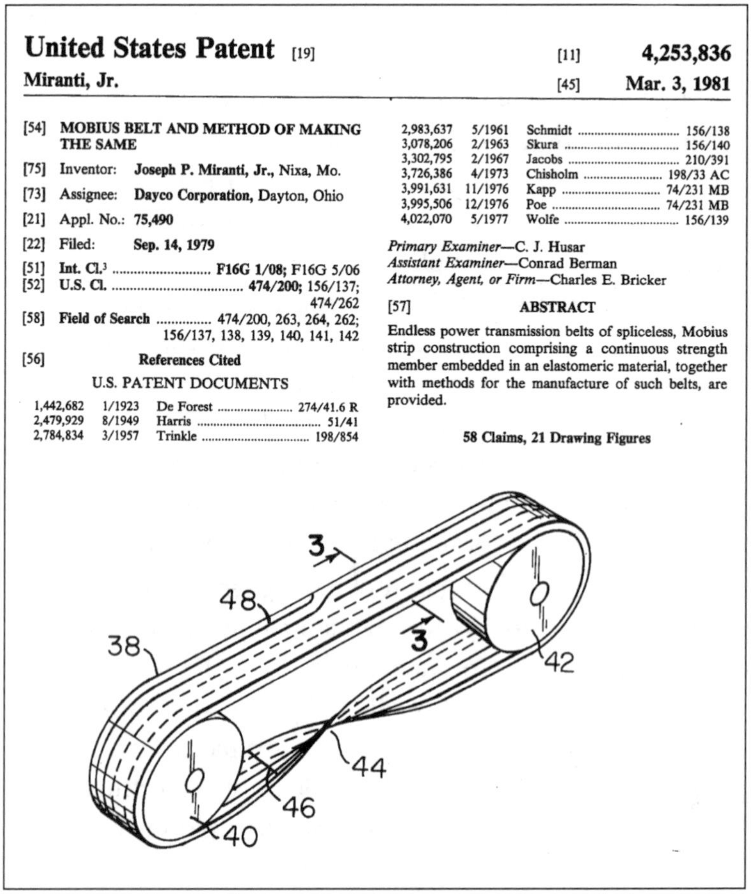

United States Patent [19] [11] **4,253,836**

Miranti, Jr. [45] **Mar. 3, 1981**

[54] **MOBIUS BELT AND METHOD OF MAKING THE SAME**

[75] Inventor: **Joseph P. Miranti, Jr.,** Nixa, Mo.

[73] Assignee: **Dayco Corporation,** Dayton, Ohio

[21] Appl. No.: **75,490**

[22] Filed: **Sep. 14, 1979**

[51] **Int. Cl.**³ **F16G 1/08;** F16G 5/06

[52] **U.S. Cl.** **474/200;** 156/137; 474/262

[58] **Field of Search** 474/200, 263, 264, 262; 156/137, 138, 139, 140, 141, 142

[56] **References Cited**

U.S. PATENT DOCUMENTS

1,442,682	1/1923	De Forest	274/41.6 R
2,479,929	8/1949	Harris	51/41
2,784,834	3/1957	Trinkle	198/854
2,983,637	5/1961	Schmidt	156/138
3,078,206	2/1963	Skura	156/140
3,302,795	2/1967	Jacobs	210/391
3,726,386	4/1973	Chisholm	198/33 AC
3,991,631	11/1976	Kapp	74/231 MB
3,995,506	12/1976	Poe	74/231 MB
4,022,070	5/1977	Wolfe	156/139

Primary Examiner—C. J. Husar
Assistant Examiner—Conrad Berman
Attorney, Agent, or Firm—Charles E. Bricker

[57] **ABSTRACT**

Endless power transmission belts of spliceless, Mobius strip construction comprising a continuous strength member embedded in an elastomeric material, together with methods for the manufacture of such belts, are provided.

58 Claims, 21 Drawing Figures

Fig. 2.46 U. S. Patent #4,253,836. A power-transmission belt employing the *Möbius Strip paradigm.* The half-twist in the belt is intended to make the belt last longer and wear more evenly.

The Möbius strip is, perhaps, most powerfully imprinted as a paradigm by M. C. Escher's illustration of a gridded Möbius strip with ants walking across its surface. As you follow the path of the ants, you soon see how they end up on the "other" side of the strip without changing direction. The Möbius strip has been the basis of many designs and inventions, and is particularly applicable to two-sided devices wherein only one side is typically used.

So when a fan belt for an engine is manufactured in the form of a Möbius strip, the belt surface is effectively doubled, leading, we hope, to longer lasting fan belts. Patents have been filed for Möbius-strip-band saw blades, roller coasters, and a host of other devices. Architect Peter Eisenman has even designed a building based on the Möbius strip.

The Möbius strip is the basis for the international recycling symbol, designed by University of California, Berkeley, student Gary Anderson for a 1970 Earth Day contest, which was sponsored by Container Corporation of America.[25] The symbol is composed of three arrows representing collection of used materials, production of new products reusing the materials, and consumer demand for recycled products. For recycling, the Möbius strip is taken as a metaphor for the transformation of waste into useful products and the realization that our planet does not have two sides, one for consumers and one for wastes. Recycling acknowledges that we must coexist with our wastes.

Fig. 2.47 Illustration by M. C. Escher. The ants on the Möbius strip convey the concept of the infinite surface. The Möbius strip is intentionally rendered in the form of the "8"-shaped infinity symbol.

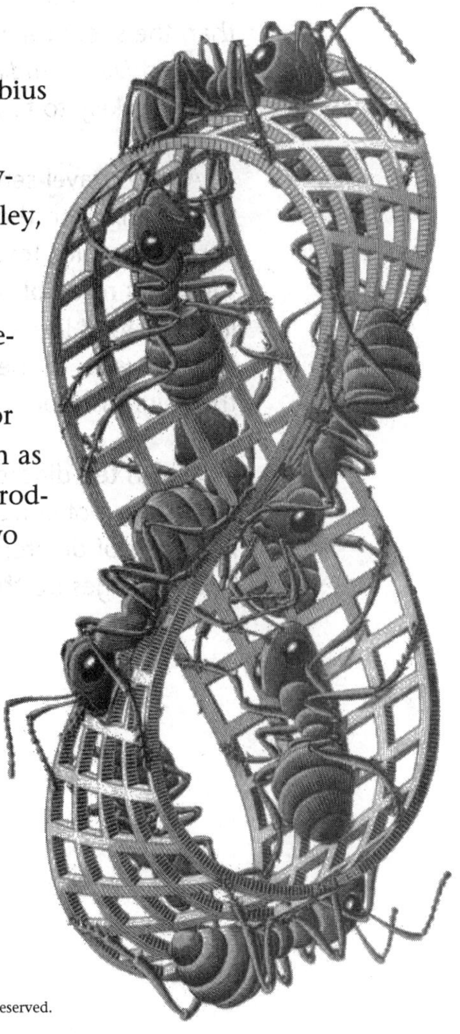

Questions

1) The U. S. Mint produces all of its coins as discs. What advantages does the disc form offer for coinage? What disadvantages can you think of?

2) List three foods that come in sheet form, other than the sheet cake example. Do the same for the *Ball* and *Disc paradigm.* What simple shapes are you not likely to find used for food? Why?

3) A large travel-services company has asked you your opinion on the design for their new 60-story corporate office tower. You notice that the plan of the floors resembles a large airfoil. The entire building is shaped like a wing, intended by the architect as an allusion to their aircraft business. Explain why this might not be a good idea.

4) Sketch ten different design variations for a chair constructed of corrugated materials. Consider corrugations of different sizes. What advantages and disadvantages do the corrugations present?

3

Enclosure

Enclosure paradigms involve the ways that things are held, encased, wrapped, and sheltered. Enclosure can imply shelter, as it does with buildings. It can also imply containment, either protecting the contained, as with a shipping container, or protecting the environment outside the container, as with enclosures for nuclear waste. In all cases, enclosure is about separating the enclosed from everything else, and in many cases the enclosure also serves to maintain a different environment from its surroundings. An enclosure might serve to preserve or protect from environmental variations, such as atmospheric content, temperature, pressure, light levels and qualities, the presence of chemicals, and the presence of radiation or magnetic field. We also enclose things to prevent the spread of organisms in or out of the enclosed area, ranging from wrapping a wound with an adhesive bandage to keep it sterile to fencing in an entire city to enforce a quarantine.

Cup

Consider a cup of milk. While the cup is held upright, it contains the milk and keeps the liquid from leaking out. Most applications of the *Cup paradigm* rely on gravity, achieving containment of liquids or solids by providing a hollow surrounded by rigid, non-porous walls. There are two primary types of cup forms. The first is free-standing, with double-walled cups. This includes such manmade objects as bowls, cups, pitchers, and the giant

Fig. 3.1 A ceramic coffee cup.

Fig. 3.2 A pitcher also fits the *Cup paradigm*. Despite its larger size, it may be used in the same ways as a cup.

cauldrons used in making steel. The second type is a cuplike depression in a larger, usually fixed, object. This type of cup appears, for example, on large office copiers as a place to put paper clips. It also includes most standing bodies of water, whether natural or manmade, including swimming pools, reservoirs, and lakes.

Of the many design paradigms that exist within, or can be formed with the human body, several of these can be formed with the hands. Of these, perhaps the most important is the cup or bowl. We learn early in life to form a cup with our hands, to drink from, to carry marbles, or to hold a pet frog. Experience soon teaches, however, that whereas the cupped hands worked fairly well for holding water or marbles, the frog can jump and easily escape. Consequently, the frog's action provides an early lesson on using design paradigms: The failure to contain the frog is not due to the inability of the hands to make a good cup; rather it's caused by the misapplication of the paradigm. Because frogs can jump, a fully enclosed container would be a better retainer. A cup can be used to contain an animal like a frog, but the side walls of the cup must be higher than the animal can jump and must not provide footholds. Many zoo enclosures for bears, lions, and other animals are, in effect, cups. Simple depressions with smooth, high walls contain the animals and yet allow them to live and be viewed in a more natural, open-air environment.

Fig. 3.3 a,b Cup-like depressions on these copiers provide places to hold paperclips.

Numerous cup forms are found in nature. Many flowers fit the paradigm with respect to their shape, and some are even adapted to catch and hold rainwater. The New World pitcher plant (family *Sarraceniaceae* order *Nepenthales*) has specially evolved leaves that form cup shapes that traps and digest insects. Insects are attracted to the nectar at the base of the pitcher and enter the cup. The surface of the neck of the pitcher is lined with inward-pointing hairs, making it fairly easy to enter but difficult to leave. When the insects reach the lower part of the pitcher, they step onto a slippery surface and slide into the liquid held in the bottom of the pitcher, where they drown and are digested by enzymes the plant secretes.

Cups are occasionally used in ways other than containment based on gravity. They can also be used with their open side against a flat surface, thus fully enclosing the contents, such as when a cup is turned over on a table and traps a fly. Cups made of thick Styrofoam® are used this way to protect outdoor faucets from freezing. Similarly, "flight-deck" hearing protectors used in such environments as airport tarmacs are made with foam-lined cups attached by a wire spring, much like earmuffs. The cup, enclosing the entire ear, provides the most effective hearing protection generally available.

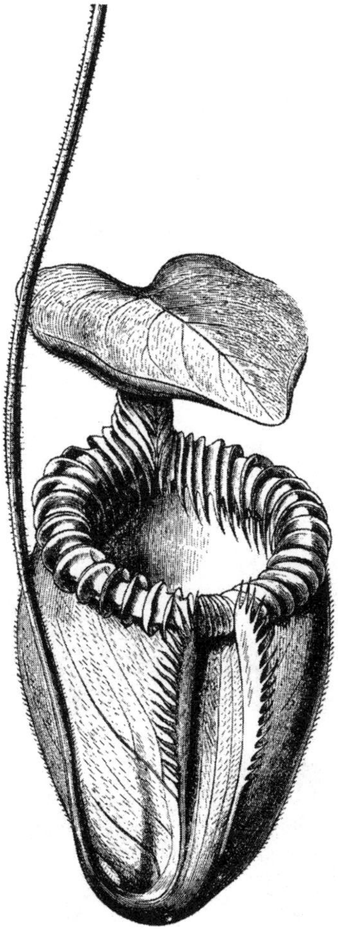

Fig. 3.4 The pitcher plant utilizes a cup form as a liquid-filled insect trap.

Jar

A jar is a container with a lid. Jars are usually made of nonporous materials capable of holding liquids and have wide mouths. Among the objects fitting the paradigm are tiny vials and test tubes, food jars, 50-gallon metal drums. If we place a lid over a cup, we can seal the contents, but the cup is no longer functionally a cup; it becomes a jar. Similarly, taking the lid off a jar effectively makes it a cup. In this manner we can change the functional properties of cups and jars, although we don't usually start calling a jar a cup merely because it has its lid off. One exception, though,

Fig. 3.5 A jar of olives.

are the Mason jars used in home canning. Without their lids, these jars make quite good cups, and are used to serve drinks in a number of homes and restaurants.

Jars make very effective enclosures, and can be used to contain things that can easily become lost (like parts or marbles), fly away (like bugs), or evaporate (like paint thinner). They can also be used to contain a space of a different humidity from the surrounding atmosphere, and so are sometimes used as cigar humidors. A jar can also be used to protect its contents (like food) from damage by animals, insects, bacteria, and air. They are, consequently, popular for storing and preserving foods.

Bottle

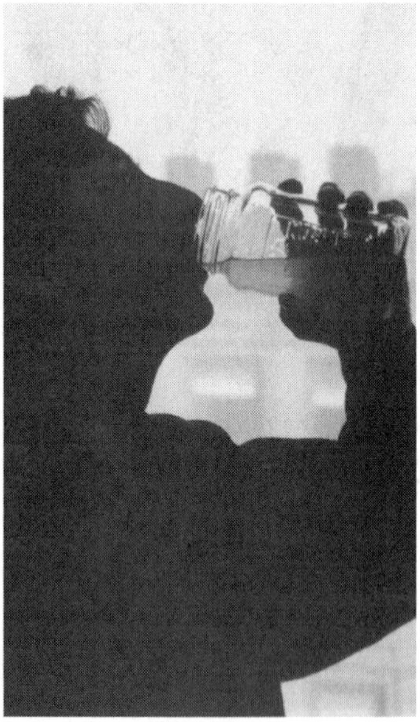

Fig. 3.6 A Mason jar sometimes finds use as a cup.

The *Bottle paradigm* is quite similar to the *Jar paradigm*, but bottles have tapered necks. Bottles are used almost exclusively for liquids. The tapered neck (see also the *Bottleneck paradigm* section in Chapter 9) provides better control when you pour liquids, and also makes it difficult to use the bottle for applications other than liquids.

Most bottles are poured to empty their contents. Sometimes, as with a soft drink, we might use a straw. A bottle may also be attached to a hose to drain the contents, as in an IV (intravenous) bottle. Spray caps may also be used when desired to disperse the contents.

Most bottles are made of glass or plastic. Bottles are occasionally made of skin or leather, as in the *bota*, which is Spanish for a leather bottle often used to hold wine. Bottles are commonly sealed with a crimped-on cap (like soda and beer bottles), a screw-on cap (like plastic bottles), corks (like wine bottles), or nipples (like baby bottles).

Some bottles have special properties. Most are intentionally manufactured of materials that will not react with the contents. Some bottles are intentionally tinted

Fig. 3.7 a-g Some of the many familiar bottle types. Beyond suggesting containment, each is evocative of an activity, a time, and a place.

or opaque to block some or all light in order to protect their contents. Some have markings to indicate the volume of the liquid contained inside. Vacuum bottles are double-walled bottles with an evacuated space in-between, which results in thermal insulation.

Nature provides many parallels to the bottle, because storing and dispensing liquids are crucial to so many creatures. Mammals have in common the ability to produce milk to feed their young. Bottle-like breasts with nipples are a common but not universal solution to the need to store and dispense the milk. The duckbilled platypus is one exception. Because this animal lacks teats, the milk drips down hairs on the mother's abdomen, and the young feed by licking the milk from the hairs.

Among the many fluids human bodies must store and periodically drain, another that everyone is directly familiar with is urine. Perhaps most resembling the *bota,* the urinary bladder also functions in a bottlelike manner.

Fig. 3.8 Soap and chewing-gum bubbles are examples of double-sided bubbles.

Bubble

Bubbles are familiar as the round, thin, soap-film spheres children blow out of hoops, but in consideration of the *Bubble paradigm*, it is important to recognize that, as with the *Cup paradigm*, there are two fundamentally different types of bubbles. The familiar soap bubbles are double-sided, with a thin film or shell encasing an air pocket. There are also single-sided bubbles, however, that are formed by a pocket of air within a solid, liquid, or gel medium. Single-sided bubbles naturally occur usually as gasses are released in, or pass through, a liquid, and as mechanical action folds air into liquid. We find such bubbles rising in ponds, for instance, as gasses are produced and released as a result of metabolic and respiratory processes of the creatures living in it. We also see single-sided bubbles in soft drinks when the carbon dioxide absorbed into the liquid under pressure is released. Bubbles can also be produced by chemical action, such as when vinegar and baking soda are combined.

Single-sided bubbles tend to be lighter than their surrounding medium and as such are visible rising through liquids. This property is exploited in spirit levels, which are horizontally positioned liquid-filled glass tubes that indicate if a surface is level with the ground. Any tilt of the tube that causes one side to be higher than the other is visible as the bubble floats to the higher position. Seaweeds exploit this property by using bubbles as floats to support their structures. The bubbles support the weight of the plant, keeping the leaves spread out. Since the plants have no rigid supporting structures, without the bubbles, they would sit as crumpled heaps on the bottoms of lakes and oceans.

The air inside a bubble can be valuable for other purposes as well. The water beetle *dytiscus* brings a bubble of air with it as it dives below the surface of the water, enabling it to breathe for extended periods of time under water. As the water beetle breathes from the bubble and exhales into it, its time underwater is somewhat extended by active processes

Fig. 3.9 Bubbles have long featured prominently in mythologic imagery, perhaps because as minimal and transparent structures they represent the quintessence of minimal enclosure.

at the surface of the bubble. As the carbon-dioxide level builds up with the bubble, it tends to diffuse into the surrounding water, and oxygen tends to diffuse in as the level drops within the bubble. Other aquatic beetles extend their time under water by capturing oxygen bubbles to breathe from, as the bubbles are produced by algae and rise through the water.[26]

Bubbles formed inside a liquid can become permanently trapped as the liquid solidifies. We find such bubbles in

Fig. 3.10 When a diver exhales, single-sided bubbles are released. Divers must carefully track their depth and the length of their dives to avoid decompression sickness, caused when nitrogen bubbles are released into the bloodstream.

glass, amber, and metal. In metallurgy, much attention is focused on avoiding these bubbles, because they tend to make metal weaker. Sometimes bubbles are introduced intentionally to lighten the weight of a material while preserving its exterior form, as is sometimes done with chocolate. Introducing bubbles into chocolate bars gives the appearance of larger bars while reducing the amount of chocolate and hence the cost to the manufacturer.

While bubbles rising from suspension in champagne or soda are enjoyable, bubbles can be life-threatening when they form in the human body. When you breathe in a pressurized environment for any period of time, an increasing amount of nitrogen is absorbed into the blood and tissues. When you return to a lower pressure, this gas is released and can form bubbles if the pressure is reduced too quickly. This is known as *decompression sickness*, or *the bends*.

Double-sided, free-floating bubbles like those we form by blowing through rings dipped in a detergent solution are usually associated with children playing. These bubbles sometimes form spontaneously as one-sided bubbles rise to the surface. They can also form spontaneously as we speak and air is trapped in bubbles of saliva. These free-floating spheres can take on other shapes as they adhere to point-, line-, or plane-shaped items, or other bubbles.

These bubbles are minimal surfaces; they are held together by surface tension, so the surface of the bubble naturally tends to reduce the surface to the minimum area required to enclose a given volume. The tendency of two-sided bubbles to form minimal surfaces has led to the extensive study of them for potential use in architectural, industrial design, and aerospace applications. A design for a structure like a space station might begin with a concept of a metal framework and the necessity of providing a "skin" over it to protect the occupants. A minimal surface is attractive for the property of using the minimal amount of material necessary to enclose the volume, hence the smallest load necessary to lift from the earth. Studies of this type are sometimes performed by dipping a metal framework into a detergent solution and examining the bubble forms that emerge.

When many small bubbles are produced close to each other, they join together to make foam, which takes on its own set of properties (see the *Foam paradigm* in Chapter 5).

Blister

A blister is a bubble or pocket of liquid affixed to a surface or trapped between two surfaces; in other words, a blister is not free-standing. Since it is adjoined to a surface, it does not tend to move. Blisters occur in human skin as a result of burns or irritants, when liquid or gas accumulates in pockets between layers of skin. Blisters also appear in leaves as a result of disease, fungus, or insect activity, such as when the gall wasp *Biorhiza pallida* lays its eggs in oak leaves. The developing insects living between the layers of the leaves produce substances that cause the surrounding leaf cells to grow substantially larger or to divide faster, thereby making the layers blister outward and providing the developing larva with both food and shelter.

The *Blister paradigm* has been quite successfully employed in packing material: Bubble Wrap®, sheets of plastic blisters,

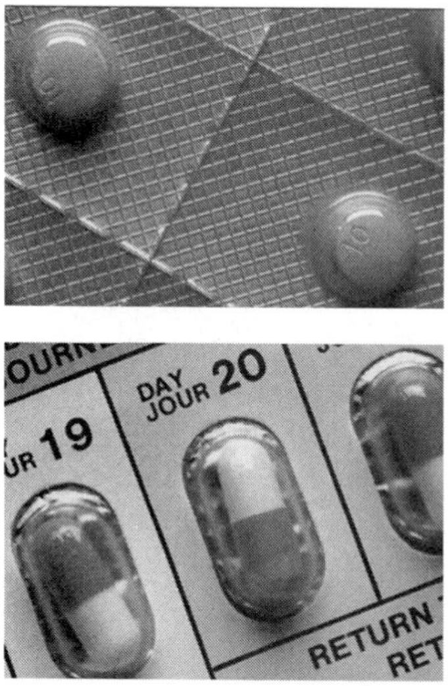

Fig. 3.11 a, b Blister packaging is effective and popular for medicines. Blisters keep each capsule or pill individually wrapped and protected until ready for use, and prevents spills. Packages can be made tamper resistant, and the base card can be marked to indicate the intended date for each dose.

Fig. 3.12 Blistering on a leaf is a natural consequence of irritation from insect activity.

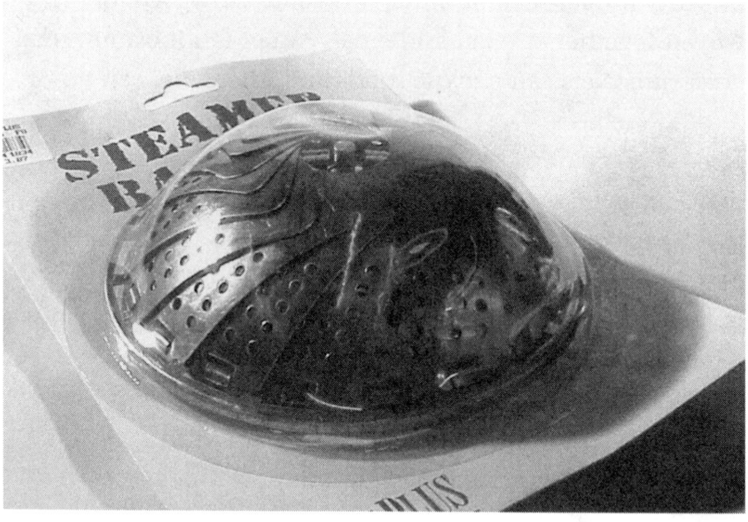

Fig. 3.13 Blister packaging.

Fig. 3.14 Bubble Wrap® uses air blisters sealed between two layers of polyethelene as an protective cushioning material.

is a most effective cushioning material. Blisters have also been used to package individual pills, keeping them from exposure to air and moisture, as well as simplifying dispensing. Larger blisters are used to attach a wide range of products to cards, typically with a clear-plastic blister material. The attractiveness of this type of packaging comes from the combination of the card material's attributes, particularly that it can easily be printed upon, and the enclosure and transparent attributes of the blister (Fig. 3.13).

Net

A net is a porous, fabric mesh, made of string, cord, wire, or other similar materials that are knotted, twisted, or woven together at regular intervals. A net is a most minimal enclosure. Nets can enclose solids and, therefore, can be

Fig. 3.15 a-e Icons representing several common types of nets.

used to separate solids from an air or liquid medium that passes through the net. For this application, fish nets and butterfly nets might first come to mind. Nets are also frequently used to tie down cargo on ships and trucks, and even in car trunks. Nets can be used as barriers, such as the nets used in games like tennis, on the sides of playpens, and in place of tailgates on pickup trucks.

A most familiar natural net is the spider web. A spider web filters insects from the air, enhancing the web's operation through its stickiness. The web also acts as a sensory device, transmitting the vibrations of the struggling insect to the hungry spider. The use of a web as enclosure is even clearer when a spider wraps its prey in silk to prevent its escape. Various other enclosures are made of silk, including spider-egg sacs and the cocoons the larvae of butterflies and moths spin.

Fig. 3.16 The spider web is the quintessential natural net.

Fig. 3.17 Fishing with a net is a process closely analogous to the spider's web. Similarly we manufacture our nets, and spread them out in the path of our prey. The net then separates our prey from that medium.

In a manner analogous to the sensory aspects of a spider's web, we refer to a system of interconnected communications wires as a "net" or "network" (or simply "Web") as well, such as the Internet. Many types of cloth are also net-like, for example a knitted scarf, stockings, and tulle, which is a fine soft netting used for curtains and wedding veils. Netting is also used for the linings and pockets of bathing suits to prevent them from catching and holding water.

There are rigid and semi-rigid equivalents of nets, for instance chain-link fencing, which is essentially semi-rigid netting attached to periodically placed poles. A screen door fits the paradigm as well. Like the spider's web, a screen door separates insects from the air that passes through the mesh. Also related to the net are sieves and colanders, which are usually rigid, whereas nets are flexible. Sieves can perform many of the same functions as nets and are used in such applications as sifting the lumps out of flour or separating cooked pasta from water.

Fig. 3.18 a, b Electric sockets serve not only to provide electric connections, but also to enclose those connections, thereby protecting the consumer from burns and electric shocks.

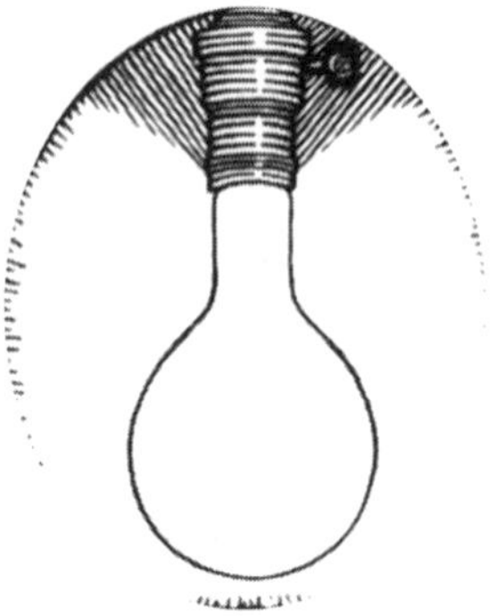

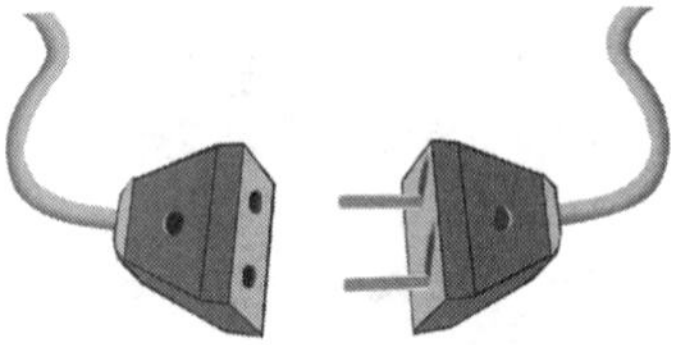

Socket

A socket is a hole or opening in a body of determinate size into which usually fits a plug (cylindrical) or a ball (spherical). So, in essence, a socket is a type of enclosure, albeit frequently only for its counterpart. Sockets will be discussed in greater detail in later chapters for their roles in joining, bending, and flexing, but deserve brief mention as an enclosure paradigm as well.

Among the familiar sockets are electric sockets into which we insert electric plugs, socket wrenches, and ball and socket joints (see Chapter 4). The human body employs sockets as the enclosure for the eyeball, and in the ball and socket joints of the shoulders and hips. We also refer to teeth as sitting in sockets.

A socket joint resembles a sexual relationship between the socket and the plug, and, consequently, we refer to such parts using gender terms. For example we refer to the "male"

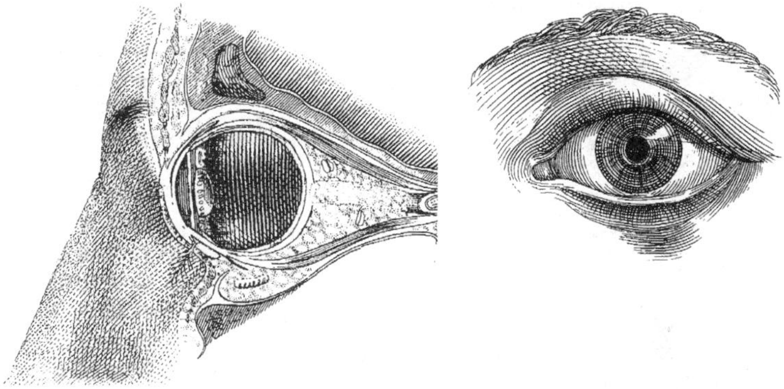

Fig. 3.19 a, b The eyeball rests in a socket that both protects the eye in a recessed enclosure, and enables its free rotation.

and "female" ends of an extension cord (See the Plug and Socket paradigm in Chapter 7). While the primary purpose of an electric light bulb socket is to provide an electrical connection to the bulb, the enclosure aspect is certainly important as well. A well-designed socket on a lamp encloses the metal part of the bulb to protect the consumer from electric shock. And while it may seem that allowing the eyeball to move freely is the primary purpose of the eye socket, it certainly serves a protective function as well, as the eye's enclosure.

A socket is employed as a protective enclosure in the unusual reproductive strategy of the Surinam toad *Pipa pipa*. As the female lays eggs, they are fertilized by the male and pushed up onto her back. The eggs become encased in tissue on her back, forming individual sockets for the creatures to develop in. The young toads later break through her back skin to emerge from the sockets.

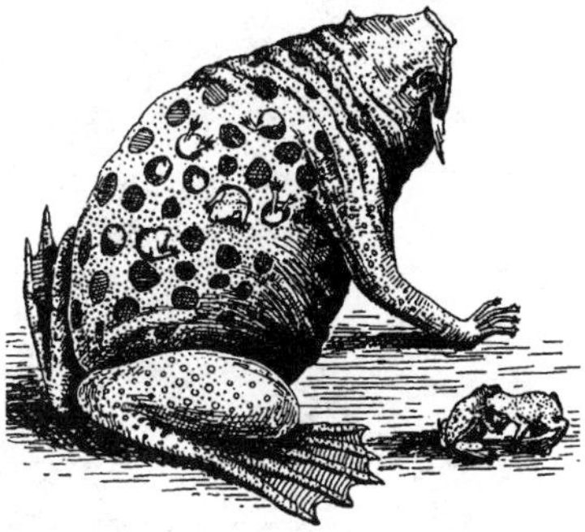

Fig. 3.20 The female Surinam toad (*Pipa pipa)* with her young emerging from sockets in her back.

Skin

Skin is an outer layer or a set of layers on an animal, plant, or mechanical device that serves to enclose and protect its contents. Skin is remarkable stuff. Human skin is a sensory organ sensitive to heat, touch, moisture, and so forth. Skin provides a means of cooling ourselves, through the evaporation of sweat. Further, our skin gives us a resilient, self-repairing, constantly regenerating envelope for

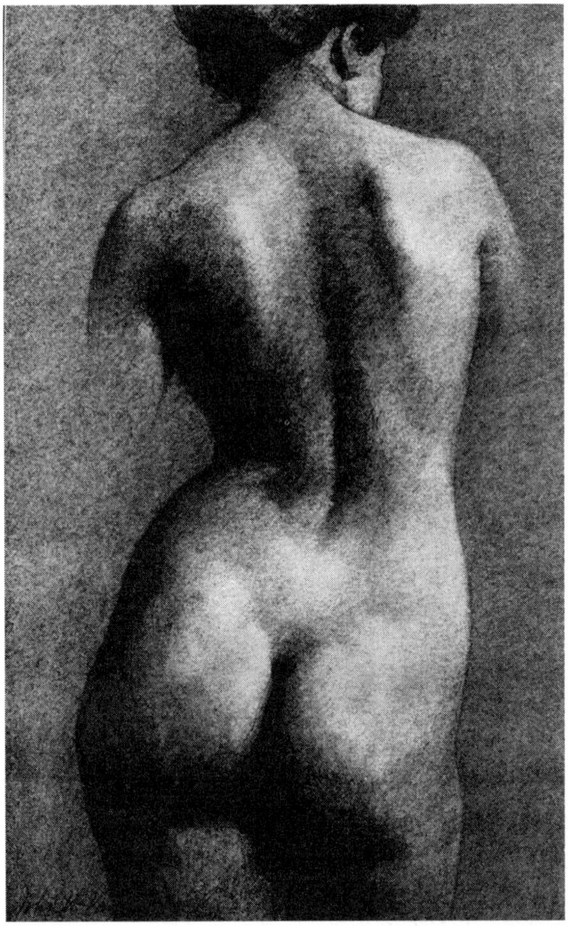

Fig. 3.21 Human skin is often described as our largest organ. It serves to modulate our liquid balance, cool us, and sense pressure, heat, cold, and sharp stimuli.

our mostly liquid bodies. Certain animals are even able to breathe through their skin. For example, the *Plethodontidae* family of salamanders have no lungs, their skin serves all their respiration needs.

Our skin is made of many layers (Fig. 3.23), and we continually wash, rub away, and otherwise lose the outer layer; consequently, we keep a fresh layer exposed. While we are usually unaware of losing so much skin, we are clearly shedding a lot of material. By some estimates, 75% of household dust is made of dead skin cells.[27]

The multiple-layer and protection properties of skin are sometimes emulated in restaurants. Multiple layers of thin plastic are placed over tables as tablecloths. Each time the uppermost layer is soiled or otherwise damaged, it is merely lifted off to reveal a new clean layer underneath. A similar approach is used in the stomach lining. The stomach produces hydrochloric acid, one of the most powerful corrosives known. How does the stomach lining protect itself from the acid it needs to break down food? Employing the same paradigm, the stomach continually sheds its lining, producing a new one approximately every three days.

Fig. 3.22 We also use the term "skin" to refer to the outer enclosing surface of airplanes and buildings. Navy photo.

Clothes often perform skin-like functions. This is particularly evident in skintight stretchy materials like Lycra® sportswear. For comedic effect, the Three Stooges developed a skit based on the multi-layer aspect of the *Skin paradigm* wherein Curly is grabbed from behind, ripping his suit off him, only to reveal him with a complete suit of clothes under the suit that was ripped off. This is repeated several times for effect. Similarly, various animals shed their skins,

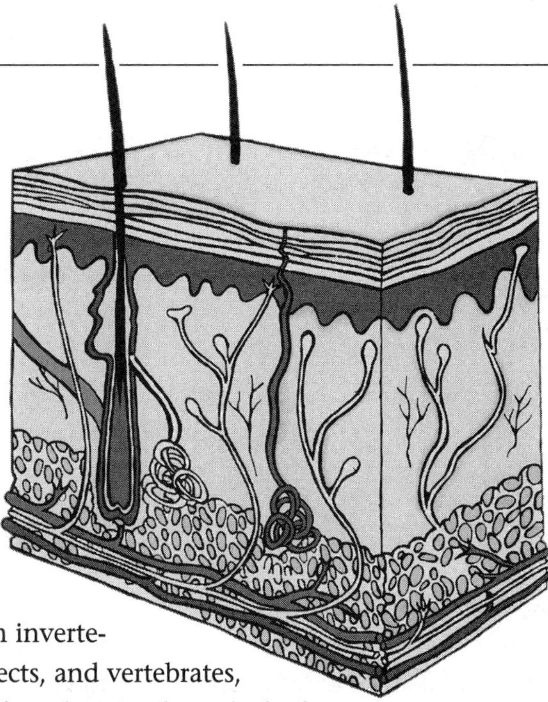

Fig. 3.23 (left) Human skin shown in cross-section.

including both invertebrates, like insects, and vertebrates, like snakes. Although animals can't shed their skins as quickly as Curly to avoid danger, there are some parallels in the way lobsters molt. Barnacles sometimes form on a lobster's back, out of reach. A lobster's periodic molting enables it to escape these pests, leaving them attached to the lobster's old skin on the ocean floor.

Most skins are flexible, effective barriers to liquids. Consequently, when we want to protect something from rain, it might make sense to try to stretch a skin over it, which is essentially what we do when we use a Tyvek® car cover (see Fig. 3.26). We use the term "skin" to apply to a range of outer surfaces, when those surfaces are different from the rest of the given body. For example we speak of a skin forming on ice or on pudding, and call the outer surface of an airplane its skin. Skin's flexible and waterproof properties have made the term "skin" synonymous with containers made to hold liquids, such as the Spanish *bota* (see the *Bottle paradigm* discussed earlier in this chapter), which is traditionally made of animal skin.

The resilient and self-repairing qualities of human skin are more difficult to emulate in manufactured products, but some materials come close. Some plastics heal when cut, as

Fig. 3.24 Animal skins have been used since ancient times as containers for liquids.

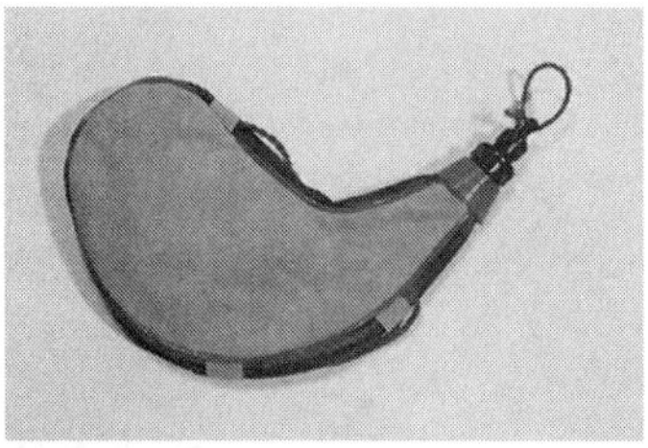

Fig. 3.25 a, b The Spainsh *bota*, an animal skin container, is used to carry beverages, particularly wine or water.

Fig. 3.26 Car cover. Tyvek is well suited to this application. Like skin, it is resilient and water repellent, yet it allows moisture vapor to pass through to help prevent condensation.

the adjacent sides re-fuse. Such surfaces are sometimes used as protection for furniture and as cutting surfaces. Designers of reconnaissance and fighter aircraft have also discovered that use of gelatinlike, resilient skins on aircraft results in a surface less likely to reflect radar waves, thereby helping to hide the aircraft in flight.

Fig. 3.27 a) Cicada shedding its skin. b) The skin it leaves behind, often found clinging onto tree bark. c) The adult Cicada.

Wrap

Wrapping, as in gift wrap, might be considered a subset of the *Skin paradigm*. Similarly, wrapping is usually a thin layer around something, but wrappings are usually discontinuous from their contents, whereas skins are usually integral to their contents. Various food products sold in supermarkets are wrapped in paper rather than put into plastic containers, including meat, fish, and cheese, when these items are cut to order. Various wraps are used in the household, including gift-wrap, waxed paper, plastic wrap, and aluminum foil. Many manufactured products come with wrappers, such as

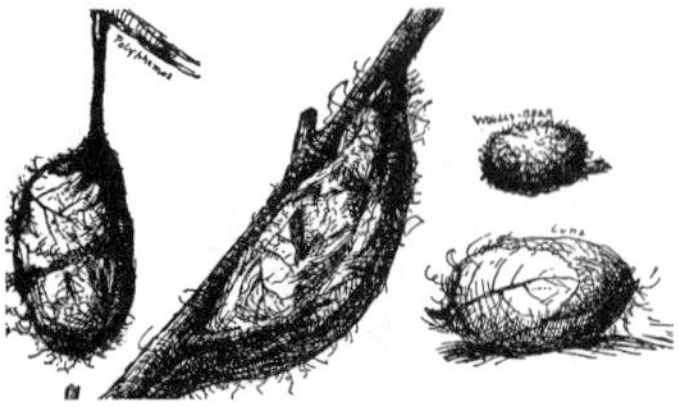

Fig. 3.28 Many caterpillars create a protective enclosure by wrapping thousands of windings of silk around themselves.

candy bars. Wrappers can be used to guarantee sterility, separating the product from the atmosphere, as is the case with bandages. Wrapping is sometimes used more to convey a message of cleanliness rather than sterility, as when hotel glasses are wrapped in paper bags. Wrapping can also convey safety by indicating that the product has not been tampered with, as with collars around aspirin bottles, as well as parents' instructions to children to eat only factory-wrapped candies on Halloween.

In clothing, a wrap is an outer garment like a coat. We can also wrap ourselves with scarves or blankets to keep warm. Similarly we wrap insulation around pipes or water tanks to avoid heat loss. We can wrap things with tape to protect them and provide support, which we do when we bandage an arm, or to change the surface characteristics, which we do when we wrap the handle of a tennis racket.

Among the creatures that wrap themselves are various types of worms and caterpillars. The caterpillars of several species of moths of the genus *Bombyx*, the silkworms, are perhaps the most famous. Each caterpillar wraps a cocoon around itself made from thousands of windings of silk. These cocoons provide a home for the caterpillar as it transforms into a moth, or can be harvested and unwound to make silk cloth.

Fig. 3.29 a, b Wrapping is employed to protect things for shipping, and for decorative purposes in gift-giving.

Fig. 3.30 Wrapping is popular in traditional Japanese culture, not only for gift-giving, but also in such areas as clothing design, food preparation, and religious ceremonies.

Coating

Coatings are usually applied by spraying or painting a liquid onto the outer surface of an object or by dipping the object into a liquid. Sometimes these coatings might dry or freeze to form a hard shell. Thicker coatings, particularly rigid, clear coatings of ice, glass, or sugar, are sometimes called *glazes*. A wide variety of coatings is employed to provide protection from a range of different perils. Paints, for instance, typically protect things from rain, sun, corrosion, and insects. Plastic coatings are often used to increase resistance to both abrasion and electricity. Mineral compounds, metals, organic substances, and all manner of chemicals are also widely employed as coating materials for a myriad of purposes.

Some coatings are used to affect the friction and bonding properties of a surface. A Teflon™ (polytetraflouroethylene resin) coating or a spray of cooking oil protects a cooking surface from having food stick to it. Similarly, waxes are applied to the bottoms of skis to modulate the frictional properties according to the snow conditions. Coatings are also used to increase friction, as when an adhesive and sand coating is applied to a walkway to ensure safe footing.

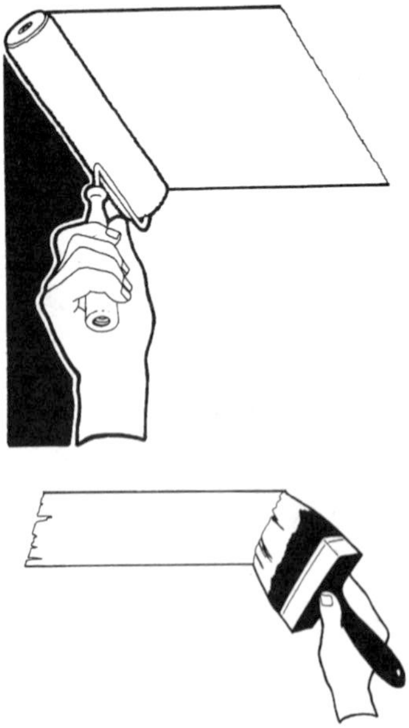

Fig. 3.31 Paint is a coating that helps to decorate and protect surfaces, sealing out moisture and preventing damage by insects, light and oxygen.

Coatings can also be used to harden or strengthen materials. Hard anodizing aluminum leaves a durable coating that is nonreactive and stick-resistant, popularized in recent years by Calphalon® cookware. A coating of diamond dust or tungsten carbide on a drill bit dramatically improves its hardness and cutting ability.

Some coatings exhibit skinlike properties. Latex paints can enclose a form like skin; further it can even possess a human-skinlike resiliency. If the surface being painted is not properly prepared, the paint can be stretched and peeled away, much like a layer of sunburnt skin.

Coatings are often used as insulation, providing protec-

Fig. 3.32 Lidded jar, Ming dynasty, China. Ceramics are often glazed. A ceramic glaze is a glasslike permanent coating that fuses with, and protects, the baked clay surface. Colors are achieved by intermixing various minerals, enabling highly decorative effects.

tion from heat, cold, or electricity. Plastic and rubber are widely used for this purpose, though many materials provide some degree of insulation. One of the more surprising applications is the use of ice as thermal insulation. Water is sometimes sprayed on crops to protect them from a hard freeze; plants are coated with ice, giving them some degree of protection.

Coatings are often used to change the visual appearance of things or in other ways to control their interaction with light. For example, a coating of paint can be used to change the color of a house from white to blue. A more elaborate paint job is used to camouflage a tank. Similarly, makeup is a coating intended to change the appearance of the skin. Sunscreens and other compounds are used to control the transmission, rather than the reflection, of light; applying a layer of sunscreen to your skin blocks ultra violet radiation. Coatings are sometimes applied to car win-

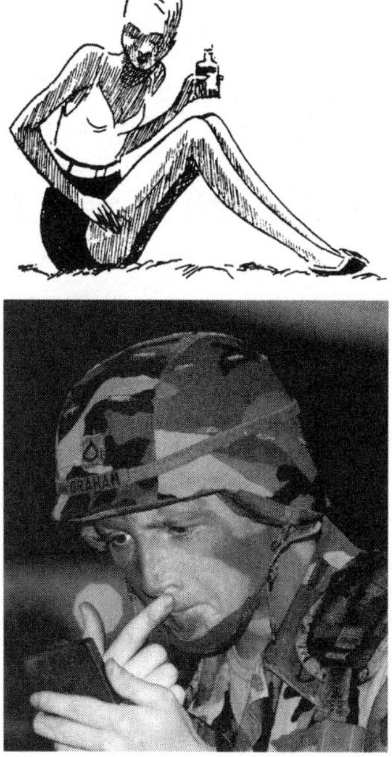

Fig. 3.33 Skin coatings. a) Suntan lotion is applied to block the ultraviolet rays that cause sunburn.
b) Camouflage paint helps to hide soldiers and equipment, even when in plain sight. DOD photo.

dows to reduce glare and sun intensity. Coatings are also widely used in the production of optical lenses. Most fine optics receive several coatings to balance the properties of the light transmitted through the lens, thereby compensating for certain types of distortion introduced by the shape and composition of the lens.

Capsule

Perhaps "medicine" comes to mind first when you hear the word "capsule." Certainly you think of medicine capsules as small, closed shells with a substance, either liquid or powder, inside. A capsule is usually a rigid enclosure, unlike a bubble. The conventional shape of a capsule is a cylinder capped with hemispherical ends, familiar from medicines, although capsules can be other shapes as well. Many capsules can be opened to load or unload them. Most canned goods, such as cans of soup, can be considered capsules. Time capsules are containers loaded with mementos of a particular time, sealed and left for later generations. A "space capsule" is another term for a "space

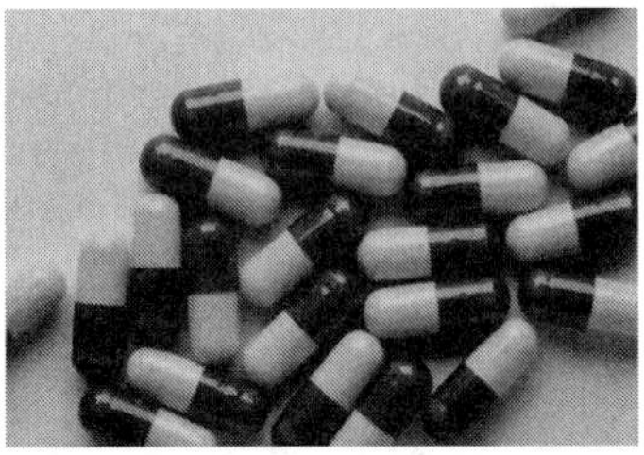

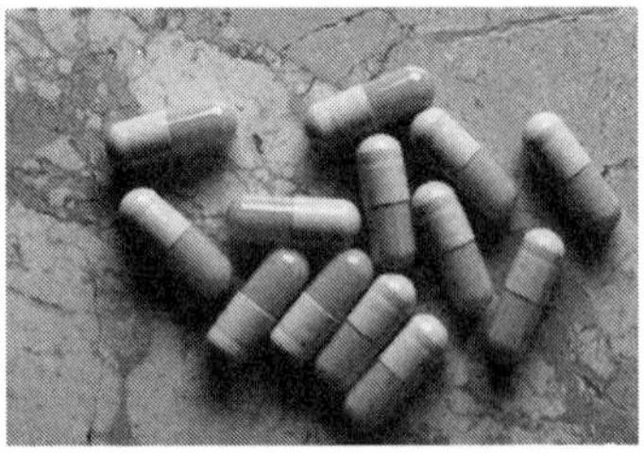

Fig. 3.34 a, b Medicine capsules.

Fig. 3.35 Space capsule. As a capsule, it served to enclose and protect the astronauts, separating its contents from the harsh conditions of space and ocean, while maintaining a life-sustaining environment within. NASA photo.

ship," implying the rigid shell enclosing its human cargo and environment. A car driving down the highway, is, effectively, a capsule. An egg, particularly one with an embryo growing inside it, is a classic, natural example of a capsule, with the growing creature and virtually everything it needs to survive (except perhaps climate control) sealed within.

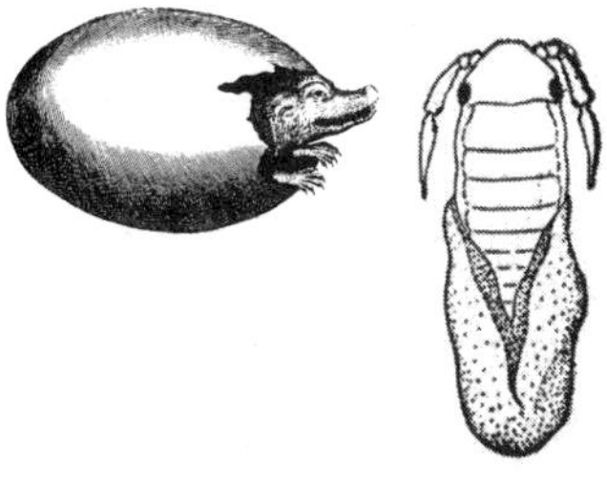

Fig. 3.36 a, b Eggs as capsules. The egg provides a controlled, sealed environment and sustains the growing creatures until they are ready to hatch.

A number of products are packaged in traditional capsules. Although medicines and food supplements are most familiar, plastic capsules are widely used in gum machines for dispensing small toys. The Hanes company established brand awareness for their L'eggs® pantyhose by packaging its product in egg-shaped capsules. Silly Putty® is also packaged in an egg-shaped capsule.

Capsules imply independence: when we consider more than one capsule, in almost all cases they are considered independent from one another. There is no direct corollary to the way bubbles join to become foam, except perhaps a jar full of medicine capsules. If we were to arrange and attach capsules in an orderly matrix, they would no longer be capsules, but rather cells.

Fig. 3.37 A jail cell functions as containment (of a prisoner) within an enclosure. A larger structure (the jail) is made up of a large number of cells, repeated in a matrix.

Cell

A cell is much like a capsule, but it is usually part of a larger structure, arranged in a regular matrix. A classic cell structure is the honeybee's comb. Each cell is a space, or an enclosable compartment, that can be sealed with honey, used as a storage compartment for pollen, or can serve as the home for a developing pupa (see the *Honeycomb paradigm*, in Chapter 10). Most biological structures are composed of cells; living organisms, for example, are made up of one or more cells. Cells of many types, performing different functions, can be present in a single organism. The human body is composed of more than 200 types of cells.

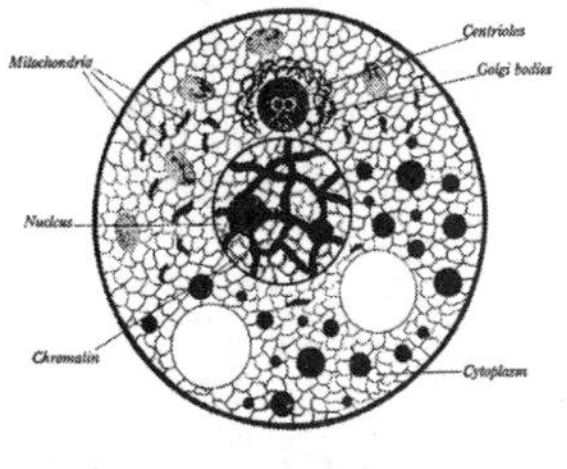

Fig. 3.38 Plant and animal cells similarly contain the nucleus, protoplasm and other components of the cell. Repeated similar cells form larger structures such as flowers, organs, and muscles.

Cells of different types can be of radically different sizes, ranging from microscopic red blood cells, to an ostrich egg

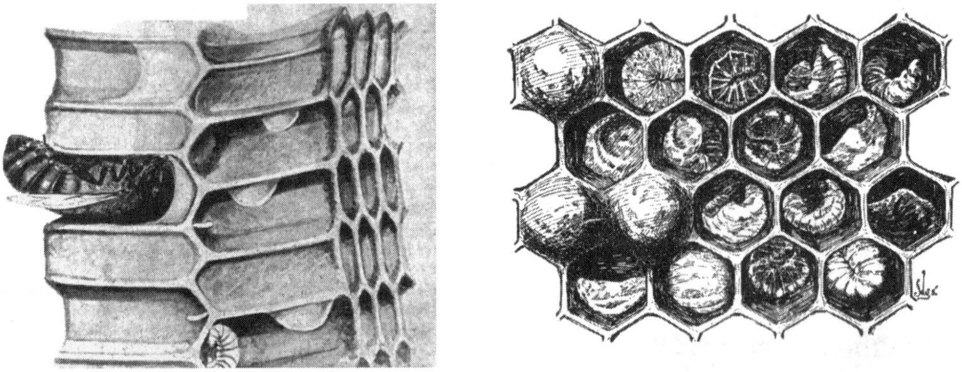

Fig. 3.39 a, b Honeycomb as a collection of cells for the growth of individual honeybees.

weighing more than 3 pounds, but we usually think of cells of a given type as being more or less the same size as each other. Consequently, the rooms of a jail are appropriately called cells, as are the monks' rooms at Swiss architect Le Corbusier's convent of Sainte-Marie-de-la-Tourette at Eveux-sur-Arbresle, near Lyon, France; these rooms are of regular size and arrangement.

Fig. 3.40 a, b Pringles chips and drawing leads are among the products sold in segments of pipe or tubing.

Pipe

Pipes are commonly used to *convey* liquids or gasses (see the *Pipe paradigm,* in Chapter 9), but they can also serve as enclosures and containers. Short segments of pipe or tubes are used to hold products, such as pencil leads and cigars. Larger tubes are used to store architectural drawings.

This storage/containment aspect comes into play even with the piping used in building plumbing systems. These pipes are passageways for water into your house from a water main or a well, but when you open the faucet, you don't have to wait for water to travel from the source to your faucet, as you do when you turn on a garden hose. The pipes are already loaded and ready to dispense because they are functioning as water-storage and containment vessels, not only as passageways. While this might seem obvious, it is an important consideration in the design of systems. Consider for example, a sprinkler system for a large building. Are the many pipes feeding through every room of the building already loaded with water and ready to spray when needed? If so, will the water standing in the pipes hasten corrosion within the pipes? How much more will the building weigh with all of these pipes filled with water rather than air? In practice, many sprinkler systems are filled with compressed air rather than water. Tripping a sprinkler head causes a drop in the pressure that triggers an automatic gate to fill the system with water.

Box

Boxes are ubiquitous in the manmade world. Around the home we encounter boxes big and small holding anything from diamond rings to refrigerators. As a paradigm, the box has several important attributes. Most important, it separates its contents from the rest of the world. We say "box-shaped" to refer to the rectangular-prismoid solid that most boxes are, and often refer to particular types of boxes in describing forms: *"The United Nations building in New York City is shaped like a cereal box."* Boxes need not be rectangular prismoids, however. Light bulbs, for instance, are often sold in hexagonal-prismoid-shaped boxes. Boxes have rigid or semirigid flat walls. Most boxes stack neatly, and some types can be folded flat when they're empty. Boxes are commonly made of cardboard and

Fig. 3.41 a, b Wooden and cardboard boxes.

Fig. 3.42 Wooden Shaker boxes. The Shakers used wooden boxes like these to store sewing and quilting supplies and kitchen dry goods. They doubled as dry measures and so were available in graduated sizes. They consequently nest like Russian dolls (see Chapter 11).

Fig. 3.43 The overall form of many office buildings may be described as *"shaped like a cereal box."*

wood, but they are occasionally made of other materials as well, including plastic, metal, and glass. Boxes are usually closed with flaps, or with a lid that can be hinged or separate.

While the term "box" is likely to first make you think of packaging, functionally, many items in daily life are boxes. A refrigerator, for instance, is a box with an integral cooling unit that was once merely a block of ice, hence, an "icebox." In furniture, chests and various other storage units are boxes. In transportation, we find that many trucks and railroad cars are functionally boxes, consequently, the term "boxcar." Thinking of these units more literally as boxes than as trucks shaped like boxes led to the development of containerized shipping, wherein these large boxes could be separated from a truck, and loaded and stacked on a cargo ship or train.

The British celebrate Boxing Day on the first weekday after Christmas. This holiday has nothing to do with boxing, the sport. On Boxing Day holiday leftovers and other gifts are placed in a box and given mail carriers, errand boys, and the needy. Boxes may be gift items in their own right as well, independent of their contents. Lidded wooden Shaker boxes for instance (Fig 3.42), are prized for their fine yet simple wooden construction and their nesting ability, much like the Russian Dolls (see Chapter 11).

While we might be hard-pressed to identify naturally-occurring boxes, we can easily identify boxlike structures in nature. Since many of the more familiar boxes are made of paper and wood, we can look first to the very material of these and find that the cellulose structure of wood exhibits properties similar to those of manufactured boxes. Most cells in a living tree are dead. The parenchyma cells that make up much of wood are, much like cardboard boxes, blocklike, made of cellulose, rigid-walled and neatly stacked (albeit joined and sharing common walls), and keep their contents separated from the outside. Similarly we find various marine animals such as Stony corals (order *Madreporaria* or *Scleractinia*), sharing these properties of rigid walls and stacking.

Trunk

The *Trunk paradigm* is a subset of the *Box paradigm*, encompassing boxlike enclosures with closable, usually attached, and often lockable lids or doors. Trunks employ walls that sturdy and rigid. Among the familiar trunklike containers are rigid luggage items, such as chests and steamer trunks, safes, and freezers. Most trunks are independent objects, although some trunks are parts of other objects, such as the trunks of cars. As independent objects, trunks are usually rectangular and stackable.

Trunks and chests are widely used for storing items and protecting their contents from a range of perils. For example, cedar chests protect woolen clothes and blankets from moths. Chests made of plastic- or metal-coated gypsum pro-

Fig. 3.44 a, b Trunks, a variation on the *Box paradigm*, usually include a lockable hinged lid.

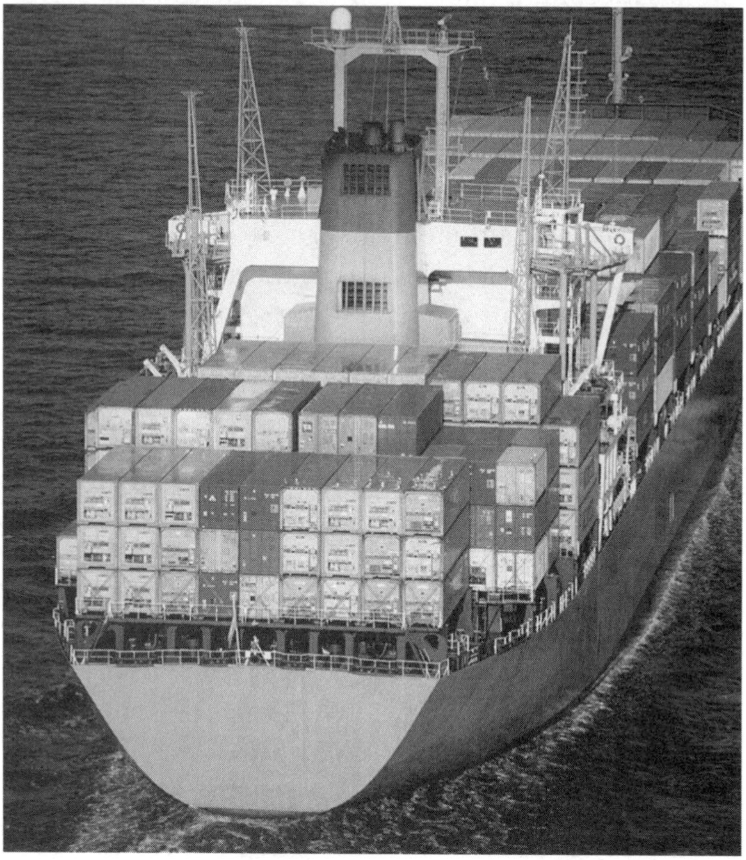

Fig. 3.45 Containerized shipping uses a standard box unit that can be carried by truck, train, or cargo ship. Each box on this huge Japanese freighter is essentially the trailer of an 18-wheeler, minus the wheels.

vide protection from fire. Safes are meant to protect their contents from a variety of dangers including attempts to open them. Many freezers are chestlike, and may even be equipped with a lockable lid. At the larger end of the scale, the boxcars used in trains and containerized shipping also fit the paradigm.

Cave

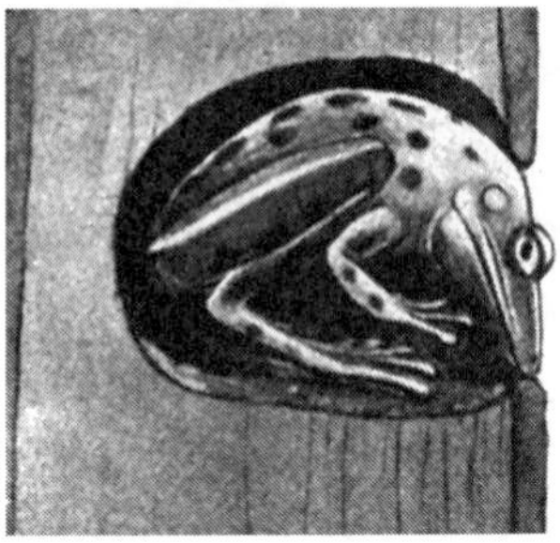

Fig. 3.46 Many animals, such as this tree frog, make their homes in cavelike spaces dug into dirt, trees, rock, or other materials.

A cave might be home to various creatures, but unlike a building, we distinguish this category as a hollowed-out space within a solid. Closely related are a burrow, which is a cavelike home dug into the dirt, and a tunnel, which is a cave open at both ends.

Caves have been widely used as dwellings, by humans, bats, bears, and other creatures. Caves are important for a number of food-preparation and storage purposes, like wine maturation, where temperature and humidity are ideal for long-term storage. Roquefort cheese is produced only in the limestone caves of the southern France town of Roquefort, where the cool, damp environment promotes the growth of the *Penicillium roqueforti* mold that gives the cheese its distinctive taste, texture, and color. Caves and abandoned coal mines have also been used for growing mush-

Fig. 3.47 18th Century coal mine. As a paradigm, caves are enclosures hollowed out of otherwise solid forms.

rooms, where the conditions promote the growth of these *sporophores,* and the closed environment prevents infiltration of spores of inedible or toxic species.

The human body has several cavelike spaces, including the vagina and the ear canal. The ear fits the enclosure paradigm because it can enclose a hearing aid, holding it in place. Some protozoan creatures, lacking mouths, create a cavelike enclosure around their intended food. Once the food is enclosed in a cave within the creature, the opening is tapered and then closed, leaving a food *vacuole* enclosed inside the creature for digestion.

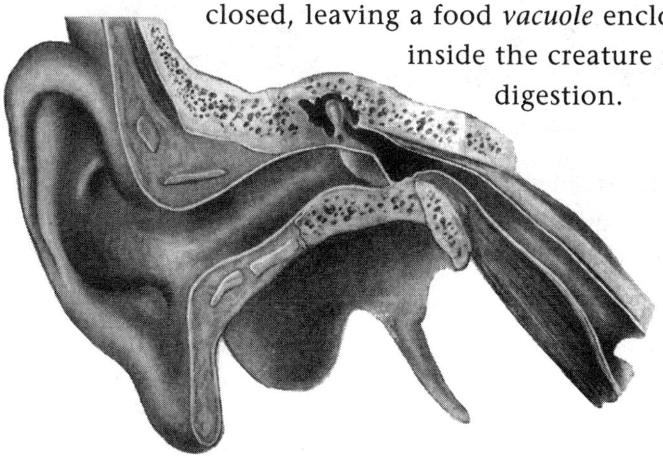

Fig. 3.48 The ear canal is one of the body's cave-like spaces.

Building

The essence of a building is enclosure. Perhaps the foremost function of buildings is to separate the inside from the outside. A building's inhabitants are sheltered from rain, sun, heat, cold, wind, and at least the psychological threat of wild animals. The *Building paradigm* implies an enclosure that is constructed of smaller parts, providing an enclosed and protected interior space. Most buildings are free-standing, rigid, and relatively permanent, although exceptions to all of these exist. Most buildings enclose their contents flexibly, allowing a fair amount of flow in and out of people, air, drinking water, heat, and sewage. Some buildings, such as prisons or bank vaults, however, are meant to restrict that flow, with an emphasis on keeping what is inside *in.* Conversely, fortresses and homes with security bars on the

Fig. 3.49 Windsor castle. Buildings usually function as enclosures. Some buildings enclose to keep what is inside in, others to keep what is outside out. Some enclose and shelter people while others serve primarily to house animals, machinery, or materials.

Fig. 3.50 In some cases, buildings are enclosures less for humans and human space than for equipment, with enclosure also implying sealing out the environment. This is the case with lighthouses, as depicted here by Edward Hopper (1992–1967) in his painting *Lighthouse at Two Lights*.

windows are meant to keep what's outside *out*, at least with respect to unauthorized entry. Some buildings are meant to prevent flow in either direction of air (a center for disease research), radiation (a nuclear-power plant), or water (an aquarium building). These buildings would be discussed as separate building paradigms in a full treatment of architectural types.

Bag

Like the boxes in the *Box paradigm*, the bags in the *Bag paradigm* are familiar in many forms in everyday life. Similarly, a bag's primary function is to separate its contents from the outside world. Among the most common reasons to bag things are to protect the bag contents, to package measured quantities of the contents, and to make the contents easier to carry. Bags of all sizes, shapes, and materials are familiar in retail shopping,

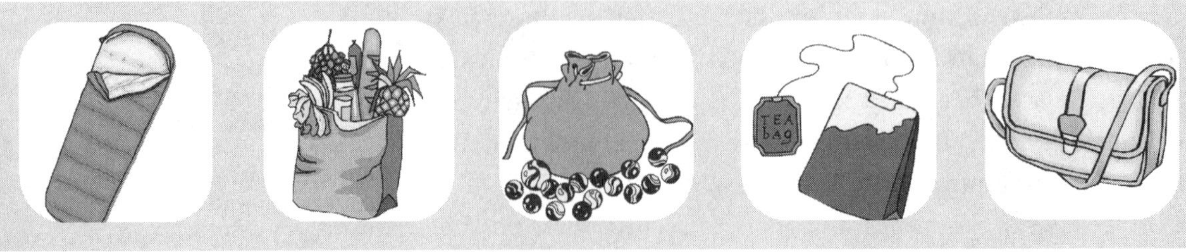

Fig. 3.51 a-e Icons representing several types of bags and pouches.

from supermarkets to hardware stores, but also find use in a wide variety of other areas. Bags are widely used in industry for packaged materials, such as cement, sand, and animal feed. Bags may even be used in a crude construction technique. Sandbags, for instance, may be used to quickly build a dam to hold back floodwaters; without the bags, the sand would be useless for the purpose.

Unlike boxes, bags usually feature flexible walls and do not stack neatly when loaded. A box is generally a compression structure; it is intended to resist crushing through its rigidity. In contrast, a bag is a tensile structure that is usually suspended, for instance, by a handle at the top. As tensile structures, bags, like bubbles, utilize a minimal amount of material to enclose or carry things. While a grocery bag affords almost no protection against crushing for the tomatoes, crackers, and other items it might hold, you can make a bag crush-resistant by inflating and sealing it, as is done with potato-chip packages. Inflated and sealed, bags can provide substantial resistance to crushing and bursting because pressure on the sides is resisted by air pressure inside and the tensile strength of the material. With strong tensile materials, this can be thousands of pounds, in the case of automotive air bags (see the *Balloon paradigm* in Chapter 5). Closely related to the *Bag paradigm* are pouches.

Fig. 3.52 Bags used as packaging can incorporate several features including transparency to show the product, and opaque areas printed in color. Airtight bags can be made crush-resistant by inflating and sealing them.

Pouch

Pouches are a subcategory of bags. Pouches are typically small and made of flexible and often stretchy material. Pouches are usually closable at one end, often with drawstrings. Pouches are consequently less dependent upon gravity to hold their contents than paradigms like cups and many types of bags. A pouch is, therefore, a better choice than a cup to contain a frog or a rambunctious joey (baby kangaroo). Consequently we find natural pouches in the cheeks of some of the creatures which eat frogs, and on the abdomen of the female kangaroo.

Fig. 3.53 Flexible, stretchy, and closable at one end, the Pelican's pouch is an excellent example of the *Pouch paradigm*. As the pelican flies low over the surface of the water, it dips its beak down to catch fish in its pouch. After the water is squeezed from the pouch, the fish is swallowed whole.

Fig. 3.54 a) A female kangaroo, carrying her joey in her pouch. b) A belt pouch, precursor to modern fanny packs. c) (below) Pouch used for packaging freeze-dried foods.

Pockets are pouches and are, of course, present on clothing, but also on the sides of lounge chairs, car doors and seat backs, and knapsacks.

Envelope

Envelopes are another subcategory of bags. Envelopes are usually made of paper or plastic and are not stretchy. Most envelopes are intended for fairly flat items, although some envelopes equipped with bellowslike sides (see the *Bellows paradigm* in Chapter 5) to enable them to expand to hold odd-shaped objects. These envelopes are used for such applications as mailing film to processing houses.

Envelopes are usually sealable and have long been associated with private, personal communication, although this association is eroding as personal communications are increasingly taking place via electronic media such as email.

Fig. 3.55 a-c Envelopes through the ages. Envelopes have long been a potent symbol of private personal communications. Among the earliest known envelopes is the clay tablet shown below. Encased in an outer layer of baked clay in Assyria in 2000BC, this envelope has kept the message within private for 4000 years.

Questions

1) The next time you buy groceries, identify the enclosure paradigms employed by each product you've purchased. If you notice a packaging-related failure, such as a leak, consider whether application of a different paradigm might solve this problem.

2) Christo, the artist known for large works such as his 1976 *Running Fence* through Marin and Sonoma counties, California, surprised the art world in 1985 by wrapping the Pont Neuf (bridge) in beige cloth. In 1995 he wrapped the Reichstag in Berlin in metallic silver fabric. While these projects were for art's sake, list five or more practical reasons to wrap a building.

3) Liquid medicines are usually dispensed in bottles. Design a liquid medicine package utilizing a blister system similar to the type used for packaging pills. What advantages, disadvantages, and challenges does the design present?

4) You have been asked to suggest some ways to protect houses in a region of Florida that is prone to wildfires. Sketch 5 different approaches to protecting the houses that employ Enclosure paradigms.

4

Bending and Flexing

In this chapter we explore things that alter their shape by bending and flexing. Many things change shape when we use them. When we use our hands or when we walk for instance, our joints flex and bend, and our bodies change shape continually. The ability to change shape is critical for creatures or devices with rigid skeletons or exoskeletons so that they can move. It is also important in enabling changes of size or configuration. Bending and flexing are essential aspects of our being. We can easily take bending for granted until we find that a condition, such as rheumatoid arthritis, can rob us of our ability to bend. Our ability to walk, to sit, to write and draw, to hug, to shake hands—almost every physical activity imaginable—involves bending our various joints. This is true of almost all higher animals, and to some extent, plants as well.

Bending is also important in the design of many objects. While the term bending is clear when we're talking about a knee joint, it is somehow less clear when talking about man-made objects, suggesting more a bend in a coat hanger wire than a mechanical equivalent of a knee joint. But just as flexing a knee changes the angular relationship between two rigid members, similar transformations must be accommodated in such applications as lifting the boom of a crane, raising a drawbridge, or installing a section of metal electrical conduit.

Consideration of the *Flexing* and *Bending paradigms* introduces a broad repertoire of connection and form-modifying techniques that are important in all but the simplest objects. Flexing and bending are simple form changes, compared to the overwhelmingly complex transformations in a process such as metamorphosis, wherein caterpillars turn into butterflies. Even though a bendable joint is conceptually simple, it is essential to many designs and is a component of larger changes. Consequently we'll not only explore the different types of bending and flexing in this chapter, we'll also revisit joints in Chapter 5 (*Arms and Legs* as a *Bigger and Smaller paradigm*) and Chapter 7 (*Ball and Socket* as a *Joining paradigm*).

Sapling

Fig. 4.1 The sapling is a symbol of the resilience of youth, and the ability to bend under forces that would break the larger and stronger.

Saplings, or baby trees, demonstrate a natural springiness and are frequently cited as examples of the benefits of springy bending. In a severe wind or ice storm, you can often find a giant tree split or broken by the storm, while a sapling sits next to it undamaged. The reason, of course, is that the sapling bends under the weight and pressure while a giant oak cannot, so it cracks.

In manufactured goods, leaf springs (usually strips of steel) are frequently employed when bending is required in this manner. Other types of springs are also explored in Chapter 2, *Coil* as a *Simple Shape paradigm*, and Chapter 5, *Spring* as a *Bigger and Smaller paradigm*. Since saplings exemplify the bending paradigm, we're concerned with the way various springy materials can bend, then return to their original shape and position. The sapling illustrates some of the nature and purpose of bending within an elastic range, that is, where things can bend and snap back to their original position. Many materials enjoy this property, including plastics, rubber, metals, and wood.

Gumby

This design paradigm features a wire core and a soft material around it, named for the posable Gumby® toy. Having a metal wire core inside a soft rubber body enables these toys to be bent into various shapes and retain poses they are set into. A similar technique is used in sculpture. Clay models are frequently made with a wire armature at their core, which helps to hold the shape, giving the model strength, and allowing bending when necessary. The paradigm also finds serious application in curve-drawing tools used in mechanical drafting. These tools typically use a lead core with a soft plastic shell. The tools are easily bent into the desired shape, then a pencil or pen drawn along the side of the plastic housing places the curve onto the paper.

The *Gumby paradigm* also includes pipe cleaners. A pipe cleaner is a thin wire pair, twisted with flocking between them to look something like a cat's tail. Pipe cleaners are sometimes used to clean smoking pipes. Their ability to flex enables them to follow a curved path through a pipe, while their flocking serves to scrub the surfaces of the passageway. But any kindergartener can tell you that the real purpose of pipe cleaners is to bend them, twist them together, and make things out of them.

Fig. 4.2 Gumby and Pokey. These and other flexible toys incorporate an embedded wire armature that enables the plastic figures to be bent into various poses.

Fig. 4.3 Most metals will bounce back from a small deformation (elastic range) but will hold a shape when more substantially bent (plastic range, *Gumby paradigm*).

Fig. 4.4 A flexible curve-drawing tool. Like Gumby, a flexible metal core enables it to hold the desired shape, while a plastic coating provides the desired surface characteristics.

Nitinol

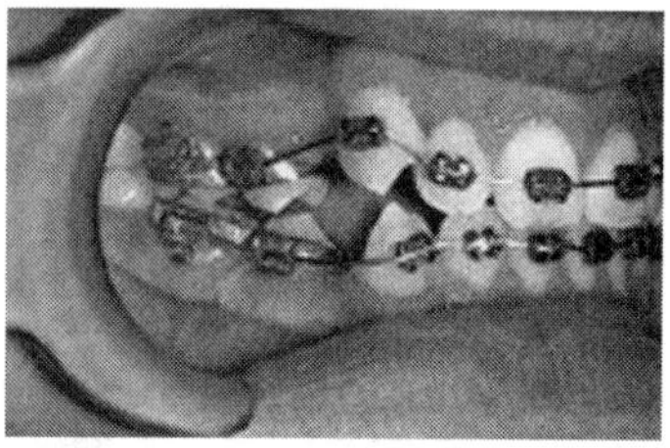

Fig. 4.5 Orthodontic braces. Nitinol wires may easily be inserted when cold. Upon heating, the wires pull into their original shape, in turn applying pressure to move the teeth into line. 3M Unitek Photo.

Nitinol is a nickel-titanium metal alloy that has some very unusual properties. First developed at the Naval Ordnance Laboratory (the *nol* in Nitinol) in 1968, Nitinol is called "the metal with a memory." It can be formed into shapes such as a helical spring. It can then be pulled out of that shape, for example stretched outward. When the part is heated (usually to between 60°C and 100°C) it returns to its original formed shape, in this case, the helical spring.

Nitinol is used in a wide variety of medical and surgical applications. Its memory property enables parts to be deformed to allow easy insertion, and a brief heating restores their shape once they are in place. One such application is orthodontic braces. Wires can be deformed to thread them through the braces on individual teeth, whereupon heating the wire results in an internal force pulling the wire back into a straight line, which is usually the desired alignment of teeth.

Hinge

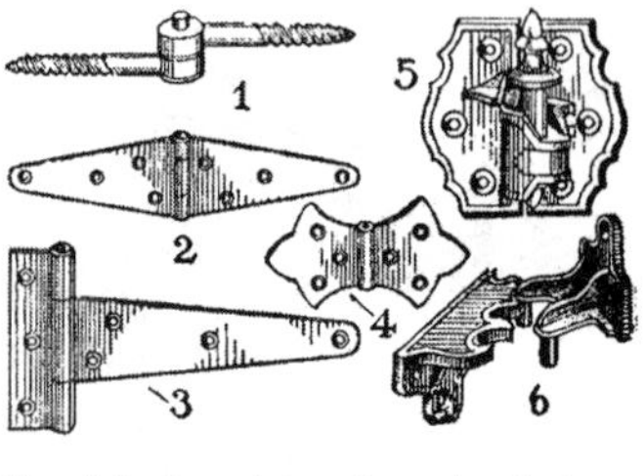

Fig. 4.6 A variety of mechanical hinges.

Hinges are devices that permit bending at the joints of rigid elements. The most common type of hinge is a pair of metal plates with interlocking fingers wrapped around a pin. These hinges facilitate rotation of one or both plates around the axis of the pin. Hinges come in a wide variety of sizes beyond the common door hinges. There are also miniature hinges, which are used to open secret compartments on rings; very long hinges, which are used along the edge of grand piano tops, and huge hinges, which are used in very large doors and equipment.

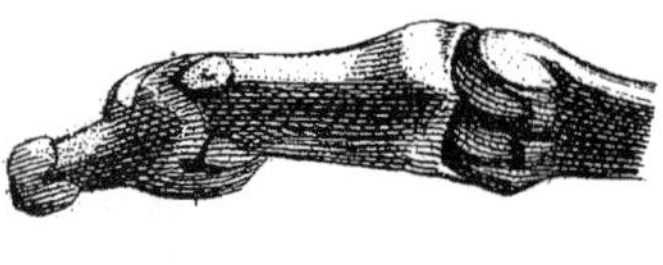

Fig. 4.7 Certain of our joints, for instance in the fingers, are hinge joints. Like mechanical hinges, they provide for bending only in a single plane.

Pinless hinges are commonly made of flat, flexible materials, such as paper, cloth, leather, and plastic. Old suitcases, for instance, often employed leather straps around the cases to hold them closed while in transit. Firmly attached to the top and bottom sections of the case, these straps allowed the top to pivot backwards as the leather bent; consequently,

Fig. 4.8 a) A piano lid is usually attached with a piano hinge, a long hinge running the length of the connected edge. b) An old suitcase, with leather straps serving both as hinges and as a means of closure.

they functioned as hinges. Plastic boxes are sometimes molded in a single piece, with a semirigid bottom and lid connected by a thinner and more flexible hinge section. The flaps of corrugated cardboard boxes are hinged by flattening the corrugations along the intended fold line, thus removing the resistance to bending along these folds.

Natural hinges are fairly common. A number of joints in our bodies are called hinge joints. Among these is the connection of the skull to the first vertebra, which allows us to nod our heads, and between the bones of the fingers (phalanges). Like mechanical hinges these joints enable rotation in a single plane. Instead of pins, however, they employ ovoid surfaces on left and right sides of the contact surfaces of the bones that can slide against mating surfaces as the joint bends. The second type of hinge, a flexible material that bends with the flexure of the joint, is commonly found attaching the shells of bivalves, such as razor clams, which are mollusks of the family *Solenidae.*

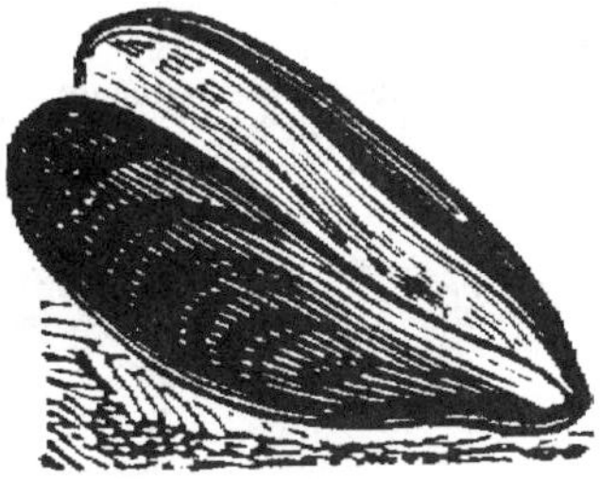

Fig. 4.9 Bivalves such as clams and mussels have two-piece shells connected by a hinge at the back.

Flexstraw

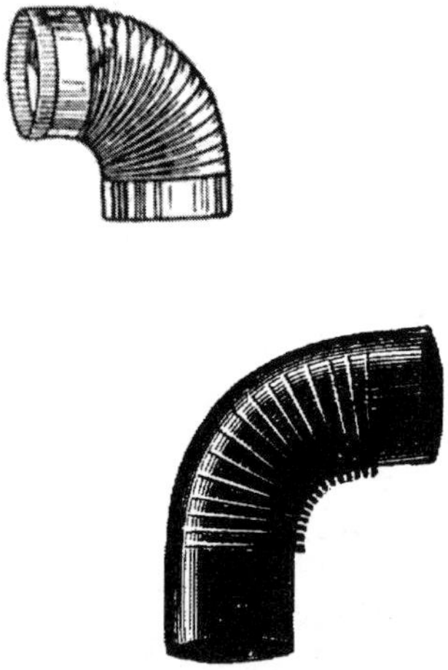

Fig. 4.10 Incorporation of the Flexstraw paradigm allows ducts and pipes to be easily and smoothly bent where they would otherwise kink.

The *Flexstraw paradigm* is used for bending an external structure, or exoskeleton. The exoskeleton form is well suited to situations wherein a substance, different from the substance of its surroundings, is to be contained and possibly conveyed. A flexible straw wouldn't work well with an internal skeleton and joint like the human leg. While the bone and joint could provide support and flexing, they would impede the flow of the liquids. A skin-type surface could be used to retain the liquids passing through this contrivance, but it would have to be fortified so it wouldn't buckle under the flow. If the skin were rigid, a means of flexing the skin would have to be introduced. Consequently we turn once again to the flexstraw minus the superfluous knee joint in our hypothetical contrivance.

Flexstraws are similar in appearance to the bellows, but whereas the bellows is primarily intended to accommodate changes in size and length, the flexstraw is primarily intended to accommodate bending. The *Flexstraw paradigm* can be found in nature in the jointed bodies of animals having exoskeletons. These include such animals as crustaceans and insects. A great lesson in creating flexible exoskeleton joints

Fig. 4.11 a, b While the flexible connections between subway cars (a) and bus sections (b) are frequently described as accordion-like, they serve to accomodate bending rather than changes of length, indicating the *Flexstraw paradigm*, rather than the *Bellows paradigm*.

can be learned from studying the joints of lobster legs and claws.

Besides drinking straws (see Fig. 9.2), the paradigm finds use in hoses, ducts and pipes, including some aftermarket auto exhaust pipes, and as a flexible connection between train and bus sections.

Gooseneck

A goose's neck is notable for its length and flexibility. Functionally, a gooseneck is a flexible form that *maintains its length* while protecting a cylindrical space within, and its contents. While a gooseneck is flexible with respect to bending, it is not flexible with respect to torsion, or twisting. The contents, as well as the neck itself, serve to connect a base or body with another part, such as a head. In the case of a goose, the contents of the neck include such vital parts and pathways as a spinal column, windpipe, esophagus and arteries.

Other natural examples of the *Gooseneck paradigm* include the vertebrate spine, a snake's body, and a millipede's exoskeleton. A swan's neck might be a better example of the paradigm than a goose's, since it is a more pronounced part of that animal's anatomy, but the functional requirements embodied are the same. Presumably we call it a gooseneck because of the more widespread abundance of geese compared to swans.

We use the term gooseneck to refer to a number of man-made objects, often based on a flexible metal conduit, such as a flexible microphone stand or a gooseneck lamp. The gooseneck here is a close analogy, preserving the flexibility and constant-length aspects of the literal goose neck, and providing a protective enclosure for the similarly critical contents of the cylindrical space, the electric wires. The gooseneck lamp usually also incorporates a headlike bulb and cowl, and a weighted base, or body, further reinforcing the visual analogy.

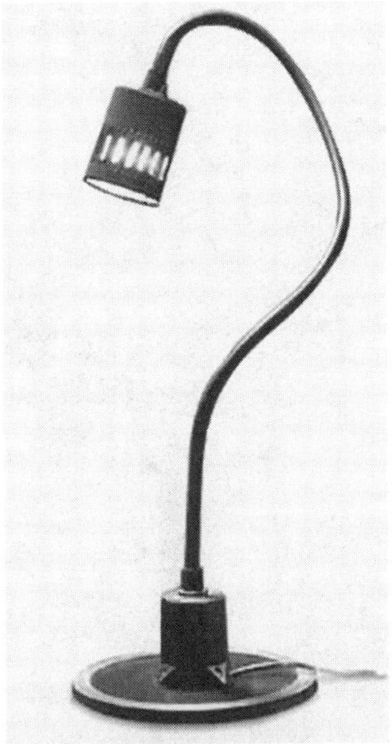

Fig. 4.12 a) A gooseneck lamp. Like a goose's neck, the neck of the lamp is flexible, maintains its length, and maintains a space inside that doesn't kink when the neck is bent. b) (below) gooseneck flashlight.

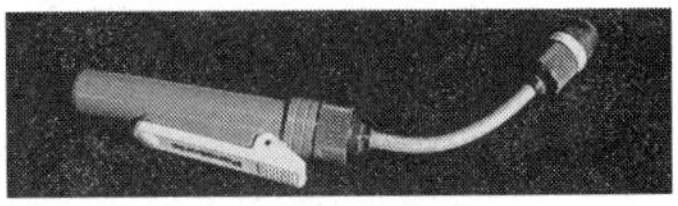

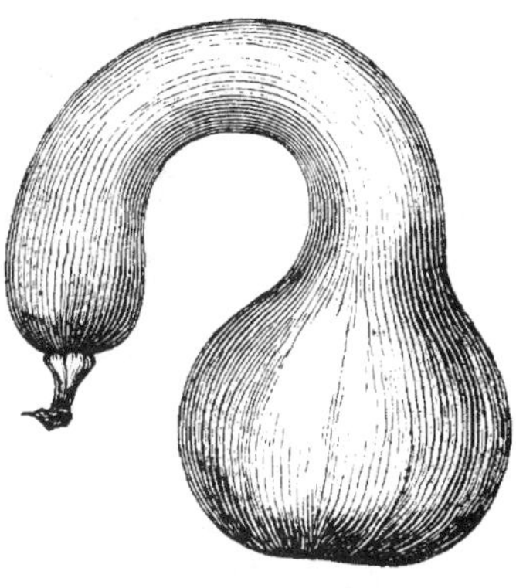

Fig. 4.13 The "gooseneck" term is also applied to a number of inflexible forms such as this squash that resemble the curves of a goose's neck.

A wide range of objects and devices might easily fit the *Gooseneck paradigm* including products based on flexible tubing or hose such as the suction device that hangs over your lip during dental work. Larger embodiments of the gooseneck paradigm allow flexible ends on devices used for pouring concrete, and air ducts that may easily be routed past obstacles in building ceilings.

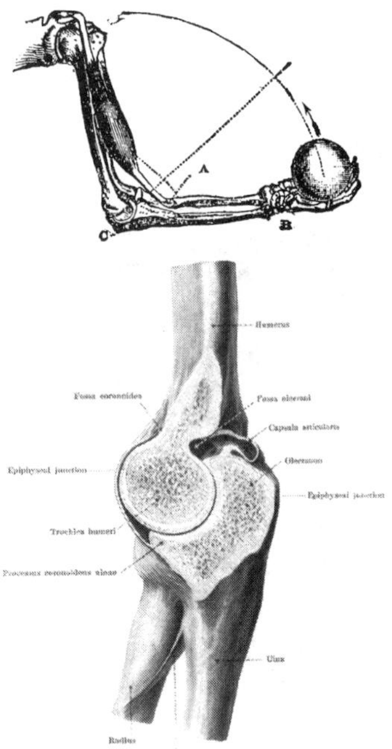

Fig. 4.14 a, b Human elbow joint.

Fig. 4.15 Elbow joints used in plumbing. The term "elbow" here implies a bend, rather than the flexibility of the human elbow.

Elbow

Elbow joints operate much like hinges. In anatomy, the elbow is known as a *hinge-type* or *ginglymus* joint. These joints enable you to bend your arm to change its configuration from extended fully to drawn tightly against the body. Most people can flex their elbows nearly 180 degrees, making it one of the most bendable of the human body's joints, but like a hinge it bends around only a single axis, thereby allowing motion on only a single plane. We have similar joints elsewhere in our bodies, like those in our fingers and knees, but the elbow is the paradigm because the term "elbow" has become synonymous with bend. At a place where a bend is to be introduced in plumbing, for instance, we place an "elbow," which is a curved section of pipe. Similarly, elbow macaroni describes a pasta shape with a bend.

Elbows and other hinge joints differ from hinges in some important ways. Rather than being held together by a pin passing through overlapping sockets, the bones meet end-to-end, and are held in place by ligaments, with a concave, rounded surface meeting a matching convex surface.

Ball And Socket

A ball-and-socket joint connects one part terminating in a ball shape with another terminating with a ball-shaped socket. Among the most immediately familiar of ball-and-socket joints are our hip and shoulder joints. Like the elbow, the ball-and-socket joint enables a wide range of motion, but not merely around one axis. Ball-and-socket joints afford both lateral and vertical freedom, tracing a semispherical, rather than planar range of operation. While this gives us a great deal of freedom in our reach, as well as in the positioning of our legs, employing ball-and-socket joints universally would present difficulties. If we replaced our knee joints with ball-and-socket joints, for instance, our knees could bow inward or outward as well as in the conventional forward plane bend. This would require constant

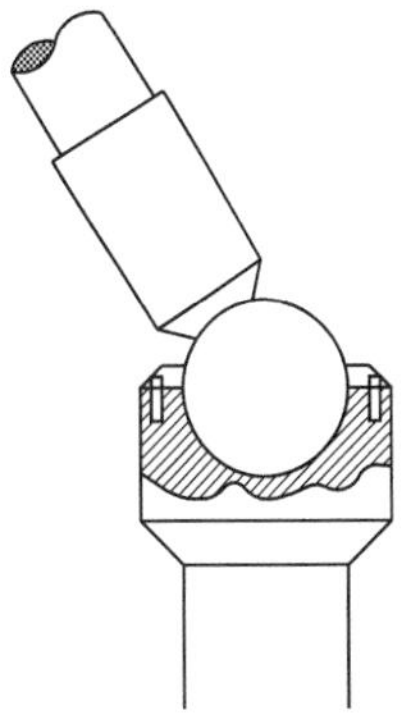

Fig. 4.16 Classic mechanical ball and socket joint. The joint is indicated where flexibility and freedom of movement are desirable.

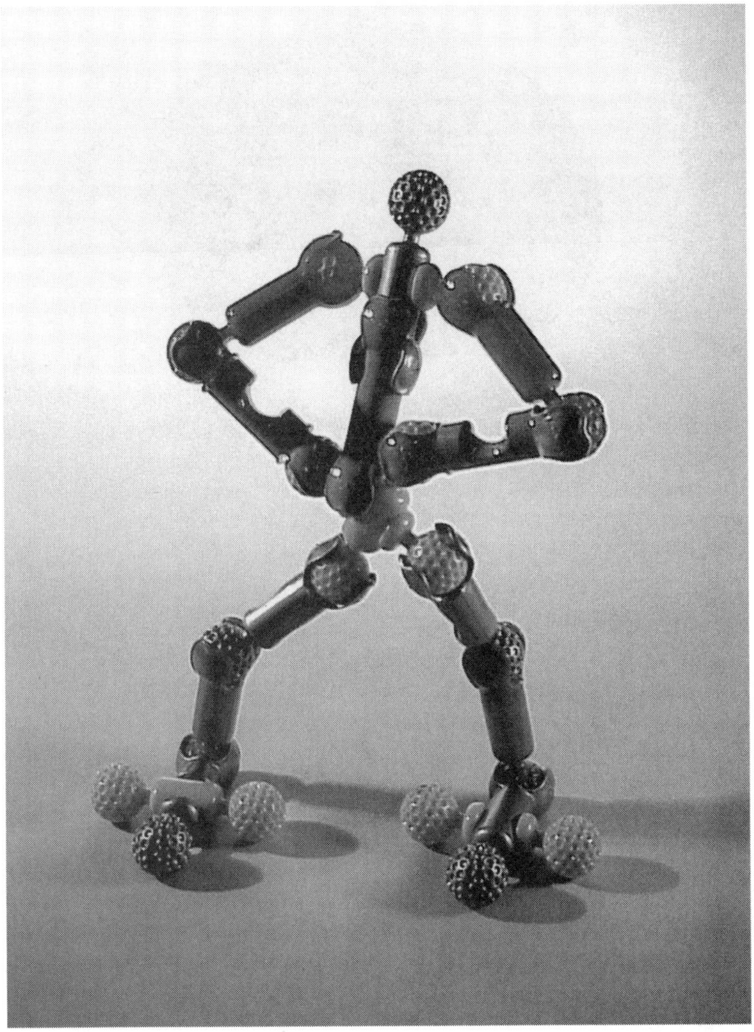

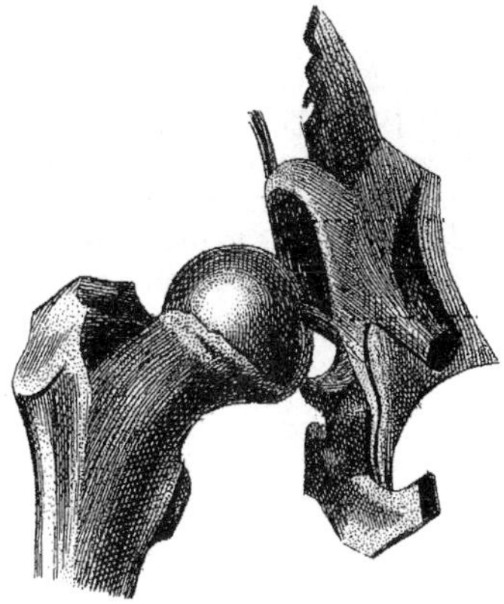

Fig. 4.17 The human hip joint is a ball and socket, allowing this joint the greatest range of movement of any of our joints.

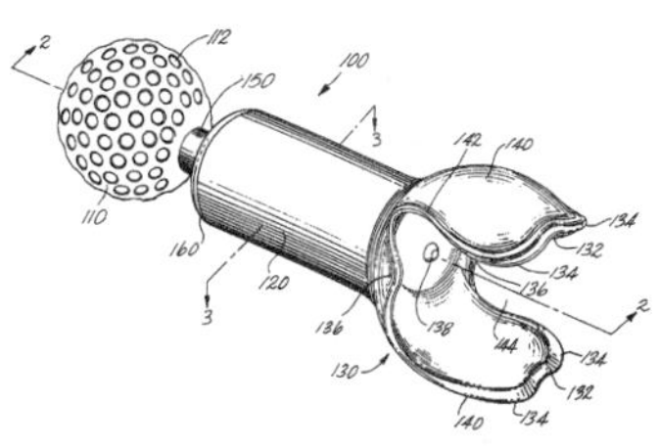

Fig. 4.18 a, b Ball and socket joints make the Zoob® construction toy easily configurable into a variety of shapes. While the ball and socket joint itself is not novel or patentable, the construction toy system based upon this paradigm is.

muscular tension to keep our legs from bending in these directions when these are not the desired actions. Further, it would take additional sets of muscles to oppose these forces.

Ball-and-socket joints are found in many vertebrates, enabling flexible joints not only on arms and legs, but also in the vertebrae of fishes, amphibians, reptiles, and birds. Ball-and-socket joints are also found in invertebrates, for instance in the *Echinoderms. Ball-and-socket* joints enable the brittle spines of sea urchins to freely move in any direction.

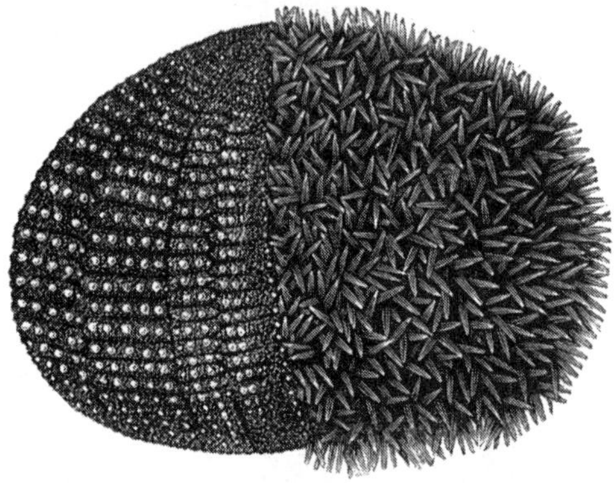

Fig. 4.19 A sea urchin shown with and without its spines. The brittle spines, made the same material as the shell, are able to move freely and independently because each is joined to the shell by a ball and socket joint.

Questions

1) What Olympic sports depend upon devices that bend in the manner of saplings?

2) Bending is common in small objects, mechanisms, and machines. Can you also identify situations where spaces for people, including vehicles and buildings, must bend, and how that bending is accommodated?

3) Closely examine the spine of a hardcover book. What accommodations are made for bending as the cover and pages are opened? What paradigms are employed?

4) Keeping your arm and body straight, move your arm through the range of positions afforded by the shoulder joint. Determine the shape of the volume describable as "all possible positions of my arm." Measure and sketch this shape, paying particular attention to the edges at which the arm can move no farther.

5

Bigger and Smaller

In both the natural and manmade worlds, many things must change between a bigger and smaller state as part of their normal functioning. We can look at birds, for instance, and observe how they expand their wings to catch the air and fly. We also notice on a cold day how the same wings are pulled close to the body, along with the head, legs, and feet, to conserve heat.

Things are made larger for a variety of reasons: to reach higher, to fill more volume, to span farther, to look scarier, to provide more cooling surface, and to catch more wind. They are made smaller for a number of reasons as well: to fit into a smaller space, to become harder to see, to minimize wind resistance, and to minimize heat loss. Things that can change between the two, becoming bigger or smaller as needed, can enjoy the benefits of both the large and small sizes, avoiding what would otherwise be at best a design compromise, or at worst a threat to their very existence. What if a bird couldn't make itself larger or smaller as needed? We can imagine a bird with fixed wings that, like most airplane wings, were always extended. Such an unfortunate creature would probably be rather clumsy when hunting for food on the ground because it couldn't make itself small to get through tight spaces. It would find it difficult to cuddle its young, and would seem rather pathetic on a cold day because it wouldn't be able to pull its wings against its body to conserve heat. Further, with its wings always in an extended state, such a bird would be more easily spotted by predators. Clearly, there are substantial benefits for many biological and mechanical devices, systems and creatures to have both large *and* small states. The essence of the *Bigger and Smaller paradigms* is that objects and animals employing these paradigms enjoy the benefits of being both big *and* small, long *and* short, and wide *and* narrow.

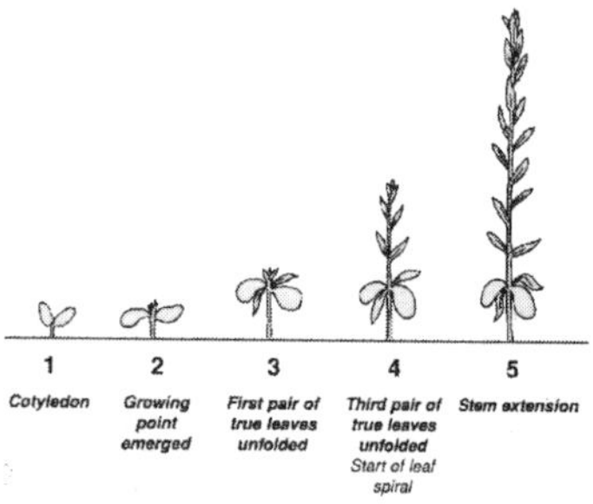

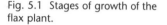

Fig. 5.1 Stages of growth of the flax plant.

Growth

Growth is one of the most familiar ways in which things in the natural world get larger. Growth in size is one of the primary signs of developing life; in other words, when we see that something is growing, we suspect it is alive. While on first consideration we might think that growth entails things simply getting bigger, growth, of course, occurs in many forms. As a baby grows into a child, for instance, it changes dramatically in proportion, not merely in size. A tree's growth involves not only getting larger, but also progressive branching and adding to its wood mass in what appears as concentric rings in a cross section of its trunk and branches. Snails and the chambered nautilus grow with their shells in logarithmic spirals. As they grow, their shells continue to wind around their centers. Growth often occurs within a space of fixed size; consequently growth might be a trigger for an event. For example, a chick growing inside an eggshell of fixed size will reach the point one day at which it won't have any more room to grow, and the eggshell must give way. Similarly a tree root growing into a crack in a rock might eventually split the rock.

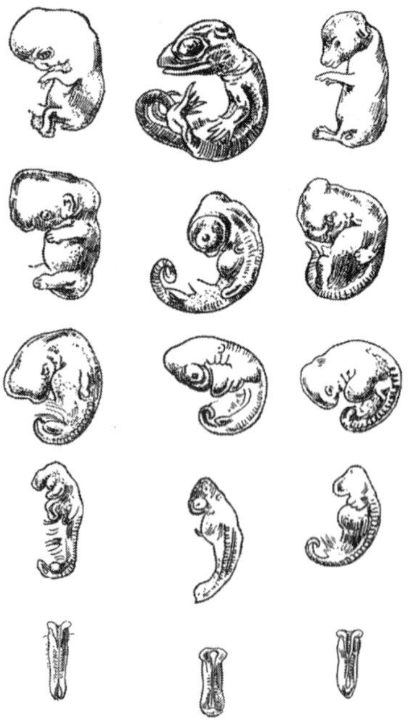

Fig. 5.2 a-c Stages of growth for a human, lizard, and rabbit. The more profound change between the different stages is arguably *size*, rather than form. Shown in actual relative sizes, the early stages would be only tiny dots.

Growth in nature isn't limited to the biological world: crystals grow, too. Some grow in long, slender needles; some, in angular blocks, and still others, in fine fibers. Stalactites, stalagmites, and icicles grow also, as dripping water either freezes to the outer surfaces of the icicles or leaves mineral deposits on the surfaces of the stalactites and stalagmites. We also speak of a fire growing, as a small fire *grows* into a large one.

Fig. 5.3 Stalactites and stalagmites are among the non-living things that change size by a process we call "growth." We also refer to the growth of a crystal, a fire, and a city.

In the manmade world we also find the *Growth paradigm* directly applied as a manufacturing process. Crystals are a most literal adaptation of this natural process. They are regularly grown from solutions to create products ranging from rock candy, to artificial rubies, to the silicon substrate for microprocessors. Candles can be "grown" as well, when a wick is dipped repeatedly in melted wax, leaving successive layers around the wick.

We can also characterize growth as the achievement of an increase in size by the structured incorporation of available raw material, where the process is self-organizing and independent from the observer. This definition allows us to use the term "growth" to describe an expanding city, an economy, or a population.

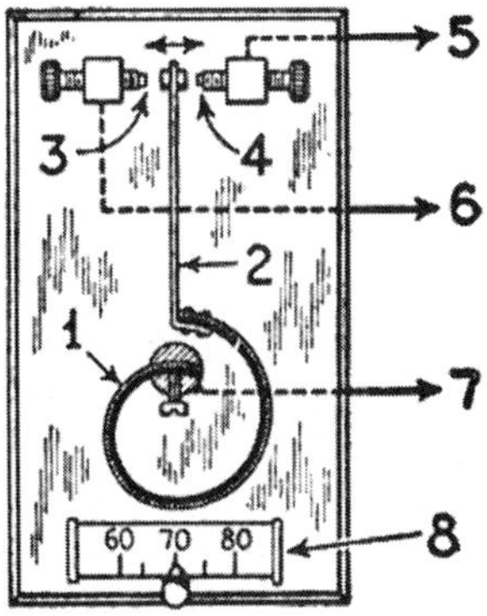

Fig. 5.4 As different metals heat, they expand at different rates. Consequently a coil made of two different metals laminated together will tighten its curl when the outer metal expands faster. This property is exploited by thermostats to turn off the heat at a preset temperature.

Expansion and Contraction

Some things simply get larger (expand) or smaller (contract), often as a result of temperature change. Metal is notable for this property, although most materials exhibit some degree of size change as heat or other energies pass through them. Metals expand and contract quite predictably as the temperature changes, and different metals expand at different rates. This property is exploited in the design of thermostats, in which a coiled sandwich of two metals becomes more tightly coiled and thus can turn a switch, when the outer layer of the sandwiched metal expands more rapidly than the inner layer.

Quartz and certain other crystals expand and contract when an electric field is applied and released or reversed. The opposite is true as well: When an impact is applied to the crystal, electricity is generated. Consequently, these crystals might be used to convert between electrical and physical phenomena. A microphone is one example, where sound energy is captured as motion of a diaphragm, which in turn hits a crystal that generates an electrical signal. This signal, which is usually amplified along the way, can then be applied to another crystal in another location, causing it to vibrate. If the crystal is attached to a paper cone, causing the cone to vibrate, a sound duplicating the original sound will be created. This is the basis for telephones, radio, intercoms, and a host of other products.

Swelling and Squashing

Another basic and most familiar means by which things get larger is for them to simply swell up. Many things that swell, such as a sponge placed in water, can also be made smaller by squeezing or squashing them, thereby giving them less room to exist in, and usually removing air or liquid from internal spaces in the process. Some things will stay squashed, while others will swell again because of their own tendencies to recover their original shape. This sometimes requires the reintroduction of liquid or air.

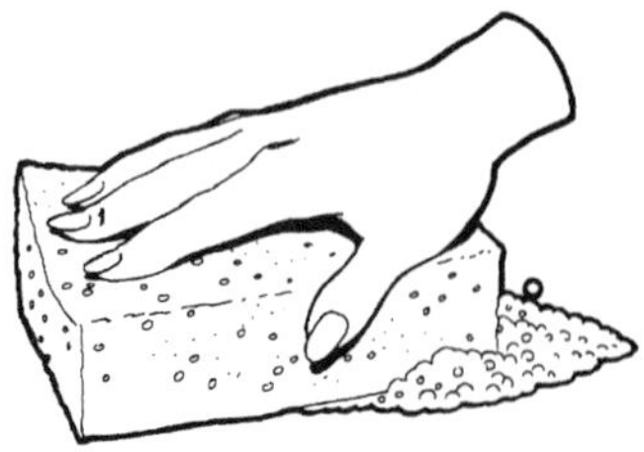

Fig. 5.5 A sponge can simply be squashed to make it smaller, and it will swell when air or liquid is allowed to re-enter its cells.

Sponges are a common example of this paradigm. Both the natural and manufactured varieties are valued for their absorbency, as well as for the ability to compress them into a fraction of their original size by simply squeezing them in your hand. Artificial sponges are usually made of open-cell foam plastic or cellulose. The open-cell structure of these sponges means that the air spaces within the sponge tend to be open to each other, thereby enabling air or liquid to pass easily in and out of the sponge when it is squeezed or released.

Sponges exemplify equally the "squashable" and "swelling" aspects of the paradigm; both are very much a part of the way we use them. We squeeze the air out, then release the sponge in liquid, for instance, and it swells as it draws in a spilled liquid. While sponges return to their original forms when we release them, this is not true of all apparently similar materials, such as a loaf of fresh bread.

A sponge can be made to stay compressed, however. If a dry sponge is extremely compressed, with perhaps a small amount of starch or other water-soluble and at least slightly adhesive material, it will remain in the compressed form until it is dipped in water. Sponges compressed in this way become extremely compact, they can be as thin as a shirt cardboard, yet will expand to their original size when water is added. The form and surface of a pressed and starched sponge become paperlike and suitable for printing upon with advertising or brand-identity messages. These properties can be exploited where motion, opening, or closing is desired based on the presence of moisture, although the process is not repeatable without changing parts.

Fig. 5.6 The *Swelling and Squashing paradigm* includes aerosols and compressed air. Compressed air will simply swell when the pressure on it is released. Conversely, it is fairly straightforward to compress air by "squashing" it. Releasing the pressure on compressed gasses absorbs energy. This produces cold, and is the basis for refrigeration equipment.

Hydration and Dehydration

In the *Swelling and Squashing paradigm*, we considered how a sponge can get smaller by compressing it and larger by releasing it. A wet sponge can also lose water weight via the nonmechanical process of evaporation. Dehydration is an important means of reducing the size or weight of things having a significant water component. Under ideal circumstances, we could take a product, reduce its water content, and later have the original product upon replacing the water component. This is very important in food processing for such applications as frozen orange-juice concentrate. Transporting a reduced-water product lowers transportation

Fig. 5.7 Fruit gets lighter and smaller as it is dried, and the sugars in the fruit become concentrated. Dried fruit will enlarge when soaked but is quite altered from the original fruit; stewed prunes are not plums. Freeze drying is an alternative process that enables dehydration and subsequent rehydration with a minimum of alteration of the food.

costs and minimizes packaging materials, as well as the need for store-shelf and freezer space. In practice, the reconstituted product is rarely indistinguishable from the original, but methods like freeze-drying, used in preparing dehydrated meals for camping, are coming increasingly closer to this objective.

Dehydration has some other properties as well. Dehydrated food products are less susceptible to spoilage; consequently, dehydration serves to preserve. The process of evaporation also has a cooling effect, which is an important benefit of sweating during exercise. The *heat of evaporation,* or energy, it takes to convert the sweat to vapor is heat that is drawn off the body.

Hydration and dehydration have important roles in the germination of seeds. Hydration is one of several important triggers for seed to germinate, along with such factors as temperature. The combination of these factors serves to ensure that germination coincides with the ideal springtime growing conditions. Many seeds, such as those of corn, require dehydration to trigger a state of dormancy in order for them to sprout. This process serves in part to ensure that the seeds do not sprout while still on the cob on warm, moist autumn days.

Fig. 5.8 Cracks in dried mud. Cracks form as the mud dries because it reduces in size, causing tension that eventually breaks apart the mud.

Spring

Closely related to the *Swelling and Squashing paradigm* are springs. A coil spring, like a sponge, gets smaller when it is compressed and expands by itself when it is released. Springs are important as a design component, and different enough from things like sponges to deserve separate mention, both as a simple shape (see the *Coil paradigm* in Chapter 2) and as a *Bigger and Smaller paradigm*.

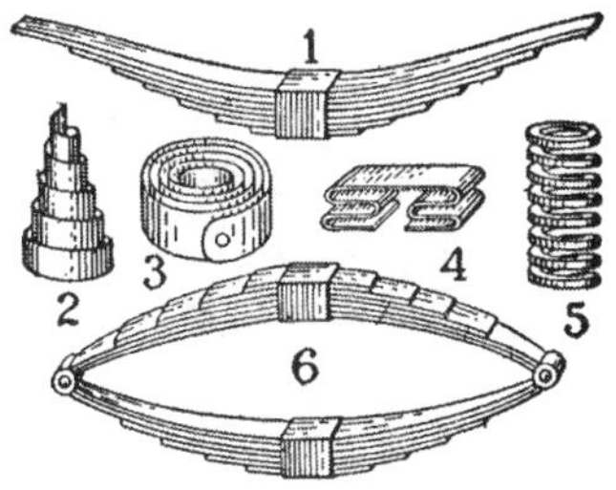

Fig. 5.9 Several types of springs. Springs trade off size for energy. As force is applied, the spring gets larger or smaller (or flatter or more tightly coiled). As the spring is released, it releases energy and returns to its original size.

Springs are familiar in many forms, though the coiled springs found in products ranging from ballpoint pens to automobile suspensions might first come to mind. Also found in auto suspensions are leaf springs. These are layers of curved steel that are bent into a flat position while resisting the vehicle's load.

Springs get smaller when compressed and bigger when stretched. This is true of many things, however. What is more notable as a *Bigger and Smaller paradigm* is the way springs get bigger by themselves after releasing the compression on them, and they get smaller by themselves when tension is released. Springs do much more than become larger and smaller, though. In fact, it is often their *resistance* to becoming smaller or larger that we value, as in the case of automobile suspensions. If they could be compressed without effort, they would be useless for absorbing shocks or holding up the weight of the car. It is the resistance to compression that causes the compressed spring to return to its larger original form, and the resistance to stretching that causes the stretched spring to snap back to its smaller form. In a stretched or compressed state, springs can store energy, making them good as a power source for windup toys and clocks.

Extension Ladder

Fig. 5.10 The *Extension Ladder paradigm* involves flat pieces that are connected and slide against each other to extend reach.

Ladders primarily serve to extend the reach of a climbing person. While a ladder extends your reaching ability, the extension ladder extends the *ladder's* reaching ability, and so leaves a more profound visual impression on us. The basic mechanism of the extension ladder consists of two ladders attached to one another, where one can slide against the other while remaining attached to it, with mechanisms to prevent its accidental collapse. Similar mechanisms are widely used in other applications where variable length and support are desired. Supports for kitchen drawers are one example. Dining-room tables sometimes employ a similar approach to extending the table, as an alternative to drop-in leaves. Instead, the leaves are permanently attached over or under the primary table surface and slide out, extension-ladder style, to extend the size of the table when desired.

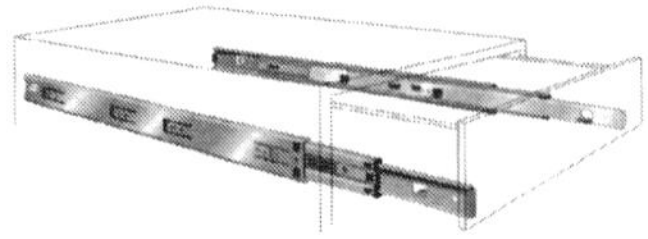

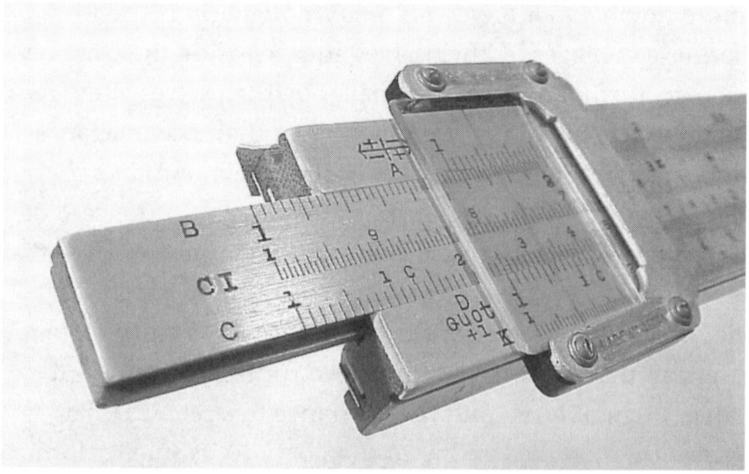

Fig. 5.11 a) (above) The *Extension Ladder paradigm* employed in drawer slide hardware. b) (right) A slide rule, the mechanical precursor of the electronic calculator. The center piece slides outward, in a variation on the *Extension Ladder paradigm.* This changes its length, and brings different points on logarithmic scales into juxtaposition with each other.

Wedge

A wedge by itself usually isn't something that gets larger or smaller, yet that is effectively the function of wedges. While the wedge, of course, stays a constant size, its cross section gets larger as we progressively consider sections starting with its narrow side and moving toward its wide side. Consequently, as a wedge is banged into a log, a larger and larger section of the wedge is pushed into the wood until the log splits (Fig. 5.12). Similarly, a wedge doorstop is pushed under a door until a wide-enough section is compressed beneath the door to hold it in place.

A wedge can function by moving it through another medium, as with the log-splitting example, or by moving a medium over the wedge. An example of the latter is a building-access ramp. This type of ramp serves as a wedge that raises people to a higher elevation as they move across it.

The classic wedge shape is rectangular in cross section and triangular in side view. For the purpose of this paradigm, however, we can include other tapered shapes, such as cones and pyramids when they are used as wedges. Both a cork and a drain plug are examples of a truncated cone wedge. When a drain plug is pressed into a drainpipe, we employ the *Wedge Bigger and Smaller paradigm,* as an increasingly wide section of the plug is pressed into blocking the hole. This in turn creates greater compression and a better seal.

Fig. 5.12 A wedge splits wood as an increasingly larger section of the wedge is forced into the wood, as Abe Lincoln here demonstrates.

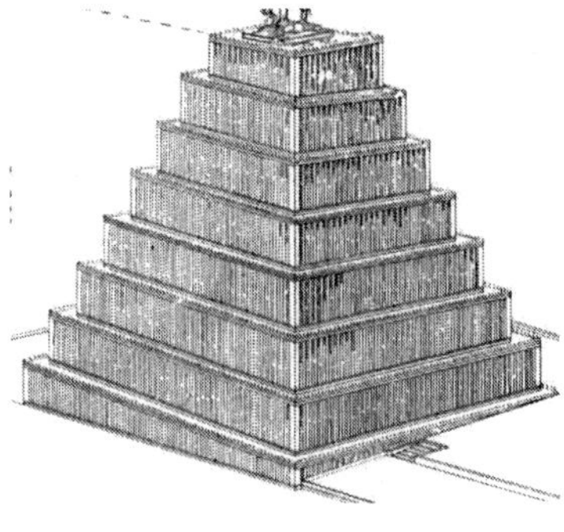

Fig. 5.13 a, b A building ramp is a wedge. As people pass across it, they are raised to a higher level. This is especially clear in buildings such as the spiral minaret at the Congregational Mosque of Samarra, Iraq (left), built 849-851 A.D., or an ancient Mesopotamian Ziggaurat (above). These buildings consist mostly of ramps wrapped around conic or pyramidal forms.

Among the many wedges found in nature are teeth and claws. A lion's pointed teeth permit the easy penetration of the teeth into the prey at the small, sharp end. As the creature bites its prey, the increasingly wider sections of the teeth cause separation of the bite from the whole.

Fig. 5.14 Many animals with spines or quills employ the *Fur paradigm*. By raising fur, quills, or spines, an animal can enlarge the psychological, visual, and in the case of the porcupine, physical, zone of personal space and protection around them.

Fur

Drop a rubber spider on the floor in front of a kitten, and you'll see a most remarkable transformation as the kitten seems instantly to double its size. The kitten's reaction illustrates *fur* as a *Bigger and Smaller paradigm*. When startled, the kitten's skin tightens, making its fur stand straight up, thereby greatly increasing its apparent bulk. The reverse effect results when a kitten is wet. With its fur slick against its skin, a kitten seems to shrink to half of its normal size.

Fig. 5.15 A cat seems to get larger when its scared, as it arches its back, and its fur stands up on end. Conversely, cats seem shrunken when wet.

Many animals employ some variant of this paradigm to enlarge the defined space around them. This might be a primarily visual effect as with the kitten, or it might be an active deployment of a defense system, as when a porcupine raises its quills in response to a perceived threat. The porcupine thereby not only positions the quills for possible defensive use, but also enlarges the protective envelope around it defined by the sharp points.

A similar approach is sometimes employed in hairbrushes designed to compact for travel. The bristles of the brush are attached flexibly to a base, then pass through a movable plate. When this plate is aligned over the bases of the bristles, they stand straight up, when it is moved to the side, the bristles all lay flat.

Stretching and Shrinking

Stretching and shrinking are a fundamental means by which things can get larger and smaller. We refer to things that stretch larger and stay stretched as plastic, while we call things that snap back to their original form elastic. Another category comprises things that shrink and do not become larger again (which includes a number of sweaters and sweatshirts I've purchased over the years). A number of products, such as heat-shrink tubing, make use of this property. A tube resembling a segment of soda straw is easily slipped over a splice in two wires. When the tubing is heated, it shrinks tightly around the wires and the splice, providing a tight air- and moisture-proof covering (see Fig. 8.13).

Elastics constitute a large category of objects, materials, and forms that share the ability to stretch to a larger size, then shrink back to their original size. We can consider elasticity in one, two, or three dimensions. A bungie cord exemplifies 1-D elasticity, in other words, it stretches in one dimension only, length. When you connect the ends of a bungie cord to form a circle, you have, in effect, a rubber band, a 2-D construct: as it gets larger, the circumference increases. This type of elasticity is also exemplified by an elastic sheet, such as an Ace bandage. When we wrap the sheet into a cylinder, as we do wrapping the Ace bandage around a leg, we have a 3-D elastic surface, a cylinder. The cylinder increases in both height and circumference as it gets larger. This 3-D elasticity is also exemplified by balloons.

Fig. 5.16 Bungie jumping employs a variant on the *Rubber Band paradigm*. An elastic rope is tied to the body, then one jumps from a high place. *"Kids, don't try this at home!"*

Rubber Band

A rubber band is complex as a *Bigger paradigm* because it can be stretched bigger in at least three different ways. First, when we fold it flat and stretch it between the fingertips of both hands, it becomes longer as we apply tension to it. Second, we can stretch it into a bigger ring shape as we do

Fig. 5.17 a, b Stretch fabrics like Lycra are widely used in sport clothing, including bicycling pants, bathing suits, and exercise wear.

to hold plastic wrap over a jar lid. Third, when we stretch it into a larger circle, the space inside the band gets larger as well as the band itself. This would exemplify the *Openings paradigm*.

Stretching and contracting under elastic conditions constitute another fundamental means by which things get longer and shorter or of greater or smaller circumference in both the natural and manmade worlds.

Elastic Sheet

An elastic sheet is perhaps most familiar as a sheet of kitchen plastic wrap that is stretched over a bowl to seal the contents. Similarly, elastic sheets are used extensively in packaging, where a stretched, clear membrane holds an object in place, often to a sheet of cardboard. In some cases the tension in the membrane is created by stretching the membrane over the supporting structure, but in packaging it is often accomplished by heating the membrane, causing it to shrink. This property is also sometimes used in weatherproofing windows. Windows are covered with plastic sheets secured at the edges, then shrunken using the heat of a hairdryer to remove wrinkles.

Many fabrics are valued for their elasticity, in garments such as sweaters and Lycra® sport clothing. The fabric's ability to stretch locally gives the wearer great freedom of move-

Fig. 5.18 A trampoline is an elastic sheet. Jumping on the surface stretches it, exchanging size for tension. The tension propels the jumper back up as the sheet returns to a flat surface.

ment because the clothing essentially becomes larger and smaller as needed. Certain materials, notably rubber and plastics, are intrinsically elastic. Fabrics can be made stretchy by making the cloth out of elastic yarn, or by having an inelastic yarn in a loose knit with elastic threads running through the fabric, as is done with underwear waistbands. A third method is to use an inelastic yarn that is knit in a particular fashion so that the pattern of the threads, rather than the threads themselves, provides the elasticity.

Balloon

Balloons are familiar as colorful playthings for children, but if we consider the general category of elastic, tensile, inflatable surfaces, we can easily find many other examples of balloonlike structures, both manmade and natural. At the smaller end of the scale, the surgical procedure *balloon angioplasty* uses a balloon small enough when deflated to fit inside a small tube, or *catheter,* that is threaded through arteries toward the heart. The balloon is inflated at the site of an obstruction, thus stretching the artery, clearing the way for blood flow. This size-change feature of the balloon makes it a good choice for this application: the balloon needs to be small to be inserted in the artery, and must get larger to perform the stretching task. The procedure

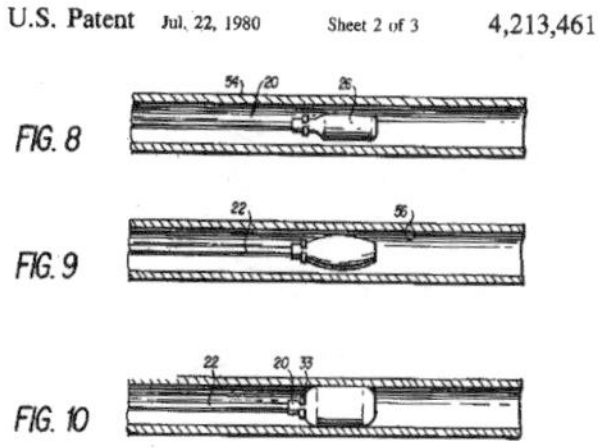

Fig. 5.19 Among the inventions based on the *Balloon paradigm* is the balloon catheter. A miniature balloon is placed inside a tube (catheter) that may be threaded through veins and arteries. It is inflated at the desired location as shown above, in order to temporarily block the artery or to stretch the walls to improve bloodflow.

Fig. 5.20 The Goodyear® blimp, an airship that functions like a large balloon. Bouyancy comes from filling the blimp with helium.

can be used for some patients in place of bypass surgery and is far less traumatic.

Larger balloons are used as automotive airbags. Here the size-change aspect solves the problem of these safety devices being small and unobtrusive when stored, but largely filling the passenger compartment when in use. At the upper end of the scale are blimps, which are essentially large helium-filled balloons.

Among the many balloons found in nature are the puffer fish of the family *Tetraodontidae*. These fish, when scared, can inflate themselves with air or water, then float upside down, thus discouraging predators. The porcupine fish *Diodon hystrix*, a relative of the puffer fish, not only inflates itself, but also is covered with spines and becomes a spiked, inflated ball when provoked.

Fig. 5.21 A hot air balloon inflates as hot air rises into it and is trapped by the balloon membrane. Unlike a rubber balloon, the material is not stretchy.

Balloons divide space into two regions, the areas inside and outside the balloon. These two regions are distinguished by more than their names. The inside of the balloon is pressurized and can be of a composition different from than the surrounding atmosphere. For example the balloon's interior can contain water or helium. The balloon must be impervious to the materials—generally gas or liquid—contained inside or kept outside the balloon. The balloon can, therefore, be used as a barrier, as in the case of a condom.

Fig. 5.22 a-c Balloonlike inflation is fairly common in the animal kingdom among fish, amphibians, and birds.

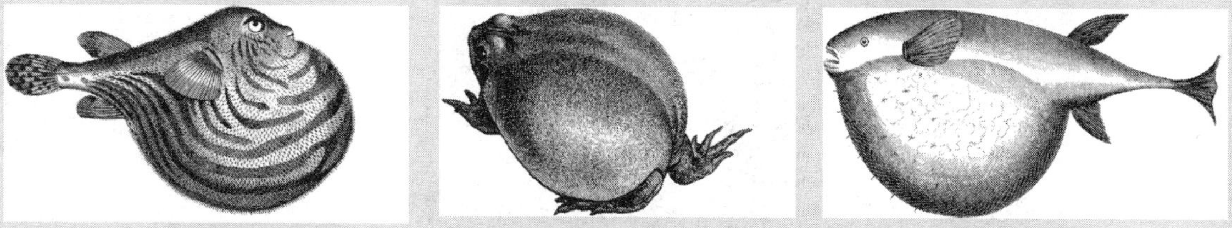

The *Balloon paradigm* is related to the *Bubble paradigm*. Like bubbles, balloons are minimal structures that use the minimal amount of material possible to enclose their contents. The *Balloon paradigm* differs from the bubbles in that we generally consider bubbles to be of fixed size, and we more typically think of balloons as things that enlarge and shrink as their relative internal pressure changes. Consequently, once we tie the end of a balloon, its properties resemble those of a bubble.

The *Balloon paradigm* is also related to the *Bellows paradigm* discussed later in this chapter. The balloon differs from a bellows however in that it is only a tensile skin. Furthermore, although like a bellows, a balloon compresses its contents, unlike a bellows it cannot be used in reverse to create vacuum. Also unlike a bellows, a balloon maintains a more or less similar shape as it changes in size.

Fig. 5.23 Children learn early that they can use their arms and legs to make themselves larger, and to extend their reach.

Arms and Legs

The legs and arms of animals serve many purposes. While arms and legs might first call to mind hugging, kicking, jumping, and swimming, let's think for a moment

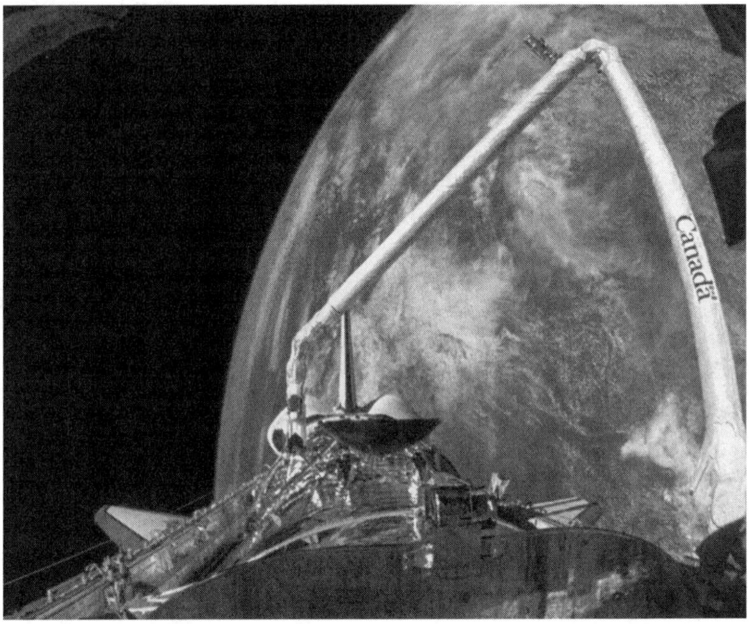

Fig. 5.24 The Robotic arm on the space shuttle uses the *Arms and Legs paradigm* as a means of folding compactly when not in use, and extending reach when necessary for tasks such as satellite deployment. NASA photo.

about what arms and legs have to do with size. With our jointed shoulders, elbows, wrist, hips, knees, and ankles, we can make our bodies compact to avoid danger, make ourselves tall or short, or extend an arm to pull a piece of fruit from a tree. Arms and legs exemplify structures that fold compactly or extend flexibly to achieve length and height changes by extending straight elements that are connected by flexible joints. Secondarily, *arm* also implies *hand*; an arm is used to extend the reach and operating range of the hand.

Fig. 5.25 Concrete pumping truck. Concrete is pumped continuously to where it is needed on the construction site, obviating the need to carry individual bucket or wheelbarrow loads. The *Arms and Legs paradigm* is employed to provide a smooth and unimpeded passageway for the concrete through a jointed plastic pipe.

Similarly, while our legs easily fit the folding and reaching aspects of the *Arm paradigm*, legs also imply such functions as supporting, standing, walking, running, and kicking. If we're talking about a utility truck, for instance, a reference to "extending the arm" of the truck would be quickly understood as referring to the cherry picker. This is the basket a worker rides in which is attached to a flexible, armlike structure that is used to reach and work in high places. If, however, we said "extending the legs" of the truck, we would more likely look for structures that extend to help support or steady the truck. We think of bears, monkeys, and raccoons as having arms and legs, while dogs, sheep,

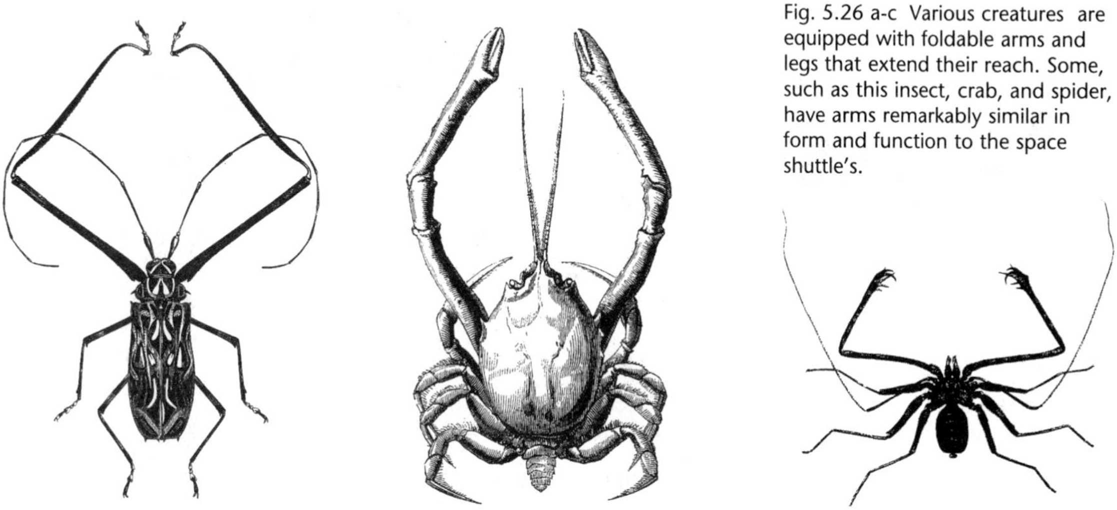

Fig. 5.26 a-c Various creatures are equipped with foldable arms and legs that extend their reach. Some, such as this insect, crab, and spider, have arms remarkably similar in form and function to the space shuttle's.

and lions have only legs. The distinction seems to have more to do with the use of the limbs than the body geometry. In other words, we think of bears, monkeys, and raccoons as having arms because of the presence of dexterous paws or hands at the end of them.

We find the concept of arms quite literally translated into various products such as the mechanical arm used on the space shuttle to remove and position objects in its cargo bay. Similarly, robotic arms are used in various manufacturing processes and in hostile environments, such as nuclear power plants. Arms and armlike structures are also found in certain tools and instruments, for instance, in the expandable bow compass or the folding rule. While we think of most Western furniture as having legs, furniture legs are mostly named merely for their role as supports, without the jointed extension feature. There are occasional exceptions, however, such as the foldout, jointed structures used in making patio lounge chairs, in which the compactness of the folded form is the motivation for the introduction of the joints to the chair.

Wing

A wing expands upon the *Arm paradigm* by stretching a skin across the straight elements, bones, or "ribs." While the internal structure of the wing might be similar to an arm or cherry picker mechanism, the stretched skin is the important distinction in the *Wing paradigm.* Rather than variable length, the objective of the *Wing paradigm* is to provide a dramatically variable surface area, with a tensile membrane well-supported by a rigid structure. The skin can serve to catch wind, water, or soil, while the ribs act to support the skin, transmit forces to the body, and, perhaps, to support nails or claws at the edge of the wing. The *Wing paradigm,* of course, occurs in nature not only as the literal wings of birds, bats, and insects, but also as the webbed feet of such animals as waterfowl, beavers, frogs, platypuses, and moles. Fish fins, and many leaves and petals fit the paradigm as well.

Fig. 5.27 An important aspect of bird wings is their ability to fold, thereby changing size. Huge wings such as these would otherwise handicap the bird when it is not in flight.

Fig. 5.28 The bat's wings are the perfect exemplars of the paradigm. Whereas a bird's wings are hidden by feathers, the bat's wings clearly show their structure, a thin skin stretched over a riblike framework.

Fig. 5.29 Umbrellas and parasols also fit the *Wing paradigm.* They are designed to spread wide when they are used to block rain or sun, yet they fold compactly when not in use.

Fig. 5.30 Yurts. These structures, which are still used in Mongolia, fit the *Wing paradigm,* as do most tents. Yurts are designed to expand to a large building composed of a membrane stretched over a thin rib framework, or to fold compactly for travel or storage.

The *Wing paradigm* is very useful in designed objects, because of its variety of utilitarian properties. Among the many uses of this paradigm are boat sails and hang-glider wings. Surprisingly, though, modern-airplane wings do not fit the *Wing paradigm.* Rather than a soft skin stretched over a rigid skeleton, modern-plane wings have an exoskeleton-like, rigid skin more akin to a lobster's claw than a bat's wing. They do, however, fit the *Airfoil paradigm* (see Chapter 2).

Beyond serving the familiar purposes of flying, digging and swimming, a stretched skin, given rigidity by ribs, can also become a shelter. The skin can resist such forces as wind and rain. The properties of the wing enable *Wing paradigm* objects to fold compactly, and they can be constructed with minimal weight. Among the manmade *Wing paradigm* objects used for purposes other than flying are umbrellas, tents, awnings on buildings, and convertible automobile roofs.

Bellows

Many children who watch an accordion player are transfixed not only by the sound of the instrument, but also by the spectacle of the instrument itself. A large bellows is compressed and expanded by the player's hands, thereby forcing air past reeds that produce its sounds.

The *Bellows paradigm* usually entails a flexible membrane over ribs, enclosing a volume of air or liquid; however, a bel-

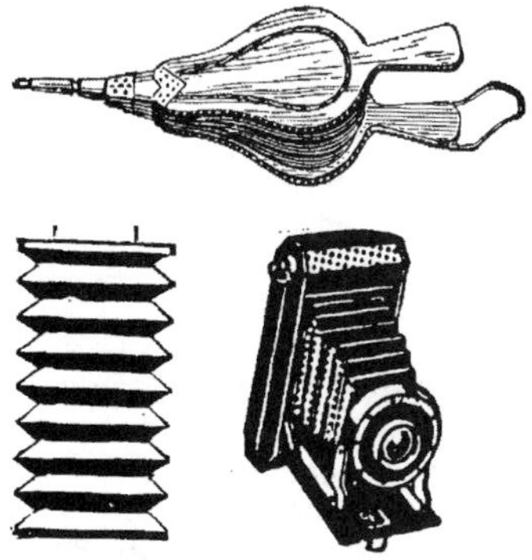

Fig. 5.31 a-c The *Bellows paradigm* combines enclosure of a space with a variable size. Because the space is enclosed, compression of the bellows implies a change in pressure or expulsion of the contents.

lows might alternatively be an exoskeletal bellows, wherein the plate surfaces of the bellows itself give it rigidity. Compression of a bellows creates a positive internal pressure, while expansion of the bellows creates a vacuum. The classic bellows is a two-handled device used to blow air into a fire to encourage combustion.

Just as the *Arm paradigm* was expanded upon by stretching a skin over it to form a wing, the bellows may be seen as an expansion of the *Wing paradigm* wherein the wing is stretched, folded, and sealed to enclose a volume.

Among the natural-bellows structures is the "sucking stomach" found in spiders. This stomach, made of a rigid cuticle material, is a classic bellows with sides that fold inward as the stomach is compressed by muscular bands that encircle it. A second set of muscles attaches to the inner fold of the sides to pull them outward, thus creating a suction that the spider uses to draw in food.[28]

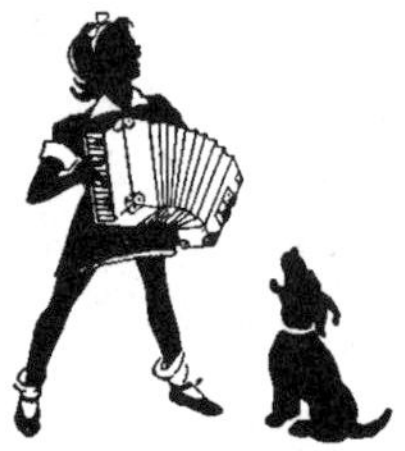

Fig. 5.32 The accordion is a classic example of the Bigger and Smaller *Bellows paradigm*. It perhaps is enjoyed as much for the visual spectacle as for its music.

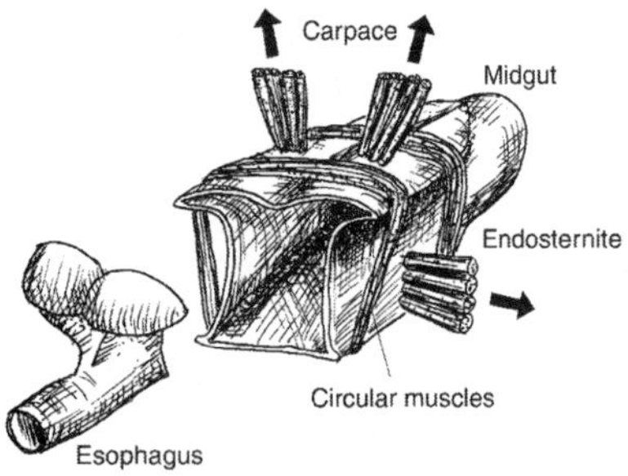

Fig. 5.33 The spider's sucking stomach employs the *Bellows paradigm*. After Kaestner, 1969.

Scissors

The *Scissors paradigm* refers not so much to the scissors we use to cut paper, but rather to the scissors mechanisms employed in automobile jacks, makeup mirrors and a variety of other devices. When you move the ends of the implement's two legs together, these mechanisms can extend to many times its original height. Because the scissors mechanism can operate while maintaining many points of attachment, it lends itself to such uses as

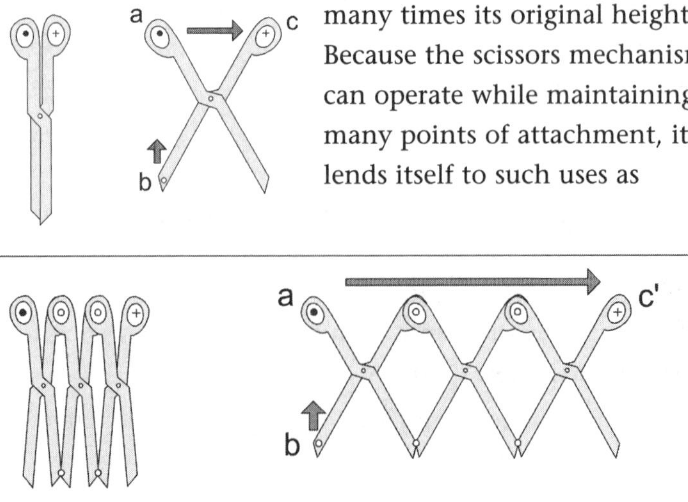

Fig. 5.34 a, b As point *b* on a scissors moves toward fixed point *a*, point *c* moves away from point *a*. The power of the scissors paradigm comes from attaching many scissors with flexible pin joints, as shown in Fig. 5.34b. Here, the same motion of point *b* toward point *a* multiplies the motion of point *c* from point a by the number of scissors units; hence, the distance from point *a* to point *c′* is three times that of point *a* to point *c* shown in Fig. 5.34a.

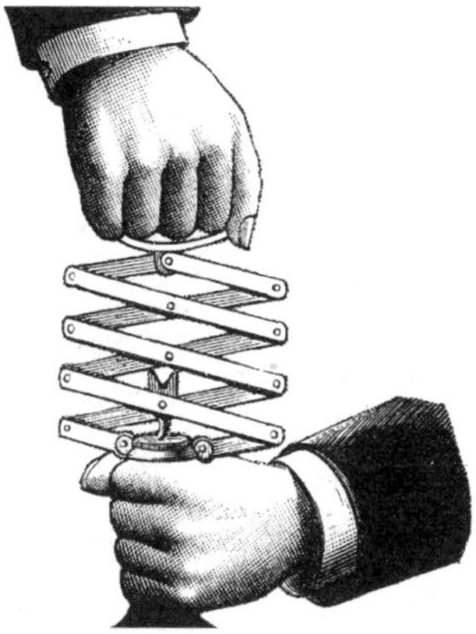

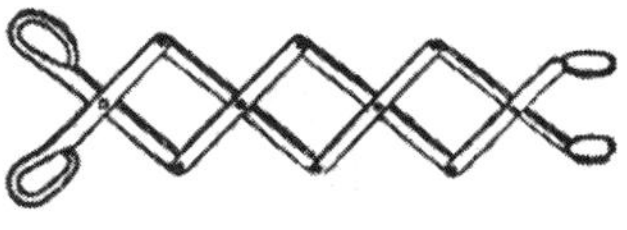

Fig. 5.35 a-c Among the products employing scissors mechanisms are a cork puller, tongs, and lift. Scissors mechanisms trade off force for distance.

expandable supports, gates, and railings. And its structural integrity need not be compromised in the process of making it larger or smaller. While this paradigm is widely employed in manufactured goods, this is not a paradigm directly found in nature, although it is related to arms, legs and wings.

Telescope

The word "telescope" has come to imply not only the optical instrument used for viewing distant objects, but also the system of nested, interlocked tubes that spyglass-type telescopes employ to extend their length. This system is found in the design of many other objects, in which it is desirable to have both a compact and an extended form. Among the many objects with telescoping parts are hydraulic elevators and camera-tripod legs. Telescoping is

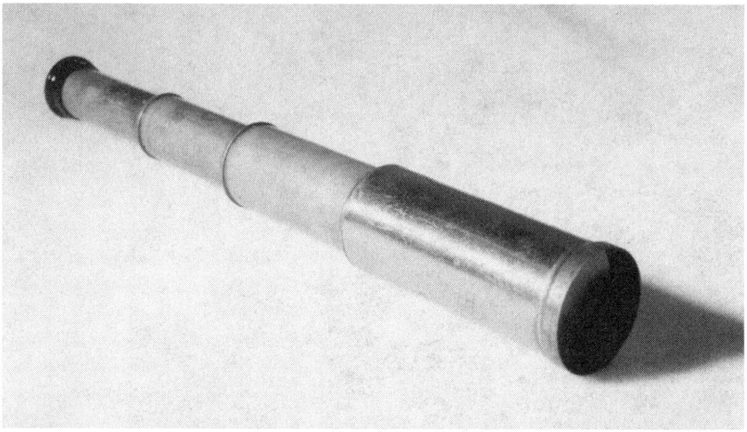

Fig. 5.36 The classic telescoping telescope. Ironically, many telescopes do not have telescoping parts.

Fig. 5.37 A collapsible cup packs compactly for camping and travel purposes. The *Telescope paradigm* enables its size change.

easily applied to exoskeleton-type forms, consequently leaving an inner space of varying length.

One circumstance when an inner space must be lengthened is in airports. *Jetways* are extended to airplanes to give passengers easy access to the planes. Telescoping, combined with pivoting, enables the opening to be aligned with the planes, no two of which will pull up to the terminal in exactly the same position. This prevents what would otherwise be a much more difficult task: parking the plane tightly against a fixed surface. The enclosed form of the Jetway is desirable to provide the travelers with a space protected from exhaust fumes, heat, rain, and so forth. An alternate or supplementary connection based on the *Bellows paradigm* is sometimes employed as well.

Since the telescope encloses a variable volume, if the telescope is air- and liquid-tight, it can be used to create pressure or a vacuum. One special case of the telescope form, in which a single solid or a sealed form slides within an outer cylinder is the *Piston and Cylinder* (see the *Sexual Connections paradigm* in Chapter 6). A tight-fitting piston moving within

Fig. 5.38 Jetways provide a variable-length enclosed walkway between a terminal and an airplane enabled by the *Telescope paradigm.*

a closed cylinder creates vacuum or pressure within the cylinder. This principle is employed in hypodermic needles as force applied to the telescoping piston creates vacuum to draw a blood sample, or pressure to expel an injection.

Alternately, pressure or vacuum within the cylinder can cause the piston to move. This is the basis for most automobile engines; gasoline burns within a cylinder, creating pressure that causes the piston to move (telescope) outward. This energy is converted into a circular motion that eventually is transferred to the wheels. Similarly, the cylinders used in the brake system, the shock absorbers and struts, and the strut lifters used on hatchbacks also employ telescoping pistons and pressurized cylinders.

Various grasses and members of the onion family like the leek (*Allium porrum)* display the telescoping nature. Growth in concentric tubes enables an interior section to grow at a faster rate than an outer cylinder, emerging from the harder fully-grown sheath already in place.

The collapsed telescope is related to the *Russian Dolls paradigm* (see Chapter 11), given that it's composed of self-similar nested shapes.

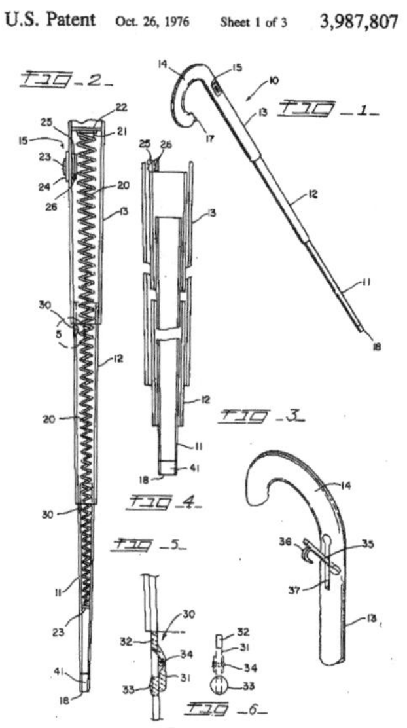

Fig. 5.39 Patent for a telescoping cane. The Telescope paradigm may be applied to many such devices that might benefit from having both a compact, and an extended, form.

Screw

As a screw is turned and enters a piece of wood, less of the screw is exposed. This process is, of course, reversible by changing direction. The same principle is at work in legs and feet used in furniture and appliances, in which a foot attached to a threaded rod may be turned in order to adjust the length of the legs. Similarly, old-fashioned piano stools were typically mounted on threaded rods, so the height of the stool could be adjusted by simply turning the seat. Screws used for height adjustment have the disadvantage of being rather slow for this purpose because the screw element must be turned continuously until the desired height is achieved. This is, however, something of an advantage

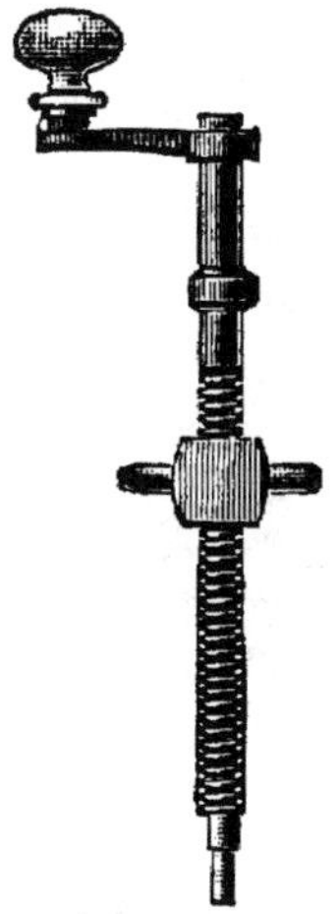

Fig. 5.40 Screws are often employed in devices to change height or length. A height adjustment mechanism such as this raises or lowers whatever is attached to the collar, when the handle is turned.

Fig. 5.41 The piano stool is a familiar example of the *Screw paradigm* used to change height or length.

when they are applied in such applications as floor jacks. Requiring many turns to raise the height of the jack provides a great mechanical advantage.

Flower

We might first think of flowers as things that smell nice or are pretty, but among their other important attributes, most flowers notably open up (bloom) to a wide display from a more compact state. If we look at the structure of a tulip opening, we find overlapping petals that move outward to create a large cuplike structure. Other flowers, like

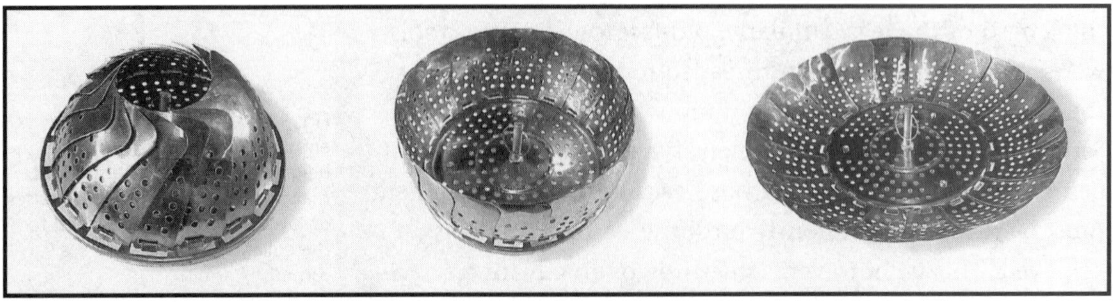

Fig. 5.42 Steamer baskets are among the devices that open like flowers, enlarging by spreading petals outward.

Fig. 5.43 Tulips are among the flowers that open to enlarge a cup-like form.

the marigold, open up to create more of a ball shape. Enlargment by unfolding petals is a useful technique for manmade objects as well. One such application is in the design of folding colanders and steamer baskets in which overlapping, stainless-steel "petals" unfold to form the basket or fold inward for compact storage. This technique is also sometimes applied to the design of satellite antennas.

Order and Disorder

Generally speaking, things take up less space when they're neatly ordered. If you look, for instance in the silverware drawer in your kitchen, you'll probably find teaspoons neatly stacked (see the *Nested Spoons paradigm* in Chapter 10). If you remove them and toss them back in haphazardly, however, they won't fit in the same compact space. Similarly, if you unwind an entire roll of paper towels, you'll end up with a pile that takes up more space than the roll you started with. We can expand the volume of a wide variety of things by decreasing the order and structure. Imagine a stack of children's blocks that are each a 1-inch cube, the stack measuring 1 foot on each edge. If we shake the cubes loosely into a bag, the gross volume of the bag will be greater than that of the neatly stacked blocks. Conversely,

Fig. 5.44 A classic primate intelligence test, "the monkey and the banana problem." Can animals understand and apply design paradigms? In order to reach the food hanging from the ceiling, the animal must realize that stacking blocks results in a taller structure to climb. This indicates a rudimentary understanding of *size through order*, a key concept of the *Order and Disorder paradigm*.

we can decrease the volume of the blocks by restacking them into the 1-foot cube. These examples illustrate the concept of *size through disorder,* that things generally take up more room when they are not neatly arranged.

Interestingly, though, we can also make something *larger* out of the blocks, by neatly stacking them. This is the basis for building masonry walls and buildings; here we achieve *size through order*. Conversely, we refer to breaking down walls as *reducing* them to rubble; in other words, we *reduce the size through disorder*. This principle is applied in the design of safety glass for automobile windows. When broken, the large pane of glass that might otherwise be dangerous in a crash, reduces when broken, into thousands of tiny cubes of glass.

The realization that stacking blocks produces something larger than the individual blocks is so fundamental that it is used as an animal intelligence test, known as "the monkey and the banana problem." A chimpanzee is placed in a room with several large blocks with a banana dangling from the ceiling. In order to get the banana it desires, the chimp must stack the blocks and then climb them.[29]

Many of the *Multiple Object Relations paradigms* (see Chapter 10) are also illustrative of *Order and Disorder* as a *Bigger and Smaller paradigm*. There are several special cases within the *Order and Disorder* category that deserve special mention as *Bigger and Smaller paradigms*, notably *Boiling and Freezing, Explosion and Implosion, Shredding,* and *Fluff.*

Boiling and Freezing

When we boil water, it expands into steam, taking many times the volume of the water. This expansion is so predictable and powerful that it became the basis for all manner of powered devices, from the steam engines of a century ago to the turbines of electric power plants today. Unlike most of the *Bigger and Smaller paradigms*, while steam achieves large and measurable increases in volume, there is no clear form we can speak of. In other words, it is *amorphous*. The process of making steam is reversible as condensation, which occurs when cooling is applied. In some cases pressure is interchangeable with temperature for boiling processes. Hence, we can cause many liquids to boil by creating a vacuum around them, and we can cause liquids to condense by compressing them. It is important to remember that while the water expands into steam and the body of

Fig. 5.45 Expansion due to boiling is easily converted to mechanical power. Widely used in coal and wood-fired steam engines in the 18th century, steam is still widely used in power generation today.

Fig. 5.46 Geyser. Expansion due to boiling causes periodic water and steam eruptions. Old Faithful geyser in Yellowstone Park, Wyoming, spouts approximately 10,000 gallons some 170 feet in the air every 65-70 minutes.

steam gets larger, the remaining quantity of water gets smaller. In cooking, *reducing* a sauce is to concentrate it by boiling off excess water. When making maple syrup, collected maple sap is *concentrated*, by boiling, thereby raising the percentage of sugar in the syrup.

Liquids can be converted into mists, with a steamlike increase in volume, by a variety of means other than heat. Mechanical action can also create mist, as it does around Niagara Falls. Ultrasonic waves can also create mist, and are employed in some household humidifiers.

Water also expands when it freezes; consequently liquid is its most compact state. The expansion of water as it freezes is a powerful force. Small cracks in large boulders can expand and eventually split the rock as water that seeps into the cracks repeatedly freezes and thaws. Concrete building foundations are poured below the frost line for a given locale to avoid having frost form underneath the foundation that will literally lift the building up, cracking the foundations and the wall surfaces. Reversing the process, we can also reduce the size of many solids by melting them; this is usually the preferred method of removing a body of ice. As with boiling, temperature is also somewhat interchangeable with pressure in the case of freezing. The weight of our bodies applied to ice along a thin blade of an ice skate produces enough pressure to momentarily liquefy the ice, enabling us to glide smoothly on a cushion of water.

Fig. 5.47 Among the greatest and most visible size changes is the huge volume of smoke and gasses that fires can produce.

Fire and Chemical Reactions

As with steam, fire and various chemical reactions also produce gasses with a dramatically larger volume than the fuel burned. Among the most dramatic common examples of this is the relatively small tank of gasoline in a car. When burned, gasoline expands into gasses filling millions of times the volume of the original liquid. When gasoline is burned in the cylinders of the engine, this expansion lifts the cylinders, turns the crankshaft, which in turn powers the wheels.

Fig. 5.48 Fire produces a large volume of flame, heated air, and smoke, while simultaneously reducing the volume of what is being burnt.

This change in size enables the conversion of the chemical energy stored in the gasoline into mechanical energy.

Fire also reduces the size or bulk of the fuel, which is sometimes the motivation for burning, as when trash or brush is burned, leaving only a fraction of the original weight in ash and unburnable remains. Some fuels, such as pure alcohol, burn cleanly, leaving nothing behind.

Numerous chemical reactions other than fire also produce a change in volume, such as mixing vinegar and baking soda, which instantly produces dramatic foaming (see the *Foam paradigm,* below). Foam-producing chemical reactions can be brought about by biological processes. A familiar example is yeast living in fermenting beer or rising bread dough. As the living yeast consume and metabolize starch, they produce many times their body size in carbon-dioxide gas, which produces the bubbles in the bread or beer. Less dramatic, but more troublesome, is the fact that when iron rusts, it also changes in volume. Consequently, you'll find raised rust spots lifting the paint on old cars, and you'll find it difficult to remove rusted nuts from bolts, on which rust has filled the spaces that had once existed between the nut and bolt, fusing them.

Explosion and Implosion

Because steam, fire, and various chemical reactions result in an increase in volume at normal atmospheric pressure, constraining the space allowed for the reaction produces an increase in pressure. This pressure might cause the failure of a containment vessel, resulting in an explosion. Similarly, the failure of a vessel containing a vacuum will result in an implosion. Explosions and implosions are the most dramatic of size changes. In a fraction of a second there may be a multi-millionfold change in volume. The effect can be devastating, such as when a bomb goes off or a water boiler explodes, but explosive processes can be important design elements as well. Automotive airbags are one example, employing an explosive discharge, instantaneously inflating the bags to cushion the passengers in the brief moment of opportunity available after a collision has been detected.

Explosions happen naturally under many circumstances. At the micro scale, cells sometimes burst as their internal pressure changes from chemical or biological infiltration. Macro-scale explosions range from volcanoes blowing their tops, to *supernovae*, violent explosions of large stars, that can produce more than a billion times the luminosity of the Sun.

Fig. 5.49 a, b Explosions and implosions are the fastest and most dramatic types of size and volume changes. While explosions such as bombs are dangerous, explosions can serve many constructive purposes as well, for instance in airbag deployment or excavation. Volcanos (right) and supernovae are examples of powerful natural explosions. DOD photos.

Fig. 5.50 A shredded newspaper takes substantially more space than a neatly folded one.

Shredding

Most cat owners can probably describe at least one thing shredded by their cat, whether a sweater, a chair, or a rug. The shredded area enlarges as the fibers are separated, bent, and pulled out of the more orderly structure they were in. Shredding seems to amuse the cat, as it does children when they eat string cheese. Children are fascinated with the cord of cheese that separates into fibers with some gentle pressure of the fingers and, almost as an afterthought, tastes good, too. Shredding increases volume. For example, running a ream of paper through a paper shredder can create a large bag of shredded paper. Shredding is generally applicable to fibrous materials. Among natural, unprocessed materials in this category are asbestos and similar minerals that can be shredded to make a sort of wool. Wood can also be shredded, as is quickly seen when a dog chews the end of a stick to shreds. Mechanically shredded or shaved wood (excelsior) was once widely used as a stuffing material in seat cushions and as a packing material for protecting fragile items. Shredded materials are often good insulators as well.

Fig. 5.51 Shredding enlarges this stick of string cheese.

Fluff

Fig. 5.52 Fluffing increases the volume of feathers in a pillow and makes it more comfortable.

A good bed pillow, whether it's a firm or soft style, is fluffy and full. As it is used, the feathers tend to align themselves flatly against each other, thus taking up less space and making the pillow flatter. Fluffing the pillow moves the feathers back out of alignment, so that with many feathers at right angles to each other, it gets larger and softer. In fluffing a pillow, it gains *size through disorder.* It differs from the *Shredding paradigm* in that before and after fluffing we are dealing with a collection of usually soft, independent elements, as in feathers. With shredding, start with a single element and might or might not still have a single element after shredding. Shredded large feathers are sometimes used as a coat or pillow filling, but this material is inferior to smaller fluffed feathers or, best of all, down.

Foam

Foaming is a powerful means of expanding the volume of a liquid. Gas bubbles injected into certain liquids can expand their volume by millions of times. When gas bubbles expand a heated substance that is solid at room temperature, such as plastic, glass, or rubber, the foam might harden with the bubbles in place, yielding a substance with properties distinctly different from those of the unfoamed substance. Foamed plastics like polystyrene and foam rubber are widely valued and employed for their light weight, insulating properties, and impact resistance. Foams are formed in the natural world both by inanimate processes and by chemical and mechanical actions of organisms. While foams are sometimes merely a useless byproduct of other processes, several species use foams constructively as a building material. The spittlebug, for example, makes a home out of foam that protects it from predators and is even resistant to rain.

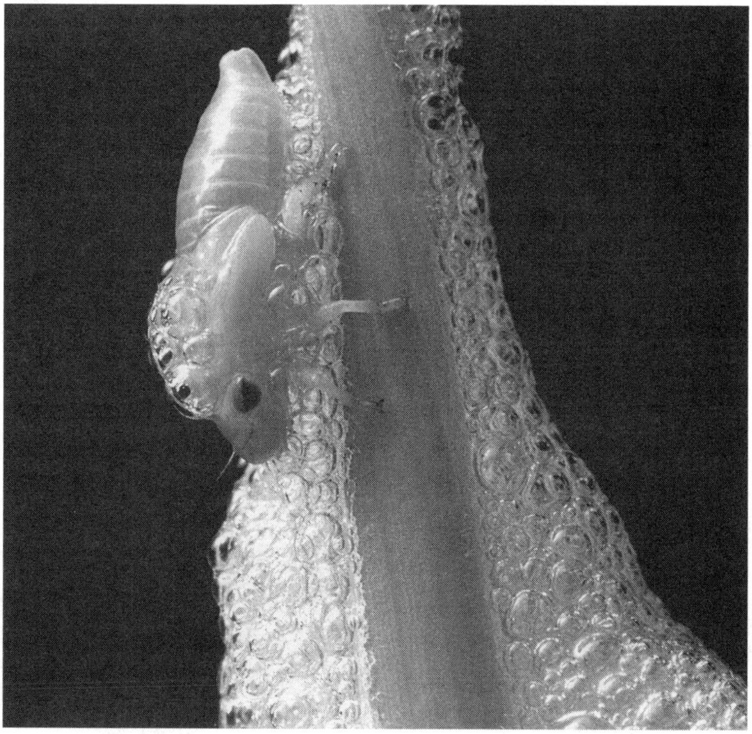

Fig. 5.53 A spittle bug making foam. Kenneth Gardiner photo.

Fig. 5.54 Plastic foam has many beneficial properties, it is lightweight, economical, strong, and insulating. Foamed plastics such as styrene are widely used for packaging. Higher density plastic foams are used to manufacture computer cases and other goods.

> "Exuded from the alimentary tract by spittlebugs, nymphs of the *Cercopidae* family (i.e. spittlebugs) are spittle masses commonly found on stems of meadow plants. The spittle fluid is voided from the anus after it has been mixed with a mucilaginous substance excreted by the epidermal glands of the seventh and eighth abdominal segments. Air bubbles are introduced into the spittle by means of the caudal appendages of the nymph. Immature spittlebugs rest head downward on the plant; as spittle is voided, it covers the nymph and is not easily dislodged, even by heavy rains." [30]

Fig. 5.55 Foaming makes materials lighter, which is desirable in many food products including bread, whipped cream, cake and mousse. Foam also forms as carbon dioxide is released from soft drinks and beer.

Enlargement by foaming gives the spittle the ability to span between branches and grass blades, embracing the nymph much as a cocoon would.

Foam is also used in firefighting. Products like 3M™ Light Water™ are effective against gasoline and fuel oil fires, where water alone is ineffective because it sinks below the surface of the burning fuels. When foam is sprayed on burning materials, it smothers the fire by keeping fresh air from

Fig. 5.56 A chain gets larger or smaller by adding or removing links.

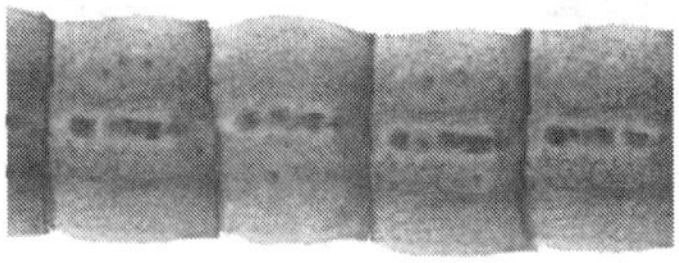

Fig. 5.57 The tapeworm, an intestinal parasite, exhibits the *Chain paradigm* in its form and function. As its body grows, it adds more "links," thereby getting longer. It periodically drops sections as well, enabling its eggs leave the host's body to find new hosts.

circulating into it. It also tends to stay in place, helping to prevent reignition of the fire. Further, unlike water, firefighters can still breathe when covered with these foams.

The process of expansion followed by hardening of plastic foam makes it ideal for filling odd cavities. Insulation foam in a can such as Great Stuff® (*Polymeric diisocyanate, polyol resin* and *hydrocarbon gas* mixture) can be sprayed in an odd opening. The foam then expands to fill the opening, sticking to the sides, and hardening in place. Further, its good insulation properties keep cold from passing through.

Chain

Chains exemplify the many things that are made longer or shorter by adding or removing modular links. Most anyone can tell you that to shorten a chain, you simply remove some links. Similarly, many metal watchbands are lengthened and shortened in the same manner. As a train travels, it can get longer or shorter as cars are added or removed from the train at various points along the way.

Among the natural examples of this paradigm are tapeworms. The adult phase of the life cycle of the tapeworm *Diphyllobothrium latum* begins with a head, which attaches to the intestine walls. It grows by extending its body as a sequence of chained segments. Each segment, called a

Fig. 5.58 Like a chain, a train gets larger or smaller by adding or removing cars.

proglottid, is sexually independent and has its own male and female sexual organs. As segments mature and fill with eggs, they detach from the rest of the worm to continue their life cycle, thereby shortening the remaining tapeworm "chain."

Openings

Openings are a rather tricky kind of *Bigger and Smaller paradigm.* As the children's riddle goes, "What gets bigger, the more you take away?" The answer of course is *a hole.* Indeed, as something opens and closes, a hole or opening gets bigger and smaller. But opening and closing can make objects larger and smaller, too, not just voids.

Clam Shell

For example, as a clam shell opens, we can observe two changes: the opening gets larger, as does the area of the exposed surface. Once open, the outside as well as the inside of the clamshell are exposed. This property is exploited in "flip-open"-type mobile phones, where it is desirable to compactly fold the phone to fit in a pocket

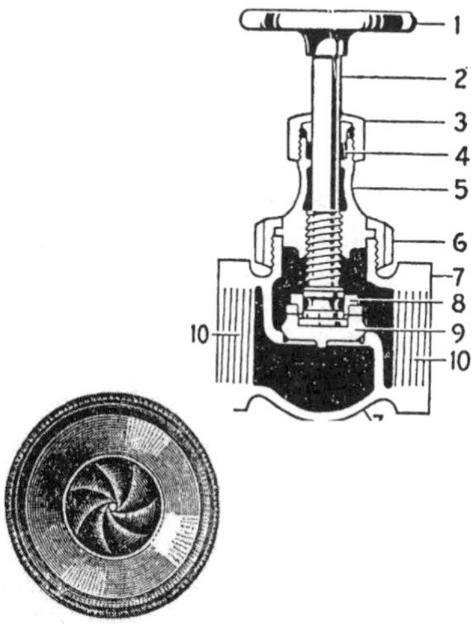

Fig. 5.59 a, b Devices such as valves and camera irises serve primarily to modulate the size of an opening, and in turn, the passage of water or light.

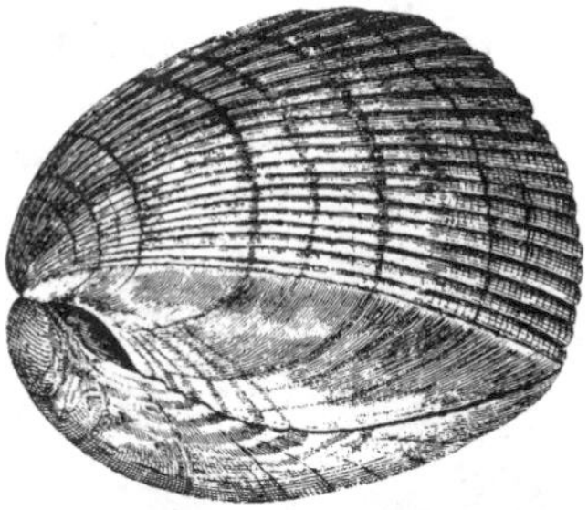

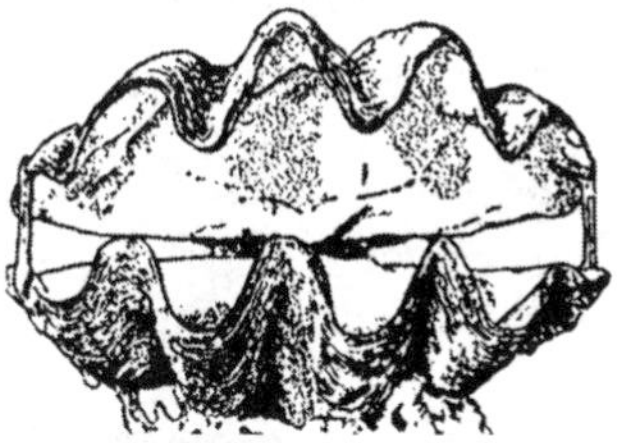

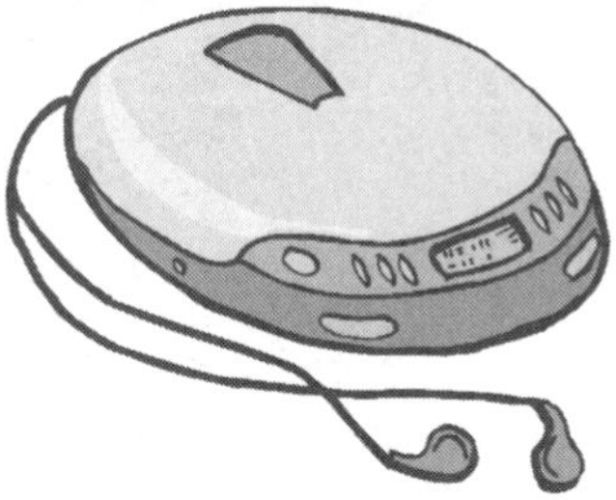

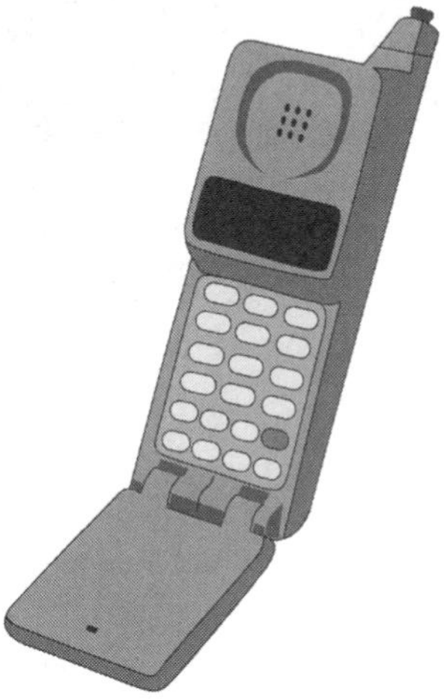

Fig. 5.60 a-e Clam shells, and the *Clam Shell paradigm* in designed objects. As technology enabled increasingly smaller cellular telephones it became necessary to invent ways to make the phones larger when in use, to span from the mouth to the ear. Recognition that when clam shells open they increase not only the size of the opening, but also the exposed area, led to designs based on this paradigm.

Fig. 5.61 Sandwich boxes made of cardboard or plastic foam are also derived from the clamshell design.

Fig. 5.62 The mouth is a negative space, if we say someone is, or has, a big mouth, we are referring to the size of the opening, rather than the flesh of the mouth itself.

and yet be large enough when unfolded to span between the ear and the mouth. *Opening* effectively enlarges this type of phone.

Drawstring Purse

Many openings are designed to change size. Windows, for instance, are opened according to how much air you wish to let through. The opening of a drawstring purse is similarly variable, we close it by pulling the strings tight, thus reducing the size of the opening.

Many variably sized openings are found in biology as well. Our bodies have many openings that change size, for example, our eyelids and mouths. *Sphincters*, the variable size openings found in our digestive tracts, rectum, and other locations, are tightened by annular muscles in the manner of the *Drawstring Purse paradigm*.

Fig. 5.63 Windows, blinds, curtains, and shutters serve to modulate the openings between buildings and the outside with respect to air and light.

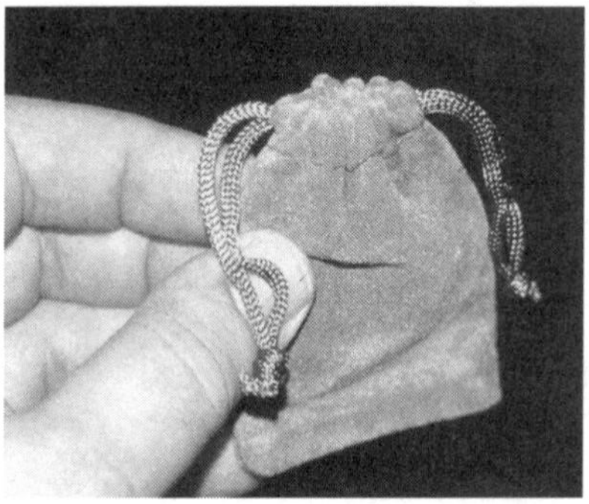

Fig. 5.64 a, b (right) Drawstring pouch and purse. Pulling cords draws an opening tighter.

Questions

1) How does a building grow over time, and how can this growth be accommodated and planned for in its design?

2) Is growth reversible? Is decay the opposite of growth? If not, what is?

3) Your basement occasionally floods, and you need a means of turning on a pump when water enters the room. How can you use a sponge to turn on the pump?

4) A foam pad makes a good sleeping surface and can be squashed compactly for storage. How can it be made to stay squashed, and consequently compact, until it is ready for use?

5) The next time you see a crane at a construction site, look at its various parts and list each of the *Bigger and Smaller paradigms* you can see employed in its design.

6) Design a camera tripod that is compact for travel that will support a camera at eye level, yet does not employ the *Telescope paradigm.*

6

Binary Object Relations

Things that fit the *Binary Object Relations paradigms* have two different parts that must be used together in order to perform a task. Binary objects typically will not work properly, if at all, if both parts are not present. This is usually not a byproduct, but rather a conscious aspect of the design, as with a lock and key. The operation of a lock without its key is not only typically impossible, it is the whole point of having locks and keys.

Two of the classic frameworks for dealing with *Binary object relations* are *figure-ground,* and *yin-yang*. Figure-ground concepts were developed as part of Gestalt psychology. The basic concept is that our visual system is tuned to perceive a figure against a background. We can often consciously switch our perception of which is the figure and which is the ground. The classic example of figure ground appears as Figure 6.1, which can be read as an image of either a vase or of two faces. This is a powerful conceptual tool for design, such as when it is applied, for example, to architecture. In looking at a plan, we may think of the walls as the figure and we might manipulate the wall forms. Alternately, we can think of the spaces between the walls (the rooms) as the figures, and manipulate these forms. Understanding this framework, then, is useful in experiencing architecture as well. We can walk into a room and appreciate the form of the space of the room, as well as the form of the building that encloses the space. So, too, the architect might consciously decide to alternately call attention to a space within a building, or the building elements enclosing and describing that space.

The yin-yang relationship shares some superficial properties with the figure-ground framework. It can certainly be looked at as a black figure against a white circle or vice versa, but this misses the point. The yin-yang symbol represents tension and balance between the black (yin) and white (yang), which represents the many equal but opposing forces in the world. These include dark and light, feminine and masculine, contracting and expanding, downward and upward, and cold and hot. The black figure is not entirely black, and the white is not entirely white. The form of the two suggests motion: the black is eternally moving into the white, and vice versa.

Fig. 6.1 Vases and faces. A classic example from Gestalt psychology, whether you see vases or faces depends on which you perceive as the figure, and which you perceive as the ground.

These two frameworks help to categorize the binary relationships. Some of the binary-object relations, we will see, relate in a figure-ground manner. The *Hammer and Anvil paradigm,* for instance, consists of the hammer as figure, against the anvil as ground. In some cases the figure-ground relationship can facilitate our perception of relative changes between the figure and the ground. Watching the motion of a second hand on a stopwatch, for instance, depends upon the binary relationship between the hand and the face of the watch to give it meaning. Without the face and its marked increments, we would not be able to tell how far the hand had moved. Other paradigms, like the *Oil and Water paradigm,* behave in a yin-yang fashion.

Fig. 6.2 Yin-yang symbol. The black and white figures represent tension and balance between equal but opposite forces.

Some binary relations have an active object like the lock, and an enabling object, the key. Others, like oil and vinegar for a salad dressing, consist of equal contributors. Sometimes the inability of certain things to work without both parts present is exploited as a means of keeping things safe or easy to handle. For example, many compounds, ranging from epoxy glue to nerve gas, are shipped as binary components. These materials are designed to present little risk or consequence to handling either one of the elements until they are mixed.

Sexual Connections

Perhaps the most basic binary-object relationship is sexual union, the joining of male and female parts. The essence of the *Sexual Connection paradigm* is the relationship of the penis and vagina, with a convex male element that protrudes and fits into the concave female form. While these elements are widespread in sexual relationships in the natural world, their presence is certainly not implicit to sexual fertilization. Male sea urchins, for example, being contentedly attached to the ocean floor, fertilize their partners without making direct contact with them. They accomplish this by releasing a cloud of sperm into the water, which currents carry over the sea urchin beds. But the penis- and vagina-based sexuality is found in creatures ranging from simple worms through mammals. Some creatures, complicating the more familiar 1:1 relationships usually suggested by sexual connections, are hermaphroditic, having both male and female sex organs. Tapeworms are not only hermaphroditic, but can also have male and female sex organs on each segment of the worm, which can be fertilized by sexual contact with other segments of the same worm. In both nature and in manufactured goods having male and female parts, the sexual connection is usually intended to be a temporary connection.

Fig. 6.3 Human love represents a connection on many levels, including spiritual, companionship, financial, and sexual.

In industrial applications, the *Sexual Connection paradigm* is useful for describing and labeling all sorts of connectors, plugs, sockets, jacks, and so forth. We speak of the male and female ends of an electrical extension cord, indicating the sexual-connection structure of the jacks and plugs. There are many such applications in electronics, (see the *Plug and Socket paradigm* described in Chapter 7 for greater detail). Pistons and cylinders relate in a sexual fashion and usually involve an exchange between pressure in the cylinder and travel of the piston within the cylinder, as discussed earlier in the *Telescope paradigm* section of Chapter 5.

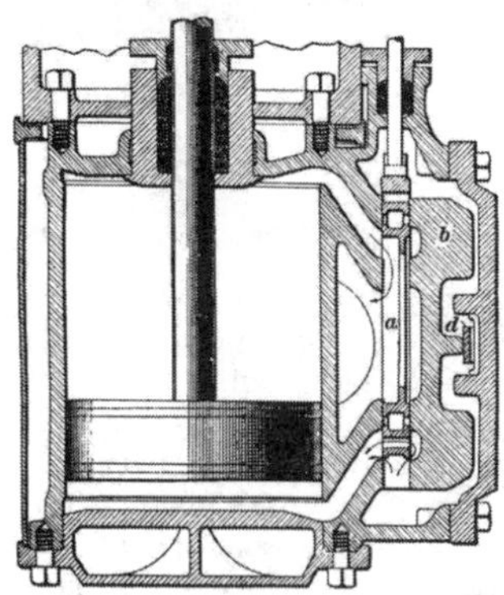

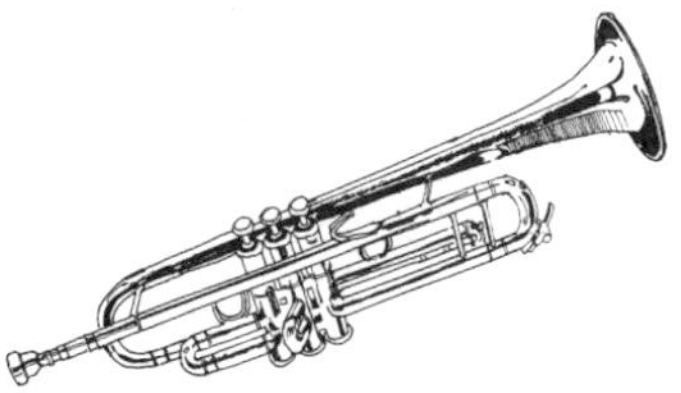

Fig. 6.4 a, b Pistons and cylinders, including those employed in the valves of trumpets, exemplify the *Sexual Connection paradigm.*

Fig. 6.5 Seeing identical twins challenges our conceptions of self and identity. Approximately 25% of identical twins are mirror image twins. Their features and even their body organs are mirror images of each other, yet we accept this within our definition of "identical."

In hardware, we find the paradigm employed in hook-and-eye closures, locks, latches, and nuts and bolts. In clothing, we see this paradigm in snaps. As with electrical connections, snaps are used where closure is intended to be temporary, or frequently opened and closed, as an alternative to a more permanent attachment like sewing.

Identical Twins

The human species has a strong bias toward biaxial symmetry. Studies have shown that subjects regard as beautiful faces that are measurably most symmetric.[31] Much of our anatomy is in matched pairs: our eyes, ears, arms, legs, hands, feet, breasts, nostrils, teeth, and so forth. Partly for this reason, twins have a special meaning to us. Seeing a pair of identical twins together adds another dimension to the perceived symmetry, both the biaxial symmetry of the individual, and the symmetry of the twins themselves. We see not only a matching left arm and right arm on Kara; we also see matching left and right twins, Kara and Kira.

Fig. 6.6 A longstanding interest in twins is evident in their appearance in myth, legend and art through the ages. This sculpture portrays Romulus and Remus, twins who, according to legend, were raised by a wolf, and later founded Rome.

The *Identical Twins* (or simply *Twins*) *paradigm* presents a message that *these two things are identical yet separate.* "Identical" allows a little leeway, however, with humans and other creatures, and with manufactured goods. We can consider things identical even though they are actually mirror images of each other; about one quarter of identical twins are mirror twins. Mirrors and mirror images are also metaphoric symbols of the Identical Twins paradigm.

Fig. 6.7 a-d San Francisco doors. The Identical Twins paradigm is often employed in architecture to achieve visual symmetry, or to accommodate duplicate functions.

Perceptually, the *Twins paradigm* has little meaning unless the twin objects are together. Just as with human twins, where little separates them from a crowd unless they are together, removing one twin breaks the paradigm.

The *Twins paradigm* is applied in design for a number of different reasons. Gloves, shoes, socks, and so forth are manufactured as mirror-image twins to accommodate our biaxially symmetric needs. Twin dispensers or containers are made to accommodate condiments or seasonings that are normally used or served together, like salt and pepper or oil and vinegar. Chopsticks, ice hooks, and other implements are similarly used in matched pairs to work in matched opposition to each other or to equally equip our right and left hands.

The paradigm is sometimes applied in architecture as well, as with New York's twin towers, the World Trade Center buildings, designed by architect Minoru Yamasaki. These buildings, at 110 stories, were the world's tallest buildings upon their completion in 1970. A design for twin buildings might result from zoning or other limitations, in situations where it may not be possible to build a single building large enough to meet client needs. Twin buildings might also be employed to take advantage of separate lots divided by a street. The design might be a conscious decision to clearly identify the constructions as being closely associated, and functioning as a single center, yet simultaneously suggesting some autonomy of dual clients. This might have been part of the message in the design of the World Trade Center: the client was the Port Authority of New York and New Jersey.

Fig. 6.8 The *Identical Twins paradigm* is employed to balance weight and thrust in applications such as the Space Shuttle's twin solid-fuel booster rockets. NASA photo.

Fig. 6.9 The visual impression of identical twins is intentionally evoked here by providing these London guards with identical outfits and buildings.

Fig. 6.10 The twin towers of New York's World Trade Center help to convey the nature of its twin clients, the Port Authority of New York and New Jersey.

Siamese Twins

Conjoined twins were labeled "Siamese twins" for Eng and Chang, born in Thailand of Chinese parents in 1811 (Thailand was formerly called Siam). Eng and Chang were identical twins born connected at the chest by a small band of flesh. Siamese twins are paradoxical to consider, which is why they continue to generate so much interest today, as in the nineteenth century when Eng and Chang toured the world as a curiosity. Visual cues indicate the presence of two individuals and yet their connection implies a single body. The alternating perception of *two* and *one* resonates in our minds seeking mental resolution.

While looking back with hindsight from the twenty-first century, we resolve this tension by simply saying Chang and Eng were separate individuals, knowing that surgically separating them would be trivial today. But for these men, their connection was central and overwhelming because they lived joined throughout their lives, on tour as a circus attraction in the 1820s and 1830s, and later settling in North Carolina, marrying British sisters, and raising families. They signed all legal documents "Chang Eng" and spoke of their doubts about their individuality.[32]

Fig. 6.11 a, b Human and animal examples of Siamese twins. Such twins result from the incomplete division of a single egg, and so are always identical twins as well.

Fig. 6.12 a-d Some of the many designed objects employing the *Siamese Twin paradigm.*

As a design paradigm, Siamese twins represents an important way that two things can relate: *joined and possibly separable, may be perceived as two yet handled as one*. The *Siamese Twin paradigm* is employed when it is desirable to have two things that are best attached, perhaps to ensure that one or the other is not misplaced. An example of this is children's gloves, attached by a long piece of yarn. The paradigm is also widely employed to keep two elements aligned or otherwise in place to be used simultaneously, as with a pair of glasses. While a monocle could be used and certainly two monocles could be held in place to see through, the advantages of creating a frame to hold the lenses in place and perfectly aligned are clear. The glasses can easily be put on, stored, cleaned, and so forth as a single unit, and there is little likelihood of misplacing a single lens. The bilateral symmetry of the human body generates many such opportunities for conjoined devices, including headphones for a radio, earmuffs, and binoculars.

Fig. 6.13 a, b Variations on the *Siamese Twins paradigm* frequently appear in architecture, with twin elements ajoining, or connected by bridge elements.

Other reasons to employ the *Siamese Twins paradigm* as a design strategy exist. In architecture, twin buildings can be joined via enclosed bridges to enable tightly coupled commerce between buildings resting on separate foundations and building lots. This paradigm was employed in the design of the Petronas Towers in Kuala Lampur, Malaysia, by architect Cesar Pelli. In food, Popsicles® employ the paradigm; this frozen dessert consists of two parts each on an individual stick and joined by a thin section at the middle. The use of the paradigm enables a Popsicle to be eaten in one or two separate portions, and facilitates sharing one with a friend. The paradigm also sometimes finds use in packaging for products that are used together, such as oil and vinegar, shampoo and conditioner, and the two components of epoxy glue (see the *Epoxy paradigm*).

Lock and Key

The *Lock and Key paradigm* embodies a binary relationship between the lock and the key that is sometimes called *specificity*, which is to say only a specific key will open the lock. It is important to remember that there is usually a third element in a lock-and-key relationship, which is the thing being locked. We can open a lock with a key, but that is not usually very interesting by itself. We are usually interested in what we gain access to by opening the lock. In addition to permitting physical access to something, keys can also operate switches, activating the thing that is locked. For example, a car can be driven only after it is *activated* by turning the ignition key.

Some similarities between the lock-and-key relationship and sexual connections exist. A key inserted into a keyhole is clearly a sexual connection, and the male and female nature of the key and the keyhole are obvious. Yet this aspect is not intrinsic to the *Lock and Key paradigm*. Numerous examples of the *Lock and Key paradigm* are

Fig. 6.14 a-c Locks and keys as icons. Keys usually imply access, while locks imply the denial of access.

employed independently from the sexual connection paradigm. Some locks use magnetic keys that are waved over the lock, for instance, while others are accessed by passing a card through a slot. Nonetheless, the two are often associated. We frequently find not only a sexual relationship between keys and locks, but also a lock-and-key relationship in sex. Among insects, for example, the physical appearance of the male reproductive organs varies widely by species. The geometry of the genitalia is often the most reliable way for entomologists to distinguish between species that otherwise closely resemble each other. The prevailing theory explaining these geometric differences is compared to the *Lock and Key paradigm*: "male organs are diversely proportioned for much the same reason that keys are: to keep strangers out of the house."[33] The reasoning behind this is that attempts at cross-species fertilization is discouraged by the lock-and-key relationship to avoid wasting reproductive effort, which usually would not result in viable offspring. Recent theories also take into account functional and selective aspects of the penile geometry, acknowledging the role of sexual selection in promoting genetic lines.

Fig. 6.15 The relationship of the male and female sexual gonads of many species resembles the *Lock and Key paradigm*, as do the egg and sperm. Most combinations of mating across different species are icompatible for this reason.

The lock-and-key paradigm exists in many other forms in nature as well. The action of enzymes is often compared to the locks and keys.[34] Enzymes are protein molecules that facilitate chemical reactions. An enzyme like lactase acts like a key when it meets lactose, the sugar found in milk. Upon contact, lactase unlocks the chemical bonds in lactose, breaking it down into the simpler and more easily digested sugars glucose and galactose. The enzyme remains unchanged by this operation and is ready to unlock the next molecule. Also like a key, lactase is very specific, it works only on lactose.

We have seen examples of both mechanical and biological forms of locks and keys. In some situations, we might want to combine aspects of both. One reason to develop this combination is for a machine to react to a specific biological trigger. This might be done to provide more security when a key isn't specific enough, such as when a potential intruder has gained access to the key. In such situations, systems can be keyed to specific individual traits, such as finger, retina, or voice prints.

Scissors

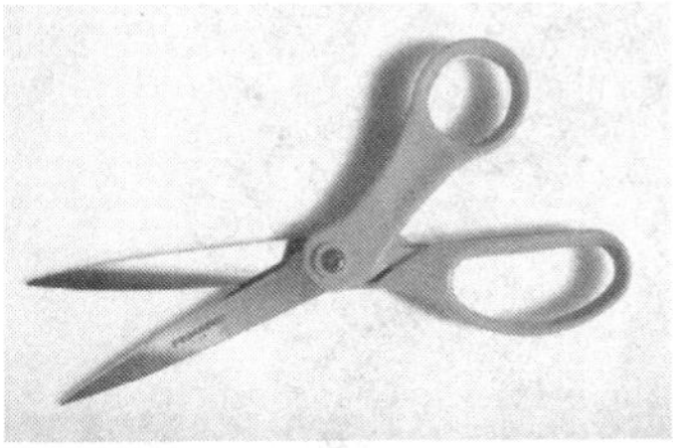

Fig. 6.16 Western-style scissors. The distinctive "X" form is common to a variety of tools.

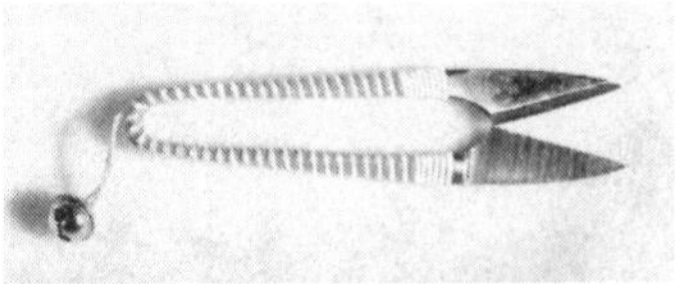

Fig. 6.17 Japanese scissors. While the body is a single piece and the legs do not cross as with Western-style scissors, the action is the same, with blades in opposition.

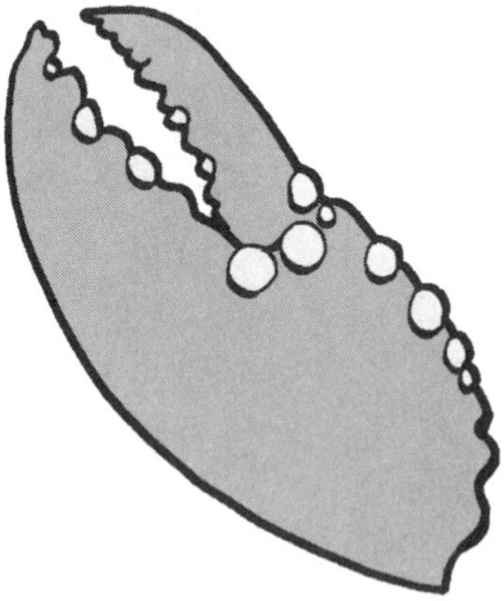

Fig. 6.18 Lobster claw. The versatility of the lobster's claw come from opposable parts, allowing it to grip and pinch.

Scissors are characteristic of a number of objects that work with two similar opposable parts that must be used together to function. One half of a scissors might work as a crude knife, but would provide little of the utility of a scissors for the task of cutting something that is not resting against a ground plane. This is true of a number of tools that similarly are usually handheld and applied to the work, such as tweezers, pliers, shears, and wire cutters. Because of the nature of the "X" form of the Western-style scissors, they change size as the handles are moved apart (see the *Scissors paradigm* in Chapter 5). For this paradigm, however, the scissors legs need not be crossed, only opposed. Japanese scissors and shears, which fit this paradigm, but not the *Bigger and Smaller Scissors paradigm*, are usually made without crossed legs.

Similarly, many animal devices depend on opposing parts for their operation. A lobster's claw, for instance, would be of little use in pinching without opposing claws. Likewise, teeth must be set against opposing teeth for most of their uses, including biting, tearing, and grinding. Also quite importantly, we use our hands in this manner for a number of tasks, such as gripping, pinching, and snapping one's fingers. Opposable thumbs enable humans to work the thumb against the fingers, which, in turn, lets us grip and hold things in a number of different ways. This ability is usually credited, along with our abilities to walk upright, reason, and use language, as being the keys to human evolution and the success of our species.

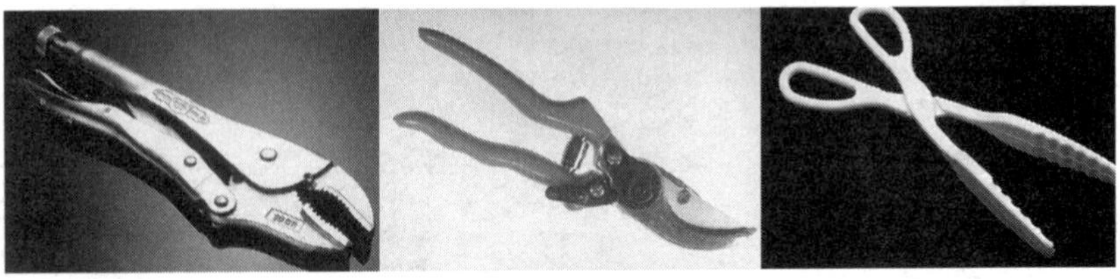

Fig. 6.19 a-c Three of the many tools that employ the *Scissors paradigm.*

Violin and Bow

A violin is one of a number of instruments usually played through the interaction of two parts, in this case, the violin and the bow. The bow, a wooden frame supporting horse-hair strings, is drawn across the violin strings, causing them to vibrate and resonate through the body of the violin, thereby producing sound. Other string instruments, such as the cello and viola, of course fit the paradigm as well, as do most applications of a bow, including archery (bow and arrow) and starting a fire with a bow and stick.

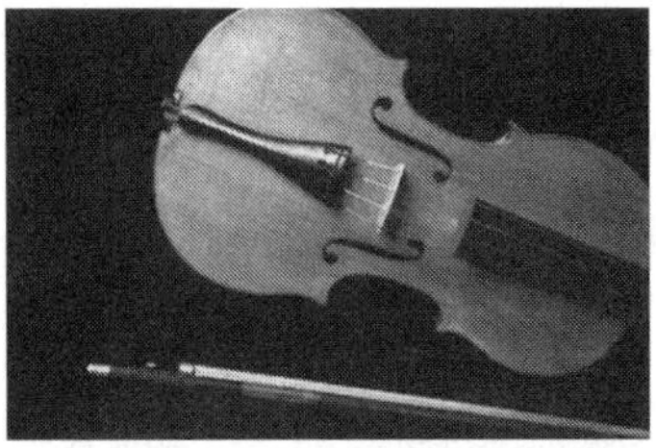

Fig. 6.20 Violin and bow. Although the violin can be plucked, in most music it is a 2-part instrument.

In the natural world, there are a number of corresponding relationships. Many insects produce sounds by a mechanism called *stridulation*: a wing or leg is rubbed or scraped (like a bow) against another body part, such as an abdominal plate or a wing, in order to cause vibrations in a distinctive pattern, frequency, and rhythm.[35] Crickets of the family *Gryllidae* (order *Orthoptera*) employ stridulation to make their chirping sounds by drawing a scraper on one forewing across a row of teeth on the opposite forewing.

Fig. 6.21 The cricket's chirp is produced through stridulation: A scraping surface on one forewing is drawn across a set of teeth on the opposite forewing, violin style.

Hammer and Anvil

The binary relationship of the hammer and anvil is one of figure and ground. The anvil, in the context of this paradigm, is the ground surface. The hammer represents any object we might pound against the ground surface. The hammer and anvil are the symbols of the smith, whether blacksmith, goldsmith, or tinsmith. These have largely become anachronistic professions, and the hammer and anvil are similarly somewhat dated, but the hammer and the anvil are powerful symbols that transcend their original purposes. In music, most percussion instruments fit this paradigm. Cymbals, drums, gongs and xylophones have a ground surface that stands more or less still while it is hit by a hammerlike object.

Fig. 6.22 The Hammer and Anvil paradigm is employed in percussion instruments: bells, drums, gongs, xylophones, and the like.

Many electrical devices employ the hammer and anvil

Fig. 6.23 a, b Blacksmith's shop. The central activity of the shop is shaping metal by pounding it between the hammer and the anvil. The power of the paradigm is evident as even a small silhouette icon conveys the activity to most observers.

paradigm, such as doorbells, emergency devices, and older telephones, wherein a small hammer hits a bell, generally triggered by an electromagnet that pulls the hammer toward the bell when electricity is applied. Within the paradigm, we find some situations where the anvil/ground surface is broken by the hammer, such as when a small hammer is placed by a glass surface to be broken in case of an emergency in order to gain access a shut-off valve, a hose, or some other piece of emergency equipment.

As metaphor, if the hammer is the rock, and the anvil is the hard place, being between the two suggests being beaten, crushed, and flattened. While the primary relationship in this paradigm is between the hammer and the anvil, it is important to remember that there is usually something between the two, whether it is a horseshoe or a gold ring.

Stone and Chisel

The *Stone and Chisel paradigm* reflects the interaction between a sharp-edged tool and the material it hits. The name refers to a sculptor carving a figure out of a block of stone. The *Stone and Chisel paradigm* is closely related to the *Hammer and Anvil paradigm*. The fundamental difference between the two is that unlike a hammer, a chisel cuts into and removes material from the surface it hits. The chisel is, therefore, acting upon the stone, whereas the hammer works on what is between it and the anvil; the anvil gives up effectively nothing to the hammer.

Fig. 6.24 While we may be inclined to focus on the point at which the hammer hits the chisel, that is not the business end. With the *Stone and Chisel paradigm*, the action takes place at the sharp end of the chisel.

Fig. 6.25 Stone and chisel. The chisel acts upon the stone, chipping the material away. The hammer amplifies its action.

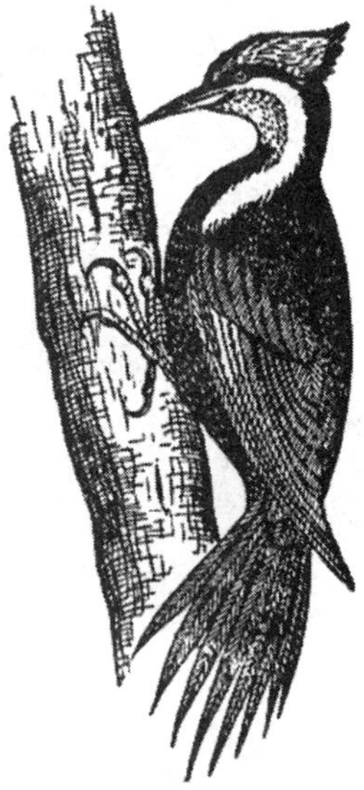

Fig. 6.26 Woodpecker. The action between the woodepecker's beak and the wood exemplifies the *Stone and Chisel paradigm.*

The *Stone and Chisel paradigm* is often employed with a hammer striking the chisel, but in most respects, the hammer doesn't change the chisel-stone relationship; it merely amplifies it. The cutting-and-chipping effect on the stone is done by the chisel. Further, a separate hammer is unnecessary if the chisel and the hammer are combined, as they are in a geologist's hammer.

In nature we find a number of examples of this paradigm, but perhaps none so striking as woodpeckers, pecking holes in a tree trunk to find grubs. While many birds repeatedly hit their beaks against a hard surface to dislodge bits of food, the woodpecker is remarkable for the amount of force it is able to apply relative to its size, and the visible impact upon trees. The pileated woodpecker *Dryocopus pileatus,* a large woodpecker the size of a crow, makes its nest inside hardwood trees, creating a hole into a tree large enough to live in using nothing but the chiseling action of its beak. These excavations sometimes lead to the collapse of the tree. The feats of beavers are no less remarkable: they can fell trees several feet in diameter. They similarly employ a chisel-like operation, using their teeth. Chisel-like incisor teeth that continually grow are a defining feature of all rodents.

Gnomon: A Stick in the Sand

Fig. 6.27 Sundial. The vertical stick, the gnomon, casts the shadow. Both the gnomon and the face are necessary in order to read the time.

A sundial consists of a face with markings, and a stick, or *gnomon,* protruding outward to cast a shadow upon the face. We can call the relationship of the two the *Gnomon paradigm,* through which we derive or convey information from the relative position or shadow of a gnomon against a face, body, or surface. The sundial is, perhaps, the simplest possible instrument. A minimal sundial is just a stick in the sand. Without moving parts, it can indicate the time; the sun over the gnomon leaves a shadow pointing to the hour. The need for both parts is clear: the gnomon alone casts a shadow, but the face is necessary to give the shadow meaning. And the face can indicate hours but requires the gnomon to cast the shadow pointing to them.

The concept that a stick placed in the sand can become an instrument that we can read information from is a powerful idea. This is so fundamental, in fact, that it at once signifies the human ability to think, imagine, and fashion instruments and machines out of found objects. The word "cognition" (to know, to learn, awareness, judgement), is derived from the word "gnomon."

Fig. 6.28 Most analog dials and instruments employ the *Gnomon paradigm.*

We find this paradigm employed in many kinds of instruments in which we wish to see a change of some sort. Dial thermometers usually employ a bimetallic coil attached to a needle. Heat makes the outer metal expand faster than the inner, causing the coil to become more tightly wound. This moves the needle across the face of the thermometer, indicating the temperature change that has caused the motion. While many of these instruments are now made with digital displays, analog instrumentation has been, and continues to be, widely used. Among the familiar examples are clocks, speedometers, tachometers, scales, and gas gauges.

While animals don't use instruments per se, many animals have information needs that are conveyed by, and read from, gnomonlike means. Think, for example, of a dog wagging its tail. The meaning the dog can express by, and which can be read from, the wagging tail is because of its gnomonlike nature. Tail-wagging is understood as happiness or excitement on the part of the dog, and is perceived as the change of position of the tail relative to the body, which is the same principle as the gnomon. The same is true when we wave an arm or point a finger.

Fig. 6.29 a-d Household products employing the *Gnomon paradigm.* A needle is read against a face. In the case of the padlock, the face moves relative to the gnomon rather than vice versa.

There is a secondary meaning to the *Gnomon paradigm* as well. This is the simple mechanical relationship of the stick to the ground. The stick jammed in the sand is held up both by compression of the sand around it, and by friction. We apply this paradigm to devices ranging from pincushions and beach umbrellas, to telephone poles and building foundations.

Fig. 6.30 a, b A stick in the sand may also be read as a sign directly, rather than by its shadow or its posion. This is enhanced by placing words on a bright panel on the stick, as with traffic signs.

Wheel and Axle

The *Wheel and Axle paradigm* is sometimes suggested as the ultimate paradigm of modern civilization, although the light bulb, the telephone, and the computer are contenders as well. The wheel and axle have clearly been instrumental for a far longer time; wheeled vehicles are depicted in Sumerian pictographs dating back to 3500 BC.

Wheels imply rolling, but rolling predated wheels by a long time. Balls roll, for instance, as do logs. But the invention of the wheel facilitated the permanent connection of the rolling part (the wheel) to the cart. The wheel attached to the cart is the basis for vehicles ranging from ancient chariots and carriages, to trains, automobiles, bicycles, and Rollerblade® skates. Even modern jets find wheels indispensable as the interface between the moving vehicle and the

Fig. 6.31 Skates are among the many forms of transportation based on axles and wheels.

Fig. 6.32 The wheel and axle are the basic units of rail transportation. Even with the rest of the train car gone, the axle and wheels seem inseparable.

ground, transferring loads, and minimizing losses due to friction.

Wheels and axles have enjoyed a "second life" beyond vehicles. They are also integral to many types of mechanical devices. Water wheels, some of the most ancient machines, helped to provide irrigation for farming and power for such processes as milling and sawing. The Industrial Revolution accelerated with the introduction of Boulton and Watt's steam engines, which turned steam-driven piston power into smooth rotary motion. This motion, which could then be transferred by belts and modified as to speed and torque, was used to drive all types of rotary machinery. Today we find that electric motors, automobile engines, and jet engines still retain both the circular motion and the internal wheel-and-axle structure. Thus, we see a common thread through all of these devices spanning thousands of years.

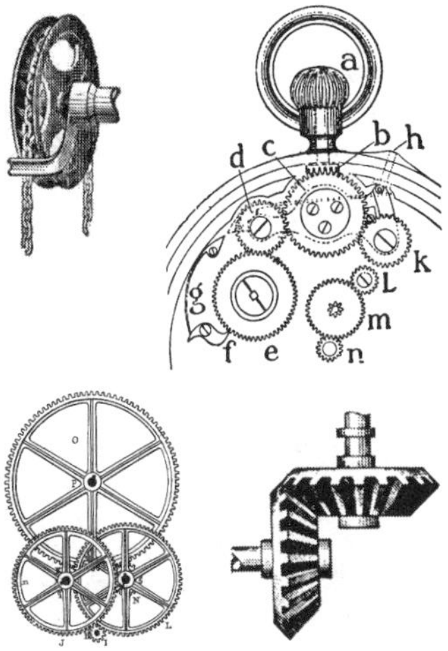

Fig. 6.33 a-d The *Wheel and Axle paradigm* is widely employed in mechanisms, with gears, rollers, and other moving parts.

Because wheels have been so important to the development of modern civilization and seem to be everywhere, artists have occasionally toyed with the ideas of fanciful creatures with wheel-like structures in place of feet, and of birds with propeller propulsion. The popular presumption is that nature has overlooked one of the favorite inventions of the human race. Indeed, it is hard to conceive of a natural mechanism to support wheels and axles. Nature seems to like to connect everything, via ligaments, blood vessels, nerves, and so forth. A freely spinning part would, therefore, tend to rip these vital connections after less than a full turn. Nonetheless, biologists continue to look for natural, wheel-like structures, and have found some good candidates. *Rotifers*, microscopic creatures living primarily as a freshwater species or as parasites, are so named for the apparently wheel-like rotation of their metachronically beating cilia. The flagellae of certain bacteria and a protozoan called "Rubberneckia" are believed to actually freely rotate.[36] While the human body has no wheellike anatomical features, it does have an axlelike structure, the pivot

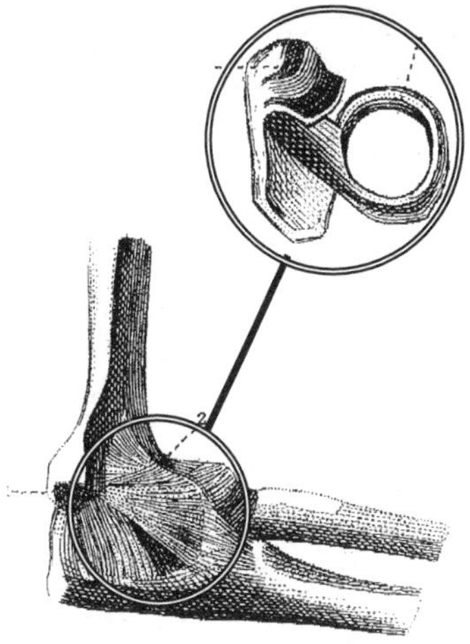

Fig. 6.34 Radio ulnar joint. While the human body doesn't have wheels and axles, the radio ulnar joints found in the arm come close. When you turn your extended arm from palm up to palm down, the two bones in the lower arm must cross, requiring one of them (the ulna) to twist. A special type of joint known pivot-type, or trochoid, accomodates this motion, allowing for spinning of an axle-like bone within a ring.

joint. The radio-ulnar joints connect the radius, the bone on the thumb side of your forearm. The end of this bone is free to spin within a ring of fibrous tissue, accommodating the turning caused when the forearm is twisted.

It sometimes seems that wheels are everywhere, but by some measures the wheel is on the decline. Wristwatches and clocks, for example, were once horologic masterpieces of wheel-like parts and gears, with tiny axles resting on jeweled bearings. These have mostly been replaced by electronic timepieces, as timekeeping has undergone a paradigm shift from a mechanical operation to information processing.

Fig. 6.35 The *Oil and Water paradigm* is always an issue when making salad dressing. An emulsifier is sometimes added to keep them mixed.

Oil and Water

The *Oil and water paradigm* is used for relationships between things that are characterized by *repellence.* Combinations like oil and water can be put into a vessel, shaken, and stirred, but will not stay mixed. Oil-and-vinegar-based salad dressing probably first comes to mind. For salad dressing, the separation of the oil and vinegar is a minor annoyance, although we can work around it by pouring the dressing immediately after shaking, or by pouring the oil and vinegar separately. Adding an emulsifier can also counteract the tendency toward separation. Emulsifiers allow the oil and vinegar to stay mixed longer, and are commonly found in commercial dressings.

Fig. 6.36 Rainwear design benefits from the *Oil and Water paradigm.* Use of hydrophobic materials helps keep the wearer dry.

In many situations, "nonmixability," or separation after mixing, is desirable. For example, cooks take advantage of the tendency of oil and water to separate. When you roast meats or poultry, the fat tends to rise to the top of the pan drippings, enabling it to be easily scooped off. Thinking creatively leads you to ask in what situations it might be beneficial to repel water or oil. Oil's unwillingness to mix with water suggests that it would be beneficial in something like a raincoat. Oilcloth, a canvas-like material treated with oil, exploits this property, and is sometimes used for this purpose. Waterfowl also use a similar technique; they preen their feathers with oil to help waterproof them.

Many synthetic materials are also *hydrophobic*, which means they tend to repel water. Rubber and plastic, for example, are consequently common for rain gear, and various chemical treatments, such as 3M's ScotchGard™, can give repellence to ordinary cloth.

Fig. 6.37 Epoxy products. Products are shipped in two parts and mixed only when needed, as they begin to harden immediately upon mixing.

Epoxy

Epoxy cement, as a paradigm, represents the category of *binary* substances, delivered as two components that become active when mixed. In the case of classic epoxy cement, two easily handled liquids, pastes, or types of putty are shipped separately. The two compounds are mixed when needed and quickly form a powerful cement. Binary components are kept separate to prevent their premature hardening or to maintain them in a form that is easy to handle, for instance, being nonsticky. In chemistry, one of the two components is usually a catalyst, something that facilitates a chemical reaction.

Among the common binary products is Bondo®, polyester-based putty used primarily for auto-body repair. Gray paste is scooped out of the can and mixed with the red catalyst supplied in a separate tube. Upon mixing, the catalyst causes the polyester to heat up and harden within about ten minutes.

Fig. 6.38 Bread machine. Yeast activates the dough, much as a catalyst activates epoxy. Some bread machines, when set for delayed breadmaking, will premix the dough, but will not add the yeast until the desired rising time.

Yeast and dough can react the same way as well. A dough of flour and water will remain stable and inactive for long periods of time, until the yeast is added. At this point, the dough will begin to rise as the yeast organisms begin to feed and multiply within the dough. Bread machines take advantage of this property to enable delayed operation. They employ various means to ensure that the yeast is not mixed into the dough until the cooking cycle calls for it to rise.

Many potentially dangerous substances are shipped as binary components as well. Because the ingredients are kept separate until needed, the materials and their handlers are often far safer than they would be if the components were mixed. One extreme example of this is binary nerve-gas weapons. Binary nerve gas was developed to allow for the relatively safe preparation and handling of weapons containing the gas. The components, which aren't particularly dangerous when handled individually, remain separate even when placed in a missile warhead. The components are only mixed in-flight as the warhead is armed.

Lever and Fulcrum

A lever is familiar as a "simple machine" that lets you magnify force through the application of leverage. The fulcrum is the support of the lever, such as the bar at the middle of a seesaw. A lever allows for a trade-off of force with distance. A pry bar can generate great force at its prying end, but move up only an inch, while you press down at the opposite end, moving the bar an entire foot. Since one end is moved 12 times the distance of the other end, the lever magnifies 50 pounds of downward force 12 times, to produce 600 pounds lift at the business end of the pry bar.

Fig. 6.39 The lever and fulcrum trades off force for distance. You can use them to multiply your force 10 times if you're also willing to move the lever 10 times farther.

Lever-and-fulcrum arrangements are use extensively in machines and natural systems. Cranes often use a lever and fulcrum to achieve a large extension of the boom of the crane with a smaller motion of motorized cables. Insects employ a similar arrangement to produce a large motion of

Fig. 6.40 The lever and fulcrum employed in the design of a backhoe. In this application, a short movement of the hydraulic cylinder at the top of the circled area produces a larger movement of the lower arm and the digging bucket.

wings from a smaller motion of muscles, to facilitate flying. Horses also employ a lever-and-fulcrum arrangement in the configuration of their lower legs.

Cam and Follower

A *cam* is a machine part that rotates or reciprocates to cause a particular motion to a part that comes in contact with it, called a *follower*. A typical cam and follower arrangement is found in the design of many automobile engines, where a rotating shaft with cams mounted on it, called a camshaft, causes valves to open and shut at precise times. When the valves open, fuel and air enter the combustion chamber. The valves then close to allow compression to form as the fuel burns.

The importance of the *Cam and Follower paradigm* is that certain forms like these might interact to convert one type of energy or motion (circular in this case) to another (vertical). This type of conversion is necessary in one form or another in many mechanical devices.

The appearance of rotating cams is distinctive for their off-center masses, frequently with a steadily increasing radius. This form, with a steadily increasing radius, is also found in the natural world in many shells, such as the nautilus. This similarity led to both the design and the naming of the Nautilus line of weight-lifting machines, in which a cam bearing uses its variable diameter to, in turn, vary the resistance of weights being lifted by the user.

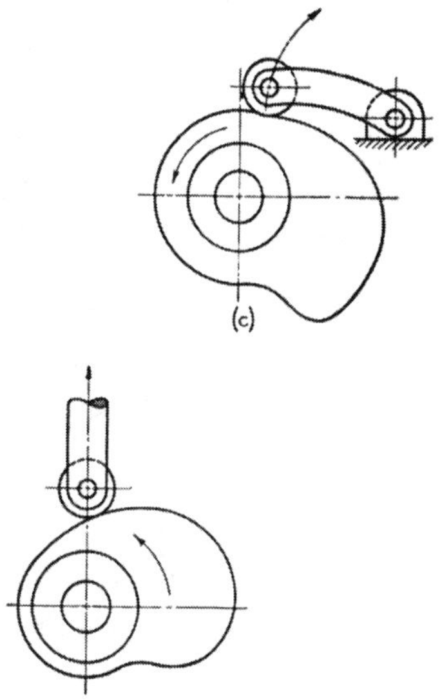

Fig. 6.41 a, b Cams and followers. Many cam and follower mechanisms serve to convert a circular motion to linear motion.

Questions

1) The *Lock and Key paradigm* operates on the principle of one key working with one lock. There are variations on this paradigm, for instance, one key that opens several identical locks. Identify two other variations on the paradigm.

2) Think of the ways two people can work together. They may simultaneously perform the same tasks, suggesting the *Identical Twins paradigm.* An athlete getting feedback from a coach might be suggestive of the *Gnomon paradigm.* What kind of working relationship does the *Cam and Follower paradigm* suggest to you? Or the *Epoxy paradigm*?

3) Salt and pepper shakers are often designed as identical twins, although their contents are quite different. Develop several alternative designs for dispensing salt and pepper based on paradigms other than the *Identical Twins paradigm.* Consider, for instance, *yin-yang* or scissors as a basis for dispensing salt and pepper.

4) Draw a seated figure and a chair in profile. Use the figure-ground technique to think of the chair as a figure acting against the seated person. Consider, visually, the weight and balance of the two forms. How does this change your thinking about the design of the chair form?

7

Joining

In this chapter we explore the paradigms for joining, which we consider separately from the *Attaching paradigms*. We can characterize the *Joining paradigms* as firmly connecting parts, each of which is prepared or designed to accommodate the joint with the other. This distinguishes the *Joining paradigms* from the *Attaching paradigms*; we can attach a piece of tape to a wall and a leech can attach itself to our skin, without any special preparation of the wall or the skin.

Joints are the devices we use to handle transitions from one object to another, or between pieces of a single object. Joints can be used to make a larger part out of two or more small parts, as when two steel bars are butt-welded and fused end-to-end. Other joints are used to connect parts at corners, as when parts are trimmed at a 45-degree angle to make a miter, which is used in woodworking. Many such joints are static; the parts are rigidly joined together. Another class of joints connects parts that can flex because of varying loads, or expanding and contracting due to thermal changes, such as the expansion joints used in roadways over bridges. A third class of joints provides for parts to be firmly connected, yet free to move angularly or rotationally, as with knee joints or the universal joints used in automotive drivetrains. This third class of joints and the flexibility they enable is covered in Chapter 4, *Bending and Flexing*.

Much of the content of a number of professions, such as plumbing, cabinet-making, and welding, is devoted to joining parts in various ways. The many types of joints used in woodworking alone could (and does!) fill a whole book,[37] as do knots,[38] so, unfortunately, not all of these wonderful joints can be covered here.

Dovetail

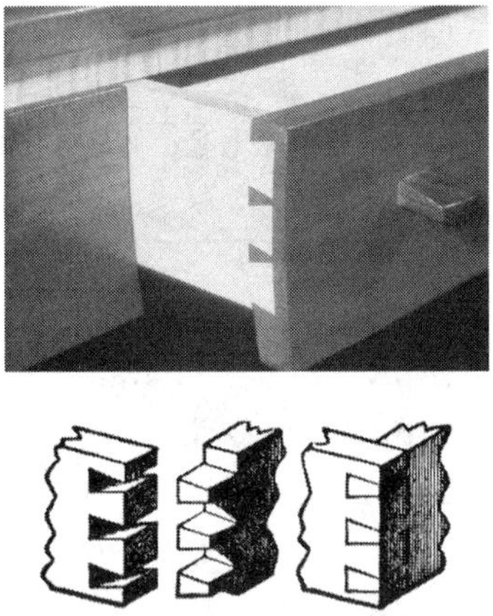

Fig. 7.1 a) Dovetail joint on a drawer. b) Dovetail joint exploded assembly. Dovetails are a sign of fine woodworking. This joint actually gets tighter as the drawer is pulled open.

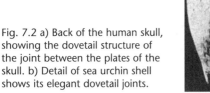

The dovetail is, perhaps the most beloved of woodworking joints. This joint is loved for both its functional and aesthetic characteristics. The magic of a dovetail joint, and part of the reason why dovetail-jointed furniture is so prized, is that it essentially fights entropy. The joint can actually get better and tighter with use. This property comes about from the wedge nature of the connections. Stress on the joints causes a wider portion of the dovetail to be pulled into its corresponding space.

Nature discovered the dovetail joint long ago. Natural dovetail joints are employed in a number of situations in which flat plates are joined and require a strong connection between them. The plates that make up our skulls are among these applications. Along the joints of the plates is a meandering line about ¼" wide made of the dovetails of each plate firmly anchored between the dovetails of the other. The plates of the sea-urchin shell are similarly connected with natural dovetail joints.

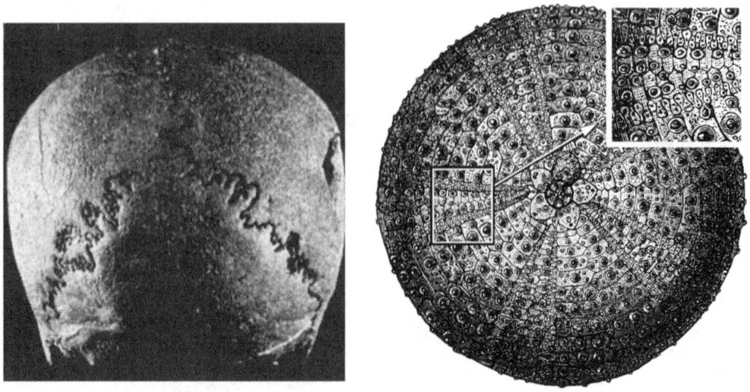

Fig. 7.2 a) Back of the human skull, showing the dovetail structure of the joint between the plates of the skull. b) Detail of sea urchin shell shows its elegant dovetail joints.

Plug and Socket

A plug-and-socket arrangement is both a sexual connection (see Chapter 6) and a means of joining two things. The *Plug and Socket paradigm* is the means by which we join two extension cords; we insert the plug of one into the socket of the other. Most temporary electrical and electronic connections are made this way. Cords terminating in plugs and sockets permit quick, uncomplicated, and electrically reasonably good connections. They are, consequently, widely used in such applications as stereos and computers to connect speakers, components, and peripherals. Because the electrical connection is by contact only, the connection is not as good as directly wired or soldered connections, so plug-and-socket connections are usually used only for temporary connections.

In woodworking, we find plug-and-socket connections are employed in dowel and mortise and tenon joints. Dowel joints utilize a section of a wooden rod (a dowel) set into a cylindrical hole to provide continuous wood fibers spanning between two pieces of wood that the woodworker wants to join. Mortise and tenon joints work the same way, but employ a section of wood with a rectangular, rather than circular, cross section. These woodworking joints are usually intended to be permanent, but only once glue is applied. The woodworker exploits the temporary nature of these joints before gluing. Fine furniture is assembled and disassembled during its manufacture to test and adjust the fit of the parts, and to sand and finish the parts prior to the final assembly.

Plug-and-socket connections are also popular in construction toys, another application in which temporary joining is desirable. Among the toys employing plug-and-socket joints are Lego® blocks and TinkerToys®.

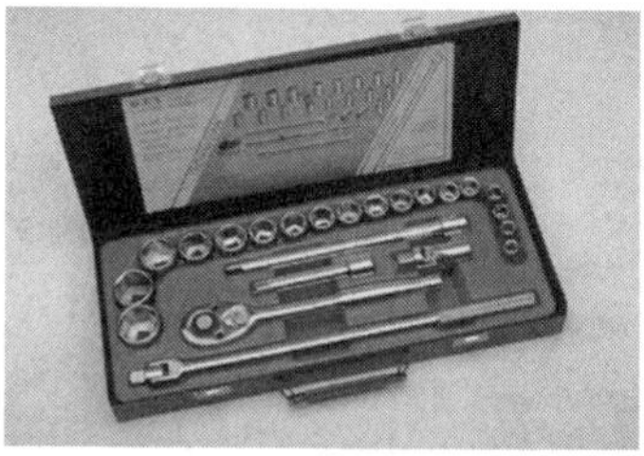

Fig. 7.3 Socket wrench set. The "sockets" are actually doubly socketed. One socket fits the nut or bolt to be tightened or loosened. The other socket connects to the wrench or its extension. All parts in the set fit together with a single type of connection, the socket. A set usually only employs only a single size of socket for interconnection of pieces, in order to maximize the compatibility of the parts.

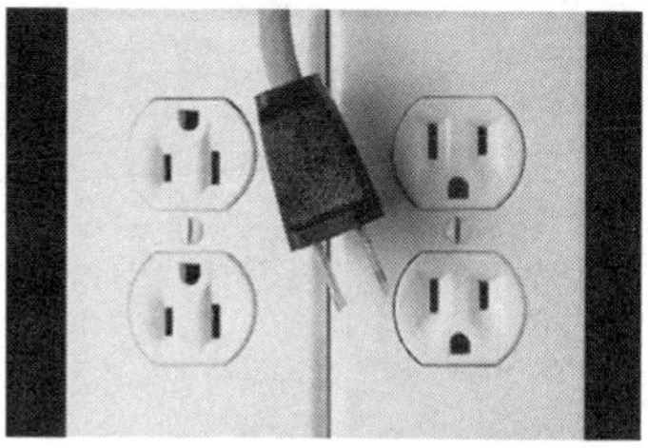

Fig. 7.4 Electric plugs and sockets. The connections that are made are meant to be effective electrically, but not physically; the socket does little to keep the plug from being pulled out.

Fig. 7.5 At the heart of the hundreds of shapes of Lego blocks and the infinite variety of constructions that can be made with them is the *Plug and Socket paradigm* joint.

Ball and Socket

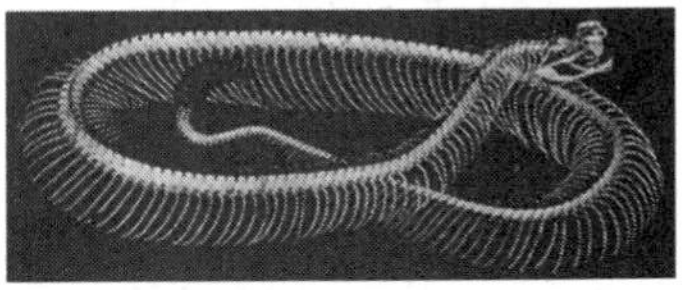

Fig. 7.6 Snake skeleton. Vertebrae interlock with ball and socket joints serving both as a flexible joint, and one capable of withstanding tension.

Ball-and-socket joints are familiar—just think about your body and how your arms join with your shoulders. The ball-and-socket joint has a number of important properties. First, it's a very flexible joint, allowing for a great deal of independent motion of the two elements (in this case, the body and the arm) while maintaining the connection. Second, it's a method of securely joining two things. Third, although not in the case of the arm, a ball-and-socket joint can facilitate the free twisting of either element. Fourth, this type of joint can be designed to easily separate and reconnect the elements, as is the case for the snaps used in clothing, which are small ball and socket joints.

The role of these joints in accommodating Bending and Flexing was discussed earlier (see *Ball and Socket* as a *Bending and Flexing paradigm*, in Chapter 4). As a *Joining paradigm* we consider its other important properties. Providing a secure yet flexible connection is perhaps most important of these. For this reason, the vertebrae of a snake's spine interlock with balls and sockets. More so than humans, snakes are subject to tensile force on their spines, as they may frequently pull with, or suspend themselves from, the front or rear parts of their bodies. With each vertebra extending a ball that is securely held by a socket in the next, the joints are able to absorb the tension, thus preventing possible damage to the delicate spinal cord.

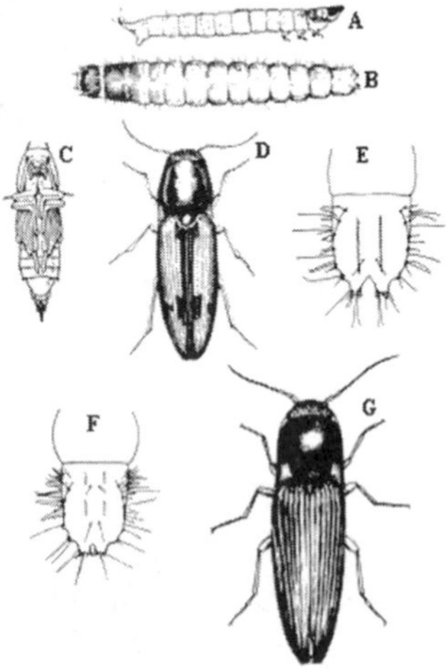

Fig. 7.7 Stages of the Click beetle. The adult is equipped with a ball and socket joint which makes a firm connection between the thorax and mesothorax. When trapped on its back, the insect dislocates this ball and socket, producing an audible clicking noise and propelling the insect several inches into the air.

Not every application requires a secure connection, however. The *Ball and Socket paradigm* also includes joints that can easily snap together and apart. Besides snaps on clothing, this usage is also popular in children's toys, such as interlocking plastic blocks. While you might cringe at the thought of an arm popping out of its socket, surprisingly, there are some instances where snap-apart ball-and-socket joints are usefully employed in animals. The adult wireworms, known as click beetles (family *Elateridae,* order

Coleoptera), have an exoskeletal version of a ball-and-socket joint. To right themselves when they are on their backs, click beetles lean their heads forward to snap a ball structure under their thorax into place in a socket in the mesothorax. They then pull their heads back until the ball snaps out of the socket, thus making an audible clicking noise and throwing their head back with enough force to propel the insect several inches into the air.

Universal Joint

A ball-and-socket joint is good for many applications, but it is not good at transferring torque. If you twist an arm that terminates in a ball joint, the ball will simply spin in its socket. Among the best solutions to this problem that human invention has discovered is the *universal joint*. A universal joint is a cross-shaped piece with U-shaped pieces connecting opposite arms of the cross to arms that are axially opposed to each other. Universal joints are widely used in power-transfer applications when a shaft comes out of an engine and the direction must be changed in order to reach the destination. Universal joints are visible underneath most rear-wheel-drive vehicles, at the end of the driveshaft.

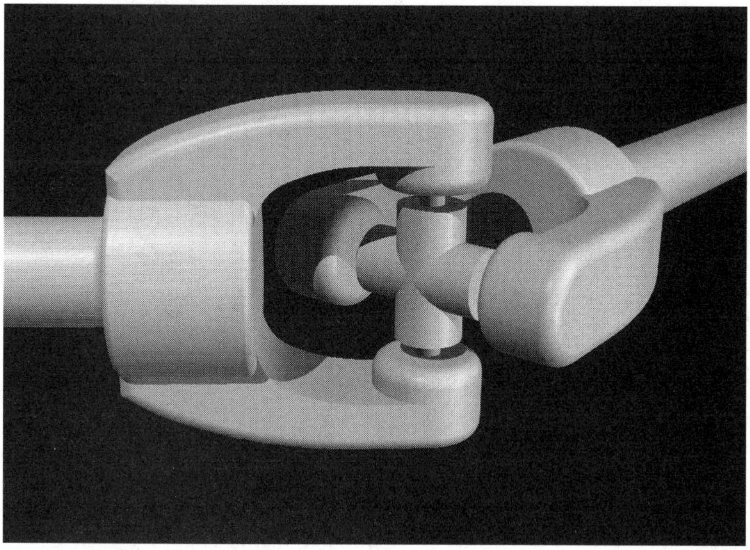

Fig. 7.8 The universal joint is a connection that allows the same degrees of freedom as the ball and socket joint, but unlike that joint, the universal joint can transfer torque. It is consequently the joint of choice for connecting axles from the engine of a vehicle to the wheels, when a change in direction is necessary.

Pin Joint

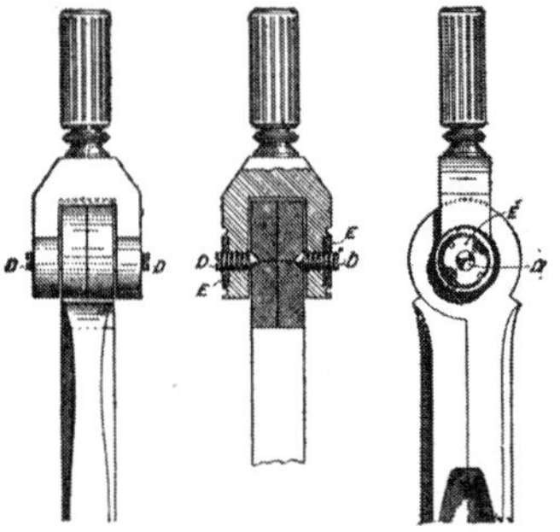

Fig. 7.9 Pin joints are widely used in mechanisms where arms are intended to swing, as in the joint of drafting compasses.

A pin joint is a simple but very widely used joint. Drill a hole through two boards, put a bolt through it with a nut loosely on the end, and you have a simple pin joint. The boards are connected at that point, but are free to move with respect to each other around the pin.

Pin joints are widely used in metal constructions where parts are intended to flex or move while remaining connected. Consequently pin joints are likely found in such applications as the connection of a ladder to a fire truck or of a boom of a crane to the cab. They are used in mechanical linkages to connect levers and extension arms. They are also used in many permanent constructions that are meant to flex, rather than move, such as the joints of a metal bridge. This helps these bridges to accommodate the varying forces they incur as they are subjected to varying loads, like when a truck drives across them. Most mechanical hinges are pin joints (see the *Hinge paradigm* in Chapter 4).

Fig. 7.10 Retractible foot on construction equipment. Pin joints enable the flexible connections.

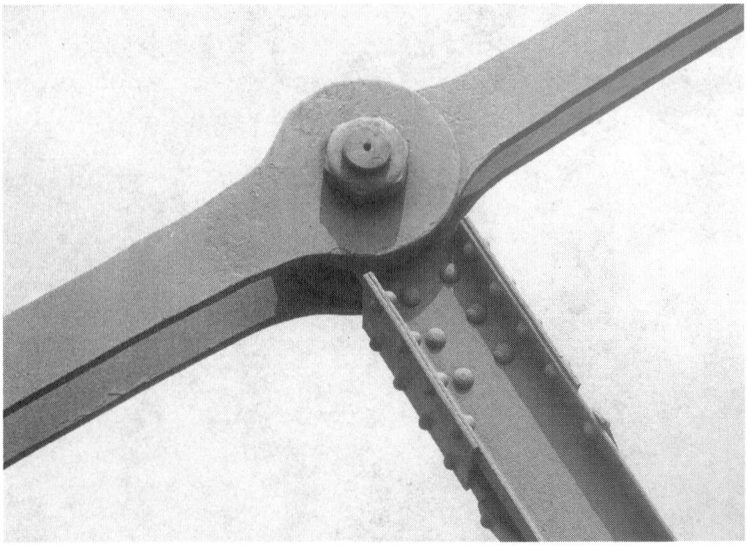

Fig. 7.11 Pin joint connecting the structural members of a bridge truss. The pin joint allows flexure as the bridge bends under loads.

Fasteners

Many things are joined using fasteners, such as nails, screws, and bolts. A bolted connection is similar to the pin joint, but it is firmly connected with one or usually more nuts and bolts. The strength of a bolted connection depends not only on the fasteners, but also on the friction between the pieces being joined. This is why the tightness of the bolts is important. Similar joints using nails depend more heavily upon the shear strength of the fasteners themselves.

Some fasteners are intended to be more or less permanent, while others are easily removable. Bolts and screws are often chosen for situations where disassembly of joint is anticipated at some point. Nails and rivets are more likely to be used when disassembly of a joint is not an immediate consideration. So, for example, auto parts like engines and pumps that might need to be periodically removed are installed with bolts, while the vehicle ID plate is riveted on.

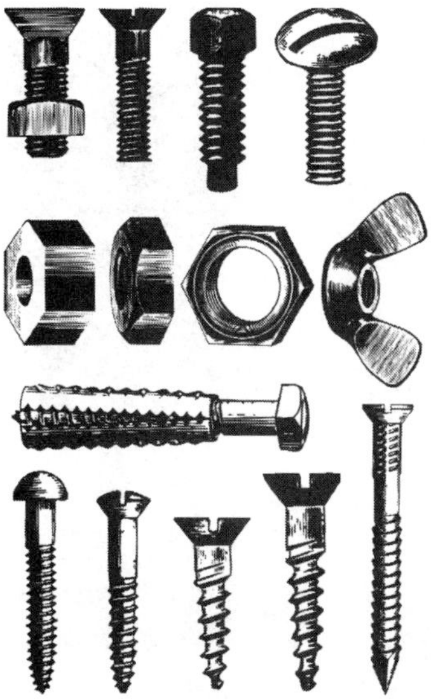

Fig. 7.12 Several types of fasteners.

Bolts usually require access to both sides of the objects being joined, one side to hold the bolt, the other to tighten the nut. Other fasteners such as screws, nails and rivets are indicated in situations where only one side of the work is accessible.

Fasteners have associations with certain materials. Nails are the fasteners of choice for wood construction, although screws and staples are widely used as well. Certain types of screws are made for sheet metal; others for wood. Special nails are also available for masonry use.

Fasteners can imply specialized equipment, from simple screwdrivers and hammers, to rivet guns, to the pneumatic or electric drivers used in building construction to drive nails and staples. Such devices are widely used in construction for installing flooring, insulation, and roofing.

Fig. 7.13 Fasteners were once popular in both light and heavy construction. Even bridges and ships were built with rivets and bolts. The World Wars brought pressures to adopt faster construction methods, and welding largely replaced fasteners in heavy construction.

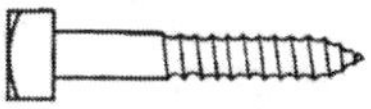

Zipper

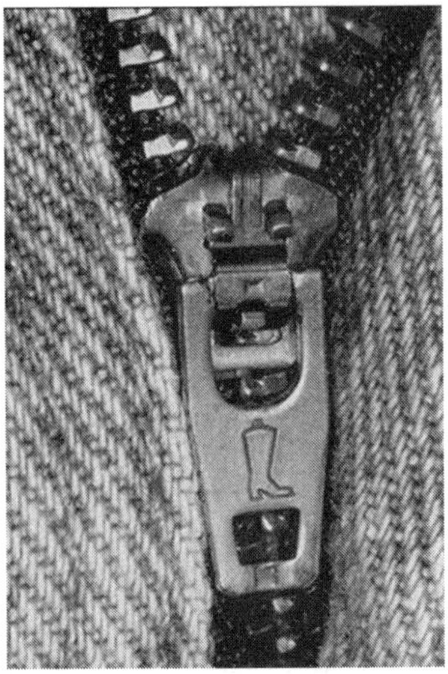

Fig. 7.14 A zipper. The zipped connection is composed of a series of dovetail joints.

A standard zipper is much like a line of dovetail joints with a device to bend and interlock the joints. The *Zipper paradigm* suggests ease of opening and closing. The zipper has few direct corollaries in the natural world that open and close as conveniently, but many corollaries that are as easily opened, such as the pods of many types of peas and beans, and the skin of bananas. One reclosable, natural seam is the zipperlike connections found on many feathers between the barbs that extend horizontally from the shaft. The feather forms a continuous, flat surface, which is resistant to air and water, but the barbs can be pulled apart with the fingers. Unlike most natural seams, though, these barbs can be rejoined via gentle preening with the fingers or a bird's beak. The mechanism at work in the feather is the tiny hook on the end of each of the barbules that branch off the barbs. With coaxing, these hooks become enmeshed. Early clothing fasteners similarly engaged a series of hooks to make a reclosable seam, although revising the design to close without hooks was such an improvement that early zippers were marketed as *hookless fasteners*.[39]

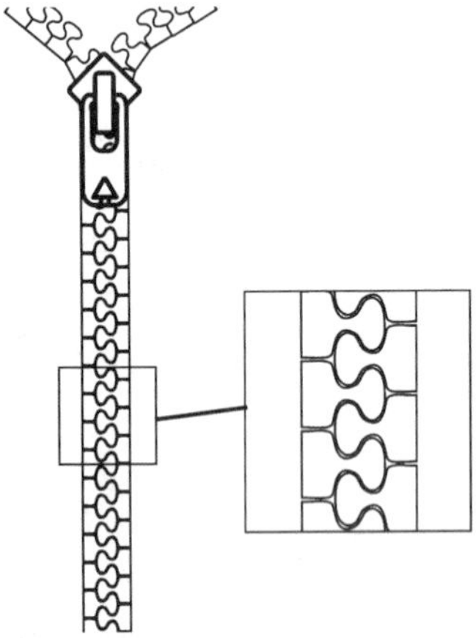

Fig. 7.15 Zipper detail showing dovetail structure (see the *Dovetail paradigm*).

Fig. 7.16 (right) A bird feather. Like a zipper, the seams along the edges of the barbules can be opened and closed. A row of hook fasteners enables this, reminiscent of early zippers and modern velcro.

Sewing

Sewing is widely employed throughout many fields of human endeavor and by a range of creatures, including insects and birds. The *Sewing paradigm* implies attaching two or more surface edges by means of running a fiber, wire, or threadlike material in loops through the materials to be joined.

Fig. 7.17 a, b Sewing machine, sewing needle with thread.

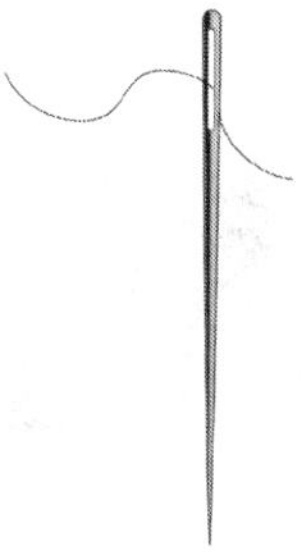

Sewing is the preferred method of joining seams in cloth for such applications as clothing, upholstery, knapsacks, and tents. It is sometimes used for joining plastics or leather in these applications as well. Sewing is also used for closing wounds, although in some situations, glues are now used (see the *Glue paradigm* in Chapter 8). A spiral notebook is also effectively sewn, via a series of loops of wire. Similarly, sections of chain-link fence are effectively sewn together and are often sewn onto poles.

Sewing is also used for some attaching tasks as well (see Chapter 8). When we sew seams together to make clothing, we are joining the pieces. But when we sew a button onto a shirt or a patch onto the knee of a pair of jeans, we are attaching them.

In the animal kingdom, we find caterpillars called *leaf tiers* that use their silk to sew the edges of two leaves together to make a home in the space between them.

> One—the silver-spotted skipper—creates perhaps the most private home of the animal kingdom. It stitches the five parts of two compound locust leaves together, every edge meeting the other to make a house of many retreats. I have often opened such a leaf and peered into the shadowy castle to find not only the five rooms but the floors matted with silver wall-to-wall carpeting.[40]

Fig. 7.18 The Tailor Bird, and the nest it sews out of leaves and plant fibers.

Among the most skilled creatures that have discovered sewing is the tailor bird of Asia. This bird makes a nest in a pouch it creates by sewing leaves together. It carefully pokes holes through the edges of the leaves and threads plant fibers through the holes to sew them together—and even ties the ends!

Velcro

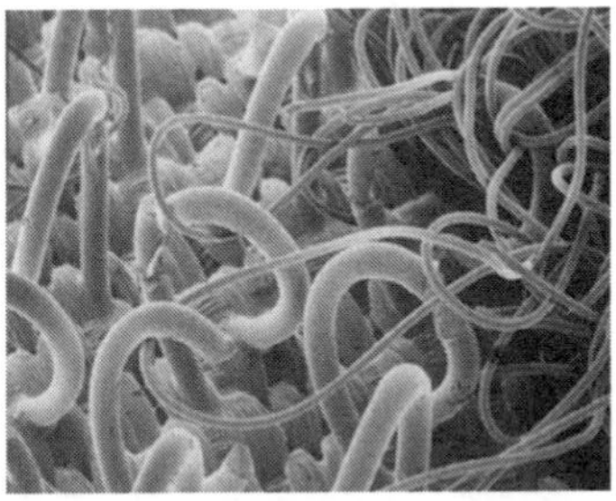

Fig. 7.19 a, b Velcro, seen under an electron microscope (Museum of Science, Boston photo) and in simulation, showing hook and loop structures.

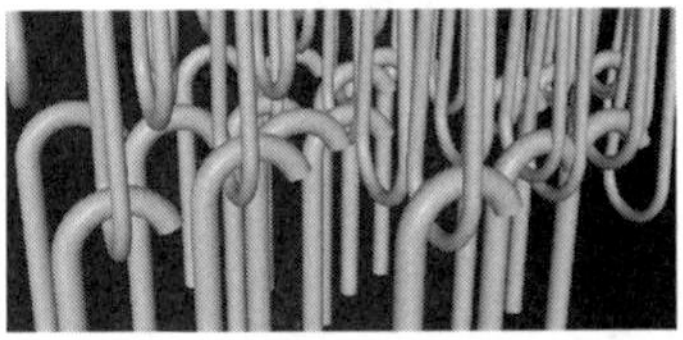

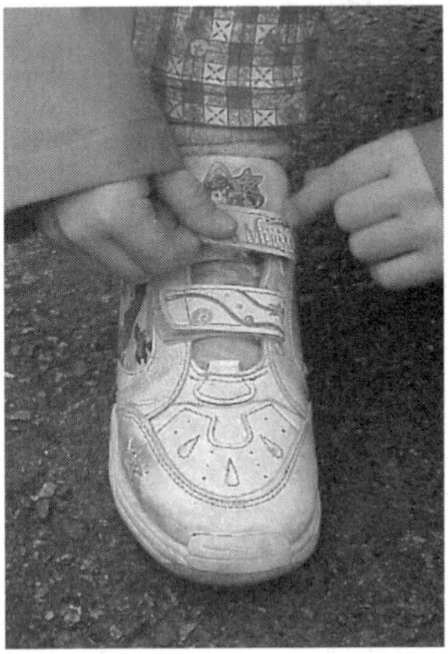

Fig. 7.20 Strips of Velcro replace laces on these sneakers. Velcro closures are easier to fasten than laces, which is important not only to the young, but also to those physically challenged by arthritis or other disability.

Velcro® is familiar as the closure material on the straps of children's sneakers that makes a distinctive ripping sound when it is opened. Velcro is a cloth closure, used as an alternative to zippers, snaps and other closures. It is a binary material, it has two different sides, one composed of hooks, and one of loops, that are essential to its operation. Accounts of the development of Velcro illustrate the Design Paradigms approach to invention:

> In the early 1940's, Swiss inventor George de Mestral went on a walk with his dog. . . . Upon his return home, he noticed that his dog's coat and his pants were covered with cockleburrs. His inventor's curiosity led him to study the burrs under a microscope, where he discovered its natural hook-like shape. This was to become the basis for a unique, two-sided fastener—one side with stiff "hooks" like the burrs and the other side with the soft "loops" like the fabric of his pants.
>
> The result was VELCRO® brand hook and loop fasteners, named for the French words "velour" and "crochet."[41]

De Mestral realized the paradigmatic nature of the burrs and developed it into a broadly applicable means of joining. He did more than adapt the cockleburr's hooks, however. His ingenious invention was to develop a counterpart loop material, and to modify the hooks to attach to these loops. Because the hook side of Velcro is designed to stick to the loop side and not much else, this distinguishes it from the cockleburrs, which are far less selective.

While inspiration for Velcro came from studying the cockleburr, there is perhaps closer analogy to be found in the interlocking hooks found on the barbules of feathers, mentioned earlier in the *Zipper paradigm*. The hooks on the barbules are selective in the same way as Velcro.

Velcro is widely used in clothing, from shoes to coats. Velcro's properties make it particularly desirable in a number of situations. Since it is a plastic cloth, it can replace snaps and other closures when it is necessary to avoid using metal. Because its use is simple, it is a good alternative to buttons and shoelaces for persons who lack the manual dexterity to manipulate these closures, including small children, and arthritic elderly. It is available in long tapes that may be sewn into seams, allowing its use down the side of a pant leg, as is sometimes necessary to put on pants over a leg cast.

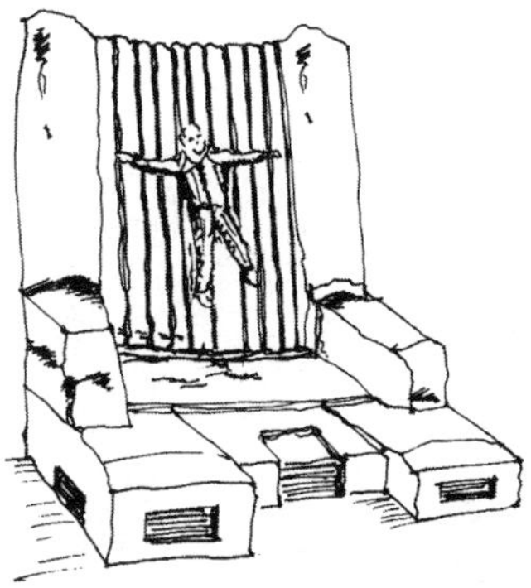

Fig. 7.21 The Velcro wall. In this carnival attraction, a participant dons a velcro suit, runs and bounces on the trampoline, and then hits and sticks to the velcro-covered wall.

Some special purpose Velcro closures have been developed, including Velcro patches for permanent placement of machine parts. Using stainless steel hooks and loops, heavy machine parts may be permanently installed on walls just by pressing them into place.

Fig. 7.22 The burdock plant. Velcro was inspired by plants like this. The "fruit" of the burdock are covered with sharp hooks, allowing them to attach to passing animals or clothing, thus spreading their seed (see the *Burdock paradigm*, Chapter 8).

Fig. 7.23 Welders use gas torches and electric arcs both to cut and to join metals. As a *Joining paradigm,* we are concerned with creating welded joints, not only of these welding processes, but also the lower temperature processes of soldering and brazing.

Fig. 7.24 a, b Arc and gas welding as icons.

Weld

Welding, brazing, and soldering are similar methods of joining metal. In all cases heat from a gas flame or electricity warms the parts to be joined and/or a filler metal, such as tin, lead, or bronze. The parts and/or the filler are melted and fused, thus bridging the gaps between the pieces being joined. Soldering is a low-temperature joining technique, using a lead or tin alloy solder. This technique is used extensively to join metal pipes and electronics, and in automotive bodywork. Brazing is a higher-temperature process, calling for a filler metal, such as silver or bronze, with a lower melting point than the metals being joined. Brazing can produce very strong joints and is used in applications ranging from casual metal repairs, to the manufacture of high-strength parts like rockets and aircraft-engine parts.

Welding is the highest-temperature process of the three, and is widely used in producing metal structures for machines and buildings, as well as various manufactured products, including steel food cans. Electric-arc, oxygen-acetylene torch, and resistance heat are the dominant types of welding. These welding techniques are a fairly recent invention, although related metal-joining techniques were employed in swordmaking in first-century Syria. Modern techniques were discovered at the end of the nineteenth century and came into widespread use during the World Wars, when the pressure was on to find faster alternatives to using bolts and rivets for steel construction.

Welding and related processes can be described as *joining by melting, fusing, and freezing.* Consequently we sometimes might speak of other meltable materials as being welded, such as plastics or glass. This definition can also include a number of similar natural processes. Ice on a lake, for instance, can crack into pieces, which can later be "welded" together as the water between them freezes. In geology, an underlying principle of plate tectonics is that the plates that make up the earth's crust fold and are remelted at some points, while at others, lava might emerge between plates, solidify, and expand. Thus, rock is a material that is periodically remelted and welded.

Knot

Knots are the preferred method of joining ropes, cords, shoelaces, and threads. Thousands of different types of knots are known and used, designed to serve a wide variety of purposes. Some knots are designed to hold tightly, others are designed to slip. Some are meant to splice rope segments, and some are meant to attach ropes to poles. Some are meant to shorten a length of rope or take stress off a worn segment.

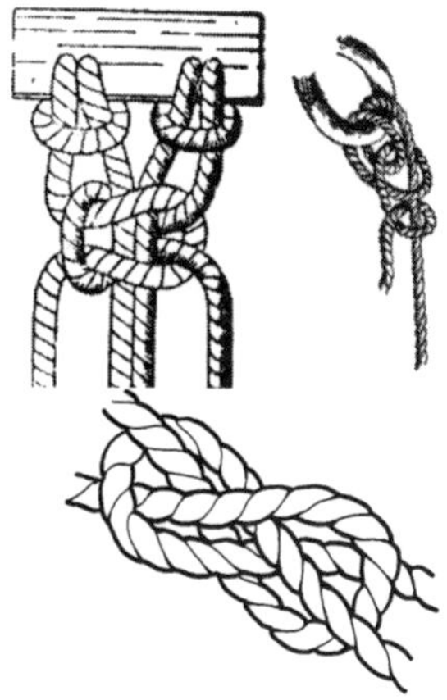

Fig. 7.25 a-c Some of the many types of knots used to join ropes.

Knots are with us throughout our lives, some literal, others metaphorical. We begin life with a knot tied to sever our connection to the umbilical cord and placenta. Learning to tie one's shoelaces is a milestone in the cognitive and physical development of children, and learning to tie a tie is often taken as a sign of a young man's entry into adulthood. We refer to marriage as "tying the knot." We speak of familial relationships throughout our lives as family ties. Knots are part of the standard training of scouts, roustabouts, surgeons, and sailors. Knots are also integral to certain crafts such as macramé, and important to others, such as sewing and crocheting. Lives depend on effective knots in applications like mountain climbing.

Fig. 7.26 Rings fashioned of gold wire formed into knots is both decorative and symbolic of marriage, as in "tying the knot."

Knots appear spontaneously in nature, wherever there are roots, vines, hair or other string or cordlike forms interacting. But these are rarely as elaborate as some of the human-invented knot forms.

Bridge

Fig. 7.27 Knots are appreciated for their beauty and are often used as ornament, as found in Byzantine architecture.

The term "island" implies isolation because a tract of land surrounded by water is isolated from the mainland. A bridge counteracts the isolation by joining the two bodies. New York City was greatly affected by bridges; it is com-

Fig. 7.28 Some bridges such as this serve to join two parts of a street that sit on opposite sides of a body of water. Perceptually the road and the commerce areas on both sides of the water can now function as a continuous stretch.

posed of five boroughs separated by rivers, bays, and the Atlantic Ocean. The Brooklyn Bridge effectively joined the borough of Brooklyn to Manhattan when it opened in 1883, facilitating commerce and movement between the boroughs.

Many other kinds of bridges also serve similar joining functions. The part of a pair of glasses that rests on the nose joins the two lenses, and is also referred to as a bridge. When a permanent tooth is lost, a dentist might make a bridge to span between the teeth on either side of the missing tooth, to support a false tooth in the space between them. A more abstract form of bridge is found in music; here, a bridge is a musical passage that links two sections of a composition.

Bridges also serve as passageways. We will revisit them as a *Passage paradigm* in Chapter 9.

Fig. 7.29 The Brooklyn Bridge. Designed by John A. Roebling and Wilhelm Hildenbrand in 1865. Roebling died during its construction and was succeded by his son, Washington, who was later struck by then-unknown caisson disease (the bends), while supervising the construction of the footings from the deep-underwater caissons.

Questions

1) Sewing has some obvious applications in joining, such as sewing seams on pants and shirts. Look around your home and try to find at least two less obvious applications: Things that are not made of cloth, but are sewn together.

2) A company has purchased two adjacent four-story buildings separated by a ten-foot wide alleyway. They wish to allow both buildings to function as a single corporate headquarters. List as many ways as you can think of to join the two buildings.

3) Design and examine three alternative techniques to join chairs into neat rows, for use as auditorium seating, that allow the chairs to be separated for individual use. Note the advantages and disadvantages of each approach.

4) Consider the problem of joining two ships in space, for instance, a space station, and a shuttlecraft bringing supplies. What requirements must the joint meet? Consider which *Joining paradigms* these requirements might suggest, and which they might preclude.

8

Attaching

There are two primary categories of paradigms for bringing things together: *Attaching* and *Joining*. The distinction between them is that *Joining* implies the cooperation of the parts, while *Attaching* does not. For instance, we may *join* hands because we both agree to, whereas a leech *attachs* to one's ankle without permission.

Many of the *Attaching paradigms* can be described as *stickers,* the class of objects that attach to other things by sticking to them. Stickers can stick to a wide variety of things, without knowing what those things are in advance. For example, tape can be stuck to paper, a wall, or the back of your hand. Most kinds of tape will stick to most things. There are always limitations with stickers, however, for instance, tape will not typically stick to a wet surface, and a suction cup will not stick to a dusty surface. Some materials, like Velcro, are specific in what they will stick to, as the hook-sided Velcro is intended to stick only to the eye-sided Velcro (see Chapter 7 for detailed information about these *Joining paradigms*).

Suction Cup

Suction cups are familiar to almost everyone both in household applications of manufactured objects, such as stick-on thermometers, and in natural examples, such as on octopus tentacles. Suction cups typically operate by pressing flat against

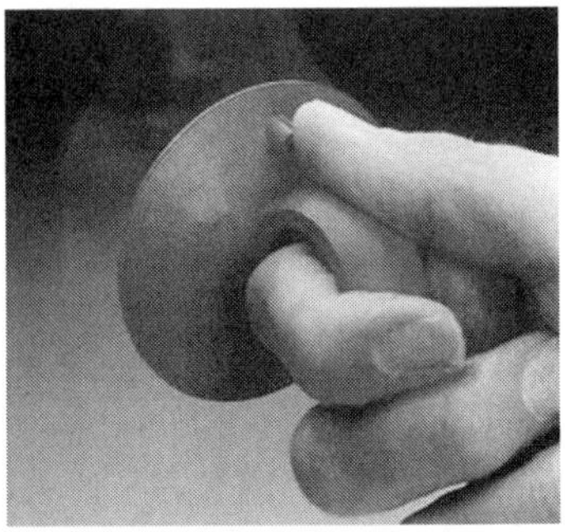

Fig. 8.1 Suction cups such as this, provided with a finger hole, are used to safely handle materials such as glass. The suction cups help prevent cuts to the hands, and help protect the glass surface from scratches and smearing.

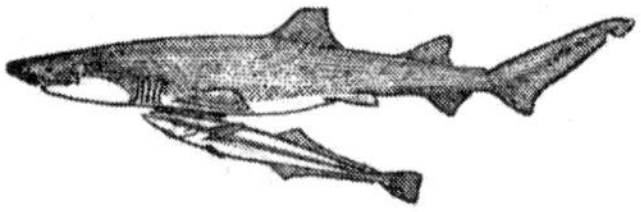

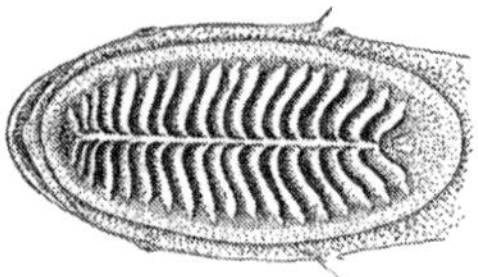

Fig. 8.2 The remora is one of many creatures with a suction cup device. Their sucking disc, at the top of their head, shown in detail above, allows them to attach to the underside of a shark. This gives them a free ride through the ocean depths, and leaves their mouth free to catch meals of passing debris from the shark's dinner.

a surface, with a suction created either by the tendency of the cup to return to its original shape, or by tension or vacuum applied at the center of the cup. Tension applied to the cup's center attempts to pull the center outward, thus creating a vacuum condition in the disclike space under the suction cup. The suction then increases as attempts are made to pull it away. Suction cups stick best to smooth, nonporous rigid or semirigid materials. Suction cups tend to work better in the presence of moisture, whereas most other means of sticking, such as tape and glue, are usually inhibited when wet. Suction cups are released by changing the geometry of the cups in a manner to decrease the vacuum, or by opening a vent to the evacuated space. Because they must be soft and flexible, suction cups are usually made of rubber or soft plastics, such as vinyl. Suction cups usually do little or no damage to the surface they're applied to.

Natural suction cups include those found on the tentacles of many cephalopods, including the octopus, squid and cuttlefish. Starfish also have suction cups on their legs, which enable them to adhere to undersea rocks as well as to the sides of clams; this, in turn, enables the starfish to pull the clams apart to eat them. Many fish employ suction cups, of several dramatically different types. Many bottom-feeding fish, such as the family *Catostomidae*, or suckers, have a mouth formed like a suction cup that lets them both feed by

Fig. 8.3 GelRelease^{tm} suction cup attached to a Beluga whale. The application of the *Suction Cup paradigm* allows attachment of tracking instruments to live whales without harming them. Making the suction cup out of a water soluable gelatinous material enables the equipment to separate from the animal at a predetermined time. Cetacean Research Technology photo.

sucking in plant and animal matter, and use suction to attach themselves to objects. The remora has a suction disc on the top of its head, modified from a dorsal fin, that permits it to attach to a shark's body, thereby catching a free ride and leaving its mouth free to feed upon passing leftover bits of the shark's dinner. The clingfish of the genus *Gobiesox* have a suction disk on their bellies formed in part by their pelvic fins that enables them to attach themselves to the bottoms of fast-moving streams. Many other families of animals employ suction cups, including leeches and the worms of the class *Hirundinea*. These creatures have a small sucker at the mouth end of their body, which they use to hold on to a passing host from which they'll suck blood. They also have a larger sucker at the other end, which they use to hold them in place on plants or other ground surfaces. Even some mammals employ suction cups, notably the disk bat (genus *Thyroptera*), so-called for the suction discs on its hands and feet that enable it to stick itself onto smooth surfaces.

Fig. 8.4 The octopus is perhaps the creature most associated with the *Suction Cup paradigm*. In captivity, these intelligent creatures are observed using their suction cups to pick up things, open containers, and whenever possible, to outwit their captors and escape from their tanks.

Suction cups are used in a wide variety of products for several different reasons. First, they are used to stick things to surfaces temporarily without damaging the surfaces. An example of this is suction cups placed on the bottom of dishes for toddlers, allowing the dishes to be temporarily adhered to a table without damaging it, while avoiding accidental spills during meals. Second, suction cups are used to stick things in wet areas, for example, such bath accessories as mats, utility hooks, and shelves, as well as items installed in fish tanks. Third, suction cups are often preferred for long-term adhesion to glass, where they work better and more simply than most other methods of attachment.

Fig. 8.5 The starfish also has legs covered with suction cups. Starfish suction cups are made of a stiffer material than those of the octopus, and they function dramatically differently. Rather than creating suction by changing the shape of the cup, the starfish employs a hydraulic system that sucks water out of each suction cup, through the legs and out the head. What starfish lack in speed, they make up for in stamina. To open a clamshell, they apply their suction cups and pull outward until the clam becomes fatigued. In 20 to 30 minutes, the shell opens.

Among the interesting applications for suction cups is cetacean research. Small radio transmitters are attached via suction cups to the backs of whales without hurting the whales. These suction cups provide for long-term attachment with a minimum of danger and discomfort to the whales. Some cups are now made of gelatin-based materials that deteriorate at a predetermined time, so the transmitter is released automatically from the whales at the conclusion of the study.

Suction cups are also used extensively in industrial processes for materials handling. Many photocopiers and laser printers use suction as a means of lifting a sheet of paper to be printed on. Larger, handheld suction cups are used to carry and install sheets of glass. In manufacturing facilities still larger suction cups are mounted on frames to lift and convey heavy materials, such as slabs of marble, glass, or steel, with a minimal risk of damage.

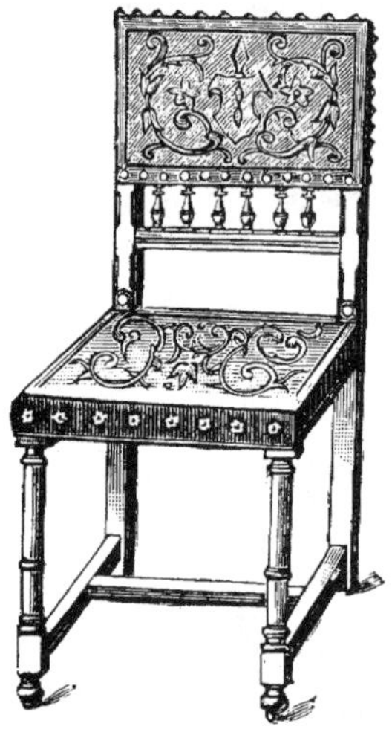

Fig. 8.6 Among the most ancient human uses of glue is to fasten furniture joints. Glue has been used in furniture manufacture since at least 3000 BC.

Glue

Glue is an important paradigm for attaching things, particularly when we know little about these things in advance. Suction cups usually require that one surface is clean, flat, smooth, and nonporous, but when one cannot ensure these surface characteristics, glue is likely a better choice. As children, we become familiar with several glues, typically white glue, glue sticks, rubber cement, and paste. We learn that these vary in terms of their drying time, what materials they work well with, and whether or not glued items can be repositioned. The possibilities of gluing greatly expand when you discover hot-melt glues, which adhere within seconds, and *cyanoacrylate* (super) glues, which can result in glue joints stronger than the materials being glued. There are also many applications for intentionally weak glues, including products like Post-it® notes; these self-sticking pieces of paper can easily be removed from anything they're stuck to.

Fig. 8.7 Electric glue gun. Plastic rods are melted and squirted where desired. The glue hardens quickly as the plastic needs only to cool, rather than dry, in order to harden.

Glues are most typically used to fuse the surfaces of objects that can be brought into contact with each other, but they can be used in many other ways as well. Glues are sometimes used to change a removable joint or fixture into a permanent joint, as when glue is added to a joint in a piece of furniture. Woodworking joints are among the first-known uses of glues, dating back to 3000 BC Egypt. Glues are sometimes used to seal holes, seams, and flaps on things as well. Some glues can also take on structural properties; they can span gaps, connecting surfaces some distance apart.

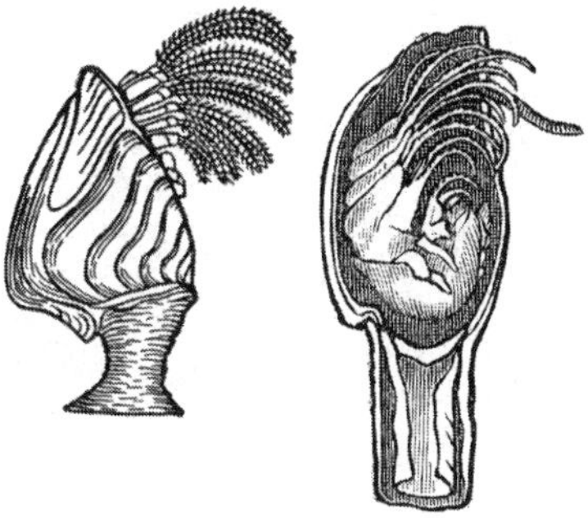

Fig. 8.8 The goose barnacle, *Lepas fascicularis.* The barnacle exudes a powerful cement to permanently glue itself to almost any underwater surface. The cement is remarkable for its tenacity, its versatility, and its ability to set under water.

Glues abound in nature; many natural substances are sticky. Glues can be derived from, for example, hides, bones, fish, milk solids, and vegetable matter. Many creatures and even plants are able to produce their own refined glues and cements, and have developed behaviors that exploit these substances to their advantage. Barnacles begin life as free-swimming creatures. At the end of this stage, they swim into an object head first, and a powerful cement is emitted from a special gland that later disappears. Unlike most other glues, the barnacles' cement will set under water and will stick to almost anything, enabling them to attach themselves to smooth stainless steel, painted surfaces, wood, plastic, and whale bellies. This natural glue has been studied for possible use in dental applications.

An African bird, the Palm Swift *Cypsiurus parvus*, produces a gluelike saliva that it uses to build a nest in the otherwise impossible support of drooping palm fronds. When the Palm Swift glues plant fibers and feathers to the fronds, the nest ends up hanging effectively sideways. But the bird makes use of it nonetheless by gluing its eggs in place and holding onto and pressing against the nest in order to incubate them.

Fig. 8.9 The male Swiftlet, *Collocalia fuciphaga,* produces a glue of regurgitated saliva that it uses as a structural material to form a nest on a cave wall. The nest is used in Chinese cuisine to make bird's nest soup.

The male Swiftlet (genus *Collocalia*), a sparrow-sized bird of Southeast Asia, produces a gelatinous glue of regurgitated saliva in such copious quantities that it is able to use it as the sole structural material for its nest. The Swiftlet "glues" the strands of saliva to the sides of cave walls and weaves them outward into a half-cup shape, and the strands harden to form a crystalline-lace basket. This nest made entirely of the Swiftlet's saliva-based structural glue is prized in Chinese cooking for making bird's-nest soup.

Fig. 8.10 Glues are widely used in construction for such applications as adhering countertops, flooring, tile, and molding.

Glue is, of course, sold as a product by itself, but it is also an integral part of a number of other products, and critical to many processes. Glue traps, for example, are used to catch roaches, mice, and other pests. Usually a bait or scent is placed so that the creature approaching the bait walks over a glued surface along the way, thereby becoming trapped. Lightly adhesive, rubbery glue compounds are sometimes used in magazines to hold floppy discs, samples, or envelopes in place, yet enabling consumers to remove them easily. A glue related to super glue (but less toxic and longer-lasting) called Dermabond™ (*2-octyl cyanoacrylate*) is now used to close wounds, as an alternative to sutures, having won FDA approval in 1998. Glue is used extensively in construction. Materials, such as floor boards, are now routinely laid with glue, replacing or supplementing nails. The resultant floor is more rigid and less likely to squeak or have boards come loose. It is consequently not surprising to find a construction adhesive named Liquid Nails®. Glue is also integral to the manufacture of many building components. Glue holds the layers of plywood together, as well as the wood chips that make up particleboard. Gluelike adhesives hold down Formica laminate on a kitchen counter, and keep linoleum floor tiles in place.

Adhesive Tape

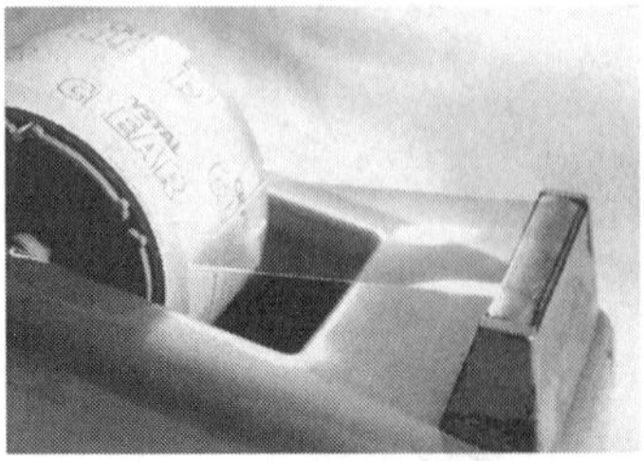

Fig. 8.11 Clear plastic tape. Many types of adhesive tape are commonly used. Most are made of plastic, cloth, or pape. Some special tapes used in photography are made of metal. Cellophane, once universally used for clear tape, is now rare.

Adhesive tape has become such a fundamental material, we can hardly imagine how people managed without it. Commercial tapes are usually made of cloth, paper, or plastic, with adhesive applied to one or both sides. Some tapes, like Scotch Magic Transparent Tape®, are almost invisible when applied to a surface. Others, used in photography, allow almost no light to pass through. Some tapes, like fiber-reinforced duct tape, are extremely strong in both adhesive and tensile strength, while other tapes, like masking tape, are intended to be both easy to tear and easy to remove.

Many natural materials, such as spider webs, exhibit at

least some of the properties of adhesive tape. While not wide and flat like adhesive tape, webs are often both tensile and adhesive in nature. A more direct, natural parallel is found in the papyrus plant. Early writing papers were made thousands of years ago by exploiting the adhesive-tape-like properties of the plant. Strips of the plant were placed down in two layers, at right angles to each other. Wetting and pressing the material permanently bonded the natural tape strips, because gluelike sap was released by the pressure.

Fig. 8.12 The *Adhesive Tape paradigm* is widely employed in first aid materials, from small adhesive bandages to body casts.

Adhesive tapes of various types are widely used in medical applications. A Band-Aid® is essentially a strip of sterile, plastic tape with a square of gauze applied in the middle. Surgical tapes are sometimes used to close wounds in place of stitches. Casts are made by wrapping the injured appendage with a cloth tape impregnated with either plaster or UV-cured plastic as an adhesive. Tapes are sometimes applied to alter surface characteristics, for instance to increase friction. For this purpose, tape is wrapped around the handle of a bat and adhesive friction strips are added to bathtubs and stair edges. Tapes are also sometimes used not for holding things together, but rather for what the tape takes with it when it is removed. We use tape in this manner to remove lint from clothing, and a similar concept is employed in strips used to unclog facial pores.

Shrink Wrap

Shrink-wraps and -tapes often have the basic properties of adhesive tapes, but in addition, they shrink after they're applied, resulting in a tighter binding than was originally applied. Heat-shrink-tubing and -tape are used extensively to protect electrical connections. Either a length of tubing is slipped over the connection or tape is wrapped around the connection, then heat is applied, usually with a heat gun resembling a hair dryer. The material then shrinks, resulting in a tight covering for the connection that will not easily slip off, and keeps air and moisture from the connection.

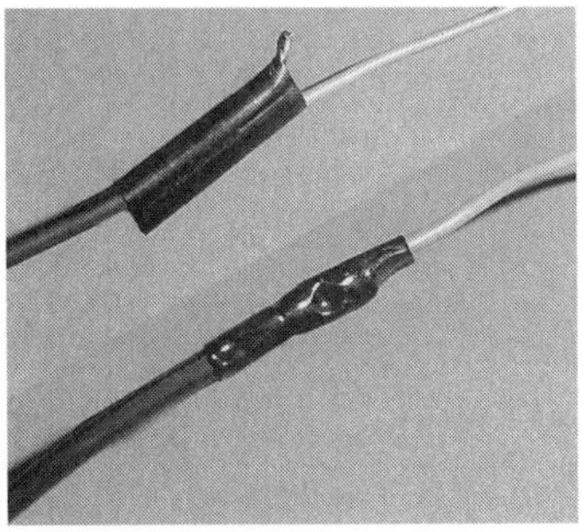

Fig. 8.13 Heat-shrink tubing. With the application of heat, the tubing shrinks to make a firm air- and water-tight joint.

Fig. 8.15 Leafroller caterpillars employ the *Shrink Wrap paradigm* to create tube-shaped homes out of leaves. Silk is wrapped loosely around the leaves. Tension builds as the silk shrinks, thus curling the leaves. Ohio State University Extension photo.

Shrink-wrap resembling food-wrap is used to hold odd collections of boxes and crates together for shipping. After this material is wrapped around the boxes, which are usually stacked loosely on a wooden pallet, again a hot-air gun is applied and the shrink-wrap shrinks, holding the boxes tightly to the pallet.

Among the creatures to employ their own "shrink-wrap" are the larvae of the *Tortricidae* family, the leaf roller moth. The larvae form leaves into tube-shaped homes by using shrink-wrapping silk. Silk is run to the edges of the leaf, usually perpendicular to the midrib. As the silk dries, it shrinks, pulling the edges of the leaf inward. The larva then repeat the process, attaching shorter silk strands that shrink to pull the sides even closer together until the leaf is formed into a tube about the diameter of a pencil.[42]

Tacks

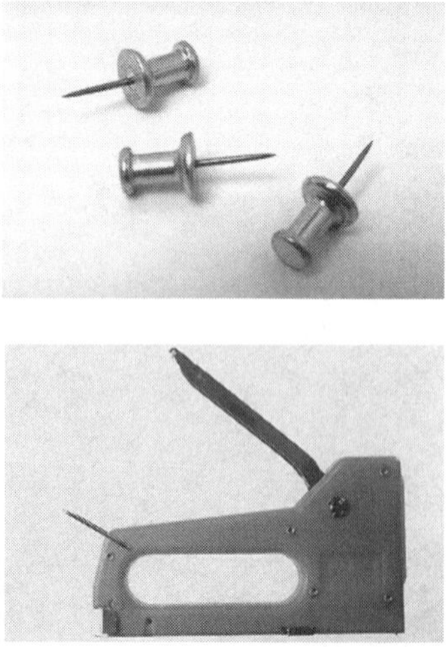

Fig. 8.16 a) Pushpins, perhaps the most familiar symbol representing the *Tacks paradigm.* b) Besides stapling paper, staples are widely used in construction for installing materials such as asphalt tiles, flooring, carpet, and telephone wires. Staples are also used in surgery to close skin or even to join bones.

Members of the *Tacks paradigm* attach by piercing with a fastener, which has a head or a bend at one end to keep the piece from slipping from the fastener. The piercing end is held in place by being embedded into a firm material, or by being bent upward after piercing the material.

Tacks, nails, pins, staples, and other similar devices are widely used for attaching things, such as when we tack a sign to a board or staple papers together. Tacks and nails find many uses in building and construction, from building a basic stud wall frame, to attaching floorboards to joists and Sheetrock® to walls. Surprisingly we find that many of these types of fasteners are used in clothing as well, from the pins used to hold hemlines or to keep new shirts neat in a package, to the rivets used in Levi's® jeans, to the nails used in shoe construction for attaching heels.

While we can quickly think of many inanimate things we might nail together, on first consideration we might think that nails would be of little use for attaching things to living animals, yet that is how shoes are attached to horses' hooves. Thorns, spines and prickers also attach in a tacklike manner.

Staples, beyond the ordinary desk variety, are used for many construction tasks, such as applying shingles to roofs. They even find use in surgical applications. A skin stapler is sometimes used as an alternative to sutures; each pull on the handle of the special staple gun inserts a staple "stitch" to close a wound.

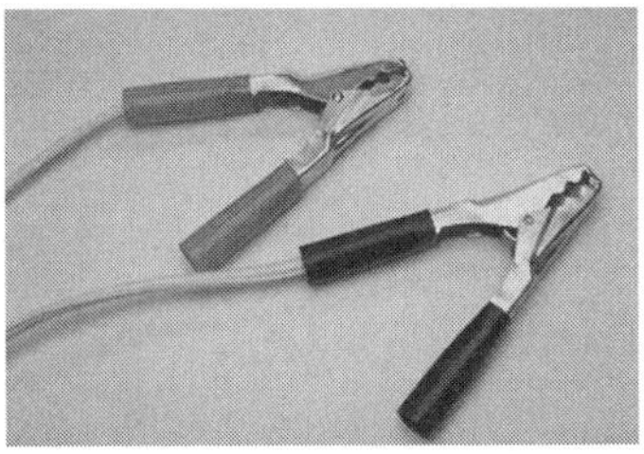

Fig. 8.17 Clips are used for many types of temporary attachments, such as electrical connections, as with these automotive jumper cables.

Clips and Clamps

A clip is usually a piece of spring metal or plastic designed to allow attachment by compression. For example, a note can be attached to a document or a book using a paper clip. Clamps also attach by means of compression. Clamps are usually larger than clips and can incorporate a device to vary pressure, like the screw in C-clamps. Clips and clamps are used for a wide variety of applications for temporary attachment. Clips might be independent, like a paper clip, or attached to a fixed surface, like a clipboard. Clips are widely used in medicine. Microscopes use them to hold slides in place for viewing. Hemostats and other clips are attached to veins and arteries during surgery to stop blood flow. Clips are affixed above X-ray viewers to temporarily hold the X-rays in place. Small plastic clips are used to stop the flow in tubing used for intravenous drip or phlebotomy (blood collection). Many military and police items also employ clips, often to fasten devices to belts.

Fig. 8.18 Clips use compression to hold things in place. Clips can be two-sided, as with paperclips, or one sided, as with this clipboard.

Among the clips found around the home are hair clips, clothespins, and certain kinds of towel holders. Clips are provided on ballpoint pens to fasten them to pockets. Small portable tools and instruments often have belt clips, including pagers, tape measures, and portable phones.

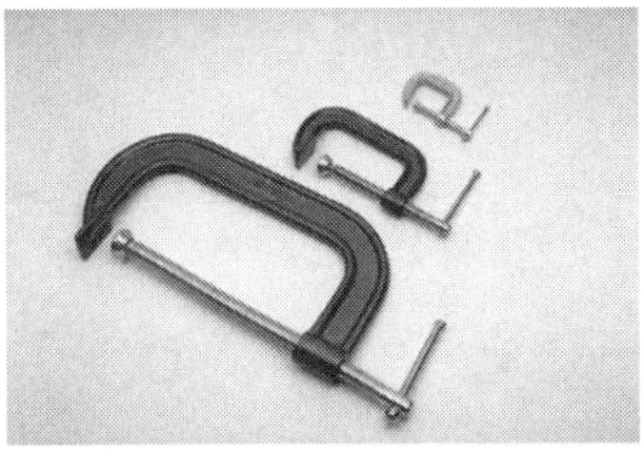

Fig. 8.19 Clamps are similarly used for temporary attachment, and to apply pressure.

Clamps are also found both as independent devices, such as the C-clamp, and affixed to other surfaces, as with a vise attached to a workbench. Clamps are used to temporarily hold things that will be subject to forces. They are widely used in wood- and metalworking. Here, work is usually clamped to hold it still during sanding or milling that would otherwise cause it to move. Clamps are also frequently employed in machine designs to attach parts that will need to be removed at some point, as with the hose clamps attaching radiator hoses in an automobile.

In the natural world, teeth, claws, and pincers sometimes work like clips and clamps, and at other times work like other paradigms. A crab might use its claws in a noncliplike manner, for instance, to eat. The crab can also can be "clipped" onto a fixed or moving object by clamping its claws shut. Similarly an ant's pincers can behave like clamps. In Africa, ants have sometimes been used for holding wounds closed in place of stitches, like surgical staples. When a live ant is held up to the wound, it clenches its pincers. The ant's body is then clipped off, leaving the head and pincers to hold the wound closed; the pincers don't release after the ant is dead. The term "clamp" is sometimes used to describe firm biting, as in "clamp down on this tongue depressor." The similarity between teeth and jaws and clips and clamps is quite evident in such devices as alligator clips, so named because they resemble the jaws of an alligator.

Fig. 8.20 Harpoons were once widely used for hunting whales, first thrown by hand, and later, shot from guns like this. Whaling has largely stopped under international pressure to protect these animals.

Harpoon

Members of the *Harpoon paradigm* attach by piercing, as do the members of the *Tacks paradigm*, but they use barbed spikes that make them more difficult to remove. Harpoons have been widely used in hunting since prehistoric times. When used in hunting, the barbs act to work the point in deeper as an animal attempts to flee, thus hastening its demise. At the large end of the scale, whales were once hunted with harpoons; these spears had barbs at the end to lodge them in the flesh of the whale, connected by rope to the ship. The harpoons effectively attached the ship to the whale, making the boat a drag weight, thus tiring the animal out for easy capture. Small harpoons are still used in fishing, particularly in scuba diving. They are also still widely used by traditional cultures like the Inuit of the Arctic regions for hunting sea mammals and fish.

Fig. 8.21 Spearguns, a variation on the *Harpoon paradigm*, are used for underwater sport fishing.

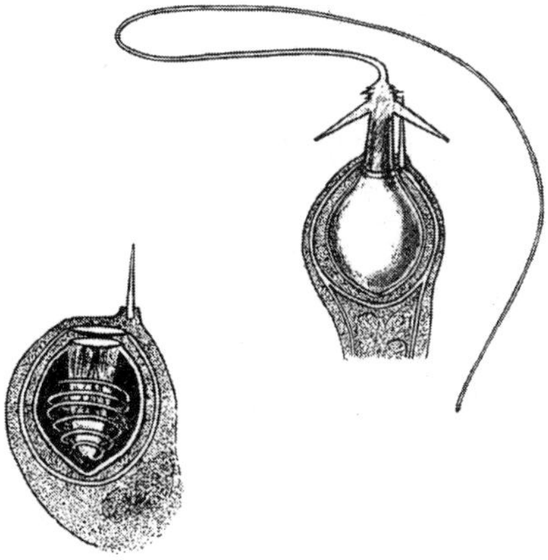

Fig. 8.22 Nematocysts are pre-loaded, often poison-charged, harpoons found in the *Cnidaria* phylum, which includes jellyfish, corals, and sea anemones. When triggered as a defensive mechanism, or in attacking prey, the capsule turns inside out, extending and uncoiling the barb-tipped thread which pierces the skin of the victim. In some species, poison is pumped through the hollow thread, paralyzing the victim.

Fig. 8.23 (left) Hunting with harpoons is an important part of traditional arctic cultures.

Some special nails and other fasteners have harpoonlike barbs to hold them into walls or masonry after being hammered or shot into the surface.

Among the natural harpoonlike structures are worker-bee stingers. These stingers are pointed to puncture the skin of the victim, and barbed to ensure the stinger remains in the skin. The poison sacs and adjoining muscles are usually then pulled from the bee, thereby remaining attached to the victim whereupon the bee's muscles continue to contract, pumping more venom into the wound. Porcupine quills and many cactus spines are also barbed, preventing them from being easily removed from a victim's flesh.

Fig. 8.24 Burdock plant, with mature fruit ready to attach to passers-by.

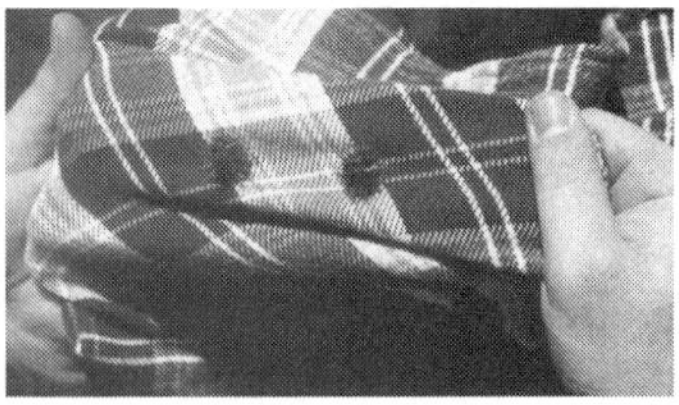

Fig. 8.25 Even careful hikers will occasionally find burdock and cockleburrs "hitching rides" on their clothing.

Burdock

Any experience with the thistlelike fruit of the burdock plant conveys clearly why this, too, belongs among the *Attaching paradigms*. The ball-shaped fruit is covered with hook-tipped spikes that enable it to easily stick to fur or clothing. It can then hitchhike for many miles, whereupon it might get planted, as the animal discovers the burdock seed and pulls the seed from its fur with its teeth. This has proven to be a very effective way for this plant to spread its seed, because as common as it now is in the United States, it is a native of Europe, having most likely arrived stuck to the sides and tails of livestock. Burdock spines are quite similar to crochet hooks. Their rigidity allows them to pierce clothing or work their way deep into an animal's fur, and the hooks let them lock themselves in place. The effectiveness of these little hooks in sticking, as found on the burdock and cockleburr, led to the development of Velcro (see the *Velcro paradigm* in Chapter 7). The primary difference between the *Burdock paradigm* and the *Velcro paradigm* is that Velcro is designed to be a binary material. Velcro hooks stick to velcro loops. Burdock, in contrast, is not selective, the hooks will stick to most any fur or cloth surface, and can even get caught on your skin.

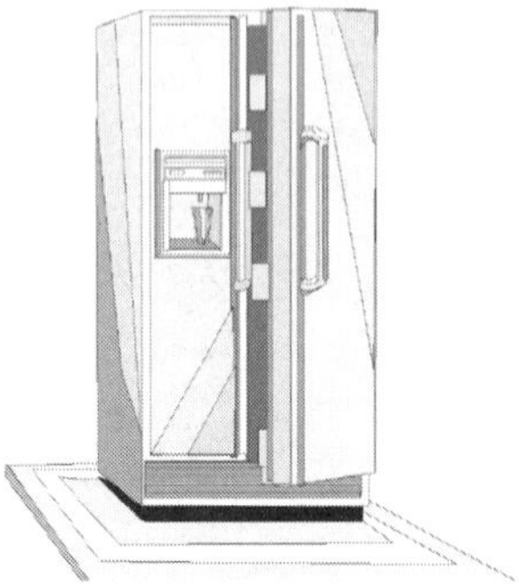

Fig. 8.26 Magnets are widely used to attach things to ferrous surfaces, for instance, attaching notes to refrigerators. Perhaps more importantly, magnets used in the gasket provide a safe, energy-efficient seal.

Magnet

Magnets are frequently used to temporarily attach things, particularly to iron and steel. Magnets, for example, are probably attaching various notes to your refrigerator. Among the positive attributes of using magnets for attachment is that they can work without harming the surface. Magnets are also simple to remove, by pulling, or in the case of electromagnets, by releasing the current. Among their disadvantages are the potential problems they cause around electronic devices, such as computers, and their applicability to only certain metals. Magnetic attachment lends itself more to environments with a large amount of exposed iron and steel. In machine shops, consequently, magnetic bases on clamps, lamps and other devices are common. Similarly, many opportunities for magnetic attachment exist on ships and submarines. Magnets can easily be used for attaching in nonmagnetic environments as well, by strategically placing a piece of steel or a magnet. For example, a magnetic strip can be attached to a kitchen wall in order to hold knives. A matching steel plate and magnet can also be set into a cabinet door and frame to hold the door closed. The many other applications of magnets are explored in Chapter 13, *Transcending the Visible.*

Questions

1) If Post-it® notes were available in rolls, it might make a good masking tape. Think of ten other uses for Post-it® material, assuming you could manufacture it in any size, shape, and configuration.

2) Look around your home and notice the things that are attached to other things. Take an inventory of the *Attaching paradigms* you find.

3) Try to think of or find three different toys that have parts that attach magnetically. Design a construction toy with magnetically attaching parts. Consider the attraction and repulsion possibilities of the magnets. Can use this to your advantage in the design of the toy?

4) You are to attach a large (12′ square) cloth banner to the exterior surface of a concrete building, where it will be subjected to rain and wind. Devise five methods of attaching the banner, each utilizing a different paradigm. Rank these according to the strength of the attachment, the ease of removal, and estimated cost. Which solution would you choose?

9

Passages

Passages paradigms imply the means by which spaces are connected *in combination with* the ways by which things are moved from one space to the other. From the term "passages," we might first think of architecture and the various openings in buildings through which its occupants and visitors pass. We might alternately think of rites of passage, the major transitions in a person's life, or *A Passage to India,* suggesting travel. In all cases passageways connect things that hold things, whether they are bodies, rooms, countries, or spiritual states of mind. And *"passage"* can refer either to the opening in the connection or to the movement of bodies or material between the connected spaces.

Passages, as a category of paradigms, are closely related to concepts presented in the preceding two chapters, on the *Joining* and *Attaching* paradigms, respectively. However passages suggest a greater degree of intimacy. If we imagine two one-celled creatures like amoebas, we can imagine them attached to each other like Velcro. They might be attached and certainly close to each other, but having a passageway between them, through which protoplasm can be exchanged, is clearly a more intimate connection.

Passages can be fairly free-flowing between the spaces they connect, but usually at least some constriction is involved. If, for instance, a theater is emptied through a passageway to an exit, a bottleneck and consequent waiting will result as people funnel thorough the passageway. The choice of the words "bottleneck" and "funnel" are intentional here, helping to reinforce the metaphors presented here and how they relate to physical objects. Several of the *Passage paradigms* have to do with this the flow restriction aspect, bottlenecks, baffles, and filters.

Pipe

Fig. 9.1 a) Many of the passages in a building are pipes, providing services such as allowing water in, and directing exhaust air and sewage out. b) Passenger car tunnels are essentially large pipes, evident in the curved walls in this image.

The pipe is the most fundamental and versatile *Passage paradigm*. Many of the other *Passage paradigm* types are variations on the *Pipe paradigm*, or can be described in relation to a pipe. The *Pipe paradigm* implies long, hollow cylinders that can be used to convey liquid, steam, smoke, or other substances. Pipes are commonly made of a wide variety of materials, including metal, plastic, glass (to avoid corrosion from acids and chemicals), baked clay, and concrete. Cylindrical sections can be connected in order to change direction, or branch off, or terminate, using elbows, T-junctions, U-shaped traps, and caps.

Pipes imply rigid walls. A pipe usually depends on a different atmospheric pressure inside the pipe relative to the outside to force contents through the pipe. Consequently rigid walls are usually required to separate the inside and the outside of the pipe, enabling the contents to be under relative pressure or vacuum with respect to the surroundings. For some applications, pipes can operate without a significant pressure differential. They can, for example, carry waste water out of a building by means of gravity, or smoke up a chimney by convection. Pressurized pipes are important, however, in such applications as conveying water upward from the basement of a building, or providing vacuum through the pipes of a central vacuum system. Vacuum pipes, or pneumatic tubes, have also been used as a sort of communications system, moving notes, small parts, and cash around buildings in small canisters.

We don't usually think of pipes as being things that people pass through, yet tunnels, for cars, subways, and pedestrians, are essentially pipes, that are rigid-walled, waterproof, and often cylindrical in shape.

Two variants of the *Pipe paradigm* are specific to the pressure conditions they suggest. A straw usually implies its use with suction, while a hose is used with pressure.

Straw

A straw implies a thin-walled pipelike object that is used primarily with suction, usually to draw small quantities of liquid short distances. Straws require rigid walls, because the walls are compressed when pulled inward by the vacuum.

Straws are familiar as things to drink beverages through. As most children discover, they can also be used under pressure, to blow air, liquid, or spitballs through. Common variations include the flexstraw (see the *Flexstraw paradigm* in Chapter 4), and "crazy straws," which are rigid-plastic drinking straws made with tubing twisted and curled in the middle section as a novelty. A familiar piece of laboratory equipment, the pipette, is basically a glass straw with graduated markings on the side.

Hypodermic needles are a variation on the *Straw paradigm*, with a sharpened end for puncturing skin. Similarly, drinking straws provided with "drink boxes" are equipped with a sharpened end for puncturing the "skin" of the box. A standard hypodermic needle uses a plunger at the end that can be drawn out to create the suction needed for filling the cylinder with medicine or drawing a blood sample. The plunger may also be depressed to create pressure to expel the needle's contents (see the *Telescope paradigm* section in Chapter 5). In place of a plunger, a rubber bulb at the end of a straw can be used to create suction or pressure, as is seen in such devices as eyedroppers and turkey basters.

In the natural world, "straw" refers to stalks of grain or grass, which usually are also rigid, hollow tubes. A number

Fig. 9.2 Drinking straws, straight and flexstraw types.

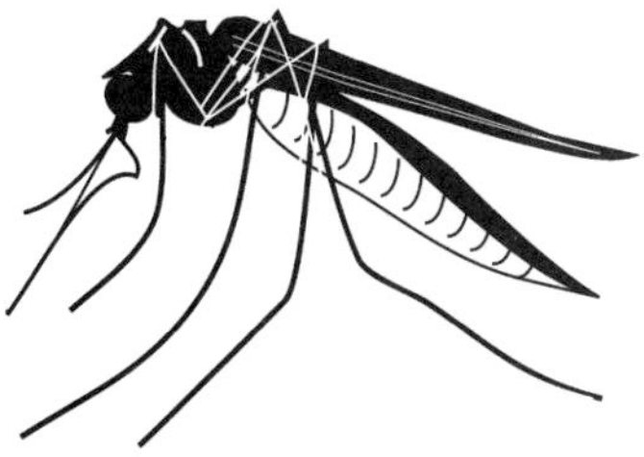

Fig. 9.3 The female mosquito uses a strawlike tube to draw a blood meal from her victims. Mosquito larvae, which live in water, also use a strawlike tube to breath from.

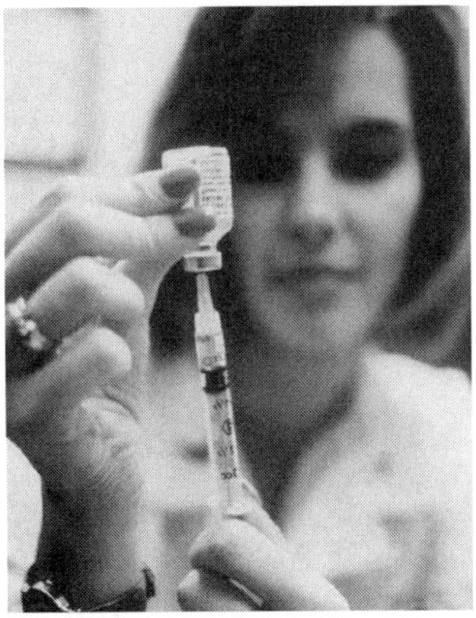

Fig. 9.4 Hypodermic needles employ the *Straw paradigm*. A sharpened hollow needle inserted through the skin or a rubber bottle seal becomes a passageway for medicine or blood. USAF Photo.

of creatures use natural strawlike drinking or breathing apparatus. Perhaps the most familiar and least liked is the mosquito. Mosquitoes constitute some 2,500 species of the family *Culicidae.* The female requires a meal of blood to mature her eggs, which she acquires through her specially adapted strawlike mouth. Mosquito larvae also use straws, but in a different way. Mosquitoes lay their eggs in water, but the larvae that develop from these eggs must breathe air. The larvae of the genus *Culex* come equipped with a breathing tube that enables them to breathe air while their bodies are below the surface of the water. Humans use a similar device, the snorkel, when skin diving. Within our bodies, the trachea functions like a straw, providing the passageway for air moving between the mouth and the lungs. The trachea's thin but rigid walls provide for both the vacuum conditions of inhaling and the pressure conditions of exhaling.

Hose

Fig. 9.5 a, b Garden hoses are for many people a fun first exposure to the *Hose paradigm.*

A hose, a variant on the *Pipe paradigm,* implies that it is made of a flexible material and is primarily used with pressure rather than with vacuum. To hold its shape with a pressurized interior, a hose must have tensile strength but need not be rigid. Consequently, a nonrigid material, such as rubber, plastic, or cloth, can be used, as with garden and fire hoses. When a soft-walled hose is subjected to vacuum, the walls collapse, preventing passage of material through the hose. This effect is used to advantage in a simple valve wherein a section of flexible rubber extends from a cylindrical opening to a flattened slot. Under pressure, the slot opens to function as a hose, while the opening is flattened and tightly sealed when under vacuum.

Since humans and other animals are composed largely of water, circulating liquids through the body is of great importance. Our circulatory system, which moves blood, oxygen, and nutrients through the body, is an obvious example. Most of our internal "piping" resembles hoses

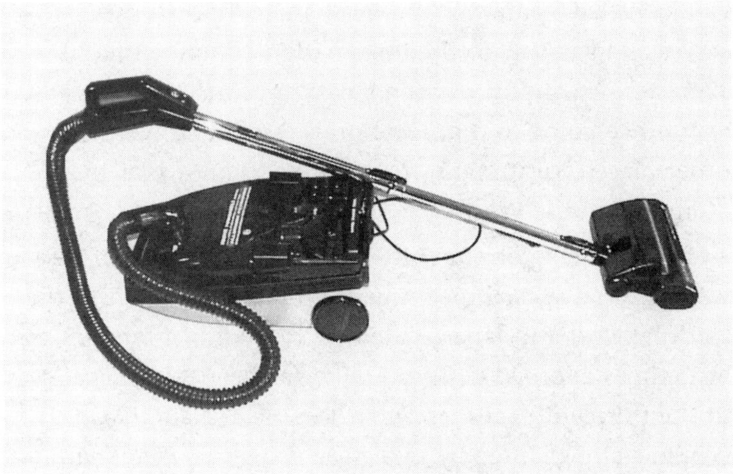

Fig. 9.6 A hose is a key component of a vacuum cleaner. It directs the vacuum to where it in needed, it connects the motor to the attachments, and it serves as the passageway for dirt to reach the collection bag.

more than pipes or straws. Soft-walled yet strong, our veins and arteries are designed to function under the pressure our pumping hearts create. Among our other many other hose-like parts are our intestines, tear ducts, and urethra, through which urine leaves the body.

Gateway

A gateway implies a passageway between two spaces, whether a literal opening with a gate, as in a fence, or metaphoric gateways, as in college, which is sometimes described as a "gateway to a good career." A gateway also implies a gate, suggesting the possibility of restricting access and, possibly, the presence of a gatekeeper. Doorways fit the paradigm; they can be passageways between two rooms, or between the inside and the outside. Windows fit the paradigm as well, but usually imply the passage of air rather than of humans. The paradigm can also include openings without doors or gates; for example, a doorway still functions as a passage with the door removed.

Fig. 9.7 A gateway, in the literal sense of the word, is an opening in a fence or wall with a gate.

Computers can serve as gateways for information "traffic" passing in both directions between a local network and the Internet. Such computers can perform gatekeeping functions, using firewall software designed to keep out unauthorized users and prevent infiltration by viruses. A Web server can be called a gateway in a more metaphoric sense: It serves as a gateway to the information contained on its Websites. An airport or even a city can function as a gateway, since going to that location is essential to getting to other places. Saint Louis, for example, is known as the "Gateway to the West."

In many religions, architectural manifestations of gateways take on special meaning as symbolic gateways to the spiritual world. In Japan, gateways to Buddhist temples are sometimes adorned with symbolic gatekeepers. The gateway to the thirteenth-century To̱dai Temple at Nara, Japan, is symbolically guarded by two gigantic figures. The *Kongo̱-rik-*

Fig. 9.8 a, b The 630-ft. tall Gateway arch in St. Louis, by architect Eero Saarinen (1910–1961), completed in 1965. The arch symbolizes St. Louis's role as the "Gateway to the West."

Fig. 9.9 *The Gates of Hell,* a doorway designed by sculptor Auguste Rodin (1840–1917) for the Museum of Decorative Arts in Paris. The sculpture is intended both as a literal gateway into the building, and as the representation of a metaphorical gateway, a reference from the third canto of Dante's Inferno.

ishi stands at one side holding thunderbolts to destroy evil, and the heavily armored *Misshaku-rikishi* stands at the other. In one of his greatest works (although unfinished in his lifetime), French sculptor Auguste Rodin designed a doorway for the future Musée des Arts Decoratif in Paris as his vision of the Gates of Hell.

In the natural world, many of the animals that build homes restrict access to a hidden or guarded passageway. The social insects, including bees and ants, employ gateways in the design of their nests. Openings are usually restricted to certain small and tightly controlled openings, complete with gatekeepers. Some species of spiders also build restricted passageways into their webs or burrows, with the equivalent of guarded doorways. Members of the spider family *Ctenizidae,* or trap-door spiders, live in a burrow in the ground, and fashion a silk-hinged door at its entrance. This serves to restrict access to the burrow and camouflages the spiders until a prey walks within striking distance.

Bottleneck

The neck of a bottle is the passageway between the body of the bottle and another vessel into which the contents is being poured, such as your mouth. It is also a potent metaphor that we use throughout our lives, referring to a wide range of situations, including traffic patterns, moving paperwork through a company, and processing data in a computer program.

Fig. 9.10 A bottleneck is the tapering of the bottle from the body to the opening. This tapering distinguishes bottles from jars, and reduces the flow capacity through the opening.

A bottleneck simultaneously implies both flow through a passageway and the restriction of that flow. The restriction of the flow in designed objects and systems is often intentional and a functional aspect of the design. In a bottle, for example, the neck design can serve to control the rate of flow and to prevent splashing (see the *Bottle paradigm* in Chapter 3).

Perhaps more often, however, the bottleneck is a problem, as when a bottleneck in computing caused by having to perform the same instruction on every element of a large data

Fig. 9.11 When traffic lanes converge, as for a bridge toll, a traffic jam often results. We refer to the convergence as a bottleneck.

set, one at a time. A common solution to bottleneck problems is to widen the neck, as when computers employ parallel processors, which perform operations on multiple data elements at one time. Alternately, in computing as well as with traffic, one can find an alternate route.

Wire

Fig. 9.12 A telephone switchboard. Though rarely used now, it remains one of the most potent symbols of wire-based voice communications. The wires embody both the physical and metaphorical connection between parties who want to talk to each other.

When you look at a wire, it's strange to think of things traveling through it, yet wires have become arguably the most important passageways in terms of the transfer of information, power, and commerce.

In its simplest application, a wire can be used like a rope, to suspend things or hold things together under tension. Imagine holding one end of a 50-foot wire, with a friend holding the other end. In a sense, the wire becomes a passageway for tension because if you pull at one end, the tension is felt at the other end. Similarly, if you yank twice at one end, your friend, who feels the yanks at the other end, might interpret this as a signal.

A wire can also transmit electricity. It is, consequently, a passageway for power. Since electricity can be modulated, it can encode information, so a wire can also be a passageway for information in an electronic form. The contemporary metaphor of the wire as a pipe for information derives from the popularity of the Internet. The use of wires to transmit information, though, has been well established for more than a century. The telegraph established the wire as a communications passageway, and wire-based terms and phrases soon entered the language such as "Send him a message by wire" and "Wire her some money." Similarly, telephones and cable television are information devices connected by wires. Metal wires for information purposes are largely interchangeable with glass fibers, which can transmit information as pulses of light rather than electricity.

Umbilical Cord

The umbilical cord is a connection between mother and child that is the child's sole source of life support in an environment that would otherwise not support its life. The umbilical cord is, consequently, a powerful metaphor and paradigmatically suggestive of a range of connections. The simplest of these is the tether. A tether is usually a strap, string, or rope that attaches something that moves to something that is relatively stationary. For example, you can go

Fig. 9.13 Spacewalk. Early spacewalks employed an umbilical cord tether connecting the astronaut to the ship, and providing life support functions. NASA photo.

scuba diving from a boat or a submarine using a tether to find your way back through murky waters. A retractable tether is often used on a belt attached to your keys to ensure that they are not accidentally left behind. Walking a dog on a leash is another use of a tether. Some games and toys employ a tether, such as tetherball, in which a volleyball-like ball is tethered to a pole and hit from either side.

Tethering is not the only function of umbilical cords, however. More importantly, the umbilical cord provides life-support functions. The umbilical veins provide the fetus with freshly oxygenated blood from the placenta, while the umbilical arteries carry away the deoxygenated blood and fetal wastes. Similarly, diving tethers sometimes include an air hose as an alternative to diving with air tanks. One of the most memorable images of the early space program of the 1960s is of an astronaut in a space walk, seen against the clouds below him, attached to the ship only by an umbilical tether (Figure 9.13).

Chinese Fingercuffs

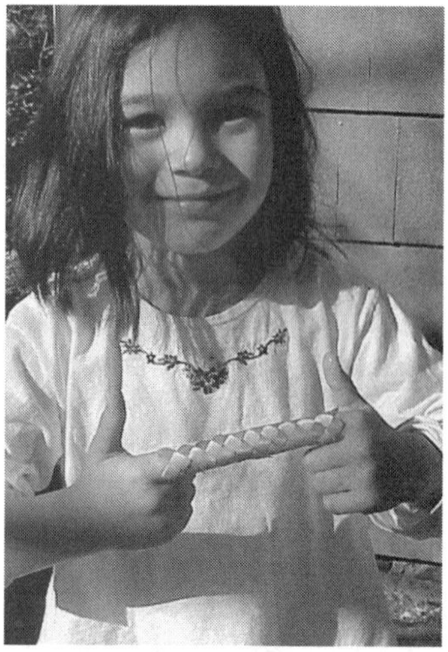

Fig. 9.14 Chinese fingercuffs. Attempting to pull the fingers out causes the tube to tighten its grip.

While most pipes and hoses are designed to maintain a constant diameter, some are designed to change in diameter, in response to such factors as pressure, temperature and tension. One example is known as "Chinese fingercuffs" or "Chinese handcuffs." This novelty is a tube that you can easily insert your fingers into, but retracting them is much more difficult. When the tube is compressed by pushing the fingers in, the diameter of the tube increases. However, when you try to withdraw your fingers, the tension on the tube decreases the diameter, tightly clamping on the fingers.

An emergency-escape device was designed based on this principle. A stockinglike tube was extended from a high floor of a building. People jumped into the tube, passed to the ground at a controlled rate, and their friction on the sides of the tube caused it to stretch downward, thereby narrowing the diameter and slowing their descent.

Braided metal sheathing is among the commercial products that employ the *Chinese Fingercuffs* paradigm. Used in the coaxial cables that provide cable television and internet service, the braided metal layer helps prevent damage to the cable. If the delicate inner conductor is pulled, the sheathing tightens around it and helps resist the tension.

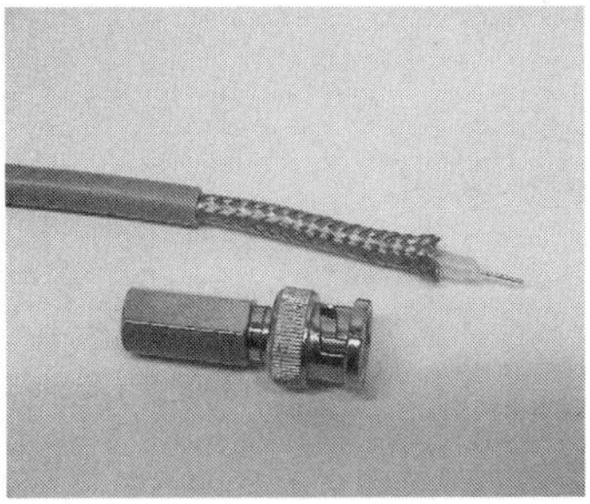

Fig. 9.15 The braided metal sheath in coaxial cable employs the *Chinese fingercuffs paradigm*. Tension on the cable tightens the grip of the sheath on the inner cable, thereby reinforcing it and helping to prevent damage.

Numerous biological passageways similarly vary their diameter, not only to accommodate contents of different sizes, but as an active process to move these contents through the passageways. For example, the birth canal must accommodate an extreme range of diameters as a baby passes through it. The birth process is facilitated by contractions of the uterus, and of the birth canal, behind the baby. This in turn helps to push the baby outward. The intestine is similarly a passageway of variable diameter. Digested matter is pushed through the intestine by muscular contractions of the intestinal passageways.

Baffle

A baffle is an intentionally indirect passageway that forces a path that weaves back and forth between obstructions. A baffle can be used either to slow down passage through the baffle, or to dampen forces. Baffles are used within an automotive muffler to force the exhaust through a series of chambers, thus dampening the sound energy. In an architectural context, baffles are sometimes used to control access to a space. Concrete barrier baffles have been placed at the entrances to some embassies, for example, to ensure that cars do not have unimpeded access to a high-security building; they must first slow down and be recognized before gaining admission.

Fig. 9.16 a, b Baffles used to modulate sun. *Brise-soleil* on a modern building, and the Taj Mahal, built by Emperor Shah Jahan for his wife, Mumatz Mahal, 1630–1653. Built in a hot desert climate, its design includes screens and lattices to modulate the sun, thereby keeping the building cooler.

Baffles are also sometimes used on buildings to reduce the glare and the heat load of direct sun. The Swiss architect Le Corbusier popularized baffles he called *brise-soleil* (sun breakers): parallel, rigid vertical panels placed over windows to block direct sunlight. Le Corbusier began applying them to his designs beginning in the 1930s, and they became strongly identified with his architecture. Sun baffles have long been popular in hot, sunny climates, such as the lattices (*shish*, or *mushrabiyah*) and pierced screens (*qamariyah*) used in India's Taj Mahal. Venetian blinds are, perhaps, the most common type of solar baffle used in the Western world.

We also have baffles in the passageways of our noses. As air passes back and through these baffles, the convoluted pathway ensures that even on the coldest days, the air reaching the lungs is warmed and moistened along the way, thereby protecting the lungs.

Filter

A filter can be described as *a passageway that is selective in allowing things to pass*. Passageways often imply filtering, because they permit some things to pass and not others. If you look at storm drains on the side of a road, for example, you see a grating integral to the passageway, intended to let water and small debris to pass, while keeping larger objects out. A "cat door" to a house has no traditional filter element, but its size effectively filters out large animals.

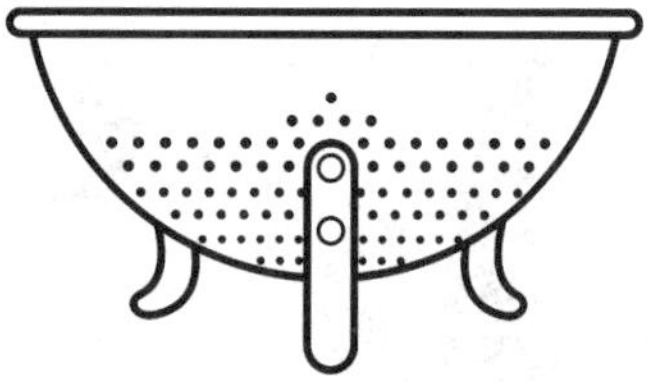

Fig. 9.17 a, b Filters are selective passageways. They include a broad range of products from sunglasses and photographic filters, to colanders, to coffee filters.

Some of the common filters you might encounter are automotive air filters, which let air, but not dirt, into the engine. Similarly, coffee filters permit liquid, but not coffee grounds, to pass through them. Sunglasses filter particular wavelengths of light, while filters in telephones and stereos filter static and noise from a signal. A person can act as a filter in a passageway; a bouncer at a nightclub, for example, filters out rowdy or underage individuals. A person can also act more metaphorically as a filter, by screening phone calls that get passed on or by censoring language in a television program.

Filters are important to many industrial processes, such as papermaking, in which the pulp that forms the paper is filtered from water, and winemaking, in which fruit pulp is filtered out of the liquid to leave a clear beverage.

Filters are also widely used in biological systems. Our noses use hairs and moist surfaces as filters to keep insects and dust out of our lungs. Our liver filters wastes and toxic substances from the blood. Many creatures use filters to gather their food, from sponges to Baleen whales, named for their filter structure (the baleen) that separates plankton and crustaceans from seawater.

Bridge

In Chapter 7 we explored bridges as a *Joining paradigm*. But a view more relevant to the average person traversing a bridge is that it serves as a passageway between two points. This view is strongly reinforced in such examples as covered bridges.

Many bridges serve to connect spaces and provide for the movement of people and things between these spaces. Bridges function as passageways for pedestrians, bicycles, automobiles, and trains. Bridges can span rivers or other bodies of water, gorges, or such obstacles as other roads. Some bridges provide passage between buildings. A gangplank is a movable bridge people use to board or leave a ship at a pier.

Among the creatures that build bridges are spiders, whose webs are used in part as passageways between the different places they connect. Ants also form bridges, primarily of ant bodies. As ants climb over each other's bodies, they may collectively span across gaps, forming a living bridge that other ants can walk across.

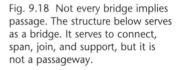

Fig. 9.18 Not every bridge implies passage. The structure below serves as a bridge. It serves to connect, span, join, and support, but it is not a passageway.

Fig. 9.19 The idea of a bridge as a passageway is strongly reinforced as one passes through a covered bridge.

Canal

Conceptually it is simple to join two bodies of water separated by land. Simply dig a trench between them. The bodies of water are joined when water can flow between them. When the bodies are separated by distance and elevation, however, such a trench could become a raging river that while effective as a connection, would not be suitable for ships passing between the two bodies of water. A canal provides for passage by controlling changes in water level using elevatorlike locks. A ship enters the lock, and doors are closed on either side of it. Water is then either admitted into the lock from the higher body of water or drained into the lower body, depending on which way the ship is going. A door is then opened to let the ship proceed on its way.

Among the greatest human engineering feats is the Panama Canal, which links the Pacific with the Atlantic, crossing 80 kilometers of jungle and rock. Because ships must fit into the locks of the canal, the size of the lock has become a consideration in ship design. This has led to a class of vessels known as "Panamax," those built to the maximum capacity of the Panama Canal.

Fig. 9.20 Panama canal. a) sketch from inside the lock. b) The Gatun locks at the Atlantic side of the canal. Each lock can accommodate ships up to 1000 feet long and 110 feet wide.

Questions

1) Examine a clothes-washing machine and dryer. Note the different types of passages and passageways they provide and utilize.

2) Think of the various types of noise that bother you. If you were designing an electronic sound control system that could selectively filter out sounds, what sounds would you include? For example, what benefits and risks would result from filtering out emergency sirens?

3) Passageways often must cross one another. Consider and sketch 5 types of passageways that cross, along with ways to minimize conflicts arising from the crossed paths.

4) Think about the examples discussed in the *Baffle paradigm*, and consider how the paradigm might apply to people. In what ways does an entourage around an important person resemble a baffle? How does a corporate hierarchy act as a baffle? Think of and interaction you've had with an institution that exhibited these characteristics.

10

Multiple Object Relations

When we consider a group of similar objects, the individual objects can rarely be considered entirely independently from the group, which usually has its own identifiable structure. If you have a large number of cattle, for instance, you perceive a herd. With trees, you perceive a forest. The grouping is often the item of most significance, as in "there is an army approaching," or "I'm lost in the forest."

Multiple objects may be organized in many ways. We can coarsely group the *Multiple Object Relations paradigms* into categories including *linear arrangements*, in which similar items are arranged in a line, such as teeth. An alternative category is *stacks*, such as pads of paper or piles of clothing. *Matrices* are arrangements of multiple objects into rows and columns of cells, such as egg cartons. *Trees* are arrangements of branches relating to a trunk, found both in literal trees, and in figurative trees, such as organizational charts. *Bunches* are groupings without a clear geometric pattern, such as bouquets of flowers. In linear arrangements and stacks, each element in the grouping tends to have a relationship or connection only to its fore and aft neighbors and/or a supporting structure. Cells in a 2-D or 3-D matrix have a relationship to more neighbors, as in an apartment building. There is a connection to next-door neighbors, as well as to the apartments above and below, in that a common wall or floor divides these spaces. Trees exhibit a one-to-many or many-to-one relationship. Thus, an organizational chart would typically show a relationship, or chain of command, between any employee (the many) and the president (the one).

Questions of arranging multiples come up in many design problems, for instance in dispensing things, such as pills or paper cups. It also arises when creating sets or kits of various kinds, or accommodating attachments for a device such as a vacuum cleaner.

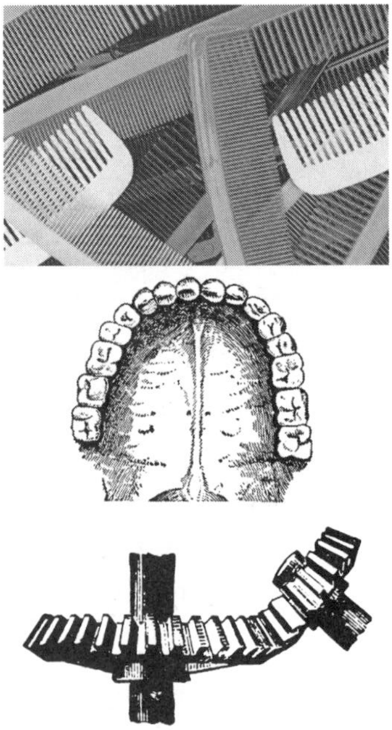

Fig. 10.1 a-c *The Comb paradigm* describes things that are repeated in linear arrangements and are joined on one side, such as the teeth of combs, mouths, and gears.

Comb

A comb, such as a hair comb, is a frame structure holding a linear arrangement of prongs or teeth. Many things are described as comblike, including a cock's comb, a fork, and the teeth in our mouths or on a saw blade. Since individual prongs on a comb are called *teeth*, you might wonder if the paradigm should be called *Teeth*. But teeth do not necessarily imply being set in a jaw, nor does a jaw necessarily have teeth. A mouth doesn't necessarily have either, as in the mouth of a river.

The ribs of animals can also be comblike. This is particularly evident in snakes, which have many more ribs than humans, and do not have sternums joining the ribs at the chest.

String of Beads

A string of beads is, like a comb, a linear arrangement. In its simplest form, a group of identical beads are held in place suspended from the string, which runs through a hole in each bead. Beads may also be of different sizes, however, and the string need not be in a straight line. In place of a string, a wire or skewer may hold items together, or in some cases, there is no string or string equivalent at all. Some objects can attach to each other rather than being held by a string, for instance, the cars on a train. *String of beads* is also used metaphorically, for instance, to speak of a conceptual linkage among a group of historical events: *"There is a common thread running through these events."*

Fig. 10.2 a) Strings of beads are popular as ornament in many cultures. They have at times been used as money, and continue to indicate wealth and status. b) (below) Shish kebab also fits the *String of Beads paradigm*.

An example of the paradigm from our own bodies is the spine. The vertebra form a linear sequence, with the spinal column running through the middle. Other examples include chains and tapeworms (see the *Chain paradigm* in Chapter 5), millipedes, and pine cones. In all of these examples, there is a tangible connection between the "beads." While a group of prisoners chained together would fit the paradigm, a line of people waiting to buy tickets does not. Without a physical connection between the elements, this would fall under the *Formation paradigm* discussed later in this chapter.

Nested Spoons

Spoons are usually designed to nest inside each other. Consequently, they can be neatly and compactly stacked. Spoons exemplify nesting as a way to relate multiple objects. Among the many other objects designed to nest neatly upon one another are paper or plastic cups, china bowls, and plates, stackable chairs, and Pringles® potato chips. Nesting provides a number of advantages. Perhaps foremost of these

Fig. 10.3 a, b Spoons, forks bowls, plates, paper cups and other products are often designed to nest well, enabling them to be stored compactly.

Fig. 10.4 Pringles potato chips. Application of the *Nested Spoons paradigm* led to a new concept in snack foods: nested hyperbolic paraboloid-shaped chips in a can. Nesting the chips provides mutual reinforcement of the easily-broken chips, thus not only reducing package size, but also reducing breakage.

is that nestable things take up far less space when stacked (see the *Order and Disorder paradigm* in Chapter 5). Another advantage is being able to handle the items as a group, such as when you pull a stack of chairs across a room, or wrap and sell a stack of bowls. Further, in the case of the potato chips, you can protect these thin fragile elements by stacking them against similar shapes. While this might seem obvious when you consider a product like Pringles, this design was a major innovation for potato chips, which greatly reduced their package size, and consequently, their case size, truck and warehouse size, shelf-space requirements, and so forth. The *Nested Spoons paradigm* is the primary basis for the success of this product.

Sandwich

The *Sandwich paradigm* involves layering dissimilar materials. Popular myths notwithstanding, the sandwich has been around a lot longer than the Earl of Sandwich (1718–1792) for whom it is named. Precursors of sushi, which in its modern form is frequently served as a sandwich of rice, fish, and toasted seaweed, are known to have been prepared as early as the second century.

The term "sandwich" is used not only in reference to food, but also in reference to composite materials. Building walls, floors, ceilings, and roofs are frequently sandwiches of many materials, for instance, plastic vapor barrier, waterproofing materials, concrete slabs, and wallboard. Wallboard is itself a sandwich of gypsum between two sheets of paper.

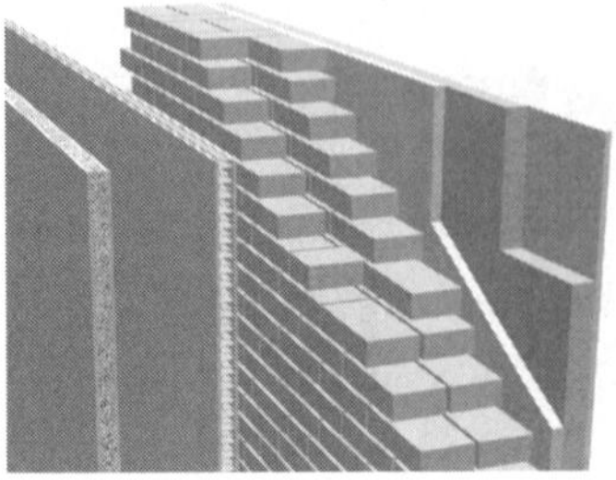

Fig. 10.5 The *Sandwich paradigm* implies an arrangement of multiple layers of dissimilar materials. In building construction we refer to the multiple layers that make up a wall, or roofing, or flooring, as a sandwich for the same reason.

In recent years, packaging materials have often been sandwiched. Drink boxes, for instance, are sandwiches of paper, aluminum, and plastic. The paper provides the desired rigidity and good printing surface, while the plastic provides air- and liquid-tight sealing of the container, and the aluminum prevents light from entering the package.

Clothing materials are sometimes sandwich materials as well, as in winter coats, in which an outer layer like Gore-tex®

provides abrasion resistance and water repellence, while an inner layer such as Thinsulate® might provide insulation, and an innermost nylon layer provides a smooth surface against the body.

Book

The *Book paradigm* is in some ways similar to the *Comb paradigm:* both have multiple elements, pages or teeth, joined at one end. Most books are stacks of physically similar pages, bound at an edge. The book form, at least the type that is read, is optimized to give the maximum surface area possible within a given volume. By maximizing the surface area, the printing area is also maximized. Some books are made for purposes other than reading, for example, a book of matches, or a book of lens tissue. There are also ticket books, coupon books, books of stamps, and scrapbooks.

Fig. 10.6 The functional requirements for books include maximizing surface area for printing and reading, and a spine to keep the pages together.

For a number of application areas maximization of surface area is desirable, such as in heat exchange. A radiator improves its efficiency in transferring heat from the radiator as its surface area increases. The *Book paradigm* is sometimes employed to accomplish this, with many pagelike fins attached in parallel to a spinelike pipe. Similarly, cooling fins are found on many things that require cooling, such as the processors of personal computers.

Books are found in nature as well. Spiders have a breathing apparatus called a *book lung*. Just as a radiator benefits from having a large surface area to effectively transfer heat to the air, a lung benefits from maximizing its surface area, thus improving its efficiency in absorbing oxygen. The book lung evolved to take advantage of the extensive-surface-area property of books. The lung extends hollow, pagelike structures into the spider's bloodstream, creating an efficient structure for the exchange of oxygen.

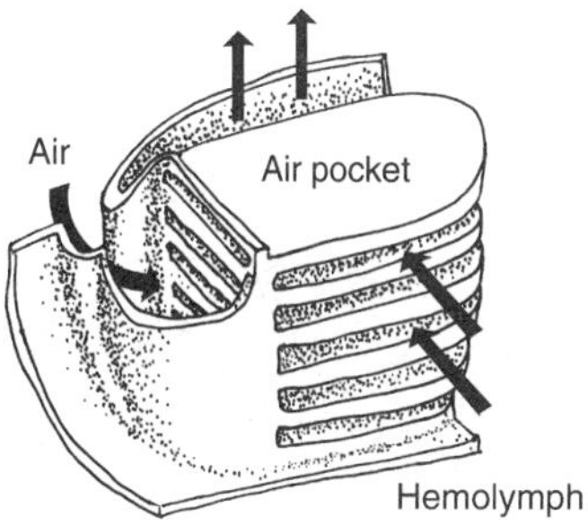

Fig. 10.7 The book lung found in spiders answers similar needs to the paper book. Similarly it maximizes surface area for efficient gas exchange, and similarly, a spine holds the "pages" together.

Matrix

A matrix is a rectangular array of rows and columns of elements. Organization into rectangular arrays is widespread in manufactured goods. Perhaps surprisingly, it is fairly common in the natural world as well. In the matrix paradigm, while we will draw upon mathematical definitions of matrices, we will be concerned only with 2-D and 3-D matrices, whereas single- and multi-dimensional matrices are common in mathematics.

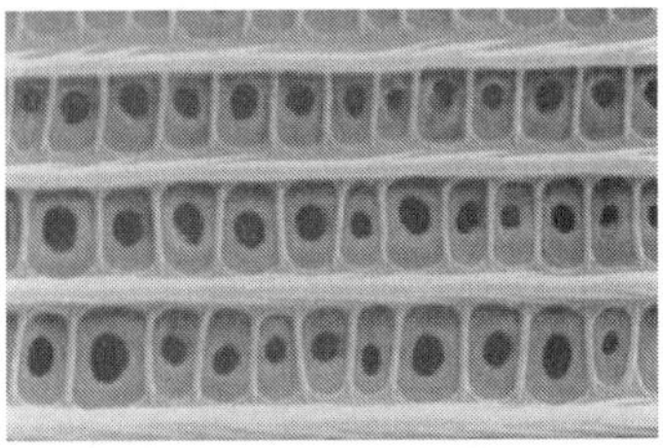

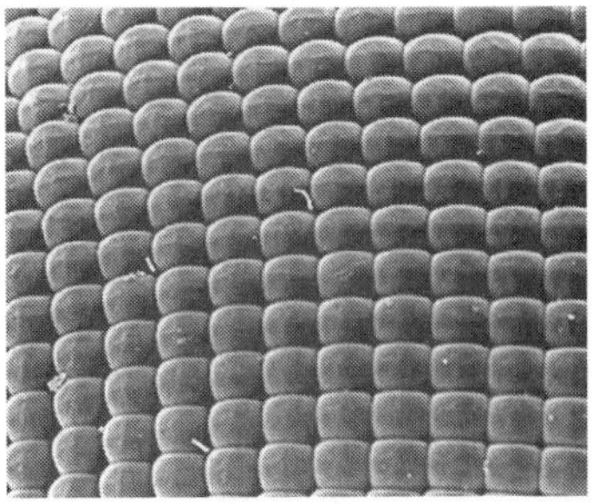

Fig. 10.8 a, b Matrices are found in plant and animal forms, particularly at the micro scale.

In mathematics, we can think of the matrix as an array of variables. Just as we may assign a value to a variable $n := 5$, with a matrix, we address an element of the matrix by its location, for instance the first row, fourth cell to the right: $m[1,4] := 5$. Similarly the seats at a baseball game function as a matrix of variables, in the sense that each seat can hold any spectator. We can assign the seat variable in the same manner as the matrix, for instance saying the seat in the first row, 4th seat over, is assigned to Jamie. *Seat[1,4] := Jamie.* A matrix implies an imposed rectangular order. This order may be imposed by a structural framework, although such a framework might not be necessary with elements that neatly align and stack without one.

In commercial products, we find a matrix structure used in products such as egg crates. Eggs are sold in a box commonly found in sizes accommodating 6, 8, 12, or 36 eggs in a rectangular array. The matrix these crates impose may

Fig. 10.9 a, b Matrices as human accommodation. Many apartments and other buildings look and function like matrices, as does auditorium or stadium seating.

extend to 3-D by stacking the crates. Walking through a supermarket, one can see many other products arranged into matrices as well. Toothpaste tubes, for instance, are placed in boxes to facilitate neatly stacking them. Rectangular arrays are widespread in architecture as well, from the organization of bricks in a wall, to the structural grid of a skyscraper, the arrangement of apartments within a building, and the arrangement of city blocks on a map of New York.

Fig. 10.10 Cubic crystals, found in minerals such as halite and pyrite, indicate an internal matrix-like structure at the atomic level.

In the natural world, crystals are a form of natural regular geometric arrays, some of which are rectangular. Rectangular crystals are an indication of an underlying atomic-level structure that is also rectangular. Among the crystals exhibiting the *Matrix paradigm* are halite and pyrite.

Numerous examples of rectangular arrays may be found in the natural world as well, including various cellular structures in plants and trees, such as the parenchyma cells mentioned in the *Box paradigm* in Chapter 2. Some seeds are arranged in matrices, as corn kernels usually are. Some woodpeckers make a rectangular matrix of holes in trees.

Besides rectangular matrices, many other regular geometric patterns may be found in nature. A full treatment of these patterns is beyond the scope of this book, however one more pattern deserves special mention here, the honeycomb.

Honeycomb

Perhaps as far as we can get from the disorder of foam and spaghetti (page 216) is the honeycomb. A honeycomb is a neat, cellular matrix organization of multiple elements. A honeycomb structure is usually imposed by some type of framework. These close-packed matrices are commonly based on a hexagonal array, as in bee and wasp nests; rectangles or squares, as in many manufactured products; or spirals, as in the seeds of a sunflower.

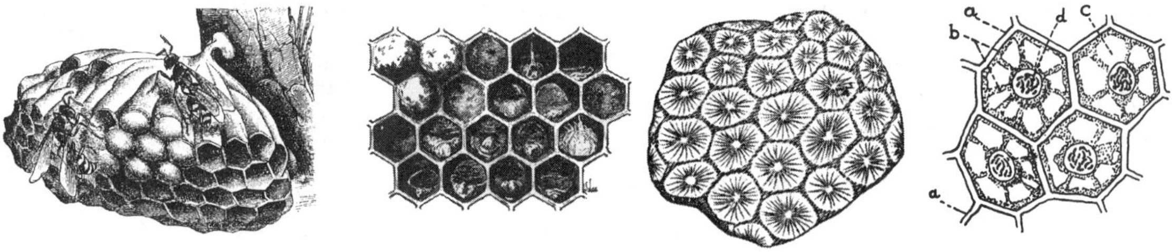

Fig.10.11 a-d Natural honeycomb structures found in a) paper wasp nests, b) honeycomb, 3) coral, 4) cells.

Although it is a 3-D object, a honeycomb is usually a 2-D organizational paradigm, as the hexagonal pattern doesn't extend in depth. While the pattern neatly and regularly expands vertically and horizontally, depth is accomplished only by adding more layers of honeycomb or by folding the 2-D array. In an actual honeycomb, additional combs are used to expand beyond a single plane.

In commercial products, we find honeycomb structures used in materials meant to span or fill spaces economically. Hollow core doors and furniture panels are often have a honeycomb center layer which provides strength, but is lightweight.

Many natural examples of honeycomb organization are found in the plant and animal kingdoms. Various insects lay their eggs honeycomb-style, where they are adhered side-by-side to some surface, such as a leaf or a plant stalk. The honeycomb pattern can come about as a result of close-packing spherical shapes, for instance groups of similarly-sized bubbles placed between two glass planes can form a honeycomb.

Tree

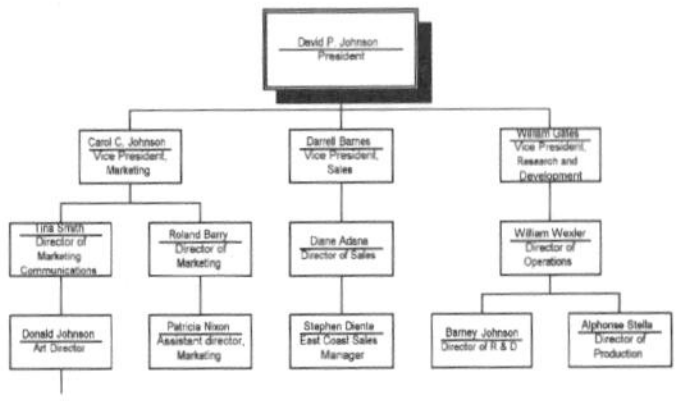

Fig. 10.12 Organizational charts, diagrams of familial relationships, and certain programming data structures are described as trees, for their internal branching.

The *Tree paradigm* as a *Multiple Object Relations paradigm* refers to the way that trees branch outward from a trunk. Branching is a means of connecting and relating many parts hierarchically. Some trees such as palms branch only at their tops, while others, like pines, have only minor branching from their sides. But the *Tree paradigm* relates particularly to the *deliquescent* trees, such as many oaks and the American

Fig. 10.13 A magnificent example of the once ubiquitous American Elm, *Ulmus americanus*. The species has in recent decades been deveas-tated by Dutch Elm Disease. A deliquescent tree, its repeated branching results in a thick crown of branches, and in the summer, leaves.

elms (*Ulmus americana*) that are distinguished by repeatedly dividing branches that form a thick crown of small branches and leaves around the tree.

In trees of this type, a single large trunk divides into increasingly larger numbers of branches. You can trace a route on the tree between any two leaves or branches on the tree. Between adjacent leaves, that path may only traverse one branch inward to a "Y" and back out on the next. A path between leaves on opposite sides of the tree, however, may require tracing inward as far as the trunk, and then back out on branches on the other side. The hierarchical structure of the tree means that you can take an action near the periphery, such as cutting off a single leaf, or you can cut off an increasingly larger number of leaves by making a cut increasingly closer to the trunk. You could sever them all from the ground by cutting the trunk itself.

This paradigm is a powerful means of structuring distribution of various types. A living tree, among other things, is a distribution system for water. Water is collected in a branch-structured root system and raised upward through the trunk, and distributed outward through the system of branches to the leaves. A similar structure is at work in our circulatory system, which is sometimes called a vascular tree. Having a tree-structured circulatory system allows a single pump, the heart, to pump blood through the entire body. Branching along the way divides the blood flow to serve different regions, the head, the abdomen, the legs, and so forth. It also allows control at various points along the way, for instance bleeding from a cut anywhere on the arm, hand, or fingers could be stopped by pressure closing arteries further up on the arm.

In a similar fashion, the plumbing for the water supply for a building begins with a main pipe at the base of the building that branches out to feed different floors and zones within the building. These pipes branch further to supply individual plumbing fixtures. Plumbing systems also have valves at various points along the way to shut off the water to an individual tap, a zone, or the entire building.

Trees are frequently applied in a more abstract manner. Many organizations structure their "chain of command" as a tree. The head of the organization, for example a president, a mayor, or a general, represents the trunk of the tree. Branches are drawn outward to the staff reporting to the head of the organization, and branches are drawn outward from these, in turn, to their reports. Tree structures are also widely used in computing, where the tree may represent connections between various data elements or program states. A tree may represent the organization of a Website, for instance, where the home page represents the trunk, branching off to the various Webpages accessed from there.

Herd

Many animals form groups, such as herds of cattle, schools of fish, flocks of birds, and swarms of bees. These entities are important perceptually, in seeing and thinking of a loose collection of similar objects or beings as an entity. These groups are important conceptually as well, in expanding our thinking about constructions and appreciating the dynamics of group efforts. In Western culture, there tends to be a strong bias toward individuality; we think of an individual as being important and complete. We need reminders that a group of creatures or people behaves differently from an individual and exhibits different capabilities. This is evident in crowded events, from the harmless "waves" that pass through an audience at a baseball game, to the potentially life-threatening anger or panic that can spread through a crowd at a political rally or other event. Beekeepers are likely more fully aware of the identity and importance of groups, since a hive of bees does not function as a collection of individuals.

A beehive is more appropriately thought of as a single living organism, with parts of that organism living in separate bodies. Individual bees are specialized much in the way our individual organs are specialized, and are not by themselves capable of the full range of behaviors necessary for survival (building a home, collecting food, reproducing). Other soci-

Collective nouns

In the *Herd paradigm*, we recognize groups as more than collections of individuals. Herds, schools, and flocks often exhibit a unique identity and character, with abilities and behaviors distinct from the individuals that make up the group. The importance of such groups is reflected in our language. There are special terms, called *collective nouns*, for such groups. Perhaps more impressive than the number of eskimo words for snow is the more than 200 collective nouns in the English language, such as:

an ***armada*** of warships
an ***army*** of caterpillars
a ***bale*** of turtles
a ***brood*** of hens
a ***class*** of students
a ***congress*** of baboons
a ***covey*** of quail
an ***exaltation*** of larks
a ***fleet*** of cars
a ***gaggle*** of geese
a ***host*** of sparrows
a ***mob*** of kangaroos
a ***pod*** of dolphins
a ***pride*** of lions
a ***sloth*** of bears
a ***staff*** of employees
a ***squadron*** of fighter jets
a ***warren*** of rabbits

Fig. 10.14 Herding behavior is exhibited by animals such as sheep and cattle. Their natural tendency to stay fairly close to other animals in the flock allows the ranchers to drive them as a group.

eties are also much more attuned to group dynamics. In Japan, for example, identity as a student in a school, worker in a company, company within a *keiretsu*, and so forth is usually given more importance than individual interests.

With respect to design, being strongly individually oriented can limit a designer's thinking. It is important to remember that many problems are solved not by a single designed object, but by several or many independent objects that work in concert with each other. As the metaphor *concert* in the previous sentence suggests, several musicians each playing different instruments and parts are necessary to play many pieces of music. Similarly, a building solution for a college or a hospital might call for a number of buildings that work together in various ways, rather than for a single building. And the design of most meals is enhanced by preparing several dishes with coordinated tastes, each served at their proper times. In fashion, designers often create an ensemble, including accessories that are intended to complement each other.

Formation

One of the most remarkable, and sometimes frightening, technological displays is fighter jets in formation. Traveling at hundreds of miles per hour, the planes fly only a few feet apart, arranged in a pattern such as a diamond or a cross. The *Formation paradigm* is characterized by groups of individual elements that are arranged into recognizable geometric patterns without the use of physical connections or frameworks. Formations can serve a number of useful purposes. For instance, the formation allows synergistic division of labor. In the case of the fighter jets, only the leader need be concerned with direction and navigation; this allows the followers to be more watchful of approaching threats. Another benefit of the formation is that it may provide greater protection to the individual. This arises through several factors. First, there is a perceptual effect on the observer,

Fig. 10.15 Jets flying in formation achieve a regular geometric relationship without a physical structure holding them in place. USAF Photo.

as the formation is perceived as a gestalt, a single, larger entity, that is often presumed to pose a greater threat than the smaller individuals. Second, there is the physical reality: The whole group can be expected to react to an attack on a single fighter. Third, attacking an individual within a group of similar entities can be confusing. Visually tracking a single anchovy is virtually impossible when it moves within a writhing school of thousands of fish in a tight ball formation.

Fig. 10.16 Geese, like fighter jets, are known for their formation flying, usually forming a V-like shape.

While an observer can see the pattern of a formation, participants within the formation can usually not perceive the pattern from their own positions within the formation. The formation therefore usually results from, and is maintained by, the cumulative effects of individual interpersonal positional preferences. For instance, army ants of the subfamily *Dorylinae* travel in a column formation that is maintained by each ant following a scent trail left by its predecessors, while maintaining a fixed distance from the ant in front of it. Among the other animals that move in formation are geese, ducks, pelicans, and cranes. These birds form distinctive V-shaped flight formations. Humans sometimes

Fig. 10.17 a, b When setting a table formally or semi-formally, silverware is placed on the table *in formation*, with a precise geometric relationship between the china and the silver. Chess pieces are also moved into a sequence of formations on the chessboard.

arrange their bodies into formations as well, as a Girl Scout or army troop might when marching in a parade. Similarly, formations are integral to the operation of a football team, as well as to the marching band that might perform for a halftime show. There are more subtle formations as well, for instance a line to buy movie tickets, or a gathering for a group photograph. While plants can't move in formation or move themselves into a formation, they often grow in geometric formations. Mushrooms sometimes grow in a circular formation known as a fairy ring. This occurs when a mushroom mycelium (spawn) sends out a radial network of underground tubular threads called hyphae. New mushrooms grow up from the ends of the hyphae, and the mycelium dies off, leaving just the fairy ring of new mushrooms. The process repeats year after year, with new growth forming an increasingly larger ring around the previous year's growth.

Objects are sometimes placed in formation as well: for instance, chairs are placed in formation in a lecture hall, creating sections and rows, and chess pieces are placed in formation on a chessboard. Dishes and silverware are placed in formation on a dinner table as well.

Cluster

Some things, like grapes growing on a vine, appear in closely-packed clusters. The *Cluster paradigm* is similar to the *Herd paradigm*, but the elements in clusters are more tightly held together than those in the herd. Some internal force is usually present binding the clusters, unlike herds. Among the forces that can cause clustering are surface tension, sticky substances, physical tensile connections (like the stems holding the grape clusters together), static, magnetism, and gravity. The arrangement of the individual elements in a cluster is typically not geometrically organized.

Fig. 10.18 Grapes are among the things grown and sold in clusters. Unlike herds, clusters are bound by an internal force, in this case, the stem.

Clustering is common where multiple objects are

involved because attractive forces of one type or another are often present. Clusters appear at the smallest and largest scales, from atomic particles and molecules, to galaxies, each of which can be considered a cluster. Among more terrestrial examples, tiny Styrofoam® balls spontaneously form clusters because of static. Similarly, when many bubbles are close enough to touch one another, surface tension causes them to form clusters; we call this *foam*. Magnetized steel balls also form clusters because they are attracted to each other by magnetism. The eggs of various creatures, including fish, amphibians, and insects, also form clusters; the eggs are encased in sticky substances that hold the clusters together.

Random Distribution and Even Distribution

One way for a group of things to be related to each other is for them to be randomly distributed over a plane or within a space. While this sounds simple and straightforward, there are often factors working against a true random distribution, such as the attractive forces that cause clustering.

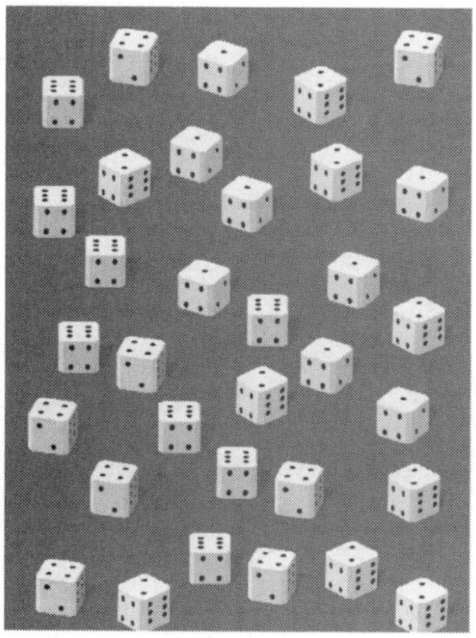

Fig. 10.19 a-c Throwing dice repeatedly produces a random distribution. Clumping clusters of doubles, 6's or other numbers are a normal part of a random distribution. Compare the random distribution pattern immediately below to the even distribution pattern below it.

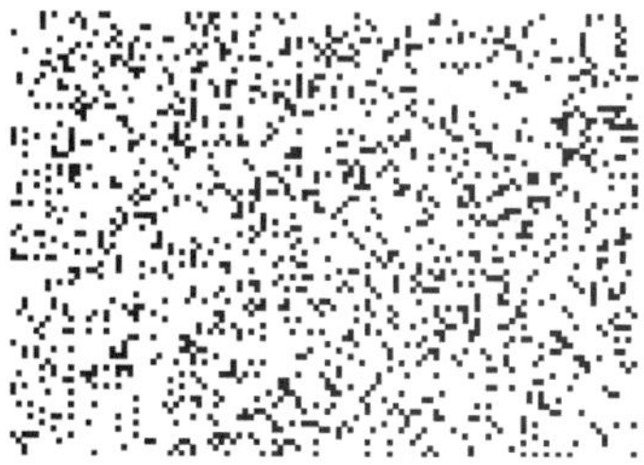

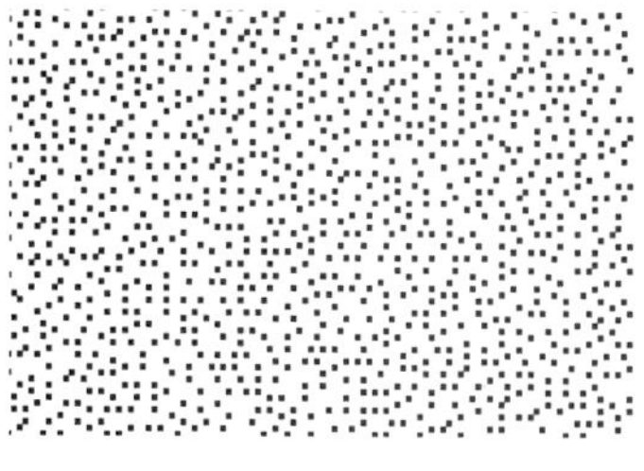

A random distribution is similar, but not identical to, an even distribution. In a truly random distribution, some clumping tends to occur. For instance, when you repeatedly roll dice and record the values, you might roll "doubles" several times in a row, whereas if the doubles were evenly distributed among the rolls, they would not appear sequentially. Computer programs can simulate a random distribution, as in illustration 10.19b right, compare it to the even distribution below it in 10.19c.

Many things that on casual inspection might look like a random distribution are, in fact, structured in various ways. A glance at the night sky might suggest that the stars are randomly distributed, whereas a view from faraway would reveal the structured form of the Milky Way galaxy. Even if stars had been evenly distributed within the galaxy, gravitational forces would have soon changed that distribution. Stars appearing close together, for example, might be pulled together by gravity, thus merging.

Sometimes random or even distribution is desirable and might be forced. A random distribution might be an initial goal in contests, for example, with a winning number under a bottle cap. Marketing and promotion firms like Einson Freeman Inc.[43] go to great lengths to ensure that the distribution of winning game pieces gives fair opportunities to all participants to win the game, but a simple random distribution might not be as fair as it initially sounds. A true random distribution of winners might result in some states having a cluster of winners while other states have none. Consequently, the strategy might be modified to distribute winning-capped bottles evenly among states, and randomly within each state. In chemical and food preparation, mixing is performed to ensure an even distribution. A random distribution of salt within a pastry might leave occasional salty clumps; mixing ensures an even distribution without such clumps.

Gradient Distribution

A gradient distribution is a change in the concentration of something from a dense to a sparse concentration. Gradients can be gradual and continuous, can sharply rise or fall or can continuously undulate. A person wearing perfume and standing in a room can create a gradient distribution of perfume molecules through a large space. As the air moves around, the scent diffuses through the space, becoming increasingly weaker the more distant it is from the source. Our olfactory systems are attuned to following gradients. Most people could find the source of the perfume, even blindfolded, by moving within the space and following a path through steadily heavier concentrations.

Distribution maps are an important tool for studying population trends. If you take a map of the United States and place a pin in the location of each McDonald's restaurant, for instance, you will see a gradient distribution, with heavy concentrations in metropolitan areas, and a thinning

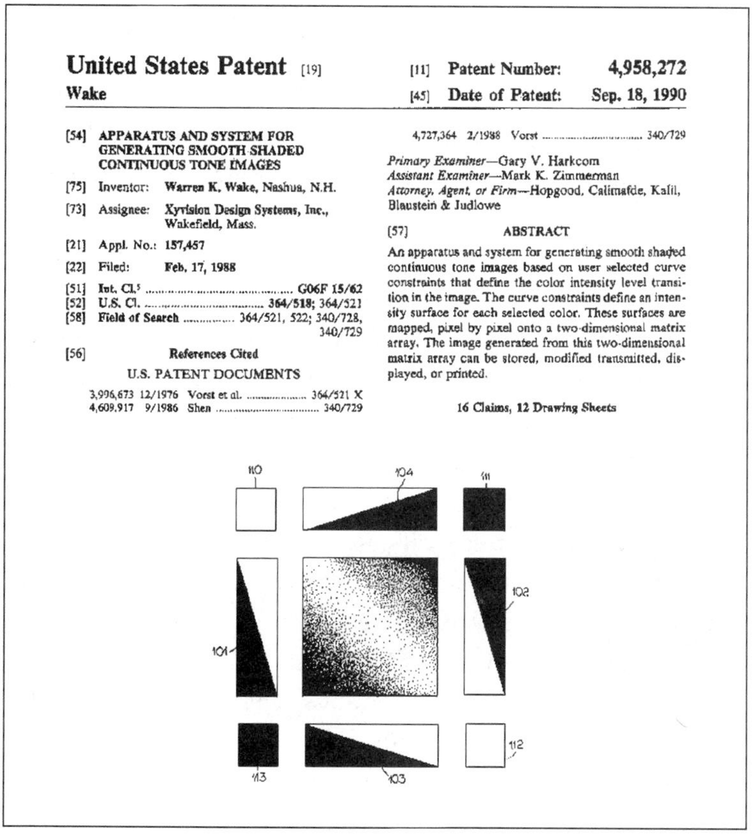

United States Patent [19]
Wake

[11] **Patent Number: 4,958,272**
[45] **Date of Patent: Sep. 18, 1990**

[54] **APPARATUS AND SYSTEM FOR GENERATING SMOOTH SHADED CONTINUOUS TONE IMAGES**

[75] Inventor: **Warren K. Wake**, Nashua, N.H.

[73] Assignee: **Xyvision Design Systems, Inc.**, Wakefield, Mass.

[21] Appl. No.: **157,457**

[22] Filed: **Feb. 17, 1988**

[51] Int. Cl.⁵ G06F 15/62
[52] U.S. Cl. 364/518; 364/521
[58] Field of Search 364/521, 522; 340/728, 340/729

[56] **References Cited**

U.S. PATENT DOCUMENTS

3,996,673 12/1976 Vorst et al. .... 364/521 X
4,609,917 9/1986 Shen 340/729
4,727,364 2/1988 Vorst 340/729

Primary Examiner—Gary V. Harkcom
Assistant Examiner—Mark K. Zimmerman
Attorney, Agent, or Firm—Hopgood, Calimafde, Kalil, Blaustein & Judlowe

[57] ABSTRACT

An apparatus and system for generating smooth shaded continuous tone images based on user selected curve constraints that define the color intensity level transition in the image. The curve constraints define an intensity surface for each selected color. These surfaces are mapped, pixel by pixel onto a two-dimensional matrix array. The image generated from this two-dimensional matrix array can be stored, modified transmitted, displayed, or printed.

16 Claims, 12 Drawing Sheets

Fig. 10.20 a-c Gradient distributions are useful in graphic arts, producing smooth color transitions over a area. The author employed the *Gradient Distribution paradigm* in the design of a software system to produce these vignettes like these.

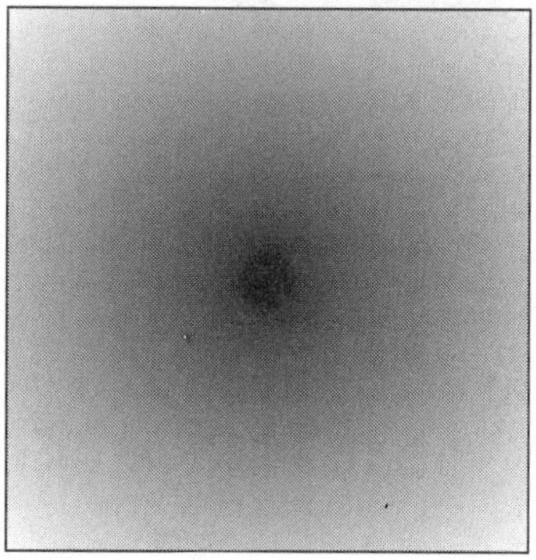

out with a move toward rural zones. The *Gradient distribution paradigm* is widely used in graphic design with color fields, called *vignettes* or *degradés*, that blend from one color to another. A patented software system developed by the author creates vignettes for use in graphic design. The software includes controls to vary the gradients between gradual and sharp transitions, and includes features of both random and even distributions to control the smoothness of the printed patterns.[44]

Most living things exist on gradient distributions at some level. Mold studies in a petrie dish, for instance, resemble distribution maps. Maps of fish in the ocean would also reflect gradient distributions around areas defined by denser concentrations around zones with good feeding conditions.

Spaghetti

Fig. 10.21 The *Spaghetti paradigm* indicates a relationship of multiple object that is characterized by a hopeless tangle, particularly of cordlike objects.

The *Spaghetti paradigm* implies things that are hopelessly intermixed and tangled. A can of worms suggests similar things, but with more negative connotations. Many situations in which we find things "organized" spaghetti-fashion are negative. For example, the term "spaghetti" is used pejoratively when it refers to a tangle of wires at the back of a computer. However some advantages to "spaghetti" do exist.

Boiled spaghetti in water behaves like a liquid. Cooked spaghetti can be poured, and when you place some in a bowl immediately, it tends to compactly fill the bowl, with little air space. When you remove spaghetti from the boiling water with a fork, the strands easily align with each other. Once the spaghetti drains, however, it behaves quite differently, in the fashion we usually associate with the word "spaghetti." If you look at a plate of drained spaghetti (no sauce), you'll see many air spaces between the strands. The individual strands are flexible, yet have both enough friction against other strands and enough resistance to bending to hold their curves. This protects these air spaces and also makes the plate of spaghetti cohesive, enabling it to be treated as a single object rather than as individual strands. A fork inserted in the plate can probably lift all of the spaghetti at once.

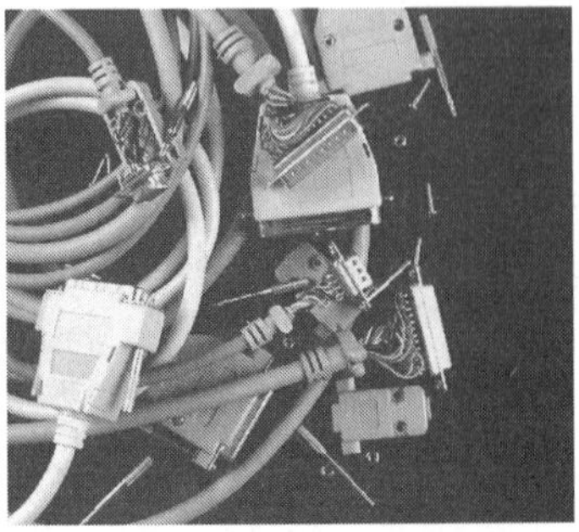

Fig. 10.22 Wires often enter the *Spaghetti paradigm*, although it becomes a problem when they do.

These principles are important in products like Fiberglas. Long thin glass fibers curled and intertwined with each other tend to hold airspaces within. This, combined with the poor conductivity of glass, makes Fiberglas an excellent insulator. The ability of the fibers to hold together is important here as well; without this property, individual strands would presumably slip and slide out of place, requiring some type of additional containment for the insulation. Numerous other similar products, often made of plastic fibers, are available and are also appreciated for their insulation value for such applications as clothing and sleeping bags, and for stuffing in toys and pillows. Cotton candy, composed of spun sugar-fibers, also employs the same paradigm, as do steel-wool pads.

Spaghetti's properties are employed in the natural world by various creatures when they make nests. Although we often speak of feathers, fibers, and sticks being woven together to make a nest, "woven" is often too generous a term. Nests made by mice, rats, and many birds employ the simpler spaghetti technique that gives their nests some degree of cohesion, plus insulation and softness.

Fig. 10.23 Many bird nests fit the *Spaghetti paradigm*. Weaving sticks, fibers and feathers through the nest helps to give it the strength to hold together against wind and rain.

Some special properties apply when a spaghettilike mass is pressed, fried, frozen, or glued together. Fiberglas embedded in plastic resin is an important construction material used in ship hulls and other recreational equipment, as well as some automotive body panels. The glass fibers provide great tensile strength in these products, while the plastic resin supplies rigidity. Tyvek® is a synthetic material somewhere between a plastic paper and a cloth that might be most familiar as tear-resistant envelopes. Tyvek is made from spun-plastic fibers, like plates of spaghetti pressed flat into sheets. Being formed from fibers gives the resultant sheet a paperlike flexibility. The long fibers of strong plastic make it tear resistant, while the small air spaces that are retained give it "breathability." Because the fibers themselves repel, and will not absorb, water, Tyvek makes an excellent moisture and vapor barrier, and is, consequently, widely used in construction as Homewrap™.

Fig.10.24 Tyvek Homewrap. Although it looks and is handled like a cloth, the secret to its strength and breathability is the *Spaghetti paradigm*. A spaghettilike mass of plastic microfibers is pressed into sheet form, yielding a material with properties of both paradigms.

Sets of Similar Objects

Sets of similar objects are usually assembled to address variations on a single task. Gathering the objects in a set reveals the complementary nature of the set. In a socket-wrench set, for example, each socket functions identically but is a different size. The set is more valuable than the individual sockets because with the set in hand, any size nut or bolt can be tightened. The paradigm would not apply if the sockets were identical; there would be no meaning to the

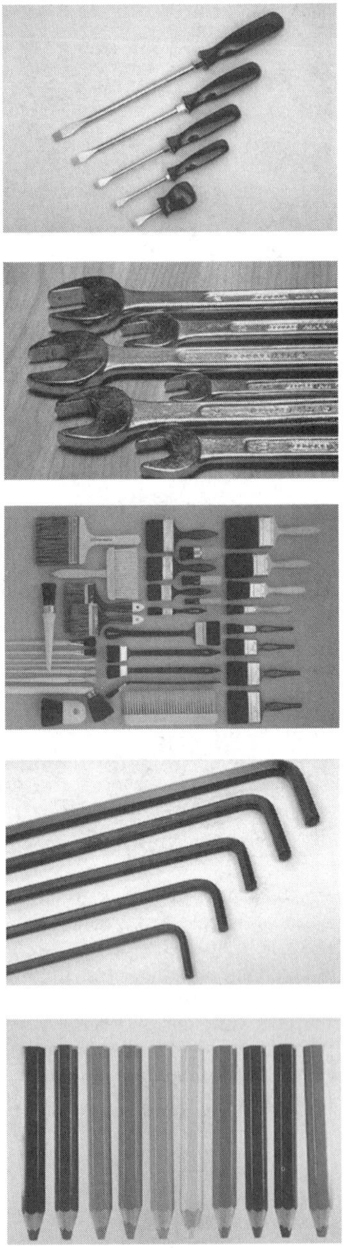

Fig. 10.25 a-e The *Sets of Similar Objects paradigm* is common in the design of tools and instruments. Individual members of the sets may vary by size, color, or other attribute.

set, no complementarity between the identical sockets, and no good reason for having 20 sockets versus one. This paradigm is widely employed in tools, including wrenches, screwdrivers, and chisels.

Many parameters other than size can be varied with a set; for instance, color, as in a set of color-sample cards from a paint store. Set members can vary by weight, as in a set of brass weights used on a balance scale. They can also vary by radius, as in a set of gouges used in turning wood on a lathe. A set of kitchen knives varies by purpose, with size, shape, and thickness variations to accommodate the widely different, food-preparation cutting tasks ranging from carving a roast, to filleting a fish, to slicing a tomato.

In the natural world there are many situations in which a grouping of similar living things varies by such attributes as size and ripeness, like apples on a tree. These would not be called sets, though. There is little complementarity between the ripe and unripe apples. The social insects, however, including many species of bees, wasps, ants, and termites, depend upon a setlike complement of specialized creatures to function properly. The different castes of insects—the workers, drones, and queens—are similar (they are all the same species), yet they vary dramatically by their functions and their equipment to perform these functions. The queen is the only sexually developed female. The drones are males that serve only to fertilize the queen and have no stingers. The workers are sexually undeveloped females and have stingers. Social insects can include more subdivisions, such as soldiers, a larger variant of workers. Some species of ants also produce winged males that fly into the air to mate with new queens, which then go off to start new colonies.

Sets of Dissimilar Objects

Dissimilar objects are assembled into sets when their use is associated by a common purpose, either in combination with each other, or as mutually exclusive alternatives. Chess pieces, for example, vary by color and shape, yet the entire set is required to play the game. Many vacuum cleaners, in contrast, come with a set of dissimilar attachments, which can be used only one at a time.

The *Sets of Dissimilar Objects paradigm* is widely employed in various disciplines. In woodworking, for example, the contents of a woodshop fits the paradigm. A set of power tools reflects division by various operations (sawing, routing, sanding, etc.), and might imply sequence as well (first cut, then plane, then sand, etc.). The paradigm is also evident at a smaller scale within the shop, for instance, the hand tools within the toolbox, or the set of router bits. In the kitchen, the paradigm is evident in the division of basic functions into different appliances, such as the toaster, the refrigerator, the dishwasher, and the sink. The paradigm is also at work in collections of gadgets and implements in a drawer, spices on a shelf, and ingredients in a pantry.

Sets of dissimilar objects are vulnerable to loss: a single card lost from a deck or a single chess piece missing ruins the set. Consequently, designers look for alternatives to this paradigm when possible. For example, a multipurpose screwdriver might employ a set of dissimilar objects in the form of four interchangeable bits. An individual bit might easily be lost, however, so various designs attempt to accomplish a variety of functions without the separate parts. Examples of these, such as the *Swiss Army Knife paradigm*, are discussed in Chapter 12, *Multi Function Objects*.

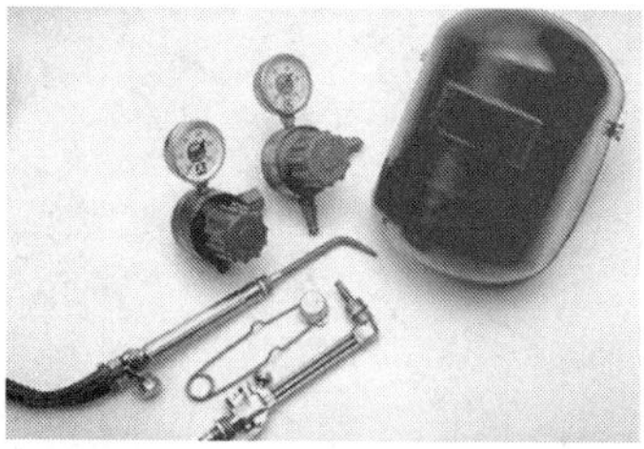

Fig. 10.26 a-d In the *Sets of Dissimilar Objects paradigm*, dissimilar objects are brought together to accommodate a group of tasks that are meaningfully associated, as for a vocation such as welding or dentistry, or a task, such as carving or cleaning. When these sets are neatly packaged, we call them kits.

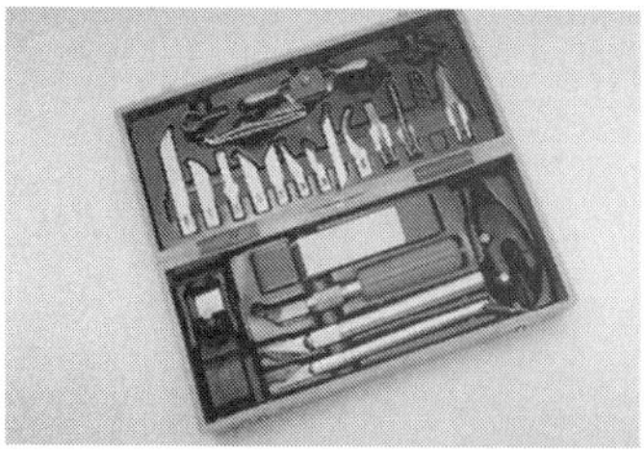

Kits

Kits are variations on the *Sets of Dissimilar Objects paradigm*. A kit implies a collection of tools or other implements for a specific purpose that is personal, packaged, organized, and portable.[45] The earliest-known kits were assembled some two million years ago, by *Homo habilis*,

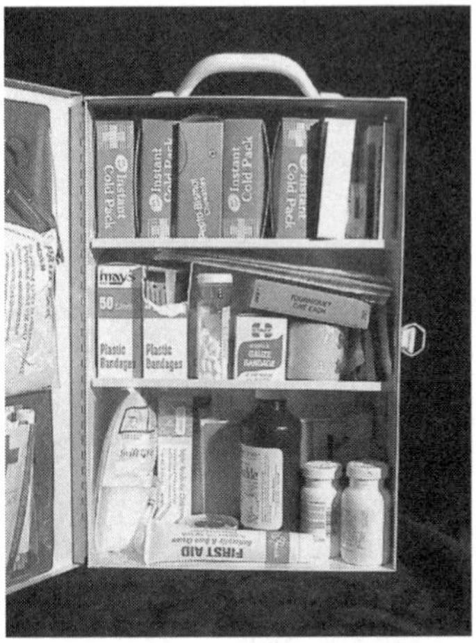

Fig. 10.27 First aid kit. The *Kit paradigm* implies more portability, plus independance or self-sufficiency, than the *Sets of Dissimilar Objects paradigm*. A first aid kit, for instance, is ideally equipped to handle all of the emergencies anticipated in its vicinity.

early human ancestors, living in the Olduvai Gorge in Tanzania[46] The ability of these creatures to assemble and carry kits is taken as strong evidence of their intelligence. Preparation of the kit indicates the cognitive ability to fashion tools and use them to expand their abilities. Furthermore, it also implies the foresight to plan ahead, anticipating the items that will be necessary in future tasks and placing these in a kit.

Because of these aspects, kits per se are used only by humans. The term is used metaphorically, however, to describe the ways certain creatures and natural processes work. Within a cell, for instance, the process of DNA replication is sometimes described as a kit of parts. These include the DNA building blocks *adenine, cytosine, guanine,* and *thymine*, and various active molecules like *messenger RNA* and *transfer RNA*. This entire "kit" of parts must be present within a cell to perform the functions necessary in transcribing and assembling the information encoded by the DNA and, in turn, cell division, and the basis of life itself.

Some kits, such as first-aid kits, can be purchased preassembled. Most kits, however, are assembled by those who will use them, such as shaving or toiletry kits. Kits are organized around a specific purpose, which is often a trade. Consequently, a doctor, a plumber, or a telephone-repair person will have a kit prepared for working at a remote site. A kit reflects the skills and abilities of the person assembling it, as well as the range of tasks anticipated in the course of the work.

Questions

1) Keeping an open mind, survey your personal belongings and count the kits you have prepared for use day-to-day. Did you include the contents of your wallet? Your backpack? The glove compartment of your car? Why or why not?

2) Collective nouns are words that indicate groupings, for instance, a "pride of lions," or a "pod of whales." Find the terms for groups of pheasants, weapons, clothes, buildings, and librarians. Which of the *Multiple Object Relations paradigms* do each of these collective nouns suggest?

3) Look in back of a standard PC-compatible computer and a component stereo to observe the "electronic spaghetti" that the wires can form. Devise three alternative strategies to interconnect these devices without the spaghetti.

4) Find a vacuum cleaner with attachments. Observe what if any accommodations there are in its design for storing the attachments. Design and sketch three alternatives that will make the attachments easy to access, yet difficult to lose.

11

Objects Within Objects

The *Objects Within Objects paradigms* involve things that have other things inside them, as a mother pregnant with a child. "Objects within objects" implies that the "mother object" acts like a container but is important in its own right as well; the "mother object" is not merely a case or a coating for the "child object."

One motivation for placing objects within objects is protection. We protect personal equipment, for instance a car, by parking it within a larger piece of personal equipment, a garage. Other motivations include convenience, minimizing space requirements, and avoiding loss of small parts. These benefits are evident in such applications as a nested screwdriver set that can be handled as a single unit by nesting the smaller screwdriver inside the larger.

Some examples of objects within objects have a single object within a larger object; others continue ad infinitum with a smaller object inside the largest, and progressively smaller and smaller objects within, as with Russian dolls (see the *Russian Dolls Paradigm* later in this chapter).

Pregnancy

Fig. 11.1 Human pregnancy instantly conveys the *objects within similar objects* concept. It is perhaps the most significant symbol of human existence. Consequently images of pregnancy are potent elements in artworks, such as Jacob Epstein's (1880–1959) sculpture "Genesis."

The most profound image of the Objects Within Objects Paradigms, and perhaps the most significant symbol of human existence, is the image of human pregnancy. The symbol most powerfully combines the image of one and the idea of two. While there is a single figure, there are two lives, two heartbeats. In a glance the image implies and triggers a wide range of human emotions, such as the love of spouse, the love of child, and the importance of life. Further, it clearly conveys the central concept of the *Pregnancy paradigm*: Objects Within Similar Objects. This concept isn't called to mind nearly so vividly with animals such as reptiles and birds, because these lay eggs. The eggs, of course, bear little resemblance, as is, to the mother.

We find this paradigm used in design somewhat differently from its role in nature. Rather than as a means of reproduction, it is often employed as a means of storing a smaller version of an object within a larger one. For example, a large ship might carry small boats on board for emergency use. A motor home was designed with a small, detachable car embedded in the rear. So, when the motor home parked, the small car was available for shopping and running errands without the need to move the larger and less efficient vehicle. Similarly, the Japanese *wakizashi* sword, sometimes worn by the Samurai, came with a smaller knife tucked into the side.

Fig. 11.2 Employing the *Pregnancy paradigm* concept of object within similar object, a large ship, the *USS Peleliu*, houses a smaller air-cushioned landing craft within. Navy Photo.

Russian Dolls

When you first see an assembled Russian-doll set, you experience a sense of wonder as the first doll is opened and the second doll is removed from it. The *Pregnancy paradigm* then comes into play. When the third doll is exposed, however, you realize that this is not the *Pregnancy paradigm.* This paradigm shift causes a ticklish and wonderful feeling, and produces a sudden urge to open the next doll, then the next.

Fig. 11.3 a, b *The Russian Dolls Paradigm*, like a recursive example of the Pregnancy paradigm, each doll opened reveals a similar smaller doll inside.

The *Russian Dolls paradigm* extends on the *Pregnancy paradigm* in a recursive fashion. Russian dolls relationship is *object within similar object within similar object.* If not for manufacturing limitations, you might expect to continue finding ever smaller Russian dolls as you keep opening dolls, until you reach microscopic sizes.

The *Russian Dolls paradigm* has been applied to a wide variety of objects. One such application that capitalizes on the wonderful feeling associated with discovering the Russian dolls, is a technique sometimes used in Japanese

Fig. 11.4 a, b Onions are a natural example of the *Russian Dolls paradigm.* As each layer of the onion is peeled off, a smaller onion is revealed within.

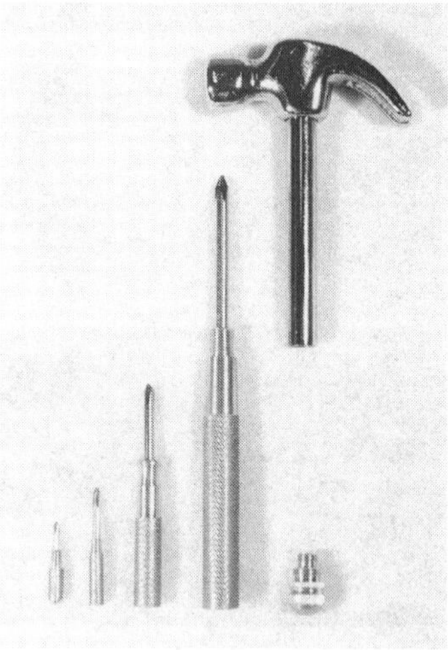

Fig. 11.5 a) A set of screwdrivers based on the *Russian Dolls Paradigm*, that fits within, and becomes, the handle of the hammer. b) A set of nesting colanders. c) Northwest Coast Stacking Tables, by Scott Schmidt. Dean Powell Photo.

gift-wrapping. One may purchase a set of nesting cardboard boxes. Something small, like a piece of jewelry, can be placed in the smallest box. The box is wrapped, then inserted into the next larger box, which, in turn, is wrapped. This is continued until the largest box is wrapped. The recipient unwraps the package, only to find another wrapped package inside, and continues opening packages until the smallest box is reached. The joy of this is presumably the extension of the process of opening presents, the wonder at where it will end, combined with the pleasure of experiencing the *Russian Dolls paradigm*.

A popular, practical application of the *Russian Dolls paradigm* is a set of nested screwdrivers. You unscrew a cap on the end of the largest screwdriver and pull out a smaller screwdriver from within that screwdriver's handle. Inside the smaller screwdriver is yet another screwdriver. This is a good use of the paradigm, since screwdrivers of various sizes are required to accommodate the range of screw sizes, and since, nested like Russian dolls, they take up less space and are easily kept together as a set.

Furniture is another area of design in which the *Russian Dolls paradigm* has been applied. A set of side tables nests to take up a minimum of space when stored nested, yet come apart to provide tables for a several people on which to rest their drinks or plates. Shaker boxes are manufactured in graduated sizes; they are enjoyed both as nesting containers and as examples of fine craftsmanship. Measuring cups and spoons sometimes come in graduated sizes as well, and might employ the paradigm, too. The *Russian Dolls paradigm* also appears in science fiction, religion, and fantasy, with descriptions of worlds within worlds, in concentric layers.

In the natural world, a clear parallel is the onion. Peeling off a layer of the onion reveals a second onion within the first, and another inside that. Similarly, pearls are formed as successive layers of *nacre* are deposited on an impurity, such as a piece of sand. Consequently, each pearl has a successive line of smaller similar pearls inside it. This is true of "cave pearls" as well. These spherical mineral balls form in pools when constant water motion prevents stalagmites from forming. Instead, minerals accrete in layers on a small piece of foreign matter, resulting in a globe of concentric layers of calcite.

Even closer to the *Russian Dolls paradigm* image is the situation, "Big fish eats little fish." Indeed, a fish can eat another fish whole that has done likewise to an even smaller one. In the sense of joy and wonder at recognizing the *Russian Dolls paradigm*, there is something that lends itself to humor. Consequently, many cartoons have been made wherein a small fish is eaten by a big fish, which, in turn, is eaten by a larger fish. In one of these, the fisherman pulls up a huge fish on his line, but it then slips off, back into the water, to reveal a smaller fish still on the line. It, too, slips off to reveal yet a smaller fish. The fisherman invariably is left with only the tiniest fish.

Peas in a Pod

The *Peas in a Pod paradigm* represents the *similar-objects-within-object* concept. This is similar in some ways to the *Sets*

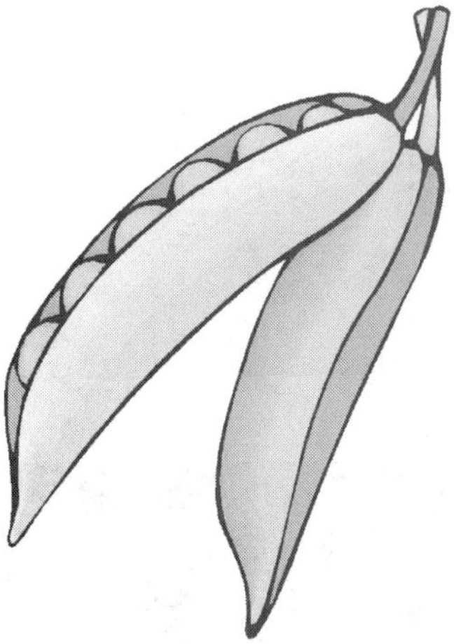

Fig. 11.6 The *Peas in a Pod paradigm* indicates multiple similar things within something else that is not merely a container. In the pea pod example, a sugar snap pea is a good example, as the pod is edible and is as important a part of this vegetable as the peas within.

Fig. 11.7 Like peas in a pod, these fighter planes sit in the hanger of the aircraft carrier *USS Enterprise*. Navy photo.

of Similar Objects paradigm described in Chapter 10, but with the *Peas in a Pod paradigm,* like the *Pregnancy paradigm,* the "mother object" is more significant, not merely a case or holder.

The term "Like two peas in a pod" means "virtually identical" and, perhaps, "raised together." The peas-in-a-pod arrangement is common in the natural world as a sort of plural of the *Pregnancy paradigm.* Multiple similar puppies, kittens, or turtle eggs are contained side by side within their mothers. Similarly, many kinds of fruit, such as pomegranates or papayas, contain seeds grouped closely side by side.

Many weapons systems are based on the *Peas in a Pod paradigm.* Guns and rifles are usually designed to hold more than one bullet in a clip or some other structure. Similarly, submarines carry many torpedoes side by side. Mechanical pencils frequently employ this paradigm, having an internal cylinder holding spare leads that can be fed through the barrel of the pencil.

Fig. 11.8 A desktop computer system. The computer is most easily understood as a system composed of subsystems, including sound, storage, CD-ROM, and graphics. Most computer repairs aim to determine the malfunctioning subsystem, such as the CD-ROM, and repair consists of replacing that whole unit.

Systems and Subsystems

The *Systems and Subsystems paradigm* can be described as *systems conceived of and decomposible into a finite number of specialized, meaningful parts.* We use this paradigm in many ways as a tool for managing complex systems. When dealing with a car problem, for instance, we try to determine if the problem is with the exhaust system, the electrical system, or the cooling system. Having determined the problem is with the exhaust system, we can narrow down the problem even further, determining the muffler to be the problem, and replace that part.

This paradigm frames how complex systems are designed, built, repaired, and taken apart. This applies to buildings, stereos, computers, cars, battleships, large software programs, and telephone systems, to name a few applications. A single individual rarely completely understands complex devices like these. Even a skilled auto mechanic, for instance, is not likely trained in the inner workings of the computer-controlled igni-

Fig. 11.9 a, b Major systems such as battleships are too complex to be fully understood or operated by an individual. Their operation and maintenance heavily depends upon a functional breakdown into systems and subsystems. Crews are trained in the operation and maintenance of these subsystems and the requirements for communicating with other subsystems. Navy photos.

tion, nor in the chemical processes at work in the catalytic converter. And no single person can even pilot, let alone understand, a device with the complexity of a battleship.

To manage this complexity, you limit your concerns to a whole at a particular level, and the parts that make up that whole. For example, someone repairing a computer should only be concerned with the computer as a whole, and the subsystems (processor, memory, hard drive, CD-ROM, modem) that make up that whole. If the CD-ROM is determined to be faulty, that subsystem should be removed and replaced without trying to repair the CD-ROM. The CD-ROM can be returned to its manufacturer, however. To the technician who receives it, the CD-ROM is the whole, and it is, in turn, made of its own subsystems (motor, door, circuitry, cache).

Biological systems are usually viewed and dealt with in the same way. The human body, for instance, can be regarded as a whole made of subsystems, including the circulatory system, immune system, digestive system, nervous system, reproductive system, the skeleton, and the organs. A general practitioner usually reviews the health of a patient only down to this subsystem level. If the doctor determines that a patient has a heart problem, the patient will be referred to a cardiologist. To the cardiologist, the heart is the whole, and within that whole are subsystems for analysis and possible therapy, including the muscle of the heart itself, cardiac rhythm, valves, arteries connecting to the heart, and so forth.

This paradigm can be applied universally, in a most literal sense, as can be seen in the wonderful 1968 film *Powers of Ten* by designers Charles and Ray Eames. Starting at one square meter of a picnic, the camera moves outward ten times farther away every ten seconds to reveal the park as a whole, then the city, the state, the continent, and the planet, and so forth, to the edges of the universe. The process is then repeated in the other direction looking at increasingly smaller wholes, to the atomic level. Many scientists devote their entire careers to concerns at specific points on this spectrum, for instance, those concerned with the universe as the whole, those concerned with earth sciences or ecology, and those concerned primarily with the atom and its subparticles.

An opposing view, however, also deserves mention. A holistic or ecological view of biology emphasizes the whole and the system in favor of a mechanistic breakdown into parts or subsystems. This approach maintains that issues such as liver disease and its treatment affect the health of the whole person, and so should not be considered separately. As author Fritjof Capra points out, "Biological form is more than shape, more than a static configuration of components in a whole. There is a continual flux of matter through a living organism, while its form is maintained. There is development, and there is evolution."[47]

Fig. 11.10 Self consumption as an image or concept is instantly understood and humorous, yet it is thought-provoking and paradoxical. The mind fights with this image, what if the dog catches its tail? What if a creature consumes itself, will it become nourished? Or will it disappear?

Self-Consumption

In this chapter we are concerned with the various ways an object can be inside another. It might be simply that one object in inside another, as in the case of pregnancy, or the containment may be recursive, as in the case of the Russian dolls. In this third category, the *Self-Consumption paradigm,* we consider how an object can be within *itself.*

There are a number of ancient tales about creatures consuming their own flesh. The Roman personification of eternity, *Aeternitas*, is symbolized by a worm or serpent biting its own tail. This image comes to mind when you sees a dog chasing and biting its own tail. The fascination with the paradigm stems from its apparent impossibility. The image is puzzling and paradoxical because a creature consuming its own flesh should at once be nourished, thus get stronger and bigger, yet at the same time, disappear, as the consumed portions pass down its throat.

Fig. 11.11 While myths of self consumption abound, one would be hard-pressed to find actual examples of self consumption in the animal world, although dogs and other animal will occasionally chase or bite their tails. One often misunderstood action, suggestive of self consumption, is the behavior of many animals which eat their placentas after giving birth.

Yet we employ this paradigm when we fold a pair of socks into itself. The neck is opened, and the body of the sock is forced backward through the throat of the sock. The paradigm is put to good use in a number of lightweight nylon jackets too. The pocket is inverted, and the jacket is progressively forced into the mouth of the inverted pocket. When the jacket is entirely contained in the pocket, the pocket flap is folded over and snapped, making a neat, compact bundle.

A more abstract application of the paradigm is found in computer programming. A *recursive program* is one that invokes itself within the body of the program. A sorting program we might call *Sort(List)* for example, can be designed to sort a list of records. When the program reaches a branch, requiring sorting group (A) and group (B), the code comprising *Sort(List)* may include instructions to *Sort(List A)* and *Sort(List B)*. By these simple instructions, *Program Sort(List)* has self-consumed; it has effectively made two complete copies of its instructions within itself.

One of the naturally occurring applications of this paradigm is the eating behavior of the amoeba. This single-celled creature, having neither a mouth nor a digestive tract, nonetheless finds a way to eat, consuming other creatures. The amoeba extends its body around the other creature, so the prey rests in a depression in the amoeba's side. The depression moves farther inside the amoeba, forming a pouch as the outer surfaces begin to close. The amoeba then closes off the pouch and rejoins its surface on the far side of the creature. As the far side rejoins, the creature is left in an inverted bubble, or food vacuole, made of what was had been the amoeba's outer skin.

Fig. 11.12 Despite the apparent paradox, the *Self Consumption paradigm* is employed practically in the design of a number of products, such as this jacket which folds into its own pocket.

Fig. 11.13 A reversible jacket. Either way it is worn, there is another jacket within the first.

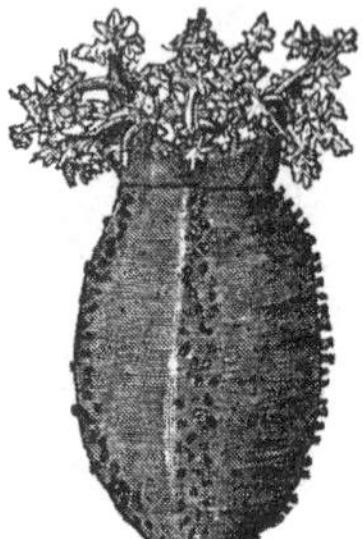

Fig. 11.14 Sea cucumber. When threatened, this creature turns itself inside out, ejecting its entire digestive system, which it later regrows.

Reversible Jacket

A reversible jacket can be taken off, turned inside out, and put back on, providing substantially different qualities from its reversed self. In effect, a second jacket resides on the inner surface of the first jacket. Thus, a single jacket can have dual personalities that might not otherwise be simultaneously possible, such as being both light and dark, or combining water repellence with fuzziness. The reversible jacket manifests the principle that the inside can be every bit as important as the outside, and the relationship between the "inner object" and the "outer object" can be reversible.

While many things can be turned inside out, revealing an inner surface to the outside, the *Reversible Jacket Paradigm* represents those things having a meaningful function associated with both states. Numerous clothing articles, including hats, gloves, and sweaters, are made this way, particularly for hunting, for which it is often desirable to have both a blaze-orange and a green-camouflage surface.

Surprisingly enough, there are natural forms of this paradigm as well, with creatures exploiting the ability to turn themselves inside out. Many of the 1,100 species of sea cucumber, which are marine animals of the class *Holothuroidea* of the phylum *Echinodermata*, can eject their entire digestive systems when stressed or threatened. Fortunately for them, they are able to regrow new guts within a few weeks. This is apparently a defense mechanism. The intestines might serve as a decoy; an attacking fish or other predator will be satisfied enough with a lunch of the sea cucumber's innards to leave the tough outer skin behind. The process might also serve to release the cucumber's natural toxins, which can confuse or irritate fish.

Questions

1) Think of or design a situation where the *Self-Consumption paradigm* can be usefully employed in the design of furniture.

2) Identify two or more examples of buildings that have smaller buildings inside them. Which paradigm or paradigms do these follow? List five reasons why a building might be built inside another.

3) Design three different types of suitcases, each based on a different *Objects Within Objects paradigm*. What purposes are facilitated by employing the paradigms?

4) Devices that employ the *Pregnancy paradigm* usually enclose something within an unused space. For instance, a survival knife might contain a first aid kit within its handle. Look at the things around you and find five things, other than handles, that could be manufactured with internal spaces to accommodate the *Pregnancy paradigm*.

12

Multi-Function Objects

Some objects perform a number of different functions depending on how they're used. To use an object for a second or third function, we might have to turn it around and use the other side, as we do with a claw hammer or pencil. With other multi-function objects, we fold out a different part to change the device, as we do with a Swiss Army knife. With still other objects, we might have to use the device in a different way to achieve a different function, as we do when we attach a hose to the blower rather than suction end of a vacuum cleaner.

Multi-functionality is certainly something humans seem to enjoy. Our hands and bodies exhibit this propensity. We pride ourselves on the versatility of our hands, and make art of the versatility of our bodies, as we do with dance.

Consequently, it is not surprising, perhaps, that many people have a strong fascination with and attraction to multi-function objects. Swiss Army knives and multi-function tools, for instance, have long been popular gift items and collectibles.

Part of the beauty and appeal of multi-function objects is the realization that we have acquired something that serves a wide range of functions, yet we have to pay for, house, keep track of, and maintain only a single object. Of these, housing, or space requirement, is often the greatest motivating factor for buying a multi-function object. Swiss Army knives and similar devices are often sold as a "A toolbox that fits in the palm of your hand."

Knife

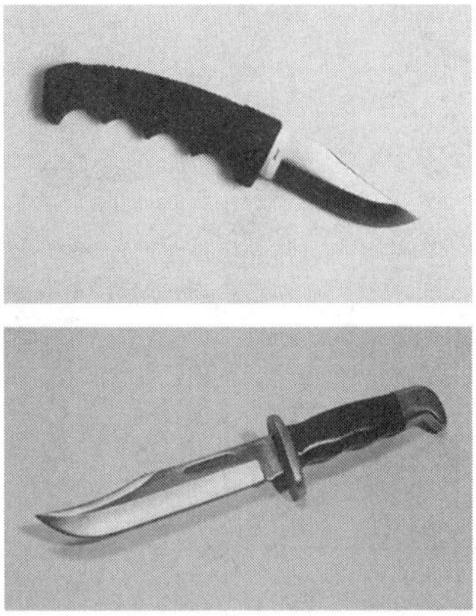

Fig. 12.1 a, b Camping, pocket, and kitchen knives are all by nature multi function tools, in the sense that we perform various functions by using the same tool in different ways.

The most basic tool for camping, survival, and food preparation is a knife. This is not because cutting tasks are so universal, but rather because a knife, in the hands of a skilled user, is a multi-function tool. A knife can be used to puncture, cut, scrape, carve, gouge, slice, fillet, pry, squash, ream, burnish, sharpen, and so forth.

The *Knife paradigm* reminds us that many objects can perform multiple functions as a result of the user's skill and knowledge, rather than because of designed-in features. This realization might have been the key to the development of our early ancestors, as rocks became the first multi-function tools. With practice, our ancestors mastered using rocks for cracking open bones, pounding, grinding, opening nuts, and as projectile weapons. In Jamie Uys's 1980 comedy *The Gods Must Be Crazy*, this theme is playfully explored as a Coke® bottle, dropped from a plane, lands in a remote African village. As the natives discover many uses for this clear, hard device (good for pounding root pulp, whistling into, etc.), they take it to be a gift from the gods.

Claw Hammer

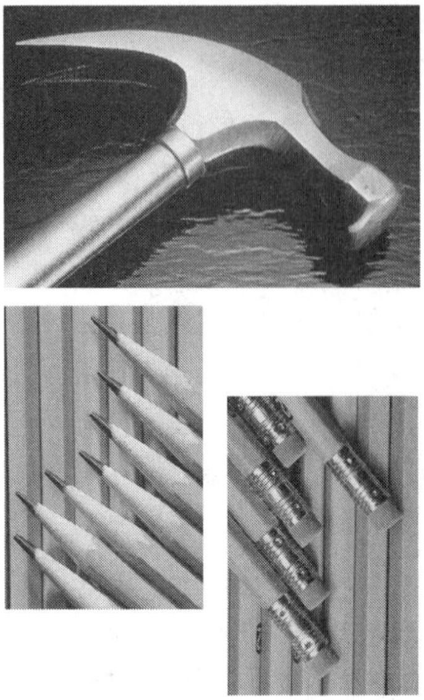

Fig. 12.2 a-c Claw hammers and pencils similarly have no moving parts, and pair complementary opposite functions opposite each other.

After the knife, the next simplest multi-function object is the claw hammer. The multi-functionality here is built into the name. At one end is the hammer, for driving nails. Turn the hammer around and there's another tool, the claw, for removing nails. Devices fitting this paradigm *have two complementary or opposite functions, and no moving parts.* Though the hammer can be used to open walnuts and the claw can be used to pry open a paint can, the essence of the tool is bi-functionality: pairing two opposite functions on a single tool (hammer nails/remove nails). The claw hammer and other similar devices accomplish their multi-functionality without the need to reconfigure the object or to add or remove parts. Such objects can be turned around, used sideways, or held upside down in order to achieve their different functions.

Other devices fitting the paradigm include the standard wooden pencil, which also serves two opposite purposes. One end is used to write, and the other is used to erase. Other examples include the "spork," a combination spoon/fork, and combination can openers/bottle-cap lifters.

Bicycle Wrench

A simple bicycle wrench is a stamped piece of metal with no moving parts, which has several hexagonal holes to accommodate nuts of various sizes and a sharpened point that can be used as a screwdriver. Numerous tools fit the *Bicycle Wrench paradigm*, some as extensions of the *Knife* or *Claw Hammer paradigms*. Some knives, for instance, have been designed with various cutouts, notches, and roughened areas to serve as bottle and cap lifters, wire strippers, and files. Similarly, hammers have been designed with screwdrivers and other functions facilitated by notches and extensions onto the typical claw-hammer form.

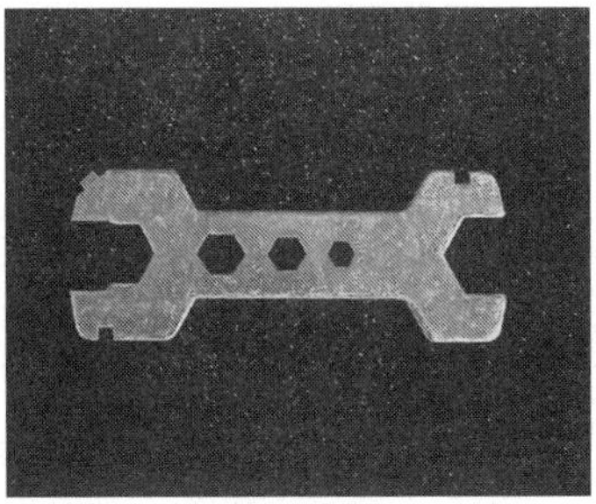

Fig. 12.3 A flat bicycle wrench. The *Bicycle Wrench paradigm* provides functions through cutouts, notches and sharpened surfaces. Devices utilizing this paradigm require no moving parts.

Fig. 12.4 A multi-purpose tool based on the *Bicycle Wrench paradigm*, designed to fit in a wallet.

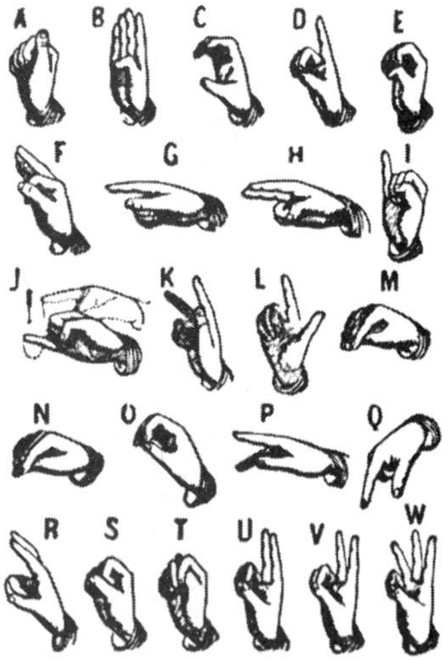

Fig. 12.5 American Sign Language for the deaf. There are few things one could do with the hands that would more profoundly convey their versatility, than to speak with them.

Hand

The hand is, perhaps, the quintessential multi-purpose tool. It is certainly the first one we become aware of, and is always the most readily accessible. We use our hands in many ways: delicately for sewing, writing, or performing surgery; and coarsely for boxing, rowing, and carrying groceries. We use our hands to grip, to throw and catch, to caress, to hit, to scratch, and even to convey words and concepts through their configuration, as when we point or gesture with them or speak in sign language.

Many of the abilities of the hand arise from changing the configuration of the hand, for instance by clenching a fist to hit something, or cupping the hand to hold water. We can further multiply the functions the hand can perform by using a given configuration of the hand in different ways. For example, a flat, open hand may be used to flatten a pizza dough, to wave, or to clap.

There are presently no near-equivalents to the hand among manufactured devices, but that may change in the near future. Much research in robotics has been applied toward developing robotic hands. This is not merely motivated by the desire to make robots humanlike; it is primarily the recognition that the hand is a wonderfully versatile device for physically interacting with the world.

Fig. 12.6 Shop type vacuums have two holes. When turned on, there is simultaneously vacuum at one hole, and pressure at the other. Whether this appliance functions as a vacuum or a blower depends on how you attach the hose.

Vacuum Cleaner

As a *Multi-Function Object paradigm,* the vacuum cleaner refers to those vacuum cleaners in which the hose is attached on one side of the machine for suction, and on the other side for blowing. The blowing side is useful, for instance, to blow dust out of keyboards. Because the vacuum cleaner is creating suction, the expelled compressed air is waste. But we need only reverse our viewpoint to see this device as an air compressor that produces vacuum as a waste product. This calls to mind a couple of expressions... "One man's ceiling is another man's floor" and "One man's trash is another man's treasure."

In many such situations, we can reverse our ideas about input and output or product and byproduct, and thus realize a second or third function. Making use of or minimizing byproducts or byproduct energy are keys to the efficiency of a system. When an automobile engine produces power, for example, it also produces exhaust and heat as byproducts. So an engine can also be viewed as an exhaust/pressure generator or a heat generator. While these are usually not the best reasons for running an automobile engine, the change of viewpoint can help us to perceive opportunities. Thus, the "waste" heat is readily applied to wintertime heating of the car interior, and occasionally even for cooking. The waste exhaust is used to turn compressors, or turbochargers, to increase engine output, and has been used to inflate airbag "jacks" to lift cars.

Nature is much more advanced in this area than humans are. In natural ecosystems there is very little if any waste. When an animal or plant dies, it is not merely waste, but dinner for other plants and animals to feed upon. Farmers tend to be more aware of this balance than most homeowners. Few farmers would dream of wasting grass clippings or potato peels, for example, preferring to recognize them as potential animal feed or at least as compost material. Even animal wastes, such as horse and cow feces, are viewed as a starting point to be composted into humus to fertilize the next season's plants.

Fig. 12.7 The *Convertible Sofa paradigm* implies a change of configuration to change the function of something. In the case of sofas, changing between a sofa and a bed requires removing cushions and unfolding a bed frame.

Convertible Sofa

By unfolding a frame tucked within, you can change a convertible sofa from a sofa into a bed. The motivations here are versatility and space conservation. A living room with a sofa can thus become a bedroom with a bed simply by configuring of a single piece of furniture. Just as important, the bed is out of sight when not in use. The convertible sofa is paradigmatic of a number of different devices that change among two or more functions by altering their configuration. This strategy is frequently applied when conservation of space is an issue. Consequently, in tight spaces, such as submarines, boats, campers, and space capsules, considerable attention is paid to the possibility of making things serve double or triple duty. A common arrangement in boats is for cushions to lift seats to reveal a storage space or a toilet. In campers, seats frequently fold down to make beds. Similarly children's transformer-type toys are designed primarily to showcase convertibility. A typical arrangement is for a robot toy to fold, legs tucked in here, arms turned in there, and the robot becomes a car, a bug, or some other form.

Among the natural examples of the *Convertible Sofa paradigm* are a cat's paws and claws. With the cat's claws extended, the paws are a potent weapon, whereas with the claws retracted, the paws are soft and gentle. The sexual apparatus of many animals is likewise "convertible." For example, the mammalian penis enlarges for copulation by engorgement of erectile tissues. At other times, it returns to its normal size and in certain species, such as the wolf, fox, and dog, is hidden by the action of retractor muscles.

Fig. 12.8 a, b The *Swiss Army Knife paradigm*, commonly applied not only to knives, but also wrenches, pliers and kitchen gadgets, imples a series of different functions realized by unfolding different blades or tools from a common handle or body.

Swiss Army Knife

Most people who have seen a Swiss Army knife will remember the first time they saw one. What at first appears to be simply a pocket knife is magically transformed, as the blade is folded in and another tool is folded out. What was a knife becomes a can opener, then a saw, then a screwdriver. So powerful is this paradigm that the Swiss Army knife has become a near-universal symbol of versatility, adaptability, and multi-functionality. As a result, the knife's image is frequently used in advertising, in which these properties are promoted for other products.

The *Swiss Army Knife paradigm* has been directly adopted

in the design of a variety of tools and implements. Wrenches and pliers, for instance, are now widely found with foldout attachments. Many kitchen gadgets are based on the paradigm, such as can openers with foldout corkscrews.

Fig. 12.9 The *Swiss Army Knife paradigm* applied to pliers.

Like the *Convertible Sofa paradigm*, the *Swiss Army Knife paradigm* is often employed in situations in which space is tight, and particularly when weight is a consideration as well. Consequently this paradigm is widely employed in devices designed for use in airplanes, spacecraft, and in activities such as hiking. Swiss-Army-knife-type thinking can be seen, for example, in the design of an airline seat. The airline seat accommodates a range of functions by changing its configuration and folding out parts, but without adding or removing parts. As such, it changes from an upright chair to a reclining lounger, and when mealtime comes, a dining table can be unfolded from the armrest. And finally, although we hope we'll never need it, the seat can usually become a flotation device in case of a water landing.

The *Swiss Army Knife paradigm* may also be applied in simpler and more subtle ways. For example, the design of some automotive glove-compartment doors incorporates a tray to hold beverage cups, that may be used when the door is open. Design touches like these are usually considered thoughtful and considerate.

Socket Wrenches

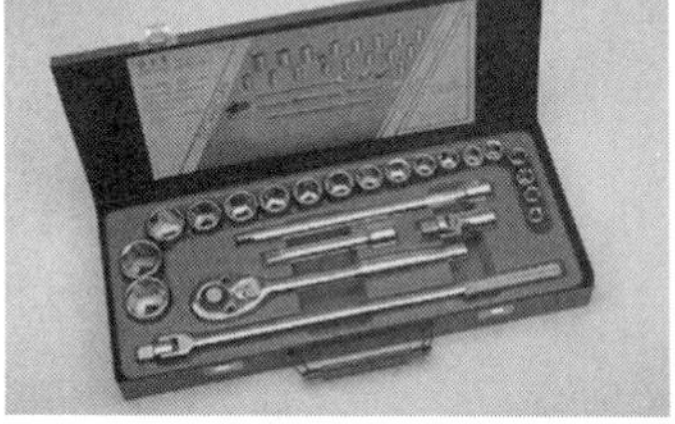

Fig. 12.10 Socket wrench set. By snapping on different parts, the tool can be made larger or smaller, can have a swivel head, and can accommodate a variety of sizes of nuts and bolts.

Socket wrenches are characteristic of a wide variety of things that require the assembly of several parts in order to function. The socket-wrench handle is virtually useless by itself, as is the socket. The strength of the *Socket Wrench paradigm* is that you can use a few simple rules—such as "handle first, then extension if necessary, then socket"—can be applied to a large set of special-purpose parts to assemble a wide range of tools as needed for specific jobs.

Various other tools and implements work in a similar manner. Vacuum cleaners, for instance, might have several extension tubes that can be used, as well as a range of attachments for the end for bare floors, rugs, curtains, and upholstery. Architects' drafting sets, although now largely replaced by computer-aided design, employed a similar modularity in the design of bow compasses. Adding a short or long arm extended the reach of the compass, and interchangeable tips changed the function from a needle divider, to a tool for drawing circles with a pencil or pen.

A significant problem with the socket-wrench approach is parts. Parts like individual sockets are easily lost, to the detriment of the entire set. This is certainly an advantage of other approaches, such as the *Swiss Army Knife paradigm*. The problem is somewhat alleviated by carefully considering the storage of the parts in the design of the system. If vacuum cleaner, for instance, requires removable parts, the well-designed vacuum cleaner will include storage places for the parts that not only hold them snugly, but also make it obvious at a glance if a part is missing.

Tractor

Devices fitting the *Tractor paradigm* achieve multi-functionality through the addition of attachments. A farm tractor is a wonderful and amazing machine. When you see tractors from a distance, you might assume that they only move through fields and down roads, slowly pulling loads. Tractors are worth a closer look, however. They are designed to fulfill virtually every conceivable power need on a farm. A variety of attachments can be easily hitched on the front, rear, side, and on top of the tractor. Most tractors provide PTOs (power take-offs) at both ends, thereby allowing the tractor's engine to power these attachments. Many provide connections for hydraulic systems as well. An attachment might change the tractor into a snowplow, a loader, a backhoe, a mower, a baler, or a sprayer, to name a few of the many possibilities.

Fig. 12.11 a, b Prior to widespread use of tractors, horses and oxen performed many of the same functions on the farm, in much the same way: by attaching different implements, such as tillers, seeders, and carriages.

Fig. 12.12 The *Tractor paradigm* achieves versatility through the hundreds of available attachments each of which transforms a tractor into something else, a cart, a sprayer, a tiller, or, as in the image at left, a lettuce planter. Power take-offs (PTO's) on the tractor can be used to drive mechanisms on these attachments.

In the natural world, the horse has also operated under the *Tractor paradigm*, and prior to the widespread availability of tractors, had performed many of the same functions. In addition to serving as the "engine" for ploughs and other farm equipment, horses also provided transportation and fertilizer. Other beasts of burden have served, and continue to serve, similar purposes, including oxen, donkeys, elephants, llamas, and camels.

Computer

The ultimate multi-function device or device controller is the computer. The power of the computer as a multi-function device comes from its ability to execute programs, sequences of instructions with conditional execution, branching, looping, and other types of control structures.

While most users no longer need to learn to program in order to make use of a program, it is evident, even through casual use, that the appearance and purpose of the computer dramatically change with each program

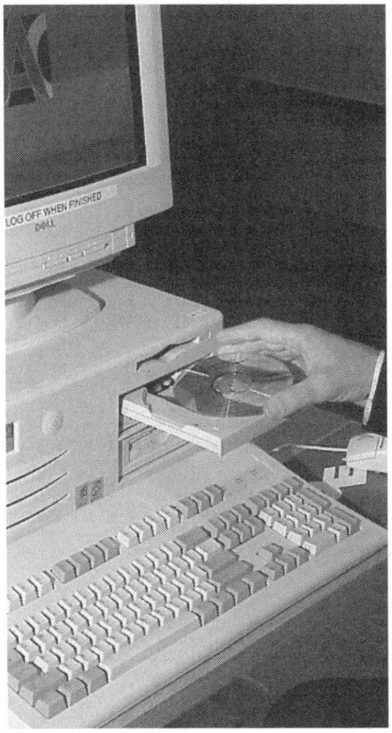

Fig. 12.13 The computer is the ultimate multi-function device of this age. At one moment it is a telephone-like communications device. With the click of a mouse it transforms into a fast-paced arcade game, and then into a French tutor. The concept of software was invented to rapidly change the function of general purpose computing hardware.

that is executed. At one moment it can be a driving-simulation game; another, a word processor; at still another, a French tutor.

Computers can also employ the *Tractor paradigm,* adding to or changing the purpose and abilities of the system through attachments. Thus, with a color printer and the appropriate software, a computer may become a greeting-card manufacturing system. With a video-recording deck and controller a computer becomes a video-editing system, and with the appropriate type of keyboard, it becomes a musical instrument.

In biological systems, learning fulfills much the same purpose as software. The behavior of many animals is "coded in firmware," and is not learned. For instance, a baby chick knows how to scratch the dirt and feed itself, and will run for cover when it sees a hawk silhouette. But the ability to learn new behaviors allows a species the ability to adapt to changing conditions or new dangers. Arguably this is much of the reason for the success of the human species, despite not being the largest, fastest or strongest animals on the planet.

Questions

1) Many devices employ more than one paradigm, and may be exemplars of multiple paradigms. Explain the *Self Consumption paradigm* of Chapter 11 using the convertible sofa as an example. How are the two paradigms different?

2) Think of your feet in terms of the *Hand paradigm*. What functions are you able to perform with your feet? What additional tasks could you perform with your feet with practice? Could you sign your name? Could you paint a watercolor? What keeps you from performing other tasks that you now perform with your hands?

3) While some rooms in a building are usually dedicated to a single purpose, such as a boiler room or a broom closet, others are intended to function as multi-function rooms. Describe the characteristics, features, systems, and materials that facilitate this versatility.

4) Choose three devices that you might use on a camping trip, and design a single device that combines the functions of all three. Can you envision the combined device working as well as the individual devices?

13

Transcending the Visible

The paradigms and forms we have considered so far have purposes and relationships to each other, for the most part, that are readily visible. Form and function are not merely about what is visible, however. Many devices and forms exist to take advantage of, or translate, a force that might not otherwise be visible or perceivable. What are some of the things that you depend on every day and yet are not visible? While air might certainly come to mind, how about time? Or gravity? Or your sense of direction?

While many such forces and concepts now appear as a digital readout on a webpage, it's important to remember that certain concrete relationships exist between these entities and the physical world. These relationships formed the basis for many of the instruments of yesteryear, and still must be considered in the design of many things. These paradigms remind us that we cannot always design for a perfect world, where everything is visible, and where everything is prepared for us and laid out with ten-digit precision. Further, what is clear and visible to a designer in a well-lit studio might not be so for the user of the design. Imagine designing a tool for the blind, for instance. If you make the handle bright orange it won't make it any easier to find when it is misplaced. Tactile or auditory, rather than visual, clues will prove more useful. You can expect to face similar considerations when designing tools and other devices that will be used in environments such as underwater, or in space, or simply things to be used at night. In circumstances such as these, you must consider that the user's vision might be obscured, and relative gravity may be reduced or absent.

Flashlights and Glowworms

Fig. 13.1 A flashlight is important not only to let you see things in the dark, but also to help others see you. Further, if you can be seen, you can also use the light as a signal, transmitting information.

Nothing more quickly modifies our perception of our environment than turning off the lights. Depending on the circumstances, our most immediate concern might be to see, or to be seen. If we can't simply turn the lights back on, our first thought will likely be *"where is a flashlight?"* In another era, the flashlight paradigm might have been called the *Oil Lamp paradigm* or the *Candle paradigm*. Today a flashlight is most likely to come to mind when we think of something portable that extends our senses by permitting us to see in the dark. The *Flashlight paradigm* is a powerful reminder that our perception of the world is dependent on such conditions as the presence of light. It is also inspirational to remind ourselves that such a simple device as a flashlight can open up perceptual worlds that might otherwise be closed to us.

Navigating in the dark is a frequent need, and is the primary reason for using flashlights and flashlightlike devices. When a flashlight is attached to a vehicle, we use the term "headlight" instead of "flashlight." Beyond cars, trucks, busses, and motorcycles, we also find headlights on airplanes, submarines, snowmobiles, bicycles, helicopters, riding lawnmowers, and vacuum cleaners.

Besides lighting the way, flashlights also commonly serve two other purposes: first, to make the holder of the flashlight visible, and second, as a signal. We find all three of these purposes served by lights found on an automobile. In addition to the headlights, side marker lights and taillights help the car be seen, and turn signals indicate directional intentions.

While these three purposes might seem obvious at first, surprisingly enough they are frequently overlooked in the design of various products. Consider a simple flashlight, for instance. Most flashlights are designed *to see with* in the dark, and not *to be seen* in the dark. Consequently the popular Mag-lite® flashlights, which were designed with black bodies, can be very difficult to find when they are dropped or set down in the dark before being turned on. This problem was addressed in the design of the Greenlee® pocket light which features a glow-in-the-dark button on the end opposite the lamp. There is still room for improvement upon this design, however, because the button cannot be energized by the same lamp; you need a second light source to energize it.

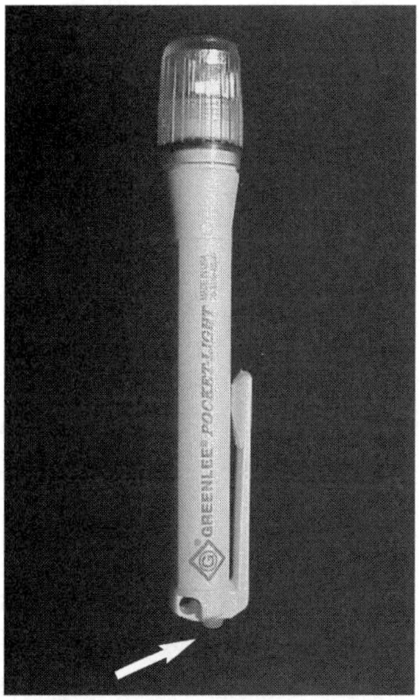

Fig. 13.2 Greenlee pocket light. A glow-in-the-dark button on the end of the flashlight helps it to be found in the dark when it is turned off.

In nature a number of approaches to the same problems, of seeing, being seen, and signaling in the dark have evolved. Various creatures have *bioluminescent* areas that serve these purposes, effectively giving them the natural equivalents of flashlights, blinking signals, or even glowing bodies. You might be inclined to think that animals that are active in the dark are better off not being seen. But their lights give them advantages in their dark environments, helping them find food and mates.

Certain deep-sea fish have developed flashlightlike appendages that help them find their way in their dark environment. Deep-sea angler fish of the suborder *Ceratioidei* employ a specially developed, fishing-rod-like spine from the dorsal fin with a bioluminescent growth that serves as bait, thereby luring prey close enough to catch. The North American firefly *Photinus pyralis*, or *lightning bug*, is probably the most well-known example employing signal lights. When conditions are right, the male flies through the dark with his tail light blinking to attract a potential mate. The female, observing from the ground, responds to a potential mate by a counter signal, flashed 2 seconds after the male's flash. A male recognizes that he has been identified and chosen by the female by the timing of the female's response, and reports to the location of the flash in order to mate.[48] Glowworms exhibit the third application of personal lighting, their entire bodies glow, enabling them to be seen in the dark caves they inhabit. The cave-dwelling glowworm

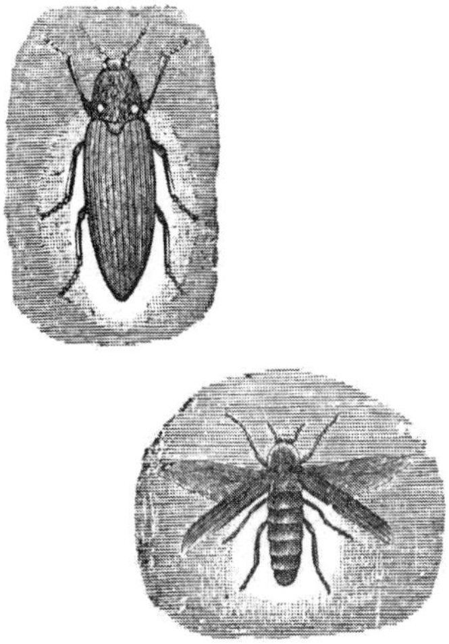

Fig. 13.3 Lightning bugs employ bioluminesence to produce their own light, used as a signal to find mates in the dark.

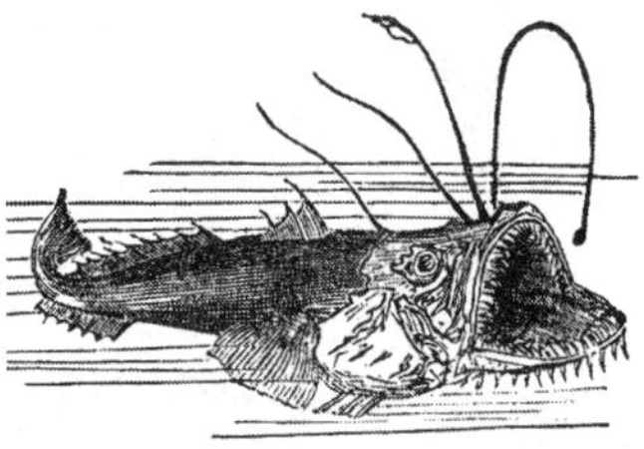

Fig. 13.4 The deep sea Angler fish. A bioluminescent growth hangs in front of its mouth, acting as bait to attract fish to within striking range.

Arachnocampa of New Zealand spins a silk web, which is attached to the cave's ceiling, to rest in. These glowworms secrete droplets of venom, that hang from the silk threads. As insects approach, attracted by the glowworm's light, they get stuck and poisoned in the web and become the glowworm's dinner.

Some other applications of bioluminescence go beyond the *Flashlights and Glowworms paradigm*. Most notably, the deep-sea lantern fish has a distinctive pattern of lights on various parts of its body that serve much the same purpose as lit golden arches and signs do for McDonald's: broadcasting its identity to attract those who might be interested. Other deep-sea fish have illuminated bottom and side surfaces that can function as a sort of camouflage. When seen from below, fish normally cast a shadow, making them easy prey. Projecting light from their undersides, however, that matches the light filtering down from above, causes the fish to almost disappear. A final and, perhaps most surprising application of bioluminescence, however, is a deep-sea squid that ejects a cloud of bioluminescent ink as a decoy to evade capture. This produces a glowing ghost to distract predators as the squid escapes; it then dissipates into nothing.

Lens

A lens is a transparent material with one or more curved surfaces that bends the light passing through it. Most lenses are used to convert the shape, size, and orientation of images, although some, such as lenses on flashlights, are used to focus light. In a certain sense it seems odd to talk about lenses in a chapter entitled "Transcending the Visible," yet this is what lenses are about. Lenses serve to transcend, or go beyond, what is visible without them. They can serve to bring a fuzzy image into focus, as do glasses and contact lenses. Magnifying glasses serve to enlarge small things, thereby making them visible. Telescopes and binoculars effectively bring the distant closer. A lens is most often thought of as having two convex sides, though optical lenses might have concave or flat surfaces as well. Fresnel and holographic lenses can be both thin and flat. For the purpose of the *Lens paradigm,* it is useful to assume a concentrating lens unless the term "diffusing lens" is specified.

From a human perspective, the most important lens is the lens inside our eyes, which enables us to focus on objects from a few inches away to far in the distance. The lens is such a basic part of our visual system that it might be difficult to imagine a visual system without one. Nature, however, has given rise to a number of alternate schemes. Eyespots, which are simple light-sensitive patches on a body surface, are found in a number of species. Eyespots form no image, providing information only about relative light and darkness. To produce a clear image, our eyes, and cameras, use lenses. A lens gathers light and forms a coherent, inverted image on the back, inner surface of the eye. Cameras typically use lenses to gather and focus the light onto the plane of the recording surface (film or electronic array). To perform these functions without a lens, a pinhole can be used instead, as in the *camera obscura,* a pinhole camera. A pinhole camera can produce a coherent, inverted image and can take a decent picture, although without a lens there is a tradeoff between the size of the hole and the sharpness of the image. To produce a sharp image, the hole must be small, and, consequently, it can take a long time to get an exposure. In the animal world, a number of creatures, such as the nautilus, have simple eyes called *ocelli,* which, like pinhole cameras, function without a lens. These eyes are typically open to the outside (yes, water can flow in and out of the eye), and light enters through a "pinhole" to focus on a cup-shaped array of photoreceptor cells.

The lens paradigm implies focusing light, but the term is sometimes used metaphorically as well, for collecting, sharpening, or studying various other things; for example, we *focus on an idea.*

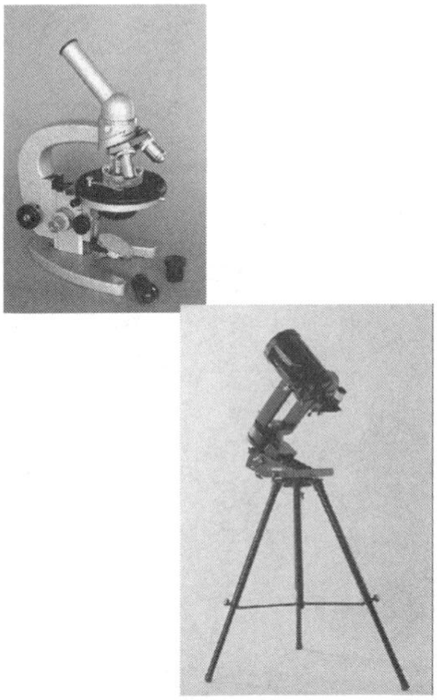

Fig. 13.5 a, b Microscopes and telescopes employ the *Lens paradigm,* helping us to see what would otherwise be invisible to us.

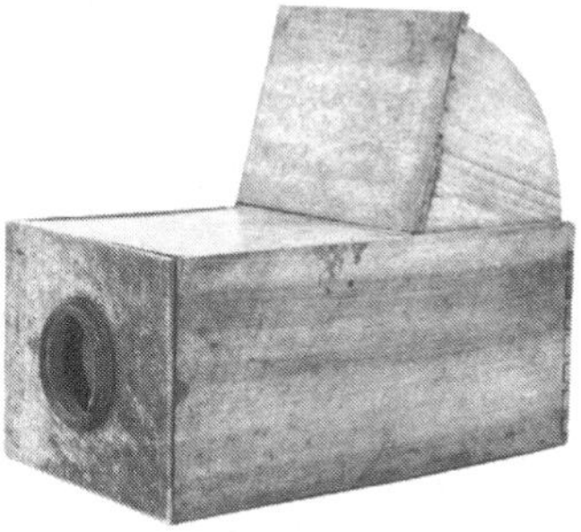

Fig. 13.6 The *camera obscura.* A small hole works in place of a lens, creating a coherent inverted image on the opposite side of the box.

Wristwatch

Modern life frequently requires that a great deal of attention be paid to the passage of time. Whether we are billing for labor on an hourly rate, or picking up a date at 8 P.M., we often need to know the time, and to measure elapsed time. We might also need to know the time remaining until a particular event starts, and might need notification at that time. Our ability to time these events based solely on our innate human senses is rather poor. Consequently, timing devices have become essential equipment in modern life, including watches, wall clocks, alarm clocks, stopwatches, and, for longer increments of time, calendars. With modern watchmaking techniques, particularly in the employment of multi-purpose, integrated circuits in watches, these functions have converged in modern wristwatches. Consequently, the wristwatch has become the paradigm of human timekeeping.

Timing is integral to the operation of many machines as well, so clocklike devices are built into many of these. Washing machines, for example, must time a sequence of events including turning on and off water, starting and stopping motors, and draining wastewater. A simple toaster

Fig. 13.7 The wristwatch is the paradigm representing timekeeping in various forms. This watch has numerous countdown timers and alarms, and keeps time in two time zones. Other timers in our daily lives control how brown our toast becomes, how long the rinse cycle runs, how long of a gap there is between flashes when we signal a left turn, and how long we can park in a parking space.

provides a timer that lets you select the darkness of the toast, and times the ejection of the toast upon completion. Tuning an automobile engine usually includes timing a spark to ignite the gas-air mixture at just the right moment within a cycle in order to provide the maximum output. A single cycle of an auto engine may take only $^{1}/_{100^{th}}$ of a second, and tuning can be performed to 1 degree (of a circle), which is consequently $^{1}/_{36{,}000^{th}}$ of a second. The finest timing in home applications is in computing. With computer clock speeds approaching 1 gigahertz at this writing, computing events that are now timed in billionths of seconds must soon be measured in even shorter intervals.

Nature has its own clocks and timers as well. As the earth turns on its axis and orbits the sun, cycles of events take place that we mark as days and years, made visible by the light-dark cycle and the changing of the seasons. Creatures and processes of the natural world have time components to their existence and, thus, perform clocklike functions. Our most personal clock is the human heart, but many other human rhythms exist as well.

Magnet

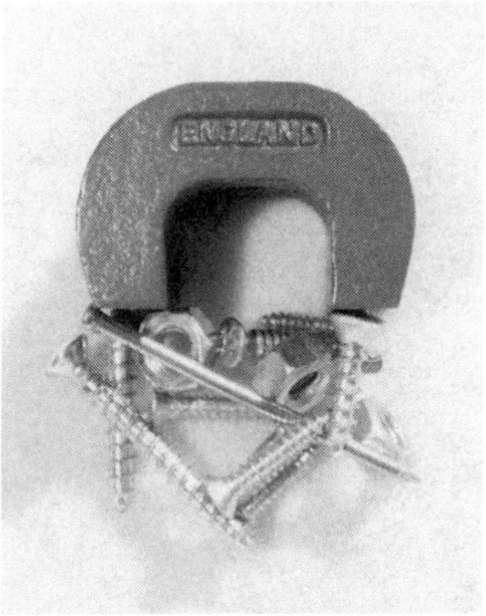

Fig. 13.8 Beyond its ability to attract and attach, the magnet acts on a world that is invisible to us. The magnet forms a field around it, as the earth does. Magnetism passes through things. much as electricity does. The lowest screw in the image here is being magnetically held in place, although it is not touching the magnet.

Magnets are familiar in many forms, beginning, perhaps, with novelty magnets stuck to the refrigerator. Most of the magnets we use daily, however, are hidden inside various devices. Magnets, of course, exhibit an attraction to iron, and this attraction is measurable in a magnetic field around the magnet. There is also an interrelationship between electricity and magnetic fields. Electricity passing through a wire creates a magnetic field around the wire, which can be multiplied by coiling the wire around a conductor. This makes an electromagnet. This is a very important property in modern life in large part because the electricity can be turned on and off at will, modulated with a variable electrical signal, or switched on and off by a timer or a computer. Further, when magnetic fields are arranged radially and alternately energized, they might induce motion in a magnetic rotor, causing it to spin—in other words, an electric motor. Magnetic force can also be used to pull at a diaphragm. When modulated with an electrical signal, this causes the diaphragm to vibrate, making audible waves through the air. This is the basis for loudspeakers. Magnetic coatings applied to plastic tape or metal discs can be used to store information by magnetizing spots on the magnetic material with a recording head. This information can then be recognized by a reading head, which treats the presence of magnetization on a spot of material as a "1" or the presence of a bit of information, and the absence of charge as a "0." This is the basis for audio- and videotape, as well as computer floppy discs and hard discs. (See the *Magnet paradigm* in Chapter 8).

Compass

The compass is a special application of magnets and magnetism but deserves separate attention here. Just as the wristwatch enhances our ability to track time, the compass is the mechanical means of enhancing our ability to determine orientation relative to the magnetic poles. The compass has been known and used at least as far back as the twelfth century in China and Europe. Compasses were likely discovered when it was noticed that lodestones resting on sticks in water always tended to align themselves in the same direction. The earth behaves like a bar magnet with magnetic poles, and free-floating magnets tend to align themselves with the poles.

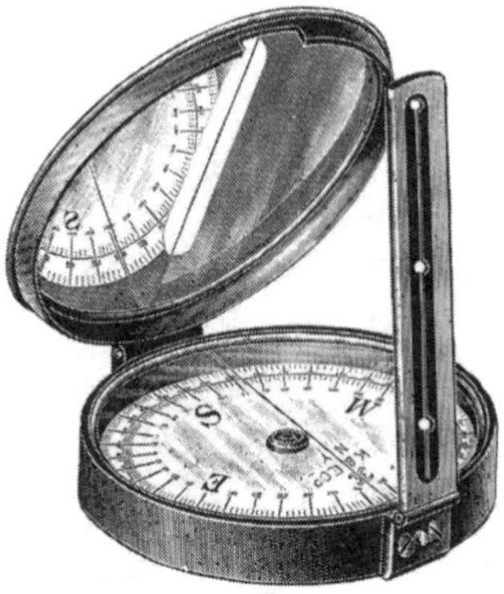

Fig. 13.9 Closely related to the magnet is the compass, the key element of this pocket transit. The compass represents the ability to determine direction, and by implication, position. Today, satellite-based global positioning systems are replacing the magnetic compass, but they respond to the same need: that of determining one's position and bearing.

Various animal species have magnetic iron deposits in their brains or elsewhere, giving them built-in, direction-finding "compasses." These include several species of migratory birds, pigeons, dolphins, and honeybees.[49] Carrier pigeons, *Columba livia*, for instance, when carried far from their homes, and released, easily find their way home due in part to their use of magnetic cues. In experiments, young birds were subjected to a distorted magnetic field while they were transported from their homes, and subsequently lost their way, indicating that their magnetic sense helped them to keep track of their positions during the outward journey.[50]

Perhaps the smallest known creatures employing compasses are *magnetotactic bacteria,* which have chains of tiny particles of magnetite in their bodies. These magnets are thought to enable the bacteria to orient themselves as to up and down, rather than north and south, because the bacteria cannot travel far enough to make use of a directional compass. The directionality of the earth's magnetic field includes a vertical component that in certain geographic locations is stronger than the horizontal component that points northward. These bacteria can benefit from orienting themselves with respect to the vertical direction because sediments at certain levels provide optimal conditions for the bacteria. At this microscopic scale, knowing up from down is a nontrivial challenge, as *Brownian motion,* which is random jittering caused by thermal energy of the surrounding medium, becomes a more powerful force than gravity.[51]

Some researchers have noted that, similarly, humans have traces of iron in the ethmoid bone between the eyes, which may help give humans a sense of direction or might be a vestige of a way-finding organ, but studies to date are inconclusive.

Barometer

A barometer measures the relative changes in atmospheric air pressure. Knowing the air pressure can be useful because it strongly corresponds to changes in the weather. Very low pressure is associated with storms, while high pressure is associated with clear weather. A barometer can, consequently, be used as a weather predictor. It can also be used as an *altimeter,* as air pressure decreases with altitude.

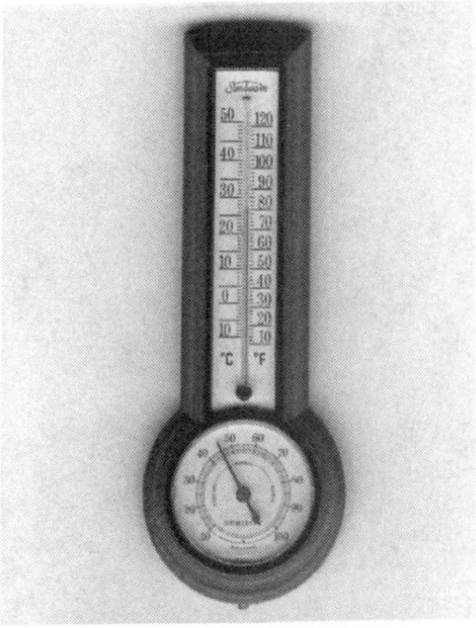

Fig. 13.10 A household barometer and thermometer. The barometer makes visible changes in air pressure that come with moving weather patterns, or with changes in altitude.

Many persons become good at predicting weather change, and these abilities might well be in part due to a bodily sensitivity to pressure change. We are all aware of at least gross pressure changes, such as when our ears pop when flying, or when driving up a hill. It is not a stretch, then, to believe that some people are more sensitive or attentive to these changes.

X ray

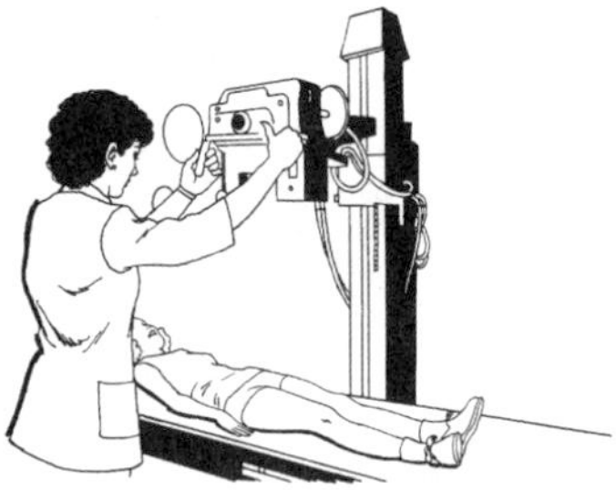

Fig. 13.11 The *X-ray paradigm* refers not only to the X ray itself, but to the concept that visual barriers have more to do with the limitations of our eyes than limitations of the physical world. We overcome these limitations through technology.

The *X-ray paradigm* implies the ability to see things that are usually hidden. On first consideration, it is easy to think of X rays as the ability to see through things. This is not usually what is of interest, though. X-ray images are interesting for what they make visible, not for what they make invisible. X rays are electromagnetic waves outside of the visible spectrum. Various other frequencies are also invisible to us, including ultraviolet and infrared, and of course, sound waves are as well.

Some things that are normally obscured may be made visible quite simply. Consider the inside of an unopened snow pea. You cannot normally see inside the unopened pod, yet you can easily do so by holding one up to a bright light source. Similarly, closing your hand over a lit flashlight can let you see through your skin and nails. More often though, we use instrumentation of various types. Imaging devices are an important part of medical diagnostic technology, and include not only conventional X rays, but also catscans, positron emission tomography (PET-scan), ultrasound, and nuclear magnetic resonance (NMR) imaging. Infrared imaging systems, once considered exotic military equipment for nighttime viewing, are now readily available through sports equipment catalogs and built in on some camcorders.

Fig. 13.12 The rattlesnake, *Crotalus viridis*, is equipped with an infrared imaging system, allowing it to perceive warm objects, even when hidden from view, or in total darkness.

The natural world is filled with examples of creatures that can see or otherwise sense things that are not visible to the naked eye. The rattlesnake *Crotalus viridis* is equipped with infrared detectors set into facial pits below the eyes. These sensory organs can sense a temperature change as small as

0.002° C. A rattlesnake can detect the infrared radiation from the body heat of a mouse even in total darkness or when the mouse is hidden behind a leaf.[52] The compound eyes of insects can see ultraviolet light. While UV light is normally invisible to humans, this is because the lens absorbs the UV light, preventing it from reaching the retina. UV light becomes visible to patients who have had their lenses removed in cataract surgery.[53]

Sail

A sail is a potent reminder that wind is a concrete reality that we must consider in the design of many things, and further that such forces can sometimes be channeled for our benefit. A sail makes wind visible as well as useful. As the sail billows outward, we can visually gauge the direction and strength of the wind by the sail's shape. That wind in the sail can push the sailboat in the direction the wind is blowing is obvious to most observers. What is a marvel to most

Fig. 13.13 a, b Which way is the wind blowing? The sail not only reacts to the wind, making it visible, it also catches it, and transfers its energy to the motion of the ship. Learning to sail, one necessarily adopts a sort of Zen philosophy that is applicable outside of sailing as well. We are surrounded by various types energy, we can stand firm and be beaten down by that energy, or raise our sails and let it take us wherever we wish to go.

people other than sailors and physicists, however, is that a sailboat can sail against the wind.

The sail passively employs the wind; it makes use of the wind by its shape and position. Among the creatures to also passively use the wind to travel—versus flapping wings—are spiderlings of many species. Shortly after hatching, spiderlings climb up stems to the tips of branches and leaves where they let out their "sail," which is usually 8 to 12 feet of spider silk. As the wind takes the silk the spiderlings release their grip on the ground and take to the air, climbing their silk. If the spiderlings get caught on a tree or building, they climb outward again to catch the wind, and repeat the process. Sailing is a remarkably efficient means through which these creatures can travel. Spiderlings have blown onto ships out hundreds of miles at sea.[54]

Questions

1) Study a modern glass window in a building. List all of the ways you can think of that the window protects you from things that are not visible to the naked eye. Visit a window manufacturer's Website as research.

2) How does the appearance of architecture change as a function of time? Consider time on different scales, from the hours of a day, to days in a week, to seasons in a year, and then year-to-year.

3) Consider three things that you have trouble finding or identifying in the dark. Devise solutions that will make these things visible or obviate the need for them to be visible.

4) What effects would a major disruption in magnetic fields have on the appliances and devices in your home? List the devices that would be affected.

14

Putting Design Paradigms to Work

Using Design Paradigms

Design paradigms can serve a wide range of purposes that for the most part can be classified as either *generative* (creating new designs) or *interpretive* (interpreting existing designs). We explored the interpretive roles in Chapters 2 through 13. In this chapter we explore the generative roles of design paradigms.

As creative tools, the paradigms can serve designers, artists, inventors, and marketing professionals. The paradigms help by providing the formal and functional inspiration for new products and product variations, as well as the categories that help to classify problems and find parallels in alternate solutions.

Design and other creative activities are often referred to as *problem solving*. However, this term has some inadequacies; it doesn't really capture the purpose of tasks in the first phases of design. The first and most important phase of design is more appropriately called *problem finding*.[55] To the designer this often means questioning an existing solution that has not been pointed out as a problem, or that is known as problematic but assumed to be intractable. A maxim of product design is *There is no such thing as a mature market.* Claims were made in the 1970s and 1980s that sneakers and bicycles were examples of mature products in mature markets, suggesting that there was little room or need for innovation in these product categories. Shortly thereafter, both categories exploded with new and radically different designs replacing the then-widespread running shoes and 10-speed racers.

As a design methodology, design paradigms might begin with problem finding or problem solving. The basic problem-solving methodology involves five steps, *reduction, selection, application, integration,* and *test.* Three additional steps, *paradigm superimposition, paradigm shifts,* and *category shifts,* are essential to problem-finding tasks. (These are described later in this chapter; see page 264.)

Reduction

The reduction phase involves breaking down a problem and/or an existing solution into specific paradigms and categories, like the sections and chapters of this book. It is important to determine whether a problem is, for instance, one of attaching or joining. It is also important to understand the underlying mechanisms of the existing solution both to find out why it worked or why it failed, and to examine opportunities for improvement.

A problem-solving task usually starts with a set of objectives or specifications. Each of these can be translated or reduced into paradigm categories. When you tackle a new problem, for which no prior solution exists, this is an important first step. In situations in which an existing solution is available for study, reducing the existing solution to its underlying paradigms provides important additional information. But this approach must not serve as a substitute for reduction of the problem itself, as this would suggest only solutions based on the preceding solution.

Selection

The selection step involves choosing a paradigm for application to the problem or an aspect of the problem. For example, a bellows is a means of spanning a variable distance. Selection can be indicated by the need to meet certain requirements. It can also be based on such factors as intuition (*I have a hunch the bellows will work*), iteration *(I have tried the third paradigm, now I'll try the fourth*), or random choice. An iterative or random assignment of a paradigm to a problem can be useful to expand the range of possible solutions. Many good solutions to problems were not initially obvious.

For an example of using random-category and paradigm assignment, consider a problem of fire safety: devise a means to protect a person trapped in a fire. Assigning the *Enclosure paradigm* (see Chapter 3) will suggest substantially different solutions than the *Passages paradigm* (see Chapter 9). This, consequently, forces you to think differently about the problem. How can people be protected from fire by enclosing them? Assign a paradigm within the category; for instance, *coating* might lead you to think of protective coatings as a means of fire protection. Barricade®, a product that does just that, has recently been released. This gel, when sprayed on to buildings, provides a fireproof barrier that protects against heat and direct flames. It is possible that a spray can of material like this might be developed so that you can spray a gelatinous fire shield on yourself to escape a fire.

Application

The application phase involves developing the design concept incorporating the chosen paradigm. The application of the paradigm can be straightforward or can require bending, enlarging, or otherwise changing the usual form of the paradigm to fit the problem at hand. The application can even be a metaphorical reference to the paradigm, looking little like the original form.

Integration

The integration phase is necessary when two or more paradigms or components are involved in a design. In this phase, the goal is to get the two parts to work well together. There is a subtle distinction between integration, which implies using more than one paradigm in one device, and paradigm superimposition, which involves synthesizing new solutions that combine features of the two. (Paradigm superimposition is discussed later in this chapter; see page 265).

Multiple paradigms are frequently required since most designs must address more than one criterion. Imagine, for example, having to design a covering for items in a truck. Requirements might include that the covering accommodate items of various sizes (see the *Bigger and Smaller paradigms* in Chapter 5), and that these items are enclosed during travel (see the *Enclosure paradigms* in Chapter 3). This might lead to the selection of the *Net paradigm* as enclosure, and the *Spring paradigm* as a means of accommodating the bigger and smaller requirement. The integration phase involves getting the net and the spring to work together. This might suggest something like a trampoline, in which springs are found at the ends of each strap forming the net.

Alternately, the springiness might be incorporated into the net material itself, which, in turn, might suggest consideration of a material like Lycra®.

Integrating paradigms, whether as part of a design phase like this or as activities in their own right, provides fertile ground for developing inventions. Certain heuristics can be applied to develop good inventions, such as combining opposites, like a pencil and eraser, or combining things that are frequently used together, like shampoo and conditioner.[56]

Test

All designs must be tested against a set of criteria appropriate for the product. Among the basic questions that must be asked are: Will the design work? Is it safe? Is it manufacturable? Is it ecologically sound? If multiple functions are present, are they compatible with each other? Do the functions support each other? Will the design be durable? Will the consumer like it? Certain products require additional tests.

The role of the paradigm must be evaluated at this point, as well as such factors as integration. Failure of the test might imply the need for refinement using the same design elements—for example, keeping the basic design, but making modifications to facilitate manufacture—or might require a return to the selection phase to try a new paradigm.

While this simple, creative methodology will produce solutions to problems, it can be improved upon in a number of ways to broaden the range and quality of ideas produced, as well as to structure the search for solutions to more effectively traverse the many possibilities. First, we examine paradigm shifts, which are rules for replacing the paradigms in new or existing solutions, then we will review *Synectics*, a related and compatible approach to enhancing creativity.

Paradigm Shifts

When you face a design problem, typically two approaches to solving the problem exist. The first is to look for a solution to the problem; the second is to look for a *replacement* for the problem. When solving problems, you might employ a paradigm whose application is obvious. It is obvious, for example, that you can solve the problem of changing the size of a tripod via telescoping. Sometimes the paradigm might be fundamentally changed by superimposing another paradigm, as when coiling is applied to shoelaces (see the *Coil paradigm* in Chapter 2). This is called a *paradigm superimposition*.

A more significant change involves replacing the expected paradigm with a dramatically different one. This is called a *paradigm shift*. Replacing the telescoping mechanism of a tripod with a mechanism based on the *Balloon paradigm* constitutes a paradigm shift.

The most radical approach to dealing with a design problem, though, is to replace it with another problem. Replacing the problem can come about through, or result in, changing the underlying paradigm category. This is called a *categorical shift*.

To return to the example of the shoelaces problem, children often find it difficult and bothersome to tie shoelaces. The problem might be assigned as "Find a way to make shoelaces easier to tie, and to keep them tied longer." You might find the assignment reasonable and embark on a search of methods of immobilizing shoelaces or (heaven forbid!) an automatic shoelace-tying machine. But you might alternately redefine the problem as "Find a way to easily close shoes and keep them closed." This type of thinking might lead you to shift *paradigms*, to consider Velcro closures, zippers, and clips as alternatives to shoelaces. Shifting the *paradigm category* results when you ask the more radical question "Why should shoes need to open and close?" Thus, you might explore shoes that do not require lacing, opening, or closing. This might lead to dramatically different designs like slip-on or stretchy, pull-on shoes, making lacing or closure a moot point. You could step back even farther, of course, and ask "Why should a child need shoes?" and start to look at alternative ways to protect feet.

Paradigm Superimposition

Paradigms can be superimposed upon each other to create new ideas, inventions, and solutions to design problems. This results in related yet substantially altered solutions through a process Weber calls *transformational heuristics*.[57] For instance, a tooth or wedge might be a starting point for an idea. This idea might then be transformed by superimposing *Multiple Object Relations paradigms* onto it. We can repeat the tooth idea regularly in one direction in the manner of the *Comb paradigm*. This might result in a saw blade. We can also repeat it in two directions in the manner of the *Honeycomb paradigm*. This might result in a potent design invention like

SureForm™ planes and rasps, popular tools for shaping and shaving wood and auto-body putty.

Weber defines several categories of invention heuristics that roughly correspond to the paradigm categories described here, including Linking (corresponding to Chapter 6, "Binary Object Relations") and Joining (corresponding to Chapter 7, "Joining," and Chapter 8, "Attaching").

Paradigm Shift

A paradigm shift involves a dramatic shift in the outlook on a problem and our basis for finding solutions for it. In his classic book *The Structure of Scientific Revolutions*, Kuhn uses the term to describe fundamental changes in the frameworks for scientific explanations, for example, moving from Copernican to Newtonian and Einsteinian physics. In each phase, these frameworks are accepted by a consensus of the scientific community, and a paradigm shift comes about when failures in the accepted model are better explained by a new model, and the consensus shifts toward the new model.[58]

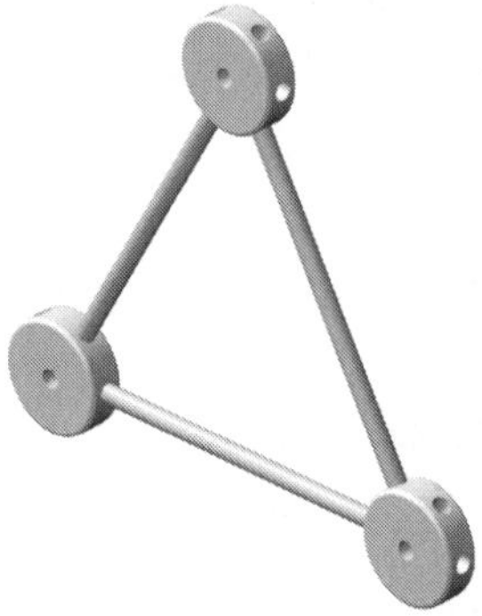

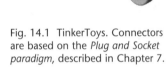

Fig. 14.1 TinkerToys. Connectors are based on the *Plug and Socket paradigm*, described in Chapter 7.

We use the term somewhat differently here, at least in examples that are not so all-encompassing. A paradigm shift in design involves a fundamental shift in the way we solve a particular problem or create a particular product, by means of changing the underlying paradigm. This results in substantially changing the public perception of that product. Telephones provide a good example. As the heavy and largely stationary objects of yesteryear changed to a wireless, portable, cellular-communications paradigm in the 1990s, the ways we think about purchasing, carrying, and using telephones and communicating with others have dramatically changed.

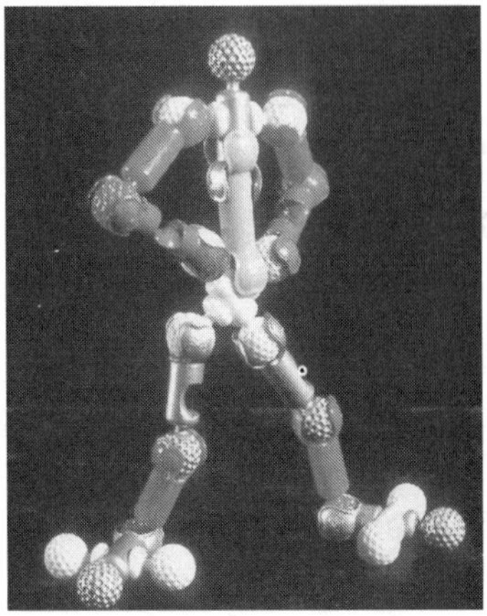

Fig. 14.2 The Zoob toy explores a similar concept for a building toy, but is an entirely new toy and invention because of the replacement of the *Plug and Socket paradigm* with the *Ball and Socket paradigm* (Chapters 4 and 7).

The paradigm-shift stage begins with *translation*, which involves replacing one paradigm with another in the same category. Translation is a conscious effort to explore alternative strategies. It is often employed as a technique to achieve variations and possible improvements on existing designs. Consider a construction toy like TinkerToys™. This toy joins parts using the *Plug and Socket paradigm*. A paradigm shift might involve replacing the plug and socket with the *Ball and Socket* paradigm. This provides a basis for developing a toy like Zoob™ (Figure 14.2), in which parts snap together with ball-and-socket connectors.

A paradigm shift occurs when the underlying paradigm is successfully and dramatically replaced to create a new solution to a problem with fundamentally different underpinnings. This, in turn, redefines the product or product category and our thoughts and conceptions about these products. Shifting picture-taking from a film-based process to an electronic process is another example of a paradigm shift. While both film and electronic methods record an image as a pattern of light and color information, the shift to the electronic image dramatically changes how we store, modify, and distribute these images, which, in turn, changes our ideas about photography.

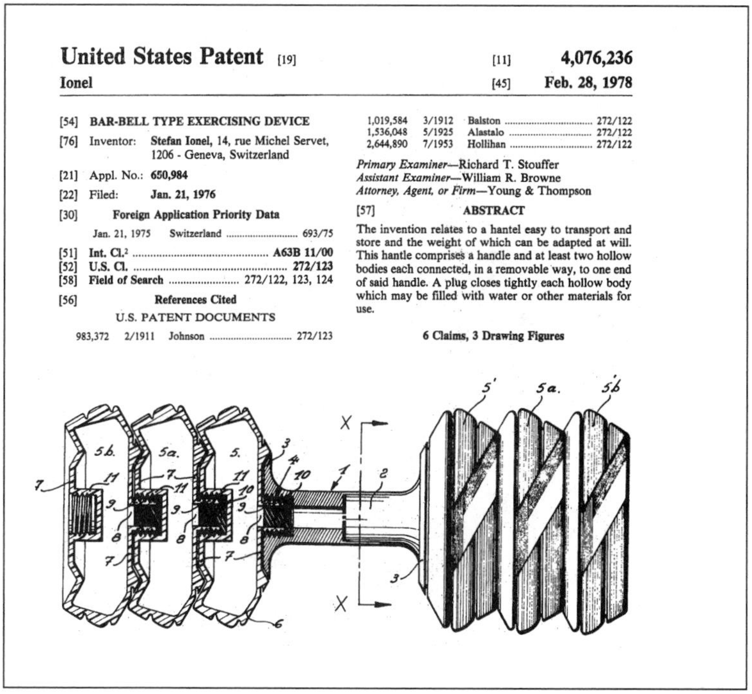

United States Patent [19] — [11] **4,076,236**

Ionel — [45] **Feb. 28, 1978**

[54] **BAR-BELL TYPE EXERCISING DEVICE**

[76] Inventor: **Stefan Ionel**, 14, rue Michel Servet, 1206 - Geneva, Switzerland

[21] Appl. No.: **650,984**

[22] Filed: **Jan. 21, 1976**

[30] **Foreign Application Priority Data**

Jan. 21, 1975 Switzerland 693/75

[51] **Int. Cl.²** **A63B 11/00**
[52] **U.S. Cl.** **272/123**
[58] **Field of Search** 272/122, 123, 124

[56] **References Cited**

U.S. PATENT DOCUMENTS

983,372	2/1911	Johnson	272/123
1,019,584	3/1912	Balston	272/122
1,536,048	5/1925	Alastalo	272/122
2,644,890	7/1953	Hollihan	272/122

Primary Examiner—Richard T. Stouffer
Assistant Examiner—William R. Browne
Attorney, Agent, or Firm—Young & Thompson

[57] **ABSTRACT**

The invention relates to a hantel easy to transport and store and the weight of which can be adapted at will. This hantle comprises a handle and at least two hollow bodies each connected, in a removable way, to one end of said handle. A plug closes tightly each hollow body which may be filled with water or other materials for use.

6 Claims, 3 Drawing Figures

Fig. 14.3 A paradigm shift applied to dumbell design. Changing the weight of conventional dumbells required removing clamps, adding additional weights to a bar, and replacing the clamps. Application of the *Chain paradigm* provided a simpler mechanism, with weight "links" screwed onto either side.

Categorical Shift

A categorical shift is a more radical paradigm change, involving a change not only of the paradigm, but of the category as well. This approach is sometimes employed in design, but might be even more important in the process of invention. In the example given in Chapter 1, a problem was stated requiring the design of a tripod that is to get bigger and smaller. The problem can be subjected to a categorical shift to the *Attaching paradigms*, which might suggest

United States Patent [19]
Olson et al.

[11] **Patent Number:** **5,637,064**
[45] **Date of Patent:** **Jun. 10, 1997**

[54] **ADJUSTABLE DUMBBELL**

[75] Inventors: **Gregory S. Olson; Carl K. Towley, III**, both of Owatonna, Minn.

[73] Assignee: **Intellbell Ventures**, Monterey, Calif.

[21] Appl. No.: **542,659**

[22] Filed: **Oct. 13, 1995**

Related U.S. Application Data

[63] Continuation of Ser. No. 13,785, Feb. 5, 1993, abandoned.

[51] **Int. Cl.**^{6} **A63B 21/075**

[52] **U.S. Cl.** **482/108**; 482/107

[58] **Field of Search** 482/93, 94, 105–109, 482/908

4,768,780	9/1988	Hayes	482/106 X
4,822,034	4/1989	Shields .	
4,880,229	11/1989	Broussard .	
4,900,016	2/1990	Caruthers .	
4,913,422	4/1990	Elmore et al. .	
4,948,123	8/1990	Schook .	
5,040,787	8/1991	Brotman	482/106
5,123,885	6/1992	Shields	482/106
5,131,898	7/1992	Panagos	482/108

FOREIGN PATENT DOCUMENTS

637365	4/1928	France .	
2452296	10/1980	France .	
384485	11/1964	Switzerland .	
1367987	1/1988	U.S.S.R.	482/108
1659073	6/1991	U.S.S.R.	482/108
1687271	10/1991	U.S.S.R.	482/107

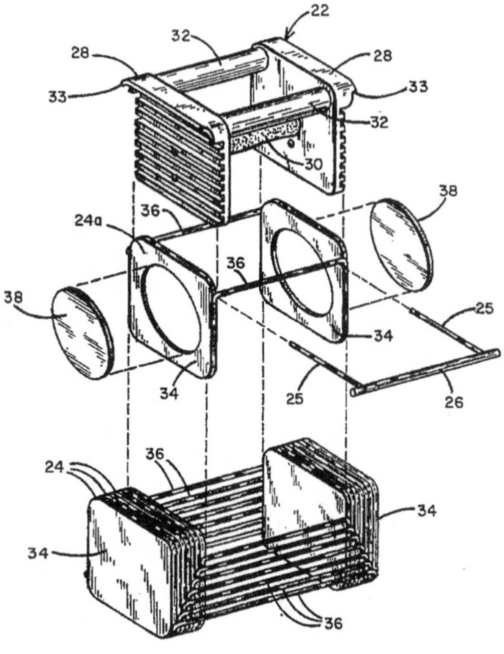

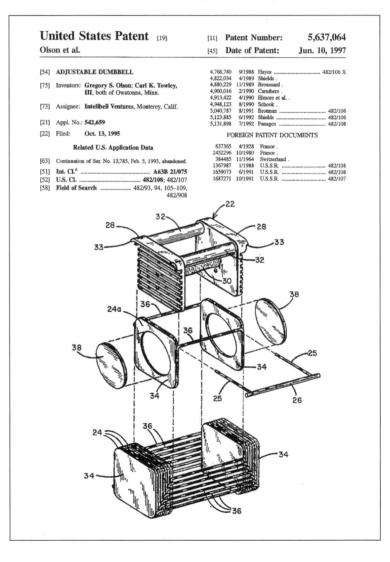

Fig. 14.4 The *Russian Dolls paradigm* is employed in this later dumbell design, resulting in a more flexible weight system with a faster adjustment mechanism. A simple clip is moved to determine how many of the nested weights are lifted along with the handle. The *Russian Dolls paradigm* is outside the Bigger and Smaller category, so this design is consequently a categorical shift.

solutions such as attaching the camera to an existing pole or tree, thereby obviating the need for the tripod. Some regard this approach as cheating, but it's an important tool of creative problem solving. Categorical shifts involve questioning the questions. Many design problems are cast in ways that suggest certain solutions and are framed in terms of certain paradigm categories, such as: "Design a better way for this device to bend so it will fit into this box." Although this problem is stated as a task of finding a means of bending (See Chapter 4), the real objective is getting the device into the box. So the problem might be better solved through a categorical shift, applying *Bigger and Smaller paradigms* (see Chapter 5).

United States Patent [19]
Damratoski

[11] **Patent Number: 4,575,074**
[45] **Date of Patent: Mar. 11, 1986**

[54] **EXERCISE WEIGHT**

[76] Inventor: **Daniel J. Damratoski,** 229 Roycroft Ave., Mt. Lebanon, Pa. 15234

[21] Appl. No.: **650,273**

[22] Filed: **Sep. 14, 1984**

[51] **Int. Cl.⁴** **A63B 21/12**
[52] **U.S. Cl.** **272/119;** 272/122
[58] **Field of Search** 272/119, 116, 122, 123, 272/67, 68, 117, 143; D21/197; D9/374, 376, 378

[56] **References Cited**

U.S. PATENT DOCUMENTS

660,962	10/1900	Kennedy	272/122
1,990,970	2/1935	Wood	272/119
4,029,312	6/1977	Wright	272/122 X
4,076,236	2/1978	Baroi	272/123
4,079,932	3/1978	Schuetz	272/75
4,103,887	8/1978	Shoofler	272/123
4,199,140	4/1980	Ferretti	272/123
4,311,306	1/1982	Solloway	272/122 X
4,322,072	3/1982	White	272/119
4,351,526	9/1982	Schwartz	272/122

OTHER PUBLICATIONS

Hand Weight sold by Brookstone Co., 320 Smithfield Street, Pittsburgh, Pa. 15219, in Jul. of 1984.

Primary Examiner—Richard J. Apley
Assistant Examiner—Robert W. Bahr
Attorney, Agent, or Firm—Grigsby, Gaca & Davies

[57] **ABSTRACT**

An exercise weight that has a handgrip and a hollow body disposed about the handgrip so that the mass of the body and of any material with which it might be filled will be evenly disposed about the hand of the user. The hand grip has a rectangular cross-section so as to engage the articulations of the hand. A flat surface is provided above the handgrip so that the weight can be rested upon the thumb and first finger of the user's hand. The outer walls of the body are sloped and join the bottom at an obtuse angle. The distance between the handgrip and one of the inner walls of the body is such that the device may be used as either a hand weight or a foot weight.

5 Claims, 5 Drawing Figures

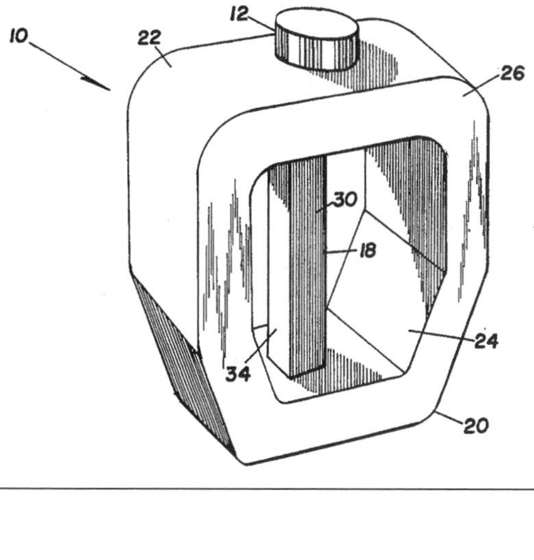

Fig. 14.5 This dumbell design, also a categorical shift, employs the *Bottle paradigm*. The weight is ajusted by adding or pouring out sand or water.

Synectics

Synectics is an approach to promoting creativity that is compatible with design paradigms. The term *synectics* comes from the Greek term *synectikos,* meaning the joining together of different and apparently irrelevant elements into a unified whole. Synectics emerged in the 1960s, with the publication of William J. J. Gordon's book *Synectics.* The method combines group interaction rules with a creative process centered around the use of metaphor and drawing analogies from diverse disciplines.

One of the key ideas of Synectics is that new thoughts, designs, and inventions can be generated by applying Synectic trigger mechanisms. These are operators such as "add," "combine," "subtract," "distort," "fragment," and "disguise." [59] A more complete listing appears in the table below:

Add	Transfer	Change Scale	Distort	Prevaricate
Subtract	Empathize	Substitute	Disguise	Analogize
Repeat	Animate	Fragment	Contradict	Hybridize
Combine	Superimpose	Isolate	Parody	Metamorphose
Symbolize	Mythologize	Fantasize		

Table 14.1: Synectic Trigger Mechanisms [60]

The operator "add" might imply extending, expanding, developing, supplementing, or magnifying our reference subject. We might make the subject bigger or find other ways to add to it. Referring to Chapter 5 "Bigger and Smaller" provides a host of specific methods to apply to this task. "Combine" implies bringing things together. We can connect, attach, unify, mix, merge, or otherwise bring together. Here, Chapter 7 "Joining," and Chapter 8 "Attaching," can be directly applied. The *Joining* and *Attaching paradigms* provide a menu of operators useful for combining things.

The "Synectic Think Cycle" involves three interrelated thinking modes that can be applied to structure these processes. Roukes describes these as the Synectic "three Rs":

> **Referring:** In this stage, the general subject and specific problem are defined. Research and background information on the problem are gathered.
>
> **Reflecting:** This phase involves the imaginative manipulation of the problem, exploring the various alternatives, possible solutions, and translations of various types.

> **Reconstruction:** This is the process of reinventing or transforming. This involves the Synectic trigger mechanisms, which can be applied as paradigm superimpositions. Reconstruction can imply taking apart the problem or its existing solution and assembling it a different way.

This process is cyclic: after the reconstruction phase, you can repeatedly return to the referring stage as you explore variations.

A comprehensive introduction to Synectics is beyond the scope of this book, but the Gordon and Roukes books are indispensable reading for those interested in Synectic methods of promoting creativity in design and other fields.

Misapplied Paradigms

"Errare humanum est, sed in errore perseverare diabolicum."
To err is human, but to continue to err is diabolical.

Design paradigms can be employed to create new designs and products. As with any approach to design, however, this can be done well, or poorly. Any new design must be tested against certain basic criteria. (This is the *test* phase described at the beginning of this chapter.) The simple application of a clever paradigm, though, can not by itself rescue a bad design.

Nonetheless, the history of design and invention is filled with examples of attempts at just that. Learning a paradigm and realizing that it can easily be applied to domains can easily leave you with a sense of empowerment and a rash of new discoveries. Much hard work, however, is required to take things from the "clever-idea" stage to the "good-design" stage, as you will see. It is instructive to look at a single paradigm to see how its misapplication can lead to bad design.

The *Swiss Army Knife paradigm* is a powerful and instantly comprehensible concept. The versatility and ease of the application of the paradigm has inspired countless designs featuring a range of tools that fold out from a single handle. Some of these, however, have not been tested against any reasonable criteria, resulting in some bizarre inventions. The paradigm is misapplied when arbitrary or contradictory functions are combined in a single object. One of the most important aspects of the *Swiss Army Knife paradigm* is the *complementarity* of the tools.

A. E. Brown and H. A. Jeffcott, Jr. compiled several examples of poorly combined functions in their book *Absolutely Mad Inventions*,[61] gathered from

Fig. 14.6 Misapplied paradigms are evident in the Combined Clothes-Brush, Flask and Drinking Cup.

the records of the United States Patent Office. The *Combined Clothes-Brush, Flask, and Drinking-Cup*[62] invention is a marvelous example. The misapplication here is the combination of the flask and drinking cup with the clothes brush. The combination suggests the unlikely prospect that people frequently get thirsty while brushing their clothes, or that they might be inspired to brush their clothes while drinking. More troublesome is the likelihood that using the invention might leave drips on the clothes or lint in the drinking cup.

Similarly problematic is the *Combined Match-Safe, Pincushion, and Trap.*[63] The problem here lies in the incompatibility of the supported activities. You might reasonably question whether matches are really needed while sewing and note that they would constitute a fire hazard. The thought of combining this with a mousetrap, though, is bizarre. You can imagine the distraction of reaching for a match or a pin and hearing the squeak of a mouse trapped inside the device. Further, many people feel uncomfortable about handling a mousetrap, so combining it with frequently handled items is a poor choice.

A final example is the *Combined Grocer's Package, Grater, Slicer, and Mouse and Fly Trap* invention.[64] Like the match safe, the incompatibility of the supported activities is the

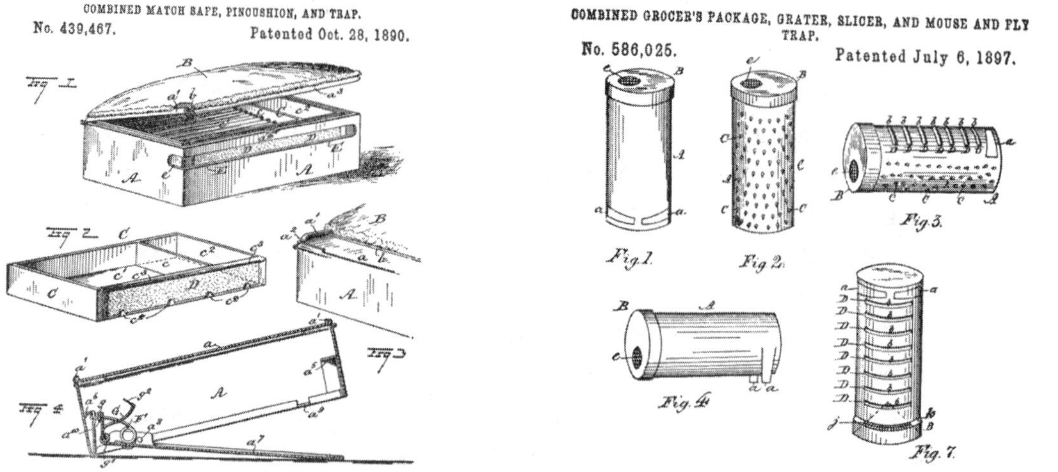

Fig. 14.7 a, b The Combined Match-Safe, Pincushion, and Trap, and the Combined Grocer's Package, Grater, Slicer, and Mouse and Fly Trap are similarly ill-thought-out inventions, and examples of misapplied paradigms.

major problem, exacerbated by the questionable wisdom of combining food preparation and pest disposal.

The lesson in reviewing misapplied paradigms is that as with any design tool or technique, they must be used wisely. The paradigms provide a language and mechanisms to explore alternatives and structure solutions, but cannot prevent their misuse. Problems like these are best avoided by ensuring careful attention to the test phase.

Finding New Paradigms

Continuing with the design paradigms approach requires an ongoing exploration to further expand and build upon your repertoire of paradigms. The categories and paradigms presented here are meant only to be a start. You might need to explore new paradigms to meet special needs, such as those encountered in space travel. Paradigms that might previously have been used on earth had to be reevaluated for use in a weightless environment. Familiar tasks, such as tightening a bolt, require reconsideration because a conventional wrench depends heavily on the torque provided by the weight of the user, weight that is not present in space.

Where do you go to find new paradigms? Since paradigms are at work all around you, the simple (but not very useful) answer is "anywhere." When you look, however, it is important to remember that the base level of structure and function within things is often hidden below surface skins and ornament. It is, consequently, necessary to literally "look under the hood" and "scratch below the surface" to see how things really work. These have long been recognized as important activies for curious and creative minds. Educational-activity guides intended to foster creativity in children frequently suggest that they literally take apart old appliances and toys to see the inner workings.

This is not necessary with all products, though. Certain classes of machines, equipment, and devices are built for utilitarian purposes and are largely free of ornament and skins that might hide their fundamental structure. This is especially true when there are severe pressures to minimize weight or maximize performance, such as camping, hiking, and climbing gear. It is also frequently true of professional and military tools and equipment, as these devices are often designed for strictly functional purposes. Devices in these categories exhibit a broad range of paradigms, with many interesting functions and mechanical relationships that can be studied without disassembly.

Military goods are produced with utility, durability, and performance foremost in mind. Military devices and equipment are usually made with their internal structure and functions readily apparent. Presumably this is partly intended to foster a good understanding of the equipment by those who must operate and maintain it. Military equipment can be seen in military-surplus stores, on army bases, and in air shows. It is also the subject of numerous magazines, books, and Websites.

Camping, hiking, and climbing equipment designs are often reduced to the bare essentials, in order to minimize their weight and size. Minimalist designs don't imply that most enthusiasts want to head to the woods with only a match and a knife, however. Most devices in this category are intended to provide comfort and convenience, with just a fraction of the weight and size of the corresponding tools and appliances used at home. Creating a minimum-weight camp stove, for example, that cooks like a home stove but packs small and light, requires sophisticated design, engineering, and manufacturing techniques. Today, camping, hiking, and climbing equipment frequently employs state-of-the-art manufacturing materials and techniques, in part because the performance demands are high, and because these sports are often pursued by persons with the discretionary income necessary for such purchases. Consequently, a camping, hiking, and climbing specialty store like EMS (www.emsonline.com) showcases devices using innovative manufacturing techniques and exotic materials, such as Gore-tex®, titanium alloys, ruby-coated glass, and carbon-fiber-reinforced structural plastics.

Professional tools and equipment. A hardware store has a wealth of interesting devices, tools, instruments, fasteners and so forth. While many or most of these things might be familiar, much can be learned by applying the paradigms framework to these devices. For example, how many ways to fasten things can you find in the hardware store? Most hardware stores have an entire section of the store (fasteners) devoted to this paradigm category, plus other sections for adhesives and tape. One may similarly explore a hardware store looking for ways to adjust the height of things, or for devices that operate in ways that aren't visible. Many tools are not found in retail stores, however, so be observant when going to the doctor or dentist's office, and take a good look at the instruments and implements around you. Also try to peek in a telephone-repair truck and a plumber or carpenter's toolbox.

The toy store. Toys are usually less transparent than tools and equipment; the inner workings are frequently hidden behind plastic and faux fur. Nonetheless, a great deal of creativity goes into the design of toys, often with the objective of finding a novel approach to a task as a point of distinction in the marketplace. You can hardly be interested in the way things work and not be fascinated by the many different ways parts fit together in a transformer-type toy, wherein 20 folds and twists might result in changing a robot into a beetle. Old toys can frequently be taken apart to see how they work. With new toys, you might be best advised to simply try the toy, play with it, observe it, and try to surmise its inner workings.

NASA. The National Aeronautics and Space Administration (NASA) develops an amazing array of technologies and techniques for the special challenges that space travel and scientific missions impose. Much of the technology developed is readily accessible through NASA's Website (www.nasa.gov) and through NASA publications.

Animals. A course in biology is highly recommended for aspiring designers. It is a good first step in exploring the paradigms found in the natural world, including humans, insects, arachnids, plants, and animals. Animals are wonderfully rich in the many adaptations they've evolved to survive and compete in the wild. Studying animals for their design aspects provides a seemingly endless stream of insights. Live animals can, of course, be studied at zoos, aquariums, aviaries, pet stores, and the like. National Geographic magazine and television specials are also wonderful sources.

Insects and arachnids. These creatures deserve special attention apart from animals. Insects account for $^5/_6$ of all known animal species. With roughly a million known species, scientists estimate there are between 1 and 4 million species yet undiscovered. Consequently, the majority of new paradigms yet to be discovered in animals will likely be found in insects. The social insects are particularly interesting, because they function as groups in ways not found in other animals. Insects deserve a second look from designers whenever and wherever they are seen, from a moth found on a porch-door screen in the summer, to a flea found on your cat, to an ant crawling across your kitchen. It is worth taking a magnifying glass along on hikes and nature walks, and looking up your finds in references like Holldobler and Wilson's wonderful book *The Ants*.[65]

Plants. Plants are also a wonderful source of design insights. Plants deserve some special trips to enjoy the diversity located beyond most backyards and local parks. Whenever traveling, try to devote at least a short time to a nature walk. The plants found even within a single city can vary widely, with changes in the dampness of the ground, the altitude, and the amount of sunlight received. The changes between large climate zones are even more dramatic, as are the differences between land, fresh water, and ocean-based vegetation. Visiting an arboretum or conservatory can be valuable, to see the amazing variety of forms and mechanisms in such plants as succulents, cacti, and orchids. Farms are also good places to see other varieties of plant forms. Something might even be gained by visiting a good vegetable market, though much of the interesting parts of the plants will rarely be found there. When studying plants from a design perspective, remember that many of the design features of plants are season-specific. The variety of mechanisms plants use to propagate their seed is a design education by itself, but might be visible only a few days per year for a given plant.

The human body. This is both the first and last source for paradigms. It is the first source we become aware of as infants, as we start to learn, for instance, the various ways to grab something (with the hand, with the toes, with the mouth, and so forth). It is the last in the sense that it is in many ways the "final frontier" of human curiosity about biological form and function. The curiosity Leonardo da Vinci expressed half a millenium ago about the inner workings of the human body continues unabated today. Contemporary efforts like the *Visible Human Project* and the *Human Genome Project* are still trying to unlock the mysteries of our bodies. The Visible Human Project, coordinated by the National Library of Medicine, is creating complete detailed 3-D models of a human male and female that can be explored through various computer interfaces. The Human Genome Project, coordinated by the U.S. Department of Energy and the National Institutes of Health, is involved in mapping the entire set of 80,000 to 100,000 genes in human DNA, and determining the complete sequence of the 3 billion DNA subunits. The project thereby aims to unlock the secrets of the instructions that create us.

Most design-degree programs require or encourage both basic biology and life drawing, giving at least a superficial introduction to the human body. A next step for serious pursuit is a course in gross anatomy. Short of that, books and videotapes on the subject are a reasonable substitute, with new resources now available on the Web as part of the Visible Human Project.

Notes

1. Descartes, Rene, quoted in Paul Jacques Grillo. *Form Function & Design* (New York: Dover Publications, 1960) 3.

2. *WWWebster Dictionary, www.m-w.com.* (Merriam-Webster, 1999).

3. Grillo, Paul Jacques. *Form Function & Design* (New York: Dover Publications, 1960) 19.

4. Ibid. 28.

5. Csikszentmihalyi, Mihaly. *Creativity: Flow and the Psychology of Discovery and Invention* (New York: HarperCollins, 1996) 363.

6. da Vinci, Leonardo. *The Notebooks of Leonardo da Vinci* (New York: Dover Publications, 1975).

7. Frost, Robert, quoted in Warren Shibles. *Metaphor: An Annotated Bibliography and History* (Whitewater, WI: The Language Press, 1971) IX.

8. *Webster's New World Dictionary of American English* (New York: Webster's New World, 1988) s.v.

9. Anderson, 1993, cited by John M. Carroll, Robert L. Mack, & Wendy A. Kellogg. *"Interface Metaphors and User Interface Design"* chapter in M. Helander, Ed., *Handbook of Human-Computer Interaction* (Amsterdam: Elsevier Science Publishers B.V., 1988) 70.

10. Aristotle, quoted in Warren Shibles. *Metaphor: An Annotated Bibliography and History* (Whitewater, WI: The Language Press, 1971) VII.

11. Edge, David. *"Technological Metaphor & Social Control"* chapter in George Bugliarello and Dean B. Doner, Eds., *The History and Philosophy of Technology* (Urbana: University of Illinois Press, 1979) 5.

12. Ibid.

13. Minsky, Marvin. *The Society of Mind.* (New York: Simon and Schuster, 1985, 1986) 298.

14. da Vinci, Leonardo. *The Notebooks of Leonardo da Vinci,* Vol. II. (New York: Dover Publications, 1970, 1883) 126.

15. Alexander, R. McNeill. *Functional Design in Fishes* (London: Hutchinson & Co. Ltd., 1967, 1974) 11.

16. Gould, Stephen Jay. Class lecture, Harvard University course: *Thinking about Thinking,* Spring, 1991.

17. Grillo, Paul Jacques. *Form, Function & Design* (New York: Dover Publications, 1960) 9.

18. Blount, Sir Thomas Pope, quoted in James Ritchie. *Design in Nature* (New York: Charles Scribner's Sons, 1937) 5.

19. da Vinci, Leonardo. Translation by Martin Kemp. *"The Inventions of Nature and the Nature of Invention"* chapter in *Leonardo da Vinci, Engineer and Architect.* (Montreal: The Montreal Museum of Fine Arts, 1987) 133.

20. Thompson, D'Arcy Wentworth. *On Growth and Form* (New York: Dover Publications, 1992) 16.

21. Alexander, Christopher. *Notes on the Synthesis of Form* (Cambridge, MA: Harvard University Press, 1964).

22. Pulos, Arthur J. *American Design Ethic* (Cambridge, MA: MIT Press, 1983) 380.

23. Ibid. 361.

24. Anderson, David and Scott Eberhardt. "How Airplanes Fly: A Physical Description of Lift." *Sport Aviation,* 48.2 (1999): 85.

25. *CERMA'S Recycled Paper Handbook, First Edition.* Edited and compiled by the Editorial Staff of Recycled Paper News (CERMA, The Center for Earth Resources Management Applications, Inc., 1991) 10, 11.

26. *Encyclopædia Britannica CD 99, Multimedia Edition* (Chicago: Encyclopædia Britannica Inc., 1999).

27. McCutcheon, Marc. *The Compass in your Nose and Other Astonishing Facts About Humans.* (New York: St. Martin's Press, 1989) 117.

28. Foelix, Rainer F. *Biology of Spiders* (Cambridge, MA: Harvard University Press, 1982) 49.

29. Gardner, Howard; Mindy Kornhaber, and Warren K. Wake. *Intelligence: Multiple Perspectives* (New York: Harcourt Brace College Publishers, 1996) 172.

30. *Encyclopædia Britannica CD 99, Multimedia Edition* (Chicago: Encyclopædia Britannica Inc., 1999).

31. Bower, Bruce. "Blinded by Beauty." *Science News* 153.6 (1998): 91.

32. Gould, Stephen Jay. *The Flamingo's Smile: Reflections in Natural History* (New York: W. W. Norton & Co., 1985).

33. Angier, Natalie. "What Do Female Bugs Want? Surprise: It's Shape, Not Size." The *New York Times on the Web,* July 7, 1998.

34. French, Michael. *Invention and Evolution: Design in Nature and Engineering* (Cambridge, England: Cambridge University Press, 1994).

35. Evans, William F. *Communication in the Animal World* (New York: Thomas Y. Crowell, 1968) 30.

36. Cooke, Robert. "In This Corner: A Tale to Make Your Head Spin," *Boston Globe*, March 20, 1984, 1.

37. De Cristoforo, Richard J. *The Complete Book Of Wood Joinery* (New York: Sterling Publications, 1997).

38. Budworth, Geoffrey. *The Complete Book of Knots* (New York: The Lyons Press, 1997).

39. Petroski, Henry. *The Evolution of Useful Things* (New York: Alfred A. Knopf, 1993) 110.

40. George, Jean Craighead. *Beastly Inventions* (New York: David McKay Company, Inc., 1970) 79.

41. Velcro Industries B.V. corporate website: http://www.velcro.com/htm/loop/invent.htm

42. George, Jean Craighead. *Beastly Inventions* (New York: David McKay Company, Inc., 1970) 78.

43. Einson Freeman Inc., of Paramus, NJ, a WPP Group plc company, specializes in creating brand awareness through promotional programs and marketing communications.

44. Wake, Warren K. *Apparatus and system for generating smooth shaded continuous tone images* (U. S. Patent 4958272, issued September 18, 1990).

45. Wake, Warren K. *Tigris: A Tool-Structured Interface and Graphic Interaction System for Computer Aided Design*. (Doctoral Dissertation, Harvard University Graduate School of Design, 1992) 178.

46. Donald, Merlin. *Origins of the Modern Mind* (Cambridge, MA: Harvard University Press, 1991) 110.

47. Capra, Fritjof. *The Web of Life: A New Scientific Understanding of Living Systems* (New York: Doubleday, 1996) 18.

48. Evans, William F. *Communication in the Animal World* (New York: Thomas Y. Crowell, 1968) 42.

49. Frier, Hellen J.; Emma Edwards, Claire Smith, Susi Neale, and Thomas S. Collett. "Magnetic Compass Cues and Visual Pattern learning in Honeybees." *The Journal of Experimental Biology* 199 (1996), 1353-1361.

50. Wiltschko, Wolfgang, and Roswitha Wiltschko. "Magnetic Orientation in Birds." *The Journal of Experimental Biology* 199 (1996), 29-38.

51. Gould, Stephen Jay. *The Panda's Thumb* (New York: W. W. Norton & Company, 1980) 309.

52. Eckert, Roger, and David Randall. *Animal Physiology: Mechanisms and Adaptations, Second Edition*. (New York: W. H. Freeman and Company, 1978, 1983) 260.

53. Ibid, 271.

54. George, Jean Craighead. *Beastly Inventions* (New York: David McKay Company, Inc., 1970) 34.

55. Csikszentmihalyi, Mihaly. *Creativity: Flow and the Psychology of Discovery and Invention* (New York: HarperCollins, 1996) 241.

56. Weber, Robert J. *Forks, Phonographs, and Hot Air Balloons: A Field Guide to Inventive Thinking* (New York: Oxford University Press, 1992) 114.

57. Ibid, 124-133.

58. Kuhn, Thomas S. *The Structure of Scientific Revolutions, Second Edition,* enlarged. (Chicago: University of Chicago Press, 1962, 1970) 119.

59. Roukes, Nicholas. *Design Synectics: Stimulating Creativity in Design.* (Worcester, MA: Davis Publications Inc., 1988) 11-13.

60. Ibid, 14-21.

61. Brown, A. E., and H. A. Jeffcott, Jr. *Absolutely Mad Inventions* (New York: Dover Publications, 1932, 1960, 1970).

62. Patent Number 490964, January 31, 1893, cited in Brown and Jeffcott, 116-117.

63. Patent Number 439,467, October 28, 1890, cited in Brown and Jeffcott, 90-91.

64. Patent Number 586,025, July 6, 1897, cited in Brown and Jeffcott, 46-47.

65. Holldobler, Bert, and E. O. Wilson. *The Ants* (Cambridge, MA: The Belknap Press of Harvard University Press, 1990).

References

Adams, James L. *Conceptual Blockbusting: A Guide to Better Ideas, Second Edition*. New York: W. W. Norton & Company, 1974, 1979.

Adams, James L. *Flying Buttresses, Entropy, and O-Rings: The World of an Engineer*. Cambridge, MA: Harvard University Press, 1991.

Alexander, Christopher. *Notes on the Synthesis of Form*. Cambridge MA: Harvard University Press, 1964.

Alexander, Christopher. *A Pattern Language*. New York: Oxford University Press, 1977.

Alexander, R. McNeil. *Functional Design in Fishes*. London: Hutchinson & Co. Ltd., 1967, 1974.

Aristotle. *De Anima, Book II*, in Richard McKeon, Ed., *Introduction to Aristotle*. New York: Modern Library, 1947.

Aristotle. *On the Generation of Animals I* in Richard McKeon, Ed., *The Basic Works of Aristotle*. New York: Random House, 1941.

Aristotle. *On the Parts of Animals IV* in Thomas Taylor, Ed., *The Works of Aristotle, Vol. VII*. London: Robert Wilks, 1812.

Bailey, Jill. *Animal Life: Form and Function in the Animal Kingdom*. New York: Oxford University Press, 1994.

Ball, John E. *Carpenters and Builders Library No. 1*. Indianapolis: Theodore Audel & Co., 1965, 1976.

Barratt, Krome. *Logic and Design in Art, Science & Mathematics*. New York: Design Press, 1980.

Beck, Benjamin B. *Animal Tool Behavior: The Use and Manufacture of Tools by Animals*. New York: Garland, 1980.

Bernal, J. D. *The Extension of Man: A History of Physics Before 1900*. St. Albans, England: Paladin, 1973.

Black, Max. *Perplexities: Rational Choice, the Prisoner's Dilemma, Metaphor, Poetic Ambiguity, and Other Puzzles*. Ithaca, NY: Cornell University Press, 1990.

Bronowski, J. *The Visionary Eye: Essays in the Arts, Literature, and Science*. Cambridge: MIT Press, 1978.

Brown, A. E. and Jeffcott, Jr., H. A. *Absolutely Mad Inventions*. New York: Dover Publications, 1932, 1970.

Bucciarelli, Louis L. *Designing Engineers*. Cambridge, MA: MIT Press, 1994.

Budworth, Geoffrey. *The Complete Book of Knots*. New York: The Lyons Press, 1997.

Bugliarello, George, and Doner, Dean B. Eds. *The History and Philosophy of Technology*. Urbana: University of Illinois Press, 1979.

Bunn, James H. *The Dimensionality of Signs, Tools, and Models: An Introduction*. Bloomington: Indiana University Press, 1981.

Campbell, Robert. *Fisherman's Guide: A Systems Approach to Creativity and Organization*. Boston: New Science Library, 1985.

Capra, Fritjof. *The Web of Life: A New Scientific Understanding of Living Systems*. New York: Doubleday, 1996.

Cardwell, Donald. *The Norton History of Technology*. New York: W. W. Norton & Company, 1995.

Cassirer, Ernst. *Language and Myth*. Langer, Susanne K., Trans. New York: Dover Publications Inc., 1946.

Ching, Francis D. K. *Architecture: Form, Space, and Order, Second Edition*. New York: Van Nostrand Reinhold, 1996.

Chironis, Nicholas P., and Sclater, Neil. *Mechanisms and Mechanical Devices Sourcebook, Second Edition*. New York: McGraw-Hill, 1991, 1996.

Collier, Graham. *Form, Space, and Vision, Third Edition*. Englewood Cliffs, NJ: Prentice-Hall, 1963, 1972.

Cook, Theodore Andrea. *The Curves of Life*. New York: Dover Publications, Inc., 1979.

Csikszentmihalyi, Mihaly. *Creativity: Flow and the Psychology of Discovery and Invention*. New York: HarperCollins, 1996.

Csikszentmihalyi, Mihaly, and Rochberg-Halton, Eugene. *The Meaning of Things: Domestic Symbols and the Self*. Cambridge: Cambridge University Press, 1981.

Darwin, Charles. *On the various contrivances by which British and foreign orchids are fertilized by insects, and on the good effects of intercrossing, Second Edition*. London, 1877.

da Vinci, Leonardo. *The Notebooks of Leonardo da Vinci*. New York: Dover Publications, 1975.

DeCristoforo, Richard J. *The Complete Book of Wood Joinery*. Sterling Publications, 1997.

Donald, Merlin. *Origins of the Modern Mind: Three Stages in the Evolution of Culture and Cognition*. Cambridge MA: Harvard University Press, 1991.

Eckert, Roger, and Randall, David. *Animal Physiology: Mechanisms and Adaptations, Second Edition*. New York: W. H. Freeman and Company, 1978, 1983.

Edwards, Edward B. *Pattern and Design with Dynamic Symmetry*. New York: Dover Publications, Inc. 1932, 1967.

Encyclopædia Britannica CD 99, Multimedia Edition. Chicago: Encyclopædia Britannica Inc., 1999.

Evans, William F. *Communication in the Animal World*. New York: Thomas Y. Crowell Company, 1968.

Fabre, J. Henri. *The Insect World of J. Henri Fabre*. New York: Dodd, Mead & Co., 1912, 1949.

Fenton, Alexander, and Myrdal, Janken, Eds. *Food and Drink and Travelling Accessories: Essays in Honour of Gösta Berg*. Edinburgh: John Donald Publishers Ltd., 1988.

Ferguson, Eugene S. *Engineering and the Mind's Eye*. Cambridge, MA: MIT Press, 1993.

Foelix, Rainer F. *Biology of Spiders*. Cambridge, MA: Harvard University Press, 1982.

French, Michael. *Invention and Evolution: Design in Nature and Engineering*. Cambridge, England: Cambridge University Press, 1994.

Fuller, R. Buckminster. *The artifacts of R. Buckminster Fuller: A Comprehensive Collection of his Designs and Drawings*. New York: Garland, 1984, 1985.

Fuller, R. Buckminster. *Inventions: The Patented Works of R. Buckminster Fuller*. New York: St. Martin's Press, 1983.

Fuller, R. Buckminster. *Operating Manual for Spaceship Earth*. New York: Pocket Books, 1969.

Fuller, R. Buckminster. *Synergetics: Explorations in the Geometry of Thinking*. New York: Macmillan Publishing Company, 1975, 1982.

Gardner, Howard; Kornhaber, Mindy, and Wake, Warren K. *Intelligence, Multiple Perspectives*. Fort Worth: Harcourt Brace College Publishers, 1996.

George, Jean Craighead. *Beastly Inventions*. New York: David McKay Company Inc., 1970.

Gideon, Siegfried. *Mechanization Takes Command*. New York: W. W. Norton & Co., 1948, 1975.

Gilfillan, S. C. *The Sociology of Invention*. Cambridge, MA: MIT Press, 1935, 1970.

Gimpel, Jean. *The Medieval Machine: The Industrial Revolution of the Middle Ages*. New York: Holt, Rinehart and Winston, 1976.

Gordon, William J. J. *Synectics, the Development of Creative Capacity*. New York: Harper, 1961.

Gould, Stephen Jay. *The Panda's Thumb*. New York: W. W. Norton & Company, 1980.

Gould, Stephen Jay. *The Flamingo's Smile: Reflections in Natural History*. New York: W. W. Norton & Co., 1985.

Gray, Henry. *Anatomy, Descriptive and Surgical, 35th Edition*. London: Longman, 1973.

Griffin, Donald R. *Animal Engineering: Readings from Scientific American*. San Francisco: Scientific American, 1948, 1974.

Grillo, Paul Jacques. *Form Function & Design*. New York: Dover Publications, 1960.

Haken, Hermann; Karlquist, Anders; and Svedin, Uno, Eds. *The Machine as Metaphor and Tool*. Berlin: Springer-Verlag, 1993.

Harrisberger, Lee. *Engineersmanship: A Philosophy of Design*. Belmont, CA: Brooks-Cole Publishing Company, 1966.

Herkimer, Herbert. *The Engineers' Illustrated Thesaurus*. New York: Chemical Publishing Co. Inc., 1952.

Hildebrandt, Stefan, and Tromba, Anthony. *The Parsimonious Universe: Shape and Form in the Natural World*. New York: Springer Verlag, 1996.

Hofstadter, Douglas R. *Goedel, Escher, Bach: an Eternal Golden Braid*. New York: Vintage Books, 1979, 1980.

Holldobler, Bert, and Wilson, E. O. *The Ants*. Cambridge, MA: The Belknap Press of Harvard University Press, 1990.

Ivins, William M. Jr. *Art & Geometry: A Study in Space Intuitions*. New York: Dover Publications Inc., 1964.

Jewkes, John; Sawers, David; and Stillerman, Richard. *The Sources of Invention, Second Edition*. New York: W. W. Norton & Co., 1958, 1969.

Jones, Franklin D. *Ingenious Mechanisms for Designers and Inventors*. New York: The Industrial Press, 1930, 1951.

Jones, Roger S. *Physics as Metaphor*. Minneapolis: Univeristy of Minnesota Press, 1982.

Jones, Stacy V. *Inventions Necessity is not the Mother of: Patents Ridiculous and Sublime*. New York: Quadrangle/The New York Times Book Co., 1973.

Kuhn, Thomas S. *The Structure of Scientific Revolutions, Second Edition,* Enlarged. Chicago: The University of Chicago Press, 1962, 1970.

Laidler, Keith J. *To Light Such a Candle: Chapters in the History of Science and Technology*. New York: Oxford University Press, 1998.

Lawson, Bryan. *How Designers Think: The Design Process Demystified, Second Edition*. Oxford: Butterworth Architecture, 1980, 1990.

Livingston, James D. *Driving Force: The Natural Magic of Magnets*. Cambridge, MA: Harvard University Press, 1996.

Lockley, Ronald M. *Animal Navigation*. New York, NY: Hart Publishing Co., 1967.

Loeb, Arthur L. *Color and Symmetry*. Huntington, New York: Robert E. Krieger Publishing Co., 1978.

Mac Cormac, Earl R. *A Cognitive Theory of Metaphor*. Cambridge, MA: MIT Press, 1985.

March, Lionel, and Steadman, Philip. *The Geometry of Environment*. Cambridge, MA: MIT Press, 1974.

Mayer, Richard E. *Thinking, Problem Solving, Cognition*. New York: W. H. Freeman and Company, 1983.

McCullough, Malcolm. *Abstracting Craft: The Practiced Digital Hand*. Cambridge MA: MIT Press, 1996.

McCutcheon, Marc. *The Compass in your Nose and Other Astonishing Facts About Humans*. New York: St. Martin's Press, 1989.

McHarg, Ian L. *Design with Nature*. Garden City, NY: Doubleday/Natural History Press, 1969.

McKim, Robert H. *Experiences in Visual Thinking, Second Edition*. Boston: PWS Publishers, 1972, 1980.

Minsky, Marvin. *The Society of Mind*. New York: Simon and Schuster, 1985, 1986.

Mitchell, William J. *The Logic of Architecture*. Cambridge, MA: MIT Press, 1990.

Montreal Museum of Fine Arts. *Leonardo da Vinci, Engineer and Architect*. Montreal: The Montreal Museum of Fine Arts, 1987.

Norman, Donald. *Turn Signals are the Facial Expressions of Automobiles*. Reading, MA: Addison-Wesley, 1992.

Norman, Donald A. *The Design of Everyday Things*. New York: Doubleday, 1988, 1990.

Olin, Harold B; Schmidt, John L.; and Lewis, Walter H. *Construction: Principles, Materials and Methods*. New York: Van Nostrand Reinhold, 1995.

Ortony, Andrew. *Metaphor and Thought*. Cambridge England: Cambridge University Press, 1979.

Pacey, Arnold. *The Maze of Ingenuity: Ideas and Idealism in the Development of Technology*. Cambridge, MA: MIT Press, 1974, 1985.

Papanek, Victor. *Design for the Real World*. London: Granada Publishing, Ltd. 1974.

Patton, Phil. *Made In USA: The Secret Histories of the Things That Made America*. New York: Grove Weidenfeld, 1992.

Perkins, D. N. *The Mind's Best Work*. Cambridge, MA: Harvard University Press, 1981.

Petroski, Henry. *Design Paradigms: Case Histories of Error and Judgment in Engineering*. New York: Cambridge University Press, 1994.

Petroski, Henry. *To Engineer is Human: The Role of Failure in Successful Design*. New York: St. Martin's Press, 1985.

Petroski, Henry. *The Evolution of Useful Things*. New York: Alfred A. Knopf, 1992.

Petroski, Henry. *Invention by Design: How Engineers get from Thought to Thing*. Cambridge, MA: Harvard University Press, 1996.

Petroski, Henry. *The Pencil: A History of Design and Circumstance*. New York: Knopf, 1990.

Pulos, Arthur J. *American Design Ethic*. Cambridge, MA: MIT Press, 1983.

Pile, John F. *Design: Purpose, Form and Meaning*. Amherst: University of Massachusetts Press, 1979.

Pye, David. *The Nature of Design*. New York: Reinhold Publishing Corp., 1964.

Radinsky, Leonard B. *The Evolution of Vertebrate Design*. Chicago: The University of Chicago Press, 1987.

Raff, Rudolf A. *The Shape of Life: Genes, Development, and the Evolution of Animal Form*. Chicago: The University of Chicago Press, 1996.

Reuleaux, Franz. *The Kinematics of Machinery*. New York: Dover Publications Inc., 1876, 1963.

Ritchie, James. *Design in Nature*. New York: Charles Scribner's Sons, 1937.

Rothenberg, David. *Hand's End: Technology and the Limits of Nature*. Berkeley: University of California Press, 1993.

Roukes, Nicholas. *Design Synectics: Stimulating Creativity in Design*. Worcester, MA: Davis Publications Inc., 1988.

Rowe, Peter G. *Design Thinking*. Cambridge, MA: MIT Press, 1987.

Shibles, Warren. *Metaphor: An Annotated Bibliography and History*. Whitewater, WI: The Language Press, 1971.

Stevens, Peter S. *Patterns in Nature*. Boston: Atlantic Monthly Press, 1974.

Street, Philip. *Animal Weapons*. New York: Taplinger Publishing Company, 1971.

Terres, John K. *How Birds Fly*. New York: Harper & Row Publishers Inc., 1968.

Todd, Mabel Elsworth. *The Thinking Body*. New York: Dance Horizons, Inc., 1937.

Turner, Gerard L'E. *Scientific Instruments 1500-1900, An Introduction*. London: Philip Wilson Publishers, 1998.

Vitruvius. *The Ten Books on Architecture*. New York, NY: Dover Publications Inc., 1960.

Vogel, Steven. *Cat's Paws and Catapults: Mechanical Worlds of Nature and People*. New York: Norton, 1998.

Vogel, Steven. *Life's Devices: The Physical World of Animals and Plants*. Princeton: Princeton University Press, 1988.

Vogel, Steven. *Vital Circuits: On Pumps, Pipes, and the Workings of Circulatory Systems*. New York: Oxford University Press, 1992.

von Frisch, Karl. *Bees: Their Vision, Chemical Senses, and Language*. Ithaca, NY: Great Seal Books division of Cornell University Press, 1950.

Wake, Warren K. *A Computer Graphic Approach to the Design and Construction of Spatially Curved Surfaces for Architectural Applications*. Bachelor of Architecture Honors Thesis, School of Architecture, Syracuse University, 1979.

Wake, Warren K. *Tigris: A Tool-Structured Interface and Graphic Interaction System for Computer Aided Design*, Doctoral Dissertation, Harvard University Graduate School of Design, 1992.

Weber, Robert J. *Forks, Phonographs, and Hot Air Balloons: A Field Guide to Inventive Thinking*. New York: Oxford University Press, 1992.

Week, David. "The Structure of CAD and the Structure of Form," *Building and Environment*, 26, no. 1., (1991) 49-59.

Weyl, Hermann. *Symmetry*. Princeton: Princeton University Press, 1952, 1982.

Willis, Delta. *The Sand Dollar and the Slide Rule: Drawing Blueprints from Nature*. Reading, MA: Addison-Wesley Publishing Co., 1995.

Whyte, Lancelot Law, Ed. *Aspects of Form*. London: Percy Lund Humphries, Ltd., 1961.

Figure Credits

Anderson, Gary: 245.

Art Institute of Chicago: 1.18.

ArtToday: 0.1, 1.3-1.11, 1.13-1.17, 1.22, 2.6, 2.8, 2.10-2.14, 2.16-2.18, 2.21, 2.22b, d, e; 2.23, 2.24, 2.28a-c, 2.30, 2.32, 2.34, 2.41, 2.42, 2.45, 3.2, 3.4, 3.7a-e, g; 3.8-3.10, 3.14, 3.15, 3.17, 3.18a, 3.19-3.21, 3.23, 3.24, 3.25b, 3.27-3.33a, 3.36-3.39, 3.40a, 3.43, 3.46-3.54b, 3.55, 4.1, 4.3, 4.6-4.8, 4.10a, 4.14, 4.17, 4.19, 5.1-5.5, 5.8-5.10, 5.12-5.13b, 5.15, 5.16 (background image), 5.23, 5.29-5.31b, 5.32, 5.35a, b; 5.40, 5.41, 5.44-5.46, 5.52, 5.55, 5.59, 5.60b-e, 5.62, 5.63, 5.64b, 6.2-6.6, 6.9, 6.10, 6.13a, b; 6.14a-c, 6.18, 6.21-6.27, 6.33a-d, 6.34, 6.36, 6.39, 6.41, 7.1b, 7.6, 7.7, 7.9, 7.15, 7.17a, b; 7.18, 7.22-7.25, 7.29, 8.2, 8.6, 8.8, 8.12, 8.20-8.24, 8.26, 9.1b, 9.3, 9.5a, b; 9.8b, 9.11, 9.12, 9.16b, 9.17a, b; 9.19, 9.20a, b; 10.1b, c; 10.2a, 10.11a-d, 10.13, 10.14, 10.16, 10.19a, 11.1, 11.10, 11.11, 11.14, 12.5, 13.3, 13.4, 13.6, 13.9, 13.11, 13.13a.

Cetacean Research Technology: 8.3. Designer: Joseph R. Olson. Courtesy of Cetacean Research Technology.

Cheimets, Peter: 2.7 a, b. Copyright 1998, Peter Cheimets.

Chicago, University of: 2.1. Copyright 1999, University of Chicago.

Corbis: 3.45, 5.18, 5.38, 5.50, 9.6. Copyright 1999, Corbis. All rights reserved.

Corel: CorelGALLERY images Copyright © 2000 John Wiley & Sons and its licensors. All rights reserved. 3.11a, b 3.25a, 3.34a, b; 5.6, 5.7, 5.14, 5.16 (background image), 5.17a, b; 5.27, 5.47-5.49a, 6.7a-d, 6.13a, 6.15, 6.19a-c, 6.20, 6.29a-d, 6.30, 6.31, 6.35, 7.3, 7.4, 7.14, 8.7, 8.16-8.19, 9.1a, 9.2, 9.8a, 10.1a, 10.2b, 10.3b, 10.6, 10.8 a, b; 10.9a, 10.10, 10.17a, b; 10.18, 10.21-10.23, 10.25a-e, 10.26a-d, 11.3a, b; 12.1a, b; 12.2a-c, 12.6, 12.10, 13.5a, b; 13.13b.

da Vinci, Leonardo: 1.3a-c, 1.4a,b; 1.13, 1.14, 1.17a,b; 2.6, 2.8, 2.11, 2.16.

Damratoski, Daniel J.: 14.5, U. S. Patent #4,575,074.

Dürer, Albrecht: 2.6.

Eisenman, Peter: 2.44. Sketch by Sally Levine, after a drawing by Peter Eisenman.

Escher, M. C.: 2.47. "Moebius Strip II" © 1999 Cordon Art B.V. Baarn, Holland. All rights reserved.

Fuller, R. Buckminster: 2.9.

Gardiner, Kenneth W.: 5.53. Copyright 1999, Kenneth W. Gardiner.

Grey, Michael J.: 4.18b, U. S. Patent #5,897,417.

Hopper, Edward: 3.50.

IMSI: The following images used herein were obtained from IMSI's MasterClips® and MasterPhotos™ Premium Image Collection, 1895 Francisco Blvd. East, San Rafael, CA 94901-5506, USA: 2.10b, 2.13, 2.14b, 2.20, 2.22a, 2.22c, 2.27, 2.31b, 2.33, 2.38, 2.40a, 3.7f, 3.11, 3.16, 3.18b, 3.25a, 3.33b, 3.34, 3.35, 3.41, 3.44, 4.9, 4.10, 4.11b, 4.13, 5.20, 5.21, 5.22a-c, 5.24, 5.26a-c, 5.28, 5.31c, 5.43, 5.47-5.49b, 5.60a, 6.12, 6.28, 7.12, 7.26, 7.27, 8.4, 8.5, 9.13, 10.9a, 10.11a, 10.17b, 11.4b, 12.8a, 12.11a, b; 12.12, 13.10, 13.12.

Ionel, Stefan: 14.3, U. S. Patent #4,076,236.

Kaestner, A: Fig. 5.33 by W. Wake, after a drawing by Kaestner A. *Lehrbuch der Speziellen Zoologie, 3rd ed.* vol. 1: Wirbellose. Stuttgart: Fischer, 1969. Fig. 10.7 by W. Wake, after a drawing by Kaestner, A. *Bau und Funktion der Fächertracheen einiger Spinnen.* Z. Morph Ökol. Tiere 13 (1929) 463.

Knape & Vogt: 5.11a. Copyright 1999, Knape & Vogt Manufacturing Co.

Lakeside Equipment Corporation: 2.29.

Levine, Sally: 2.44, after a drawing by Peter Eisenman; 7.21.

Loewy, Raymond: 1.20, 1.21.

Matho, Diego: 2.1, 2.2, 2.5, 2.19, 7.5, 7.8, 7.19b, 10.5, 14.1.

Mountain House Foods: 3.54c. Copyright 1999, Mountain House Foods.

Minnesota Mining and Manufacturing Company (3M): 4.5. Copyright © 1999, 3M Unitek Corporation. All rights reserved.

Miranti, Joseph P. Jr.: 2.46, U. S. Patent #4,253,836.

Museum of Science, Boston: 7.19a. Courtesy of the Museum of Science, Boston.

NASA: 2.3, 3.35, 5.24, 6.8, 9.13.

Ohio State University Extension, Nursery, Landscape and Turf Team: 8.15. Copyright 1999, Ohio State University Extension.

Olson, Gregory, et. al.: 14.4, U. S. Patent # 5,637,064.

Pevsner, Paul H.: 5.19, U. S. Patent #4,213,461.

Powell, Dean: 11.5c. Copyright 1999, Dean Powell.

Raphael: 1.7.

Sears, Roebuck & Co. 1.21.

United States Air Force: 2.35, 9.4, 10.15.

United States Department of Commerce, Patent and Trademark Office: 2.9, 2.46, 4.18b, 5.19, 5.39, 10.20a, 14.3-14.7 a, b.

United States Department of Defense 3.33b, 5.49a, b.

United States Navy: 3.22, 11.2, 11.7, 11.9 a, b.

University of Chicago: 1.2.

Varnell, Dennis H.: 5.39, U. S. Patent #3,987,807.

Wake, Diane: Multi-function tool, Fig. 12.4, gift to the author.

Wake, George and Ruth: Telescope, Fig. 5.36 and Japanese scissors, Fig. 6.17, gifts to the author.

Wake, Paulina: Shoe model, Fig. 7.20; Fingercuff demonstration, Fig. 9.14.

Wake, Richard: 3.1, 4.18a, 5.11b, 5.37, 5.42 (photography), 5.51, 5.54, 5.61, 8.11, 10.3a, 11.4, 12.9, 14.2.

Wake, Warren K.: 1.1, 1.11a, 1.12, 1.19, 2.4, 2.10, 2.14, 2.15, 2.25, 2.26, 2.31a, 2.36, 2.37, 2.39, 2.40b, 2.43, 3.3a, b; 3.5, 3.6, 3.13, 3.15, 3.26, 3.27, 3.40, 3.42, 4.2, 4.4, 4.11a, 4.12a, b; 4.15, 4.16, 5.16*, 5.25, 5.33, 5.34, 5.35c, 5.36, 5.42*, 5.56, 5.57*, 5.58, 5.64a, 6.1, 6.16, 6.17, 6.32, 6.37, 6.38, 6.40, 7.1a, 7.10, 7.11, 7.13, 7.16, 7.20, 7.28, 8.1*, 8.10, 8.13, 8.25, 9.6, 9.10, 9.14, 9.15, 9.16a, 10.4, 10.7, 10.9b, 10.12, 10.19b, c; 10.20 (U. S. patent #4,958,272), b, c; 10.24, 10.27, 11.5a, b; 11.8, 11.12, 11.13a, b; 12.3, 12.4, 12.7a, b; 12.8a, b; 12.13, 13.2, 13.7, 13.8.

* *photomontage.*

Index